The Jews in Poland

Thanks are due to Michael and Janet Scherer for
their help in the publication of this book
to commemorate the many members of their
families who died in the Holocaust

The Jews in Poland

edited by

CHIMEN ABRAMSKY, MACIEJ JACHIMCZYK
and
ANTONY POLONSKY

Basil Blackwell

Copyright © Basil Blackwell Ltd 1986

First published 1986

Basil Blackwell Ltd
108 Cowley Road, Oxford OX4 1JF, UK

Basil Blackwell Inc.
432 Park Avenue South, Suite 1503,
New York, NY 10016, USA

in association with the Institute for
Polish-Jewish Studies, Oxford

British Library Cataloguing in Publication Data

The Jews in Poland.
1. Jews – Poland – History
I. Abramsky, Chimen   II. Jachimczyk, Maciej
III. Polonsky, Antony
943.8′004924   DS135.P6
ISBN 0-631-14857-4

Library of Congress Cataloging in Publication Data

The Jews in Poland.
Papers presented at the International Conference on Polish-Jewish
Studies, held in Oxford, in Sept. 1984.
Includes index.
1. Jews – Poland – History – Congresses.   2. Holocaust,
Jewish (1939–1945) – Poland – Congresses.   3. Poland –
Ethnic relations – Congresses.   I. Abramsky, Chimen, 19–
II. Jachimczyk, Maciej..   III. Polonsky,
Antony.   IV. International Conference on Polish-Jewish
Studies (1984: Oxford, Oxfordshire)
DS135.P6J46   1986   943.8′004924   86-3336
ISBN 0-631-14857-4

Typeset by Joshua Associates Limited, Oxford
Printed in Great Britain by Butler & Tanner Ltd, Frome and London

Contents

Preface

The essays in this book were first presented at the International Conference on Polish-Jewish Studies held in Oxford in September 1984. Not all the papers studied at the Conference have been reprinted here. Considerations of space have meant that some historical contributions have been held over for a subsequent volume, as have all the articles on literary and ethnographic themes. The editors would like to thank Mrs Margot Levy for her assistance in editing the conference and discussion material, Miss Anna Zaranko, Miss Cecile Fox and Mr Kevin Fox for help with translations and Mr Ted Gordon for aid with proof reading. They would also like once again to express their gratitude to all those who worked so hard to make the Oxford Conference a success and to the many bodies and individuals whose financial contributions made it possible, above all the Grabowski Fund, the Lanckoronski Foundation, the Institute of Jewish Affairs, the British Academy, the British Council, the Foundation for European Intellectual Cooperation and Exchange (Paris), the John F. Cohen Foundation Institut Literacki Kultura (Paris), the Association of Jews of Polish Origin (London) and the Polish American Congress, as well as a large number of individual sponsors. This volume is the first publication to emerge from the Institute for Polish-Jewish Studies set up in Oxford as a result of the Conference. We hope it will be followed by many more.

The Polish–Lithuanian Commonwealth
(Copyright© 1962 Columbia University Press. By Permission.)

POLISH LIVONIA

R U S

POŁOCK

WITEBSK

Połock

Uła

Witebsk

Dnieper R.

Smolensk

Orsza

Mścisław

Mohilewl

MŚCISŁAW

Mińsk

M I N S K A

Rohaczew

Słuck

R O D E K

LITEWSKI

Dnieper R.

Dnieper R.

S S I A

Kiev

㉑

Żytomierz

N

A

Nowy Konstantynów

Bar

Winnica

㉒

Kamieniec

Podolski

Bracław

㉓

Chocim

Dniestr R.

Bałta

O T T O M A N   E M P I R E

Boundary of Poland, 1771

Province boundries

Boundary between Litwa
(Lithuania) and Korona (Crown)

PROVINCES OF KORONA

1	Malbork	**13**	Łęczyca
2	Pomorze	**14**	Rawa
3	Poznan	**15**	Cracow
4	Gniezno	**16**	Sandomierz
5	Inowrocław	**17**	Lublin
6	Chełmno	**18**	Ruś and Ziemia Chełm
7	Brześć-Kujawski	**19**	Bełz
8	Płock	**20**	Wołyń
9	Mazowsze	**21**	Kiev
10	Podlasie	**22**	Podole
11	Kalisz	**23**	Bracław
12	Sieradz		

miles

0   100   200

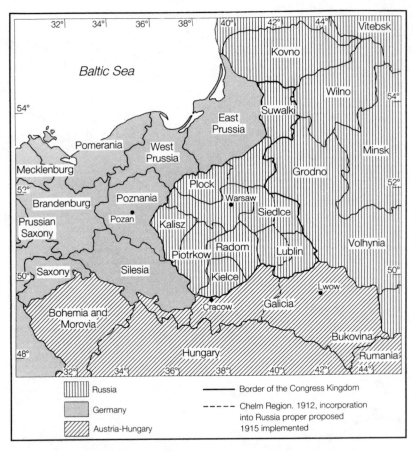

Administrative divisions in the Polish lands on the eve of World War I

The territories making up the Polish state in 1921

Introduction

Oh! All is gone . . .
There was a People, which exists no longer
There was a People, but it is no more
Gone. Wiped out

Yitzchak Katzenelson
'Lament for the murdered Jewish People'

The essays in this book describe the establishment, flourishing and destruction of one of the most important Jewish communities in the world. Since the Babylonian exile and the beginnings of the Diaspora, Jewish life has always been characterized by the emergence of major *foci* of creativity and dynamism. In the period of the second Temple and after, Mesopotamia with its *exilarch* (Resh galutha) and its great academies was an even more important area of Jewish intellectual and legal activity than *Eretz Israel*. After the destruction of the second Temple it remained a major centre to be supplanted in the early Middle Ages by the communities of Spain and the Rhineland. When these settlements lost their significance, with the persecutions which followed the Black Death in Germany and the expulsion of the Jews from Spain in 1492, their place was taken by the Polish-Lithuanian Commonwealth. By the end of the seventeenth century probably three quarters of world Jewry lived within the borders of the Polish republic. Poland – described by Jews as a haven in a world of persecution[1] – became the centre of a flourishing Jewish culture. This culture survived the decline and partition of the Polish state and in the nineteenth century those areas which had formerly made up the Polish-Lithuanian Commonwealth became the seedbed for the intellectual movements which were to transform the Jewish world: Zionism, secularism, socialism, neo-orthodoxy. Moreover, with the development of mass emigration from the late nineteenth century, the influence of Jews from the former Polish Republic was carried to Western Europe, North and South America, South Africa and the Antipodes. At the same time, the rebirth of the Polish state, although it created major difficulties for its Jewish population – ten per cent of the whole – provided a new stimulus to Jewish creativity. In 1939, before the Nazi occupation, Polish Jewry was still the second largest Jewish community in the world (after that of the United States which was largely derived from it) and was still, in many ways, the centre of Jewish political and cultural life.

This book does not provide a full account of the history of the Jews in Poland. The individual contributors were all encouraged to focus on specific themes and concentrate primarily on the relationship of the Jews to the other people, in the first instance, the Poles, with whom they lived – sometimes in harmony, sometimes in conflict. There is little on internal Jewish developments, whether the religious disputes of the seventeenth and eighteenth centuries and the emergence of *Chassidism* or the various conflicts engendered by the clash between orthodox Judaism and modernism in the nineteenth and twentieth centuries. There is also relatively little on the role of the Catholic Church, which played such a large part in determining the conditions under which the Jews lived. There is a great deal of material on how Jews fared in the period of the rise of the Polish-Lithuanian Commonwealth but much less on the impact of its economic and political decline from the Chmielnicki revolt onwards. The whole question of the 'reform' of Jewish life, how the Jews could be made more productive and useful citizens – a pre-occupation of Polish radicals from the mid-eighteenth century to the crushing of the 1863 insurrection and beyond, is not dealt with in any depth. Yet in spite of these omissions we believe that it does provide the reader with a general outline of the most significant factors in the evolution of Jewish life in Poland.

Jews first settled on the Polish lands, as Professor Gieysztor demonstrates (chapter 1), even before the establishment of a Polish state. They came both from the Mediterranean and from the short-lived Khazar state, and in every day life they probably used some forms of the Tartar and Slavonic languages. It was with the influx of Yiddish-speaking Jews, who came to Poland after the persecutions of the thirteenth and fourteenth century, that Yiddish became the most important language of normal discourse (although areas where Tartar was still spoken persisted until the seventeenth century and beyond, if one considers the Karaites as part of Polish Jewry). At this stage the size of the community was still small. As late as the end of the fifteenth century, there were only 18,000 Jews in the Polish Kingdom and 6,000 in Lithuania, located in 85 towns and constituting barely 0.6 per cent of the population. Yet at the same time the basic structure of Polish Jewry had been established in the form in which it was to persist until the decline of the Polish-Lithuanian Commonwealth. It was a community the rights of which were defined by charter (the basic instrument of medieval society) and in particular by the Kalisz statute granted by Boleslaw the Pious in 1264 and that of Kazimierz the Great in 1334. These statutes determined the legal position of Jewish communities, exempting them from German law and placing them under the jurisdiction of the *voivodes* (royal governors). In this sense, the frequently-employed description of the Jews in pre-partition Poland as a caste is quite incorrect: they were a medieval estate, with the rights, obligations and privileges of other estates, as is clearly set out in Professor Goldberg's article (chapter 3). They were a link with the outside world, both Jewish and non-Jewish, which aided them considerably in their trading activities and was one of the factors which induced the Polish Kings to invite them to their country. Their links are clearly to be seen in the charters. The Kalisz statute of 1264, for instance, is modelled on the Austrian charter of 1240.

The Jews benefited greatly from the economic upsurge experienced by Poland in the sixteenth century and linked above all with the Vistula grain trade. They were involved in all aspects of Polish trade from the most far-flung to the most local, as well as with skilled crafts connected with the rural economy, as is demonstrated by the articles of Professors Tollet and Hundert (chapters 2 and 4). Yet at the same time, they were divided from the rest of Polish society by a religious gulf, zealously maintained by both sides, which could only be overcome as Andrzej Ciechanowiecki demonstrates, by conversion (chapter 5).

Poland in the sixteenth and seventeenth century has often been described as 'heaven for the Jews, paradise for the nobles, hell for the serfs'. It is certainly true that Jews enjoyed unprecedented economic and social freedom in Poland in those years. Jewish autonomy was widened so that by the end of the sixteenth century, the Jews governed themselves through a sort of parliament, the Council of the Four Lands (*Vaad Arba Aratzot* – the four lands referred to the four parts of the Polish-Lithuanian Common-wealth; Great Poland, Little Poland, Lithuania and the Ukraine). This generally met once a year and was responsible for negotiating with the crown the level of Jewish taxation and for levying taxes on the Jewish communities. In addition, it passed laws and statutes on internal educational and economic matters and other general concerns of Jewish life. The Council of the Four Lands was a unique institution in Europe, its powers going considerably beyond the degree of self-government which Jewish communities enjoyed in other European states. One reflection of the generally favourable position of the Jews was the increase in the size of Polish Jewry, the result both of natural growth and of immigration from Germany, Bohemia and Hungary, and to a much lesser degree from Spain and Portugal as well as Italy and Turkey. By the mid-seventeenth century there were about half a million Jews in Poland, nearly five per cent of the state's population.

Another was the flourishing of Jewish religious and intellectual life. The Talmudic Colleges (*Yeshivot*) of Poland became the models for Talmudic study for the rest of Europe. Students from Germany, Bohemia, Moravia, Hungary and even Italy went to study there. From the second half of the seventeenth century, most rabbis in Germany and Central Europe came originally from Poland. At the same time, Polish masters of *Halakha* (Rabbinic law) became the dominant influence in the religious life of the Jewish world. The critical glosses of Moshe Isserles (Rama) to the rabbinic code of Joseph Karo established the mores of Ashkenazi Jews. The *novellae* on Talmudic tractates by Shlomo Luria (Maharshal) and of Samuel Eidlish remain unsurpassed to the present day. The ascetic kabbalistic ethics of Isaiah Horowitz in his book *Shnei luchot habrit* inspired both Ashkenazim and Sephardim alike, and for over two centuries his work remained the most widely distributed kabbalistic treatise. Indeed, the mystical traditions of the Kabbalah flourished more in Poland than in any other Jewish community with the exception of Safed in Palestine. In Poland Kabbalistic study was transformed from the domain of a small aristocratic elite into a mass movement. Secular learning developed too and Rabbis Moshe Isserles and Mordechai Yaffo wrote profound treatises on secular subjects such as philosophy and astronomy.

Popular religious literature also flourished on Polish soil. One need only mention the Yiddish paraphrase of the Pentateuch, the *Ze'enah Ur'enah* by Yakov of Janow, a book which has gone through innumerable editions including one recently issued in Israel and New York. Women and unlearned men gained their knowledge of the *Torah* (Pentateuch) with the aid of a Hebrew-Yiddish glossary written in Poland (*Sefer Rav Anschel*, Cracow 1534 and 1880) while there were also many editions of the Prayers in Hebrew and Yiddish. With the rise of the European Enlightenment, Polish Jews further advanced the Yiddish language – it was in Poland that the first popular book on medicine in Yiddish was printed (*Sefer Ozer Yisrael*) as was the first modern translation of parts of the Bible into Yiddish (Mendel Lefin's rendering of Proverbs and Ecclesiastes).

Of all European countries, Poland was the only one in which Jews were allowed to participate in a wide range of trades, crafts and skills. It was the only country in Europe, after the expulsion of the Jews from Spain, where Jews managed the estates of the nobility (the *Arenda* system). They were the indispensable craftsmen of the rural economy in the villages and small towns (shtetlach) – the carpenters, cobblers, blacksmiths, tailors, tar-makers, wheelwrights. This was a unique phenomenon in Europe.

The position of the Jews, however, was by no means as secure as it appeared. The failure of the Polish-Lithuanian Commonwealth to develop modern political institutions – above all a centralized and effective state bureaucracy under royal control – and the corresponding weakness of the crown made the Jews increasingly dependent on the great nobles, the magnates whose political and social influence grew considerably from the seventeenth century onwards. Jews in private (non-royal) towns were now placed under jurisdiction of their aristocratic owners and the centre of gravity of Jewish life shifted from the western and central parts of Poland to the eastern areas, where magnate influence was greater. The Jews were thus caught up in the combination of social, religious and national resentment which Polish rule aroused among the Orthodox peasantry and the Cossacks. There has been a tendency in recent years to claim that Jewish casualties in the Chmielnicki revolt have been exaggerated, although even under these estimates nearly twenty per cent of the Jews lost their lives. Certainly there can be no denying that the events of 1648–57 and their consequences both highlighted and accelerated the decline of the Polish-Lithuanian Commonwealth and, with it, the standing of its Jewish inhabitants. Economic recession was accompanied by a further weakening of the power of the King and a strengthening of that of the magnates. Parallel to these events foreign influence was growing, coming to a head with the 'dumb' Sejm of 1719 which effectively made Poland a Russian protectorate. Economic and political retrogression was accompanied by growing intolerance and a strengthening of obscurantist tendencies, above all within the Catholic Church, so that accusations of ritual murder against the Jews which had earlier been relatively rare in Poland now became much more frequent. These coincided with the increasing impoverishment of the Jewish community referred to by Professor Tollet (chapter 2) which led to growing difficulties in paying taxes and to the abolition, in 1764, of the Council of the Four Lands. Equally within the Jewish community poverty and increased insecurity provoked a reaction against the dry and rationalist character of rabbinic Judaism, which took various forms (such as limited support for the false messiah Shabtai Zvi and a subsequent outgrowth of this movement called Frankism, after its founder Jacob Frank, most of whose adherents were eventually baptized). Particularly important was the growth and development of *Chassidism*, a pietistic and originally anti-establishment religious revival which developed into a genuine religious mass movement and which is still very much alive among Jewish communities in the world today.

The first partition of Poland in 1772 led to a series of attempts to reform its political structure which were ultimately frustrated by Russian, Prussian and Austrian intervention and the disappearance of the Polish-Lithuanian

Commonwealth. These attempts at reformation included a number of efforts in line with the political thinking of the Enlightenment to 'productivize' and 'modernize' the Jewish community and convert its members into 'useful' citizens. These plans did not cease with partition but continued in the nineteenth century, both in the Kingdom of Poland, linked with Russia and established at the Vienna Congress in 1815, and in the former eastern territories of the Polish-Lithuanian Commonwealth, not to mention the Austrian and Prussian partitions. Reforms from above and from outside sometimes went hand-in-hand and sometimes clashed with Jewish attempts to reform Jewish life by introducing the principles of enlightenment (*Haskalah*) derived above all from Germany. The not very satisfactory results of this interaction, in the former eastern Polish lands, form the subject of Professor Beauvois' article (chapter 7).

Another important consequence of the partitions and the Vienna settlement was that the bulk of Polish Jewry now lived under Tsarist rule. 'Imperial Russia came to the Jews, not vice versa', it has been argued. Certainly for over a century the fate of the largest Jewish community in the world was intimately bound up with the policies and fortunes of the Tsarist Empire and, particularly in the former eastern parts of the Polish-Lithuanian Commonwealth, the impact of Russian culture on the Jewish intelligentsia was considerable, a development which led to increased tension between Jews and Poles.

Simultaneously, the attempt to regain lost independence led to a new situation in the Polish lands. How was independence to be pursued – should one work slowly within the framework of the frontiers of 1815 and seek to create the pre-conditions for an independent or semi-independent state? Or should one aim, rather, to spark off a national insurrection which would end foreign rule? How could the peasantry – the overwhelming majority of the population – be induced to support an uprising? Could the Jews be enlisted for the national cause and, if so, what sort of Jewish emancipation was required? These general questions are discussed by Professor Kieniewicz (chapter 6), while Professor Bender describes one detailed example of Polish–Jewish cooperation in the run-up to the 1863 insurrection (chapter 8).

The catastrophic crushing of that uprising ushered in a new era of Polish history. Romantic nationalism, with its hope of regaining independence by armed force, was now almost entirely discredited and the dominant ideology was positivism. This held that independence should be renounced, except as the most long-term of goals, and attempts should be made to concentrate on economic advance and to improve the positions of the peasants (who had been given their land by the Tsarist government in 1863), of women and of the Jews. Substantial economic growth did subsequently take place and the

Congress Kingdom of Poland began to experience an industrial revolution. Urbanization and the break-up of the agrarian society of pre-partition Poland were inevitable consequences, changes which inevitably affected the position of the Jews. Calls for the 'solution' of the Jewish problem by the abandonment of Jewish separateness and the adoption by Jews of the Polish language became more widespread and are described by Dr Lichten (chapter 10). It should be stressed however, that assimilation never became a mass movement and that the overwhelming bulk of the Jews remained distinct in language and dress from the majority of the population.

Concurrently with these events new forces were beginning to emerge. From the 1890s, a general European revival of assertive nationalism took place which led in Poland to the emergence of the National Democratic movement led by Roman Dmowski, Zygmunt Balicki and Jan Popławski. Like similar movements in Italy, France and Germany, the National Democrats stressed the organic character of the Nation and the unassimilable nature of the Jews. 'There cannot be two nations on the Vistula', was one of their slogans. Increasingly too, the peasantry were now drawn into political life, above all in semi-constitutional Austria. The temptation to exploit traditional anti-Jewish sentiments for political advantage became strong in Poland, as elsewhere in eastern central Europe, in order to mobilize the now increasingly important voting power of the peasantry, as is outlined in Professor Golczewski's article (chapter 9). Among Jews, the feeling became widespread that the traditional liberal panaceas of equality and assimilation were inadequate to deal with the increasingly difficult situation of the Jewish people, giving rise to movements like Socialism and Zionism and the various combinations of these ideas, which even before the First World War were assuming mass proportions. The dilemmas which the Jewish problem posed for socialists, both Polish and Jewish, before and after the Great War are set out in Professor Holzer's article (chapter 12).

The emergence of an independent Polish state in 1918 posed new and difficult problems for the Jewish community, now numbering three million and making up ten per cent of the population. Despite the intentions of the peacemakers at Versailles the prevalent climate of heightened nationalism did not favour liberal treatment of the national minorities, who constituted more than a third of the inhabitants of the new state. The Jews were regarded as only dubiously loyal, particularly in the eastern parts of the new republic where they were suspected of having been Russified and of sympathy with Bolshevism. The economic problems inherent in re-establishing a state from regions which for nearly 130 years had been integral parts of the Russian, German and Habsburg empires created major imbalances and contributed to the decline of the economic well-being of the Jews, many of whom had been deeply impoverished even before 1914 and who were, moreover, concentrated in the more backward sectors of the economy. The early years of independence were marked by anti-Jewish violence and although the situation eased from the mid-twenties, after Marshal Pilsudski's death in 1935 the impact of political and economic crises and the influence of Nazi Germany, meant that, once more, anti-semitism began to play a pre-eminent role in political life. There has been a tendency in Poland to treat these developments as essentially economic in origin and of somewhat marginal significance since no anti-Jewish legislation was introduced before the defeat of Poland in 1939. To the Jews, however, there was no doubt about the hostility of the state system to their position. As Rafael Scharf has written:

> If the question were asked, whether Poland was a country where anti-semitism grew and was rampant, the answer for every Polish Jew, an eye-witness, would be so obvious and unequivocal that he would be angered and resentful of anybody doubting it. As soon as Poland regained independence after World War I, the framework of an anti-Jewish movement began to take shape. It grew in strength and came to be for us an ever present force, filling the atmosphere like ether. The fact that the Poles were and are not aware of this – at least this is what they claim – is for us hard to believe and understand. They have either forgotten how it was or have been seeing life from an altogether different perspective.[2]

Yet at the same time, partly because of the plural character of the political system in interwar Poland, Jewish life also flourished, although under much pressure. A series of private school networks developed, reflecting the division of the community into Zionist, socialist and orthodox groupings. An extensive press in Yiddish, Hebrew and Polish found many readers. Scholarship into Jewish history and ethnography grew with the establishment of the Jewish Scientific Organization (YIVO) in Wilno and the creation for Professor Mayer Bałaban of a chair at the University of Warsaw. The paradoxes of Jewish life in Poland between the wars are summed up in Professor Ezra Mendelsohn's article, 'Interwar Poland: good for the Jews or bad for the Jews?' (chapter 11).

The Polish defeat and the German occupation sealed the fate of the Jewish community in Poland. The Nazis immediately introduced anti-Jewish legislation and soon segregated the entire Jewish population in ghettos. From late 1941 they embarked on a systematic, mass murder of the Jews which, by liberation in the second half of 1944 and nearly 1945, had led to the deaths of over ninety per cent of Polish Jewry. Approximately 50,000–100,000 Jews survived, in hiding or in concentration camps, while another 250,000 saved their lives by fleeing to the Soviet Union. It should be clearly stated that the responsibility for this horrendous crime lies with the Nazis and, in the first instance, with Hitler himself.

Inevitably, perhaps, the actual circumstances of the mass murder have led to bitter controversy and recrimination. Jewish writers have accused the Poles of offering insufficient assistance to Jewish fellow-citizens, of looking with complaisance and even approval on German actions and finally, in some cases, of actively assisting the Nazis. Poles, for their part, have argued that Jewish historians have been insufficiently aware of the brutal nature of Nazi rule in Poland, of the savage repression provoked by attempts to aid the Jews and of taking too little account of how much Poles did actually aid Jews. The Relief Council for Jews in Poland, in which Professor Bartoszewski was active and which is described by Dr Prekerowa (chapter 14) was, after all, a unique institution in occupied Europe. This controversy risks taking a too narrowly Polish perspective on events. Everywhere in the Nazi 'New Order', when faced with the plans to deport and murder local Jews, a proportion of the population attempted to aid and succour the Jews, a proportion assisted the Nazis and the majority remained inactive somewhere in between. One can only agree with Professor Bartoszewski that, from a moral point of view, 'it must be stated clearly that not enough was done in Poland or anywhere else in occupied Europe. "Enough" was done only by those who died while giving aid.'[3] The problem remains of deciding what proportion of the population should be assigned to each group. But even a willingness to aid Jews could not necessarily affect their final fate. The Dutch are generally held to have been strongly philo-semitic, yet the proportion of Jews who survived in the Netherlands was not much higher than in Poland.

The controversy surrounding the aid given by the Poles raises moral dilemmas which normal historical methods are not well-equipped to answer. The problems are aired in a balanced and open manner by Professor Bartoszewski, Dr Preker and Professor Gutmann (chapters 13, 14 and 15). The main point at issue between them appears to centre on the question of whether the impact of Nazi anti-Jewish policies led the Poles to adopt a more friendly attitude towards Jews. It is certainly true that many Poles, some of them previously strongly hostile to Jews (like the writer Zofia Kossak Szczucka or the National Democratic politician, Jan Mosdorf) came to see anti-semitism as morally totally unacceptable. Equally one cannot overlook the successes of German propaganda in isolating the Jews and inducing Poles to see them as sub-human or even not human at all. Czeslaw Milosz in his poem *Campo di Fiori* has described the indifference of Poles at the spring carnival in Warsaw to the clearly visible and audible destruction of the ghetto. Equally, it was Jan Karski, a prominent member of the Polish underground and the first person to bring an account to the West of Nazi mass murder, who in a report to the Polish government in France in February 1940 wrote of Polish attitudes:

'The solution of the Jewish Question' by the Germans – I must state this with a full
sense of responsibility for what I am saying – is a serious and quite dangerous tool in
the hands of the Germans, leading toward the 'moral pacification' of broad sections
of Polish society . . .

It would certainly be erroneous to suppose that this issue alone will be effective in
gaining for them the acceptance of the populace.

However, although the nation loathes them mortally, this question is creating
something akin to a narrow bridge upon which the Germans and a large portion of
Polish society are finding agreement.

It is certain that this bridge is no less narrow than the desires of the Germans to
strengthen and reinforce it are great.

Moreover, this situation threatens to demoralize broad segments of the populace,
and this in turn may present many problems to the future authorities endeavouring
to rebuild the Polish state. It is difficult; 'the lesson is not lost.'

I do not know how to do this, or even how to begin, or even who could do it, or on
what scale in the long run [if it is possible at all] – but might it not be possible to a
certain extent, in the face of the existence of three enemies [if, of course, one should
currently regard the Jews as enemies], to endeavour to create something along the
lines of a common front with the two weaker partners against the third more
powerful and deadly enemy, leaving accounts to be settled with the other two later?

The establishment of any kind of broader common front would be beset with very
many difficulties from the perspective of wide segments of the Polish populace,
among whom antisemitism has by no means decreased.[4]

In the immediate post-war years, the survivors of Polish Jewry found
themselves caught up in the near-civil war provoked by the imposition of a
communist government on an unwilling population. Jews provoked hostility
because of their prominence (sometimes exaggerated) in the new regime
and because of the fears of those who had taken over Jewish property that
they would be compelled to give it up. Between liberation and mid-1947
some 1,500 Jews lost their lives in violent incidents[5] of which the most
shocking was the pogrom at Kielce in July 1946 in which at least 42 Jews
were killed. This sad episode in Polish-Jewish history is chronicled by a
man who participated in it, Michał Borwicz, who had also been the highest-
ranking Jew in the Polish underground Home Army (*Armia Krajowa*) in
chapter 16. While conceding that many of these incidents, and possibly
Kielce itself, had an element of communist provocation in them and were
certainly exploited by the communists to tighten their hold on power, he
stresses the responsibility of the right-wing underground groups, and also of
those church authorities who refused to condemn anti-Jewish outrages.

By 1948, with the fall of Władysław Gomułka, a stalinist-style regime
was established in Poland and Polish–Jewish relations entered on a new
and, in many ways, paradoxical course. As Dr Hirszowicz demonstrates
(chapter 17) Jewish communists were prominent both in the Stalinist wing

of the Polish United Workers' Party (PZPR) and among the revisionists who hoped to reform the communist system. Gomułka's return to power in 1956 proved a disappointment to those who hoped he would usher in new and more open attitudes. Increasingly from the early 1960s, as his regime lost its dynamism and was plagued by persistent economic failure, the temptation grew for young, power-hungry members of the party apparently led by Mieczylaw Moczar to blame the relatively small number of Jews in the party leadership for the failures of Polish communism. This tendency came to a head in 1968 when 'anti-Zionism', ostensibly provoked by the Israeli victory in the six-day war, led to a major purge of Jewish communists and what was almost certainly an unsuccessful attempt by Moczar and his faction to seize power. Moczar failed and after Gomułka's fall in 1970, the regime of his successor Edward Gierek returned to a policy of trying to improve relations with international Jewish organizations, while periodically resorting to attempts to smear the growing opposition movement as 'Jewish' in character. This dual policy has been maintained not only during the 17 months during which Solidarity was legal but also during the subsequent period of martial law and the 'normalization' which has followed.

The history of Polish Jewry has virtually come to an end. Barely 6,000 Jews still live in Poland and although a number of institutions, such as the Jewish Social and Cultural Organization and the Jewish Historical Institute continue to perform useful and valuable work, it is difficult to see organized communal life surviving another generation. As a consequence, the history of this community, which has played so large a role in the life of both Poland and of world Jewry assumes an even more vital significance. For the Poles, it is part of their past which they are in danger of losing forever. It is true that the significance of the Jewish contribution to Polish life has not always been fully appreciated by Poles. It was the character of the Jewish writer Yitzchak Leib Peretz who, in Aaron Zeitlin's play *Esterka* tells Adam Mickiewicz, 'I know who you are, but who I am – you do not know . . .'. Rafael Scharf sees this lack of interest as the result of a superiority complex:

Did it ever occur to a Pole that in a neighbouring town, or for that matter on the very same street something was happening that could engage his attention and deserved his interest? Not in the least. The Jewish population was commonly regarded as a 'dark continent', backward and primitive, evoking feelings of aversion and repugnance. The Poles, automatically regarded themselves as something infinitely superior – each Pole to each Jew, be he a rabbi, a writer, a merchant, a shoemaker . . .'[6]

In recent years, the situation has changed. Polish interest in Jewish matters has increased greatly. The awareness of the common links binding Poles and Jews has grown enormously. Yiddish and Hebrew literature has been

translated into Polish, attempts have been made to preserve and rebuild
Jewish monuments and the study of Polish-Jewish history has become
increasingly widespread – the conference at which these papers were
delivered gave eloquent testimony to the high quality of Polish research in
this field.

There is also a moral dimension. Anti-semitism was not a uniquely Polish
phenomenon. It was a sickness of Europe and of Christianity, whose ghosts
many people have tried to exorcize. There is nothing shameful in admitting
that there are anti-semitic aspects of Polish history just as there are aspects
of the Jewish past and present which a Jewish historian must feel compelled
to criticize. On the contrary, it is on the 'overcoming of the past', on striking
a balance between what is good in a national tradition and what should be
rejected, that the path lies to true democratization and freedom. This is
clearly understood in Poland. As Marek Leski wrote in *Arka*,

The anti-pluralistic elements in Polish culture are particularly important today
when for a number of years, efforts have been made to organize society outside
officially sponsored bodies. The romantic vision of the nation-organism, the
spiritual community not open to outsiders has never been as far from reality as it is
today. Cultural diversity has become the characteristic of all modern western socie-
ties, channelling in this way more or less effectively and more or less creatively
nationalist feelings. Nationalism in its pure form, we observe only in political
dictatorships, generally economically backward as well as in political movements
with a revolutionary or autocratic character. A reckoning with Polish nationalism
and its xenophobia therefore appears an important task if our society is to become
like that of countries characterized by a political culture which respects individual
rights and civic freedoms and has a plural character. It is therefore injurious and
indeed downright harmful to close our eyes to Polish anti-semitism or to diminish its
role in our political tradition. The conviction that there is something shameful in
speaking about this subject, or that doing so will undermine or paralyze the national
will and spirit of Poles merely displays a lack of faith in the self-correcting abilities of
Polish culture. The one guarantee that we will not make such mistakes again is to
remember our past errors, the lost opportunities to make use of the intellectual and
social potential possessed by our ethnic minorities, our insensitivity to the achievements of other cultures, the laziness and sloth displayed by the glorifiers of national
self-praise.[7]

For the Jews the importance of Polish-Jewish history lies elsewhere. The
destruction of many of the major centres of Jewish life has been an amputa-
tion which has left Jewry numbed and mutilated. Memory, it has often been
said, is the mother of the muses. Jews have a need to find their own past, to
deny to the Nazis success in their bid to destroy the record of Jewish activity
in Europe and, in particular, in Poland. Jews have lived in Poland for a
millenium and many of the most glorious pages of their history have been

written there. Jewish attitudes to Poland and Poles may often be ambivalent. Yet there is no denying Jewish nostalgia for the lost centre of the Polish-Lithuanian Commonwealth. It was Jerzy Ficowski, a Polish poet, who wrote accurately of those Jews who

> 'went to Jerusalem
> and that far they smuggled
> a handful of willow pears
> and for a keepsake a herringbone
> that sticks to this day.'[8]

Similarly Antoni Słonismki wrote of the old Jew at the Jaffa Gate in Jerusalem who asked, 'Are the Saxon Gardens still there? And are they still the same?'

It was in the hope of creating the framework in which a balanced and scholarly examination of the past of our two peoples could be undertaken that the Oxford conference was held. This work is the first fruit of that conference. It is our hope that it will be followed by much further research and analysis of the many developments which have united – and sometimes divided – 'two of the saddest nations on the earth',[9] the Poles and the Jews.

1

The beginnings of Jewish settlement in the Polish lands

Aleksander Gieysztor

The presence of Jews in Polish lands before the thirteenth century and their participation in the economic life of old Poland is a phenomenon apparent from both written and other sources. Doubts expressed even by well-known academic authorities on this subject may be disregarded.[1] The appearance of Jewish communities, although almost certainly few in number, between the Odra and the Vistula by the tenth century at the latest should be considered in the wider context of their activity within Central and Eastern Europe. The economic development of the early Middle Ages focused at first on the long-distance trade between the European west and the Arabian and Byzantine east, but it soon drew into its net a third great economic sphere composed of the core of the Eurasian continent. A major role within this trade was played by communities whose religion and culture were Jewish.[2] They established themselves in many centres and countries from Western Europe to the borders of the then Moslem Asiatic world.

In the second half of the eighth century the peoples of the Eastern peripheries of Europe – Slavs, Finno-Ugrians, Turks and Mongols, some of whom had settled as agricultural tribes while others led a nomadic existence on the steppes – entered into a far-reaching trade orbit that crossed the borders of the northwestern Abbasid empire in both directions. One incentive encouraging this trade was the growing consumption and demand within the countries of the Caliphate. Another was the desire of the newly established political entities in Eastern Europe to ensure a constant supply of goods of the highest quality and in the greatest quantities possible, given prevailing technical and economic capabilities. From the end of the eighth century and throughout the ninth, the Slavonic peoples of Central and Eastern Europe began to form the first states in the region to possess a fiscal and military apparatus designed to serve the princes and the powerful. A particular characteristic of one of these states, Rus', was the process of drawing into its sphere of influence many Finno-Ugrian peoples, whether indirectly by imposing a tribute or by direct domination. The Varangians also contributed to the establishment of this state and, due to their military strength, were able to establish their own trade routes to Byzantium and the Arabian lands from the middle of the ninth century.[3]

The steppes from the Black Sea to the Caspian served as a filter, benefiting from the volume of trade conducted over this vast region by the empire of the Khazars. The empire's expansion, beginning in the seventh century, led over the next two centuries to the subordination of some of the Slavonic peoples living along the Dnieper and to control over the mouth of the Danube and the Black Sea coast. It extended, too, in the direction of the northern and eastern Turkish Bulgars on the banks of the Volga and Kama, and to the settlement of the Finnish and Hungarian peoples in their respective areas. Seeking ways of strengthening the authority of the supreme ruling group and assisting contacts with the outside world – with the Caliphate and Byzantium – the Khazar elite decided to make a declaration of neutrality regarding the two existing monotheistic religious systems, and to abandon their pagan tribal religion in favour of Judaism. (Foreign observers in the second half of the ninth century confirm that the Khazar elite had converted to Judaism.) The Khazars were distinguished among other states by their tolerance. Relations with the rabbinical Diaspora were a little distant due to the syncretic and heterodox elements that distinguished the Khazars' position, but their conversion to Judaism ensured them a place in the net of trade contacts maintained by Jewish communities in the region of the Black and Caspian Seas, as well as along the borders of the Caliphate and Byzantium.[4]

These distant markets did not escape the attention of Jews in Western Europe. In the middle of the ninth century, the remarkable and credible testimony of Ibn-Hurdadbih, head of the caliph of Baghdad's postal and intelligence service, portrays the role of the 'Radanite' Jews. This term was used to describe merchants whose trade extended over vast distances between the west and the east. They knew the Arabic, Persian, Greek, 'Frankish', Spanish and 'Slav' languages. They set out from the Frankish lands and reached the capital of the Khazars along the lower Volga. At either end of this well-travelled continental trade route and at points along its length were Jewish colonies which organized the exchange of forest products, horses and hides, swords, and slaves of both sexes from the west for luxury goods from the east, as well as impressive quantities of Arabian money, mainly in silver. The Khazar empire reached its peak at the end of the ninth century and the beginning of the tenth, assisted by the expansion of Rus' around the Black Sea and the new waves of expansion by the steppe nomads. The end of this great trading period came with the beginning of the tenth century as a result of the crisis within the Moslem world.[5]

The Jewish merchants of Central and Eastern Europe did not cast their lot exclusively with Khazaria. Established along the great road of the central continent and along a few of its offshoots – one of which reached down through Hungary along the Danube and led to Byzantium – they took advantage of local markets, contributing to their economic vitality and encouraging a widespread flow of goods. The great oriental road, beginning in Gaul with its links to Moslem Spain, passed through Verdun, the main slave market, and then through Mainz and Regensburg, reaching Raffelstetten on the Danube. From here it went through the principality of Moravia, which was already flourishing in the ninth century, and after the fall of that duchy through the territory seized by the Hungarians, where as early as the tenth century various groups of merchants, both Moslem and Jewish, were active.

Hasdai ben Shaprut, a Jewish dignitary in Spain, in a letter written before 961 to King Joseph of Khazaria, mentions Jewish communities in Hungary and their contacts with the lands of Rus'.[6] It is around this time that Ibrahim-ibn-Iaqub notes the arrival of Hungarian Jews in Prague to buy pewter, furs and slaves.[7] It is possible that some of the Hungarian Jews arrived with the Magyar migration from the Eurasian steppes, controlled by the Khazars; others may have arrived along a variation of the great Byzantine road. Another of its variations led to Kiev.

Yet another road led from Raffelstetten, or a little further north, from the banks of the Danube to Prague, which had trade relations with Magdeburg (including trade with Germany of the Ottonian dynasty) towards the Polish lands in the east. The presence of a notable Jewish community in Prague is confirmed by various tenth-century texts; trade was conducted with Hungary, Byzantium and Rus. The road then led on to Cracow over the plains or through passes along the Carpathian mountain range.[8] Excavations in Cracow, which have revealed a sizeable hoard of iron money substitutes indicating a relatively large market area, testify to Cracow's role as a trading centre in the ninth and tenth centuries.[9] It should be no surprise, therefore, that the Jews found a place for their colony here. Thanks to the records of Sefer HaDinim, which can be dated around the mid-eleventh century at the latest, perhaps even 1028, we learn of a dispute between two Jewish merchants from either the German territories or from Prague who, on their way to Russia, displayed their goods to the Jewish community in Cracow. One of the parties was accused of involving a non-Jewish authority in the dispute.[10]

The roads from Cracow and Magdeburg met at fords on the Vistula and then merged as far as Przemyśl. The latter is mentioned as 'Primis' in a text by Iehuda ben Meir ha-Kohen, probably written before 1028. The work of archaeologists and the deposits of money discovered in the area have also contributed to our knowledge of this early town.[11] The next junction of the roads was Kiev, capital of Rus', which had escaped direct Khazar patronage in the second half of the ninth century although it remained subject to Khazar influence. There are various facts which indicate that influence: the title of Kagan adopted by Prince Vladimir, and the tradition which tells of his consideration of Judaism before his decision to be christened into the Eastern Orthodox faith.[12] The name of a district in Kiev – Kozary – reveals something of existing trade relationships, as the name also occurs in Ukranian and Polish lands.[13] We know of the Jewish community in Kiev from the account of the 1113 troubles, and it had doubtless enjoyed a history previous to that.[14]

As mentioned earlier, Arabian trade with Northern and Eastern Europe was based mainly on payment in the form of silver Arabian coins and to a lesser extent in golden coins, particularly in areas towards Sweden. However, the balance of trade along the road from Regensburg or Magdeburg through the Czech and Polish lands right up to Kiev was rather complicated. The Carolingian and Ottonian west received luxury oriental goods which were paid for with arms and cloth, but also with silver coins. It is possible that the road did not reach the borders of the Caliphate but stopped in the Slavonic lands, which thus gained eastern goods both for themselves and for re-export in exchange for their own export goods as listed above, together with slaves. Halfway through the tenth century there was an increase in the flow of German money to Bohemia, Poland and Hungary. These countries also undertook the production of their own coins. Together with Arabian coins, which were often broken down into small unit weights and other money substitutes (linen rolls, iron, furs and skins), they began to circulate even in the local marketplace. The new central Europe composed of these three countries created the conditions suitable for an almost exclusively monetary trade;[15] the role of the Jews becomes particularly evident at this stage. Iehuda ben Meir ha-Kohen mentions two Jewish minters authorized by the Hungarian Queen Gisela to mint silver coins.[16] One hundred years later, we see Jews in Poland at the head of the mint producing bracteates bearing the Polish sovereign's name in Hebrew letters, together with the names of the minters.[17] Jews were also conducting land transactions around Wrocław at this time,[18] as indicated, for example, by the study of place names, which reveals a dozen or so Jewish-sounding names occurring in Polish lands.[19]

The question of the origin of Jews in Slavonic lands, and in Poland in particular, is the subject of hypothesis and discussion. The basic source of the answer to the question is primarily the rabbinical literature of the tenth to thirteenth centuries which appeared in the Western Diaspora. These texts are indicative of the whole geographical horizon of Jewish settlement at that time. The areas of settlement are described as *Sepharad* in Spain; *Ashkenaz* in Western Europe as far as the river Elbe, and eastwards from there as *Kna'an*. Southern Italy and Byzantine territories are referred to as *Yavan*. Alongside Hebrew, the language of sacred and other texts, the Sephardic Jews also used the Mediterranean Romance languages. The Ashkenazy spoke in German dialects from which – along the Rhine and in Mosel in an area they called *Loter* (from the kingdom of Lothar I) – the Yiddish language developed.[20] It is reasonable to assume that Greek was the dominant language among the Jews of *Yavan*.[21]

Enough is known about the *Kna'an* Jews to assume that their everyday language was Slavonic. From the tenth century, the general Hebrew term for the Slavs (the use of which sometimes extended as far as the Eastern German lands) was *Kna'an*. This appears to derive not so much directly from Canaan, the promised land, as from *ebed Kna'an*, 'the Canaanite slave, the non-Jew', a term used to describe the people dominated by the Hebrews in the land of Canaan. In the second half of the twelfth century Benjamin of Tudela writes of the name *Kna'an* bestowed upon the land of Isqlabonia, that is, the Slavonic lands, and comments that, 'the inhabitants of this land sell their sons and their daughters to all the peoples of the world, the inhabitants of Rus' do likewise.'[22] It is possible that the new semantic quality ascribed to the biblical *Kna'an* arose at the same time as the term *sclavus*, derived from the ethnic name of the Slavs. It came into common use at the end of the seventh century and the beginning of the eighth, when the Venetian slave market developed on the Adriatic coast. The name given to Jews which occurs in Slavonic languages provides a geographical and chronological indication of their first contacts with Slavs. In early medieval and medieval Slavonic this name appears as *židin*, *žyd*, *žid*, the first consonant indicating that the word derives from popular Latin in the Romance and probably Venetian version (the nearest form is *giudeo*). Jewish communities on the Adriatic coast may first have established contact with Karantonia and Moravia, that is to say, with the oldest organized Western Slavonic states.[23]

Was it from here that Jewish communities came to Hungary, Czechoslovakia and Poland? Their origin at its earliest phase is linked, together with *Sepharad*, *Ashkenaz* and *Kna'an*, with the fourth Jewish grouping of the Diaspora, namely *Yavan*. This name covers the Southern Italian, Balkan and Byzantine Diaspora which extended into the north. The Jews adopted local languages, Greek giving way to Latin-based dialects as they moved westwards. There were Jewish colonies in the Eastern Slavonic lands from the cultural area of *Yavan* as well as from the Khazar lands and the Caucasus, and they also adopted the local languages.[24] A letter commending a member

of the community in Rus' to the community in Salonika explains that the
protégé knew neither the sacral language, nor Greek, nor Arabic, 'as the
people of his country speak only Slavonic'.[25] So alongside polyglot
merchants travelling and trading throughout many countries, there existed
Jewish communities firmly rooted within the local landscape. A few
hundred Slavonic expressions found in Rabbinical texts of the tenth to
thirteenth centuries confirm the Jewish linguistic assimilation of Slavonic.[26]
In the most westerly parts of *Kna'an* the *Yavan* Jews coming from Hungary
or from the Adriatic coast through Karantania and Croatia encountered
Ashkenazy Jews, but maintained their own characteristic culture and
language among Czech and other communities. The complete victory of
Yiddish over colloquial Slavonic – which as a specific environmental dialect
was obviously tinged with Hebrew and Yiddish, similarly among the
Sephardim – did not occur before the thirteenth century.[27]

The rabbinical texts mentioned above also shed some light upon the
economy and even the everyday life of Jewish communities in the Western
Slavonic lands between the tenth and thirteenth centuries (before the great
fresh wave of Jews emigrated from Western Europe) since they are a
response to various expressions of doubt concerning religious and
economic questions. The texts deal not only with religious and spiritual
subjects, but also with medicine, anatomy and many aspects of human
physiology, including nutrition. There are descriptions of trading tech-
niques and methods of transporting goods and the problems of co-respon-
sibility for cargo as described by *Sefer ha Dinim*, taking a merchant returning
from a trip to Poland as an example.[28]

The oldest type of trading which drew Jewish colonies to the Slavonic
lands was the kind of exchange trading typical of the early-medieval period.
It included a few luxury articles and goods that were suitable for transport
over long distances (slaves were a self-transporting commodity, the supply
of which was guaranteed by the nature of early political organization of
countries on the Eurasian continent). This trading gained from the great
differences in economic standards: Europe exported natural resources such
as furs, skins and human labour to Arabian lands, while the Moslem world
blossomed as craftsmanship, the production of money, trade and agriculture
developed concurrently.[29] Eastern Europe's entry into this trading system
took place under less than favourable conditions, as it provided mainly raw
materials and was losing its production force by exporting slaves. The injec-
tion of Arabic silver did not prove advantageous until the tenth and eleventh
centuries, when these countries began to reorganize their economies and
reach into their metal reserves, collected back in barbarian times, reserves
which they now began to utilize in accordance with the demands of the
market.[30] Between the eighth and eleventh centuries Western Europe

traversed a long road which also led to the harmonious development of the four basic branches of economy: industry, trade, currency and agriculture. From the tenth century this development grew to encompass the peripheries of Western Europe with Central Europe and part of Eastern Europe.

Different intermediaries between the different sectors of the economy were also necessary, and were discovered in the early towns. The Jewish communities which had previously performed an outstanding organizational role were forced, in the eleventh and twelfth centuries, to rethink the basic principles governing their activities and to find a new place for themselves in Poland. Forms of trading which were to disappear in the future included the slave trade, mentioned in the chronicle of Gallus Anonimus (which describes how Judith, the wife of Prince Vladyslaus Herman, bought up slaves from the Jews before 1085).[31] New forms of trade replaced old, particularly with the development of currency. From this point onwards the Jewish communities acquired a new significance, although the number of Jews in Poland before the thirteenth century remained small, since in the earliest towns, where the task of regulating the flow of currency in the local market (*renovatio monetae*) was carried out by the princely minters, the Jews helped to bring about the development of the exchange of money and goods.[32]

2

Merchants and businessmen in Poznań and Cracow, 1588–1668

Daniel Tollet

The social development of Poland since the fifteenth century has taken place within the framework of the process of the diversification of Europe. Western Europe's economic conquest of the East European countries brought about a new division of labour, with the result that Poland became one of the principal grain suppliers for Western Europe. This transformation was made possible because the crisis facing feudal society in Poland at the close of the Middle Ages took a specific form which allowed the establishment of the manorial system known as *folwark*. This system gave the nobility excessive weight in Polish politics and economics, and thus urban growth was held back.[1] Indeed, by keeping the monopoly of the grain trade, the upper nobility hindered the establishment of a strong bourgeoisie. However the subsequent decline in Western Europe's grain purchases from Poland, at the end of the sixteenth century and the beginning of the seventeenth, disrupted the Polish economy.[2]

The period of the turn of the sixteenth and seventeenth centuries has been chosen to provide a better understanding of the form taken by the feudal mode of production[3] during the time when the seignorial taxes on the peasants and townspeople were slowly being taken over by the state. The system no longer functioned as in the Middle Ages in a strictly feudal form, yet even so it cannot be classified as a capitalist mode of production. The choice of the period of the reigns of the three Vasa kings, Zygmunt III (1588–1632), Władysław IV (1632–48) and Jan II Kazimierz (1648–68) can be justified because of their consistently benevolent policy towards Jews over a period of eighty years – long enough to allow one to trace trends and structural features.

The Jewish population at this time was extremely varied; alongside the mass of poor townspeople, craftsmen and small shopkeepers studied by

M. Horn[4] lived stewards of estates in Eastern Poland as well as bankers, tax-farmers and urban traders from central Poland. Following Yves Renouard's example, I have made a distinction between merchants and entrepreneurs, restricting the term entrepreneur (*homme d'affaires*) 'to all those whose business goes beyond the local market'.[5] I have therefore examined the social composition and the activities of these groups in terms of the size and the number of transactions handled by their members.

Before the Second World War the Polish historian Majer Bałaban realized that in view of the scarcity of Hebrew documents one had to turn to the Polish documents to study the past of the Jews in Poland. Bałaban took soundings in the official town records – *Consularia, Advocatialia, Scabinalia, Banita* – as well as in the *voivodes* documents from Cracow, Lublin and Lwów.[6] This research was mainly aimed at tracing the activities of the wealthiest Jewish merchants and entrepreneurs.

For my part, I have chosen to make a full study of only two towns, Cracow and Poznań, but I have gone beyond the 'sounding' method in order to grasp the economic activity of all the Jews who took part in business, their mutual social relations and the social relationships created within Polish society as a whole. One ought not however to delude oneself as to the actual extent of the documentation, although it bears on a period of eighty years. It is true that the entries in *protocols* are supported by those of the draft documents, but they are frequently merely a duplication. In short, there are often cases of texts which repeat themselves on one single matter, and this means we have firm knowledge of only a few transactions and merchants.

The documentation relating to attitudes of mind has not been easy to establish. To learn the Christians' opinion on the Jews, I have scoured the very abundant polemical Polish literature of the sixteenth and seventeenth centuries, which the National Library in Warsaw is patiently collecting. A great help in this task is the important research done by K. Bartoszewicz, who before World War I established a list of anti-Jewish (*judéophobes*) works.[7] Nor has it been easy to discover the Jews' own ideas about their society and about Poland, because the sources are extremely rare as a result of the destruction of Jewish libraries and archives by the Nazis during the Second World War. Thanks to the citations gathered by Majer Bałaban's pupils before 1939 I have been able to reconstitute, in the fashion of an archaeologist rather than an historian, the fragments of the lost rabbinical *Responsa*.[8] Research into the law of persons, commercial law, and fiscal decisions governing the Jews has been relatively easy because of the abundant source material published by nineteenth- and twentieth-century Polish historians.

What I have undertaken may be judged to be rash: I have reconstituted the careers of merchants while being acquainted with very few of their dealings. What value is to be accorded to a history written in mere outline? Yet if one bears in mind the almost total lack of Jewish sources – in particular the absence of account books and wills – to reject this method would have meant giving up the subject altogether. In this connection, I prefer to explain the scarcity of contemporary Polish research not by looking for anti-semitic reasons but by the thinness of the source material.

The choice of these two towns, Cracow and Poznan, is not fortuitous. They were the capitals of two great historic regions, Little Poland and Great Poland. Cracow looked to the trade of the South and of the East,[9] but had experienced a marked economic setback at the beginning of the seventeenth century because of the loss of its role as a capital. Poznań on the other hand was open to the Baltic trade and that of Central and North Germany, and knew good days at the time of the Thirty Years War.[10] There should have been added to the study of these two towns a study of Lwów, then the capital of Red Rus'. Unfortunately the present administrative situation of Lwów – in the Soviet Union – makes impossible archive research comparable to that done in Poland and for a knowledge of Lwów I have had to rely on research published before the Second World War.

Even if little is known about the demographic movements that affected Poland during this period, it is evident that up until the Cossack and Swedish Wars the Jewish population increased considerably, particularly in the small- and medium-sized towns. These people became settled thanks to the support of the property-owners (in the private towns) and of the king and the nobility (in the royal towns). The king and the nobility strove to remove the Jews from the jurisdiction of the burgesses; in turn this policy was an additional source of conflict between Christian citizens and Jews, whom the former now saw as rivals in the economic sphere, and local differences were the result of the greater or less pressure on the authorities by the burgesses. These pressures were all the stronger the older the towns and the more deeply rooted in their bourgeoisie. The towns in the Eastern Lands, of recent creation, were the most favourable for the establishment and development of Jewish communities.[11]

The economic struggle of the burgesses and the Jews forced the latter to act within the framework of a system which can be described as the Municipal Guarantee System under which the Patriciate, anxious to preserve its interests and to fight against the lack of coinage, had subjugated the town. The system prevailed over the efforts made by the very numerous entrepreneurs, who were swiftly eliminated from commercial life because of their inability to present sufficient guarantees.[12] In addition to this there were a number of discriminatory legislative measures which constituted further barriers to the activities of the Jews.

Attempts to escape 'the municipal guarantee system' by indirect means were rarely crowned by success, since the Jews controlled only a part of the commercial networks, were unable to control production and so did not carry much weight in fixing the cost price. The fact that it was impossible to make a fortune within the framework of the municipal economic system prompted certain of the most able and richest Jews (often benefiting from inherited wealth) to put themselves at the service of the state and the nobility. The resulting position of the Jewish oligarchy, which was to become permanent in the 'aristocratic Republic', marked the knell of the attempts to renew the economy through the combination of production control and marketing. The fact is that the speculations of the Jewish oligarchy benefited only those who practised them – while they enjoyed royal protection, that is. They mobilized considerable sums of money and were an important factor in the seventeenth-century decline of the Polish towns.

Despite the widely differing levels of business, it can be affirmed that during the Vasa period the ruling strata of urban society, the Patriciate, and the nobility expected the Jews to supply the market through their contracts with their fellow Jews. They were also expected to constitute a market for the sale of the Christians' products and the money they were able to earn was to be redistributed either through taxes or through consumption. Nor should it be forgotten that the Jews supplied services at a better rate – *there* lay the real meaning of the religious toleration from which the Jews benefited in Poland.

Yet certain Jews tried to escape from this role. They did not always manage to do so fully, nor everywhere. For the wealthiest among them the solution was to become even more integrated into the Polish socio-economic system by making themselves the agents of the great feudal lords and of the state and the managers of the businesses of the petty and middle nobility.

The difficulties linked to the unfavourable structure of business, to a generally negative state of affairs, to levies outside the economy, to a series of accidents (like the recurring fires and plague)[13] and incidents such as the anti-Jewish thefts and acts of violence, weighed heavily on the vitality of the Jews' economic affairs, and, particularly in Cracow, prevented the growth of new initiatives. Yet these difficulties were not the essential cause of the low level of business. The essential factor lies in the socio-economic organization: this is proved by the parallel movement of trends in Jewish business and of the Polish economy in general.

One must again stress certain important ideas relating to the careers of Jewish merchants and businessmen. On the one hand, the number of true merchants and businessmen was limited. Many of those I have come across had only an occasional part in the transactions recorded in the Town Books.

Conversely, it appears that those who managed to succeed in business, at least for a time, were those who were able to deploy a whole family's energy in such activities.

The most active merchants managed to get out of their community's economic framework. This being so, it was, for every category of merchants irrespective of their volume of business, their credit operations on which the most energy was brought to bear. It follows that the difference between merchants on a small scale and those operating on a large scale was only quantitative and very rarely qualitative. This lack of flexibility was the cause of the vulnerability of Jewish businessmen and merchants; it called for protective measures, favouritism, moratoriums or privileges. Yet these measures, for the most part taken by the king, were introduced sparingly and in the sort of crisis situation one finds after 1648. It cannot be said that the privileges and the moratoriums played a determining role, at least on the community scale. On the other hand, it is noticeable that if the most active Cracow families were able to work in symbiosis with the nobility and the magnates, this was not the case for the Poznań families: this characteristic was the determining factor. Thus the Cracow families were able to withstand the onset of the economic crisis and then the catastrophes of the Swedish and Cossack Wars, while the Poznań families, abandoned by the kings and the nobility, went into an irreparable decline.

The factors which affected Jewish business and the future of Jews as a group cannot be explained by economic facts alone. One must consider the place that the Jews occupied in Polish society, individually and collectively. The policy of religious tolerance was not supposed to be applicable to commoners, as the Jews were.[14] Nevertheless, because the Jews made up no more than ten per cent of the urban population and presented no threat to the unity of the Catholic Church, they were not made the object of excessively vigorous attacks in print. The anti-Jewish literary genre represents only 0.4% of the total Polish literary production of the period.[15] However, it must be stressed that anti-Jewish literature decreased markedly towards the end of the period, and this decline is worthy of attention because it coincided with the appearance among the population of a more violent anti-Jewish movement than had previously existed. It was no longer a question of theological speculation, of moral and economic considerations, but of pogroms.

Anti-Jewishness between 1588 and 1668 brought on the Jews in Poland the weight of a latent threat emphasized by hard times. The Jews fought against these dangers with the protections they had purchased; it follows that the wealthier a community was, the greater its chance of surmounting such clashes. The various forms of Judeophobia have methods and arguments in common but their cause and frequency vary according to the cultural environment, the local level of economic affairs and the degree of proximity of the Jewish and the Christian communities. In general terms it was the old Judeophobic feeling that predominated – that in which there was for the Christian a hope of seeing the Jew's conversion, this conversion being the way to redemption. However, certain arguments, notably the use of the notion of 'national character', were applied to the Jews, and such actions as the profaning of Jewish cemeteries indicate the view that conversion would not be enough to change a man.[16].

It must be stressed again that anti-Jewish feeling, even if it was omnipresent in Poland, showed itself in a less violent way than in several other European countries during the same period. The Jewish merchants were no doubt harassed because they were Jewish but, apart from the last phase of the Swedish Wars and the end of the Vasa period, their concerns did not suffer especially from acts of violence. Religious toleration brought about a delicate balance which stemmed from the economic and social functions of the different groups that constituted sixteenth- and seventeenth-century Poland.

The question arises whether the commercial law that governed the Jews in Vasa Poland explains the generally poor state of Jewish business, the small number of flourishing Jewish careers and the absence of large and lasting fortunes. The situation in the large towns was quite varied. One should not ignore the shades of difference which could exist between a town like Poznań, in which 75 per cent of the measures taken were for the purpose of limiting the Jews' commercial rights, and a town like Lwów, where only 46 per cent of measures taken were restrictive. On the whole, nonetheless, in the large towns the number of measures taken to reduce Jewish commercial rights was extremely low. The legislation was much more the reflection of the struggle between Jews and Christians, or even between the plebeians and the patriciate, than the result of an *a priori* intention of the legislator to trammel Jewish commerce.

The same applies to rights in the Polish-Lithuanian territory as a whole. In the private towns, the situation was rather variable but it always resulted from the proprietor's ability to impose his views on the burgesses; in return for some benefits, these owners were always well-intentioned towards the Jews.[17] It is not by considering the state of commercial law, then, that one can account for the weakness of Jewish business. The law was only the product of social and racial tensions which affected Polish society in that period. Yet these tensions may have been the cause of serious difficulties, even bankruptcies.

To this must be added the fact that while the rules were favourable to the Jews, they were not equally favourable to all Jews. The prohibitive legislation weighed heavily on the small business and the craftsmen, whereas it favoured large-scale businesses and certain renting activities according to the needs of the nobility and the royal treasury. The legislation is a factor that explains the absence of an upward social movement at the heart of the Jewish communities. A consensus was established, beyond community differences, between the ruling classes of 'the Polish Republic' and the wealthiest members of the Jewish communities.

What were the consequences of the fiscal system of Jewish affairs? The most obvious fact is the upsurge of taxation during the period of the Troubles in the middle of the seventeenth century – a phenomenon more damaging the more tax weighed on the ruined and demographically weakened populations. Nevertheless, it is essential to note that the trends towards surcharging appeared from the 1630s onwards in the East, that they became accentuated and generalized towards 1640, and that the Troubles had speeded up a process already largely under way.

Moreover, a solidarity based on community of interests grew between the state's ruling circles and the wealthiest Jewish merchants and businessmen. This solidarity was marked by the check put on the standing petitions of the nobility's provincial petty diets for increased taxes on the Jews, by the institution of the heavy *donatywum kupieckie*, which was a burden on the Christian merchants, and by the rapid increase and heavier burden of the taxes levied upon communities as a whole rather than taxes and commercial levies imposed on the Jews. Yet this solidarity reached its limits during the Troubles and later, when the richest Jews were forced to absorb the arrears of community taxes.

In the fiscal area, as in the legislative, the king was the main arbiter between the various groups as well as the main beneficiary of taxes. He showed himself anxious to favour the richest Jews through moratoriums established at the expense of local powers and by putting an even greater burden on Jewish merchants holding private estates than on those installed in their towns.[18]

It must be admitted that Jewish affairs suffered from the incessant rises in taxation, outstripping the increases in the cost of living and consequently in income, and it should be stressed that Christian merchants underwent the same experience. In the Jewish communities, the wealthiest members (those who evacuated during the Wars) were at an advantage despite the burden of taxation they found on their return; poverty had eliminated the weakest competitors. At the end of the Vasa reign, the way was open for the rare large-scale Jewish business.

The *kahal* (municipal body) was tainted by the original sin of having been set up by royal power in the interests of having a standing representative responsible for the levying of taxes. Seizing control of the *kahal* was an important matter for the merchant and business sector since the competence of this community body in legislative, fiscal and judicial matters made it an essential cog in Jewish life, after the fashion of and with the same key function as the Christians' Town Council[19]

However, if one can discern a tendency towards the over-representation of the most active merchants in comparison with their demographic importance, there is nevertheless no question of a monopoly of community rule by an oligarchy. Certain families only, certain individuals only amongst the biggest merchants held elective roles for a fairly long period. The other members of this social group, because of their absence from the *kahal*, did not display an innovating spirit in technical matters nor a particular awareness of belonging to the Polish ruling class. The spirit of protectionism, of corporation, of the collective security of the Jewish community in its confrontation with the Christian community dominated the thinking of all Jewish merchants and businessmen of the period. The difference between those who took a part in community affairs and those who did not was the expression of personal interest in the public good. However, those merchants who directed the *kahal* did so with a view to securing the interests of their social stratum, both material and moral.

With the exception of the ceremonies and specific attitudes of the Jewish religion, the life of Jewish merchants was not very different from that of the Christians. The only real originality of Jewish life, though it is of course fundamental, lies in the religious attitudes and ceremonies. These attitudes were of two kinds. One tendency led to the abandonment of Judaism through lack of interest, and integration into the Christian milieux. The other tendency was that of mysticism and messianism. On a closer look one sees that the Polish Christians were also divided between two tendencies: the 'Europeanist' tendency leading to the Enlightenment, the other towards the Counter-Reformation.

During the reigns of the Vasa, Polish Judaism was considerably transformed. The essential factor was the omnipresence in everyday life of community organisms whose initiative and control took the place of individual initiative. This model was borrowed from the Christian bourgeoisie: among the Christians, the municipal organizations ended by stifling initiative and activity in civic affairs. The very ancient question posed by the rabbis of the contradiction between enrichment and Judaism did not allow of an approach that would permit the communities to adapt to the Polish world. This outlook, though it sanctioned certain forms of the social transfer of wealth by the expedient of charity and munificence, did not allow a struggle against the assimilationist tendencies of Polish culture. The rabbis, persuaded as they were of the superiority of their religious culture over that of the Christians, did not fight against the standardization of the ways of life.[20]

It is the inevitable modelling of one town on another, of the municipal life and community structure, which gave rise to a ferment of national unification among inhabitants whose origins were very diverse. The second factor for unification was the climate of religious tolerance; although in this respect Poland experienced contradictions because of the development of Judeophobic and xenophobic feelings that were an obstacle to the assimilation of non-native people.

This analysis could be broadened by taking in other towns and other bourgeois social groups – the Scots, the Armenians and the Germans, for example, who made up other urban components more or less 'polonized'. Yet the assembled elements do allow us to think that Vasa Poland gradually settled into a general crisis as a result of the internal contradictions which undermined it. The accumulation of these contradictions, of which I have only studied certain urban aspects, contributed to the marginalization of a Poland which turned its back on the absolutism and mercantilism on which Western Europe was embarking. Poland, dominated by the interests of a few magnates and their clientele, was taking the road that was to lead, in the eighteenth century, to her disappearance as a state.

3

The privileges granted to Jewish communities of the Polish Commonwealth as a stabilizing factor in Jewish support

Jacob Goldberg

The privileges granted to the Jews in the Polish Commonwealth belong to the same category of documents as the privileges granted to the *szlachta* (nobility), the clergy and the towns, as well as to national or ethnic minorities such as the Karaites, Armenians, Tartars and Scots and to private individuals. The documents define the permissions granted by the donor of the privilege and the liberties and duties of the recipient.

The privileges granted to the Jews formulate laws defining relationships between the Jews and the rest of the population and the state, their rights to reside and trade, to erect synagogues and establish cemeteries, and the scope of the judicial jurisdiction exercised by the king or landowner in relation to that of the community (*kehilla*) organization. They also define the obligations of the Jews towards the ruling authority, and their rights and duties in respect to the burghers, as well as reaching to certain aspects of life within the community and the communal organization itself. A privilege was sought by the community or individual both when a new permission was required from the lord of the locality concerned and when the confirmation of a previous privilege was necessary (since from the Midde Ages down to the end of the independent kingdom of Poland in the eighteenth century, a document issued by a duke or a king which was not sanctioned by his successor could be deemed invalid and obsolete).[1] The same principle applied in the noble-owned towns, where the lords were accustomed to confirm the privileges issued by their predecessors. The confirmations had a particular importance for maintaining the legal validity of regulations which met with opposition from the general population.[2]

A cursory, and so far unique, source analysis and classification of the privileges of the Jews in Poland was made by Kutrzeba in his work on the history of the sources of old Polish law.[3] In an investigation of this subject over fifty years after the publication of Kutrzeba's work one should also take into account the project for a new synthesis of the history of the sources of old Polish law prepared by Grodziski.[4] Grodziski proposes to develop the classification adopted by Kutrzeba, which, although it fulfilled an important role in the study of the subject, is now regarded as pragmatic and outdated. Although Grodziski is not directly interested in Jewish privileges his classification is relevant.

Jewish privileges may be divided into general privileges valid for the Jewish population of the whole country, regional privileges, and community privileges, the latter relating to the Jewish population residing in specific towns and the localities in their neighbourhood. To the above three categories may be added confirmations of general privileges, which are more akin to codifications of earlier legislation, and finally privileges issued to individuals, which were often incorporated into the community privileges. Community privileges for Jews living in royal towns were issued by the king, or possibly the *starosta*, and those for the Jews inhabiting towns belonging to the *szlachta* were issued by the hereditary owners.

Before examining the community privileges in greater detail, reference must be made to the privileges granted to individual Jews. The practice of granting privileges to private individuals existed in the Polish Commonwealth with regard to members of all the national and ethnic minorities.[5] At first privileges were granted exclusively to individuals and only later were drawn up for the use of specific groups or social strata.[6] The Scots mostly received individual privileges, consisting primarily of trading rights.[7] (Privileges for entire groups of Scottish settlers are seldom found.[8])

The category of individual privileges, which Kutrzeba omits from his classification, is referred to by Bardach in his synthesis of the history of the Polish state and its law. All the privileges granted in Poland are here classified as either general privileges or individual privileges, the latter category including both privileges granted to a private individual and those granted to a specific town or group of people.[9]

In examining the Jewish privileges it is necessary to distinguish between those granted to communities and those granted to individuals, to establish in which circumstances the two appear together, and to discern the relationship between the rights accorded to an individual and those granted to the community: Jews who were granted individual privileges by the king were usually distinguished by their wealth or the services they rendered to the royal court and the country. In the seventeenth century the more important Jewish merchants, usually suppliers to the royal court, received privileges granting them *servitoriat* rights.[10] This meant that these Jews were included in the ranks of the royal service, and were thus placed under the aegis of the royal judiciary and removed from the competence of other courts. They were allowed to establish and maintain workshops and manufacturing concerns which were not subject to the limitations arising from the usual application of guild regulations in the towns. Germans in Great Poland in the seventeenth century received analogous rights for the purposes of production only.[11] In addition Jews received individual privileges nominating them as factors to the royal court or granting them the honorific of 'royal secretary'.[12] (The more important burghers also received this honour.) Even privileges for individual Jews which did not grant *servitoriat* rights removed them from the authority of the courts to which the rest of the Jewish population was subject and freed them from certain tax obligations.[13]

A more unusual example is a privilege granted in 1566 to Jewish booksellers, who received permission in the form of an individual privilege to print and sell books in Hebrew.[14] Non-Jewish publishers in Polish similarly received permission in the eighteenth century.[15] The number of Jews who received individual privileges greatly diminished the period of economic decline in the second half of the seventeenth and first half of the eighteenth centuries, when the Jews suffered from the general impoverishment in the state.[16]

Around the beginning of the eighteenth century, when plans were made to create a Polish-Saxon maritime trading company, no Jews with sufficiently large amounts of capital could be found in Poland and Lithuania, and stockholders were enlisted from among the Sephardi Jews of Holland and Jewish merchants of Dunkirk.[17] One of the few Jews in the Polish Commonwealth who could still be counted as very wealthy towards the end of the eighteenth century was Szmul Jakubowicz-Zbytkower, purveyor to the courts of King Stanisław August and King Frederick II of Prussia, and to the Polish, Russian and Prussian armies. However, it is noteworthy that the trade privilege he received in 1771 was granted by the Prussian Frederick II and not by the Polish king.[18]

The granting of special rights to an individual Jew sometimes became a precedent for extending these rights to all the Jews of the town. Such a development took place at the beginning of the seventeenth century in Słuck.[19] Mendel Ucielewicz, of Brześć Litewski, applied for permission from the owner of Słuck, Prince Janusz Radziwiłł, to buy land and build a house there. In his reply to the petition, Prince Radziwiłł, at the request of Ucielewicz and the other Jews, issued a privilege, on 4 February 1601, granting identical rights to all the Jews of Słuck. At the same time the prince confirmed the rights they had received from the previous owners.

Sometimes an individual privilege, especially if it was of benefit to the community, was absorbed by the community privilege, and the clauses that granted rights to an individual Jew were incorporated in it. The confirmation of the privilege granted in 1765 to the Jews of the royal town of Lublin[20] also embraced the privilege granted by Władysław IV on 16 July 1638 to Jeleń Doktorowicz in person, permitting Jeleń to build his own synagogue and enjoining the Lublin Jews not to harm him in any way. The document also interdicts the election of Jeleń as the senior of the community council since his holding of this office could have hampered his duties as royal agent. Although the last two provisions naturally ceased to be relevant after Jeleń's death, as a result of the initiative of the community elders the privilege enjoyed by Jeleń was included in the subsequent confirmations, and the Lublin community took over the right to the upkeep of the synagogue.

In turn, the granting or confirmation of a privilege to a Jewish community provided an opportunity for granting special concessions to individuals singled out by the owner of a noble-owned town. Thus the need to issue special privileges for individuals was avoided. Such was the action of Stanisław Dunin-Borkowski in 1674, when issuing the privilege for the Jews of Opole.[21] In the privilege granted to the community Borkowski confirms the rights granted by his predecessors and appends to the document an individual privilege exempting his agent Chaim Mojżeszowicz from the obligations of the other Jews in the town.

Thus the legal status and rights of the community were built on and bound up with the closely-knit ties and position of mutual dependence that existed between the community and its individual members.

Of all the Jewish privileges issued in the Polish Commonwealth, those granted to particular Jewish communities were the most important. In his work on documentary sources Kutrzeba underlines that the community privileges performed a much more vital role than the general or regional privileges.[22] Although this thesis rests only on material relating to a few larger towns, its validity is obvious for two reasons. First, apart from the inclusion of provisions pertaining to the Jews that were specified in the general privileges, the community privileges formulate many more elements of a fundamental nature. Secondly, Kutrzeba's assessment is justified not only because of the significance of the provisions framed in the community privileges, but also by reason of the increasing importance of their function in relation to the Jewish population of the state. For there exists a direct causal nexus between the growing role of local privileges and the decentralization of the socio-political structure of the Polish Commonwealth.

The increase in significance of the community privileges and their precedence over the general and regional privileges was an expression of the strengthening and growing independence of the estate power centres in Poland, a process that began during the sixteenth century in the time of the *szlachta* democracy and reached its peak during the period of the magnate oligarchy in the second half of the seventeenth and the first half of the eighteenth centuries. The expanding power of the nobility had an influence on the development of the social situation of the Jews.[23] As a result of the changes occurring in this sphere the Jews in the royal towns became increasingly subject to the authority of the *starostas* while the Jews in the privately owned towns were under the even broader authority of the hereditary rulers. The expansion of their jurisdictional powers over the Jews found expression in the constitution adopted by the Diet in 1539, which granted the owners of the private towns the exclusive right to place obligations on their Jewish populations. In addition, the Diet transferred the judicial jurisdiction over the Jews from the *voivodes* to the owners of the towns.[24] This was the first law adopted by the Diet that limited the authority of the royal officials over the towns.[25] Subsequent laws weakening the ties between the royal government and the privately owned towns in other ways were instituted somewhat later, in 1543, 1573, 1588 and 1598.[26] However, from the point of view of the interests of the lords of the privately owned towns, the 1539 constitution was of fundamental importance.

Before the passing of the act the Jews had been the only group among the residents of the privately owned towns which had the right of appeal to the royal courts. The removal of the Jews in these towns from the judicial aegis of the *voivodes* significantly expanded the area in which the nobles wielded power. The 1539 constitution is seen by Bałaban as a reaction to the continuous flow of immigration of Jews to the privately owned towns that began, according to him, in the early sixteenth century.[27] Actually, this process had already started in the second half of the fifteenth century, and did not reach large proportions until the late sixteenth and early seventeenth centuries, when the Jews were progressively ousted from the royal towns.[28] Thus the 1539 constitution was promulgated before there was any considerable increase in the Jewish population of the privately owned towns. Around the time of issue of the constitution the *szlachta* were also expanding their dominion over the population in their villages.[29] The 1539 constitution must be viewed as part of this process.

In such a situation, the elders of many of the Jewish communities realized that the general privileges issued by the king could not by themselves guarantee the rights and security of the Jews in the conditions of the Polish Commonwealth, and that each community would do well to obtain its own privilege in addition. With this aim in view the communities took steps to acquire separate privileges. Throughout the period from 1539 to 1764 the community privileges and agreements between the Jews and the burghers of a town played a greater role in the development of legislation with regard to the Jews than the general privileges and constitutions passed by the Diets during the period. However, in the Grand Duchy of Lithuania the legislation concerning the Jews there was expanded by provisions in three Lithuanian statutes, enacted in 1529, 1566 and 1588.[30] Thus in the privilege granted in 1601 to the Jews of Słuck (No. 47),[31] Prince Janusz Radziwiłł stresses 'the freedoms and laws given to the Jews in the Grand Duchy of Lithuania'. The Lithuanian statutes were in force in the Ukraine, which from 1569 belonged to the Lands of the Crown of Poland. In the privilege granted in 1614 to the Jews of Kowel,[32] Szczęsny vel Feliks Kryski states that the Jews are to 'judge according to the laws and freedoms of the Jews in the Grand Duchy of Lithuania'. These statutes incorporated elements from Polish law, and sometimes were observed in the Lands of the Crown of Poland.[33]

The need to possess a separate privilege became so self-evident that communities which did not already have one sometimes tried to fill the gap by acquiring a privilege which was merely a simple repetition of the text of the general privilege. Thus, while a community privilege might seem superfluous when granting rights to which the Jews were entitled on the strength of their general and regional privileges, its significance derived not only from the contents of the privilege but also from the fact that the community actually possessed its own document formally safeguarding these rights.

Privileges containing texts based exclusively on general privileges were acquired by the communities of Cracow and Łuck.[34] King Stefan Bathory, on 3 January 1580, granted the last-named community a privilege which consisted of the original 1264 privilege of Bolesław the Pious, sanctioned by King Kazimierz the Great, together with the confirmations issued by King Kazimierz Jagiellończyk and King Zygmunt August.[35] The privilege of Bathory declares that he is granting the Jewish community of Łuck the same rights as held by the Jews in the Lands of the Crown of Poland. In 1607, at the suggestion of the community council, the document was attested in the castle and district court records of Łuck. A note was added to the document declaring that '. . . to it had been added the privileges and liberties granted to the Jews in the Lands of the Crown of Poland by their majesties the kings of Poland who had granted the privilege of all these rights and privileges to the Jews of Łuck'.[36] This statement indicates that the rights conferred on the Jews in the general privileges acquired greater validity when they were granted again in the form of a community privilege.

The causal link between the weakening of the central authority in the Polish Commonwealth and the growth in significance of the community privileges is apparent from privileges of the Jewish inhabitants of the royal towns as well as from those of the Jews residing in the private noble-owned towns. Of the latter privileges only a small number were presented to the king for confirmation.

This fact is linked with the deeply held belief of the *szlachta* in the authority to which they were entitled and their dominial power over the inhabitants of the hereditarily owned towns. Even in the nineteenth century this outlook is voiced by Karol Kobyliński, the lord of the town of Sokołów, who, in protest against attempts to create a separate residential district for the Jews, wrote in 1822 that under the old Polish Commonwealth 'only the lords had the right in those days to grant privileges to their subjects in the privately owned towns; and those privileges could be confirmed by the king on the nobles' demand'.[37]

The situation was often analogous under the *starostas* in the royal towns since the privileges of the Jews were frequently drawn up by the *starostas*, who were recruited from among the magnates and the wealthy *szlachta*. The Jews received privileges from the *starostas* in the following royal towns, among others: Kowal in 1568[38], Lelów in 1612[39], Kowel in 1614[40], Szydłów in 1622[41], Lublin from 1636 to 1675[42], Ratno in 1661[43], Chęciny in 1668[44], Nowy Sącz in 1699[45], Wschowa in 1759[46]. The *starostas* not only drew up privileges issued by the kings but even confirmed them. In his capacity as *starosta*, Szczęsny Kryski, the crown chancellor, issued a privilege to the Jews of Kowel on 21 August 1614,[47] and simultaneously confirmed a royal privilege granted to the Jewish community of the same town.

Under King Jan III (reigned 1674–1696), there was a tendency to transfer the jurisdiction relating to the sanctioning of community privileges to the Diet. The Diet ratified in 1676 a privilege for the Jews of Nowy Sącz,[48] and in 1678 it sanctioned an analogous document for the Jewish community of Parczew.[49]

In the second half of the eighteenth century, there was a certain redundancy in this sphere. The Diet adopted several acts of basic importance relating to the Jews,[50] while the king resumed confirmation of their general privileges. In addition to the king, *starostas* and hereditary owners of towns continued to grant new community privileges or to reconfirm the old ones. Under King Stanisław August, the 1768 constitution of the Diet recognized only the validity of privileges that had been sanctioned by the Diet itself.[51] However, the 1768 law was unable to influence substantially the fixed practice in this area.

Like other documents drawn up in the Polish Commonwealth, the form and external features of the Jewish privileges were shaped by the culture and the law of the land. Relatively speaking there was little change in the traditional medieval features of the privileges in the sixteenth to eighteenth centuries. However, increasingly frequent use was made of the Polish language instead of Latin, and a different style of expression developed, while it became customary for the grantor of the privilege to sign his name by the side of the seal.[52] Up to the end of the sixteenth century the privileges are carefully formulated, making appropriate use of Roman legal terminology, but subsequently a deterioration may be noted.[53] When a copy of a privilege was drawn up, standard formulae, which were frequently abbreviated or expanded, were added certifying that the copy agreed with the original document on which it was based, or with a subsequent duplicate.

It is no accident that the introduction of new elements in the old community privileges, and the granting of new ones, become increasingly frequent from the beginning of the seventeenth century, since this process coincided with the decline of the towns in the Polish Commonwealth. The causal link is clear. The additions to the old provisions and issue of new privileges to the Jewish communities are connected with attempts on the part of the kings and nobles to make up the population losses of their towns, which had been depleted in the destruction caused by wars and the economic collapse of the country. The Jews constituted a demographic reserve, when, as a result of the Cossack uprisings and the series of other calamities, many Jewish families were looking for new places in which to live and new sources of livelihood. New Jewish settlements were initiated by the *starostas* in many royal towns, and similar action was often taken by the lords of privately owned towns. In the privileges that were issued old legal practices were renewed or new provisions were formulated to meet changed local conditions. A main emphasis in the privileges is in the economic sphere, enabling the Jews to earn a living in various branches of trade and crafts. New provisions were needed also because of the growing participation of the Jews in the production of and trade in alcoholic beverages. These features are characteristic of the privileges granted both to the old and to the newly established Jewish settlements of this period. Some communities received very similar privileges.

In addition, in a period of the intensification of the Counter-Reformation and increased religious intolerance, issues arose in the religious sphere, in particular regarding the building of synagogues and the establishment of Jewish cemeteries. Permission for this was required not only from the *starosta* or lord of a town, but also from the ecclesiastical authorities. For instance, the privilege of the Jews of Kamionka[54] contains reference to permission for building a synagogue and establishment of a cemetery granted in the early seventeenth century by the archbishop of Lwów, Jan Próchnicki.

A detailed study of all the issues involved faces various difficulties, and necessitates further research in ecclesiastical archives. However, it can be established, on the basis of fragmentary material in other archives and manuscript collections, that the procedure for settling these matters sometimes encountered considerable obstacles. The Church restricted the authority of the lords in these matters even if they came from the families of the rich and influential *szlachta*. Occasionally, several years of effort and persistence on the part of the Jews or the lord of the town were needed to gain such permission. The efforts of the castellan of Sieradz, Szymon Zaremba, provide an example of such a case. Zaremba, a pious Catholic, amassed a large fortune mainly through transactions conducted with the participation of Jews.[55] He settled several dozen Jewish families in the small town of Rozprza, which he had bought, and tried to establish a local cemetery for them.

The rights granted to the Jews in community privileges also frequently met with opposition from the burghers. In many cases the permissions bestowed in the community privileges conflicted with those in the privileges that had been acquired earlier by the non-Jewish artisan or trade guilds.[56] Although the constitution adopted by the Diet in 1504 had required the chancellors to check that documents issued by the royal chancellery were not incompatible with existing laws,[57] inconsistencies continued to occur. This happened not only in the Polish Commonwealth but also in the more efficient papal chancelleries.[58] Thus it is not surprising that the lords of privately owned towns who granted privileges to the Jews rarely bothered to find out whether the Jewish privileges conflicted with the rights held by the local Christian population. Misunderstandings and conflicts arose between the Jews and the burghers over crafts and trade practices and over the alcohol production and trade, which could not be resolved by recourse to the texts of the privileges. Other subjects of conflict concerned the apportionment of taxation and payment for the maintenance of military units.

Such disputes were usually settled by the negotiation of agreements or compacts (*ugody*) between the two sides. The constitutions adopted by the Diet in 1538, 1567 and 1568 instructed the settlement of disputes in this way.[59] References to agreements between the Jews and the burghers are found in a number of community privileges. Wincenty Skrzetuski, the author of well-known legal works in the second half of the eighteenth century, wrote that 'when complaints were made in the reign of Zygmunt August that the Jews were taking trade away from the burghers, the towns as well as the Jews were ordered to show to the Diet the trading agreements drawn up between them, and were both enjoined to behave in accordance with them. Later laws renewed these instructions, forbidding the Jews to trade without agreements with the towns'.[60] This was a reference to the 1768 constitution of the Diet, which bound the Jews strictly to respect all the economic restrictions in the agreements between them and the burghers.

This constitution imposed an obligation on all communities without privileges approved by the Diet to enter into such agreements. If this was not complied with such a community was liable to lose its rights to pursue crafts and trade. This law also established a rigorous procedure to compel obdurate burghers to reach a compromise with the Jews.[61]

The privileges granted to the different Jewish communities in the Polish Commonwealth reflect the differences in the legal and social status of the Jews living there, which was not uniform throughout the country. The privileges grant diverse rights and impose differing restrictions and obligations on the communities. For this reason they remain the most representative source for research into the social and legal position of the Jews in the Polish Commonwealth. The privileges are equally valuable for the study of different aspects of life in the Jewish community, as well as areas of the economic life of the country which concerned the Jews and in which they took an active part.

The first privilege issued to the Jews in 1264 by Bolesław the Pious, and the subsequent general or regional privileges based on it, should be regarded only as providing the broad basis for the status of the Jews in the Commonwealth, a status that developed over the centuries. The amount of matter included in the community privileges increased in the course of the seventeenth and eighteenth centuries, as an increasing number of new privileges were issued or old ones were confirmed and copied. The new provisions and expressions then introduced often yield valuable historical material. Much information can be gained from the community privileges concerning the internal affairs of the Jewish communities, as well as the relations between the Jews and different social strata and ethnic groups. They concern the contacts of the Jews with the *szlachta* and magnates, the *starostas* and the lords of the privately owned towns, as also with the burghers, the magistrates, the artisan guilds, the clergy, soldiers, and peasants, and with other groups among the Poles, Ukrainians, Byelorussians and Germans.

Often it had been the necessity of settling and regulating these relations that led directly to the drawing up of a privilege for a Jewish community. Thus the provisions included in these documents are frequently framed to resolve specific problems or remove existing conflicts and antagonisms. In effect they are similar to the judgements of the assessorial courts or to the agreements between the Jews and the burghers. The privileges therefore give information about the methods taken and attempts to overcome the difficulties that cropped up in different towns. Since most often these were linked with the economic situation of the towns, the community privileges contain much information about the professional structure and material circumstances of the Jews. The rights and duties of Jews renting inns, breweries and distilleries are extensively described.

The provisions in the community privileges that are drawn up to take into account the specific character of local conditions, as well as their formulation, differ from the legal matter borrowed from the general and regional privileges or the set formulae usually employed. On this basis it can be ascertained which parts of the text have been composed by the grantors and their plenipotentiaries and which have been borrowed from other privileges. The same can be said about parts of the community privileges that are based on the verdicts of the assessorial courts or on agreements concluded between the burghers and the Jews. An examination of the texts enables us to understand these underlying divergences and the purposes they served.

Apart from the divergences, certain uniform elements are to be found in the legislation contained in the community privileges. These originated from the general and regional privileges and the general principles of legal practice obtaining in the country, as well as from Jewish customary or traditional law.

One of the main features of the legal status of the Jews in the Polish Commonwealth was the specific category of their judiciary, originating from the privilege granted by Bolesław the Pious in 1264 and repeated in subsequent general and regional privileges. A common element in the legislation of the privileges dealing with judicial matters is the exclusion of the Jews from the municipal courts and the powers granted to the Jewish courts to adjudicate cases concerning Jews. In general, the privileges designate courts based on the principle *actor sequitur forum rei* and the jurisdiction of the courts therefore depended on whether the Jew was the plaintiff or the defendant, and whether the dispute was between Jews on both sides. A further common element is the provision concerning the powers of the *voivode* courts over the Jews and the general system of appeal against decisions of lower courts.

According to some privileges, all lawsuits involving a Jew, whether as the plaintiff or the defendant, fall within the province of the Jewish court. This was in consonance with the interest of the Jews in broadening the area of competence of their own courts.[62] Thus, instructions issued in 1775 to the towns on the entailed estates (*ordynacja*) of the Zamoyski family lay down that cases in which burghers are the plaintiffs and Jews the defendants are also to be adjudicated by the court of the local Jewish community.[63]

On the other hand, the powers of the Jewish judiciary are more restricted in the privileges of the Jews of the noble-owned towns in which it is stated that cases where the plaintiff is a burgher should be adjudicated by a Jewish court, and where a Jew is the plaintiff by a municipal court.

The Jews are placed under the jurisdiction of the municipal courts in a rare instance in Poznań in 1617 on the basis of an agreement concluded between the Jews and the municipality. This arrangement, however, met with the opposition of the *voivode* of Poznań, who viewed it as an infringement of his judicial competence over the Jews living in royal towns.[64] The question of the jurisdiction of the municipal courts in matters involving Jews has been investigated in relation to towns located in the territory of the old voivodeship of Lublin. Apparently the Jewish courts in the royal towns in this area did not usually settle cases involving both Jews and burghers because in practice it was established that such cases came under the jurisdiction of the municipal courts.[65]

However, studies of the question of the judicial jurisdiction over the Jews have to take into account the sources relating to the application of the legislation in practice. Sometimes there is a great divergence between the written law, as found in the privileges, especially of noble-owned towns, and its practice. This was especially true of cases involving Jews where the plaintiff was a burgher, who was supposed to sue the Jew in the Jewish court, yet no formal opposition was made if he lodged his complaint against the Jew in the municipal court.[66]

Some privileges specify the motives for exempting the Jews from the municipal judicial jurisdiction. The grantor of the privilege to the Jewish community of Opole declares that the Jews are free '. . . from any municipal and *wójt* jurisdiction and from all indignity'.[67] Nevertheless, even here, where the appearance of a Jew before a municipal court is called an 'indignity' (*poniżeństwo*), it appears that in reality the Jews were subject to the jurisdiction of the municipal court of Opole.[68] Similarly, the privilege granted in 1714 to the Jewish community of Szamotuły, in Great Poland, states, '. . . whereas the Jewish nation is hated by everybody, and without protection would suffer in fortune and life, therefore I, with my successors, exclude all the Jews of Szamotuły *in genere*, those living now and those to come in the future, from any jurisdiction, so that no office or superior authority should pass verdicts on them'[69] [excepting the rabbinical court]. It is not known whether in practice there were any significant deviations from the provisions of the Szamotuły privilege, as happened in the towns of the Lublin area.

The appeal system, in general, remained uniform in the royal towns, where an appeal went to the *starosta*'s court or to the assessorial court. In noble-owned towns, where the lord's court was usually the revocatory court, the privileges sometimes show variations. For example, the privilege of the Swarzędz community states that appeals against the verdicts of the Jewish courts should go before a court of equal standing in Poznań, since the Swarzędz community was dependent to a certain extent on the latter.[70] In the entailed estates of the Zamoyski family appeals could be made either to the court of the lord or to the Jewish court in Lublin.[71]

It can be seen from the foregoing that the information in the privileges helps to determine the system of judicial jurisdiction to which the Jews were subject in the Polish Commonwealth. Regardless of the extent to which the provisions were put into practice, the privileges were a step forward in stabilizing the allegiance of the Jews to specified courts of justice. As a result, an element of order was introduced at a time when considerable freedom in the choice of law court was a characteristic feature of Polish legal practice.[72] Until the end of the old Polish Commonwealth at the close of the eighteenth century no law was passed diminishing the authority of the Jewish courts of justice that had been granted by the general and community privileges.[73]

The Magdeburg law enabled the citizens of the towns in the Polish Commonwealth to enjoy a number of exemptions and freedoms.[74] Among these was the right to engage in trade, which induced even foreigners to apply for the citizenship of Polish towns.[75] However, inclusion in the roll of municipal citizens also entailed subjection to the municipal authorities and their jurisdiction, and this the Jews wished to avoid. The community privileges provided a solution to this difficulty, since they granted, either in part or totally, the same economic rights to the Jews as enjoyed by the citizens of a town but did not bring them within the municipal jurisdiction.

However, this also meant that in general the Jews were not given other rights linked with the status of citizen. They were not the only group in this position, for a substantial sector of the population of the towns remained without municipal citizenship although subject to the municipal courts.[76] This status of the Jews, which had continued over the centuries, was not sanctioned by the Diet until the constitution of 1768, which settled several matters relating to municipal citizenship. The constitution emphasizes the special position of the Jews, who, not being municipal citizens, '. . . should, however, have the right to trade without hindrance in their own Jewish towns, which have been established by privileges and in accordance with the terms of the said privileges'.[77]

The status of a person whose rights were limited to those of residence and ownership of immovable property in a town, and the right to engage in specified professions and trades, is described as *incolat*. This term, which corresponded with the scope of the rights enjoyed by the Jews, is frequently used in documents to define their legal and social status. It is employed in this sense in the agreement concluded in 1757 between the Jews and the burghers of Będzin, which is appended to the privilege of the community of that town. In it the burghers' representative declares that 'we also receive *ad incolatum* in this town the entire synagogue [i.e. the Jewish community] and each several one [Jew] individually; we grant permission for the purchase of property and permit those freedoms which we enjoy'.[78]

Inspection reports for the royal estates made in the eighteenth century also use this term, for instance that for Sochaczew, which refers to the situation in the locality in the sixteenth and seventeenth centuries.[79] The same applies to the inspection report for Chęciny which states that 'the Jews have acquired *incolatum* with the burghers and thereby have the right to close down alcohol stills'.[80]

Many of the privileges state generally that the Jews are granted the same rights as those granted to the burghers when in fact these rights are mainly limited to the economic sphere. Thus we cannot take literally the kind of formula that appears in the privilege granted by Jan III in 1676 to the Jews of Kazimierz Dolny, in which it is stated that 'all the Jews residing now and in the future in the aforementioned Kazimierz should be able to enjoy and should enjoy the same freedom as that enjoyed by the burghers and citizens of that town'. Yet a much more limited category of rights is specified following this preamble, which suggests a very different position.

The privilege granted in 1557 to the Jews of Wiślica by King Zygmunt August exempts them, along with the burghers, from paying customs dues.[81] Another privilege granted by the same king to the Jews of Tyszowce in 1567 gives them the same rights as those enjoyed by the burghers in trade, crafts, and the possession of immovable property.[82]

The Magdeburg law did not permit the Jews to participate in municipal government.[83] They were therefore deprived of the opportunity to benefit from one of the fundamental rights of municipal citizenship. However, in some instances representatives of the Jews were allowed to participate in the municipal elections. Jews participated in local elections in the royal town of Nowy Sącz and in the privately owned towns of Końskowola, Kraśnik, Łęczna and Modliborzyce in the Lublin *voivodeship* in the seventeenth and eighteenth centuries.[84] The town statutes of Łęczna of the eighteenth century even note that the municipal council was chosen by the general electorate and the Jewish community council.[85] The privilege of the community of the eastern Great Polish town of Łask, granted in the second half of the seventeenth century, states that 'the community council is to put forward two electors from among its ranks for the election of the burgomaster'.[86] However, it seems doubtful that the Jews made use of this right in practice, for the detailed regulations issued for the Jews in 1795 by the lord of Łask do not cover such an eventuality.[87] A similar interpretation must be given to the declaration by the lord who issued the privilege of the community of Opole in stating that the Jews 'are incorporated under the Magdeburg law', when he exempts them from the municipal jurisdiction in order to spare them 'indignity'.[88]

Declarations of a general kind made by the grantors of the privileges of Jewish communities in noble-owned towns are not precise legal statements and did not create the changes which the granting of municipal rights to the Jews would have brought about. Furthermore, the privilege of Opole does not mention the rights relating to municipal citizenship among those granted to the Jews of the town. Neither are they mentioned in the privilege granted in 1780 to the Jews of Wojsławice, in which the noble owner, Humbelia Kurdwanowska, refers to '. . . the Jewish merchants, inn-keepers and artisans of all crafts pressing for serfdom, citizenship and under my rule . . .'.[89] The title of citizen used occasionally for individual Jews, should be treated with equal reservation. The Jews who received this title were usually not included on the municipal roll of citizens and did not enjoy all the rights conferred by the municipal law. A few examples of Jews being accorded the basis for real municipal citizenship by the privileges occurred in the period of change at the end of the eighteenth century.[90]

The community privileges are a source of fundamental importance for study of the hitherto unexamined position of the Jews in the Polish Common-wealth regarding their rights to ownership and sale of immovable property and the changes that occurred in the course of time.[91] The references to the legal practices in this sphere that appear in other sources, such as the regu-lations issued by the kings and *voivodes*, are infrequent and scanty.[92] The documents dealing with the purchase and sale of houses and plots of land by Jews contain details about the procedures of such transactions and the property concerned without enlarging upon the fundamental law.

From the privileges it is possible to see the degree to which the Jews of a town had to adhere to restrictions that were also imposed by the owner on the burghers.[93] These restrictions were more frequent in noble-owned towns. In the royal towns most of the inhabitants, including the Jews, enjoyed relatively greater freedom in the purchase and sale of immovable property.[94] The basic restriction on property ownership in noble-owned towns was the requirement to have the permission of the lord or his pleni-potentiary for every transaction involving land and houses. The community privileges indicate that the lords did not establish greater restrictions on the Jews than on the burghers in this matter.

In certain towns, however, the Jews were limited not only by the lord's prerogatives but also by the powers accorded to the community council, which could impose its own restrictions on the members of the community. A typical regulation on this matter is found in the privilege of the com-munity of Szamotuły in which Jews buying or selling houses or plots of land in the town not only needed the permission of the lord of the town but also that of the local community council.[95]

However, there are also rare instances in which Jews received full freedom of alienation in respect of immovable property in noble-owned towns. The lord of the town emphasizes in the privilege for the community of Dobromil, that the Jews can 'sell and change their houses and property with whomsoever they wish, whether a Christian or a Jew, and neither I nor the administration may prohibit this'.[96]

The fundamental right to transfer immovable property to an heir is mentioned in the privilege of the community of the noble-owned town of Lubraniec, which contains one of the rarely found provisions on this matter. The privilege states that 'a plot of land on which a Jew builds a house with the lord's permission will serve the builder and his successors for ever'.[97] This condition merely emphasizes and formally recognizes the right of the Jew to inherit immovable property, a right which was respected in practice almost universally.

The rights of Jews to own immovable property are often restricted in the community privileges by territorial limitations. In a number of royal as well as noble-owned towns Jews are prohibited from owning houses and plots of land on the main streets or abutting on the market square. In certain royal towns also Jews are not permitted to increase the size of their immovable property. These restrictions are even maintained in instances in which the grantor declares that the privilege is issued to encourage Jews to settle in a depopulated or destroyed town and assist in its rebuilding. Some privileges of the seventeenth century limit the right of Jews in this sphere to ownership of immovable property that had belonged to Jews before the devastation of the wars in this period.

The conditions in the privileges establishing the extent of the legal and economic dependence of the Jews on the authority of the lord of a town show that this assumed various forms. Some privileges of the noble-owned towns limit or even wholly sever any bonds or contacts between the Jewish population and the autonomous municipal institutions.[98] Examples of more extreme forms of subordination of the Jewish population to the owner of an estate are also found. In places where Jews were prevented from moving to other towns without the lord's consent their status was similar to the serfdom of the peasants.[99] There are, however, milder provisions aimed ultimately at binding the Jewish population to their place of residence, as where the transfer of dowries of Jewish brides to other localities is prohibited by Stanisław Poniatowski, father of the last Polish king, in the privilege granted in 1753 to the Jews of Jazłowiec, in which it is stated that this provision follows 'the strict law maintained in other towns'.[100] The privilege also directs the Jews 'to try to settle their children in Jazłowiec with them'.[101]

On the other hand, the privilege granted in 1621 to the Jews of Swarzędź declares that the Jews have complete freedom of movement from place to place.[102] Similarly, the privilege issued in 1612 to the Jews of Dobromil states that the Jews of this noble-owned town are 'free to settle and to move out'.[103]

A great many obligations and duties owed by the Jews to the lords of a town are specified in the community privileges. Often it was the duty of Jews, mostly in the noble-owned towns, to perform the corvée – several days' work annually in conjunction with the burghers on the lord's manor. In the privately owned town of Kobylin, if a Jew bought from a burgher a house which carried the obligation of the house owner to perform work on the lord's manor, he had to continue to perform this duty.[104]

In Radzyń, which belonged to the vice-chancellor of the Grand Duchy of Lithuania, Stanisław Szczuka, the situation was similar to that in Kobylin. In this town the Jews were obliged to perform the corvée connected with the plots of land they bought from the burghers. In 1704 they sent a petition to the lord of the town stating that 'we Jews remaining in our Jewishness are not accustomed to perform the corvée ('A my Żydzi w żydostwie naszym nie przywykli pańszczyzny odbywać').[105] As a result Szczuka changed this duty to a payment of rent.[106] Probably the problem in Kobylin was solved as in Radzyń.[107] However, it is impossible to establish on the basis of the privileges whether the duties were actually carried out as stipulated or if the Jews made a cash payment in lieu.

The privileges are not merely one-sided in character, and do not refer only to the obligations and duties of the Jews towards the landowner. They also specify assistance or relief given or promised by the owner to the Jews on his estate. Among the permissions granted by the privileges are exemptions on rents for the buildings of the synagogue and ritual bath, and for the houses of the rabbi, cantor and sexton (*shammash*). Some of them include exemptions for almshouses and hostels for the sick. When he granted the privilege to the community of Jazłowiec, Stanisław Poniatowski donated the subtantial sum of 10,000 zlotys to the community, part of which was devoted to the relief of poor Jews to assist them in the development of trade.[108]

The provisions defining the powers of the community council form a substantial section in the privileges. They mainly apply to aspects of the community administration and such internal community affairs as would affect the interest of the owner of the town. Both the lords of private towns and the *starostas* or leaseholders of royal towns wanted to retain a measure of control over the local Jewish institutions. As a result many privileges contain regulations defining the scope of the lord's involvement in the elections of the community elders. Frequently this involvement was expressed in the duty of the Jews to present the candidates they elected to these posts for the lord's approval. Sometimes the grantors of the privileges also thought it proper to formulate criteria for guiding the election of these officers. The privilege granted to the Jews by the lord of Szamotuły states that although the community elders may be elected without the lord's approval they must be chosen from among those persons who 'act for the benefit of the community, are faithful to the people and love peace'.[109] In addition, the noble owners were concerned to ensure that the Jews resident on their estates should not belong to other Jewish communities.

The regulations augmenting the powers of the community council not only reflect the leanings of the grantors of the privileges but also the aims of the elders of the community to extend its powers and strengthen its position. The community council is given the right by the lord of Dobromił to issue permission to individual Jews to reside in the town, and is authorized to expel persons whom it deems undesirable.[110] The privilege of Mordy, issued towards the end of the eighteenth century, allows Jews to settle in the town only with the agreement of both the lord of Mordy and the community council.[111] The privilege also enforces recourse to the Jewish court of justice by a fine, stating that, 'if any Jew goes to the manor with any complaint, not having first applied and complained to the elders, he shall pay a fine of 20 *grzywny*'. In Szamotuły it is made compulsory for the community council to agree unanimously when immovable property is bought or sold.[112]

Such regulations are connected with the transfer by the owner of the town of some of the administrative functions concerning the Jews to the community council. Thus the functions acquired by the community council had a dual character. Some relate strictly to the internal affairs of the community and others to the execution of instructions from the lord or his representative. The community council therefore became a link in the administrative system of the lord or the *starosta*.[113]

A result of this trend was to limit the municipality's powers over the Jews, although in general it never led to a complete break between the two bodies. One example of this relationship is illustrated in the privilege granted by Stefan Czarniecki to the Jews of Ratno, in which the community representatives are ordered to supervise the finances of the municipality together with the burghers. Any auditing of the municipal accounts conducted without the participation of the representatives of the Jewish community is deemed to be invalid. Czarniecki also granted to the Jewish elders the same concessions in taxes and rents as enjoyed by the members of the municipal council.[114] These concessions should be distinguished from the exemptions and reductions granted by the community privileges to rabbis, cantors or sextons because of their religious functions.[115]

Frequently, information is given in the privileges concerning the efforts made by the Jewish communities to obtain a privilege or have it confirmed. When it was necessary to obtain it from the king, the delegates of the communities often sought support from influential members of the *szlachta* and magnates.[116] They took various measures to win the backing of individuals who had direct access to the king. The Jews also obtained access to persons with influence among the *szlachta* who took part in the Dietines.[117] The steps taken by individual Jewish communities to achieve their aims were often coordinated by the Jewish Councils of the Lands, the central institutions of Jewish autonomy in the Polish Commonwealth. This coordination did not entirely cease after these institutions were liquidated in 1765,[118] but it was weakened and only increased again during the period of the Four-Year Diet of 1788–92.

The activities of the Jewish communities to obtain these rights received much attention in non-Jewish circles and are mentioned by contemporary Polish writers. The distinguished Polish scholar Sebastian Petrycy of Pilzno, who was extremely hostile to the Jews, wrote at the beginning of the seventeenth century that they 'corrupt judges with gifts and the lords with bowing'.[119] However, the judges and lords who accepted the gifts from the Jews sometimes also accepted gifts from their adversaries.[120] In the same period Sebastian Miczyński, known for his hostile attitude towards the Jews, states that 'the Jews, indulging in the art of sorcery when presenting gifts, make Christians into great defenders and supporters', and that therefore the Jew 'has the most convenient access to all matters'.[121] Writing some years later, Szymon Starowolski states that the Jews 'enjoy greater favour in the Dietines and the Diet than the clergy, and have a defender of their rights and privileges'.[122] Jan Stanisław Jabłonowski, author of a pamphlet published in 1730, compares the Jews with the state treasurers, who were known for their corruption.[123] He writes that 'it can be truly said about them [the treasurers] what is said about the Jews: whoever speaks about them favourably receives his reward, and whoever speaks against them wishes to receive one'.[124]

However, these activities, which met with such strong criticism in contemporary writings, appear in the privileges themselves in an entirely different light. For the kings, these activities often served as a justification for the grant or confirmation of a privilege. The king who issues the document declares that he is prompted to such an action by the intervention of certain persons. King Jan III states that he confirms the privileges of the Jewish community of Kazimierz Dolny owing to the intercession of Barbara Lubomirska, wife of the crown marshal and *starosta* of the town, because of the need to rehabilitate it.[125] In other cases the request of the Jews is mentioned as the direct cause for issuing a privilege. Occasionally the

Jewish representatives themselves were received in audience by the king and could ask for a privilege for their community. This is mentioned in the privilege granted by King Michał Korybut in 1669 to the community of Kalisz, which states that . . . 'the infidel Jews living in our town of Kalisz appeared before our royal throne with a humble supplication'.[126] Such justifications were additional to those given for issuing a privilege because of the desire of the lord to repopulate or restore his town after devastations by wars or disasters, or because the document was lost.

The Jews frequently took advantage of favourable moments and situations to ask for new privileges and confirmations. Sometimes direct evidence of such actions is not forthcoming from the documents concerned but the circumstances can be deduced from their place and date of issue. King Jan Kazimierz confirmed the privileges of the Jews of Przedbórz in 1655, during the war with Sweden, when he was staying in a military camp near that town. The royal presence no doubt made it easier for the representatives of the local Jewish community to petition him.[127] It was easier to settle these matters in noble-owned towns than in royal towns because access to the town's owner or his plenipotentiaries was much simpler than to the royal residence, and contacts between the lords or their clerks and the community elders were more direct.[128]

The efforts of the representatives of the Jews did not by any means end once consent had been received for the issue of a privilege. Next came fresh exertions to obtain the widest possible rights and to see them defined in a suitable and most favourable way. The emissaries of the community tried to get in touch with the persons writing the privileges and to watch over the drafting and editing of the texts. When a privilege was to be issued or confirmed by the king the delegates of the Jewish communities concentrated their attention primarily on the officials in the royal chancelleries.[129]

It is difficult to establish the persons who drew up such documents for the Jewish communities in the noble-owned towns and where this activity took place. They could have been clerks in the service of the magnates or the wealthy *szlachta*, lawyers employed by the courts, or even local scriveners. In any case the community representatives were often able to influence the editing of the privileges. Possibly in favourable circumstances the Jews themselves dictated the text and then presented it to the issuing party for approval and signature.[130] If so, this would be analogous to the practice followed at the time of including accommodating clauses in the guild privileges at the initiative of the elders of those associations.[131] The stages through which the community privileges passed until they acquired their final form have left their mark on the arrangement, style and contents of the documents. An analysis of the texts of the privileges suggests that the major parts of the contents are by no means entirely based on stereotyped formulae but are the result of negotiations and interpolations on the part of the community representatives.

These influences are particularly noticeable in the privileges granted to the Jews settling in newly founded noble-owned towns. The contents of the privilege of the Jews of Swarzędź, issued in 1621, have been discussed by the historian A. Warschauer, writing at the end of the nineteenth century.[132] However, Warschauer did not attempt to show that this privilege was modelled on the foundation privileges which were frequently based on agreements between the lord of a town and groups of new settlers. The privilege of Swarzędź is a rare instance where the privileges granted to organized groups of settlers, including Poles as well as Germans and Dutch,[133] were used as a model to draw up a document granting rights to new Jewish settlers. When granting such privileges the lord would make an agreement with the leaders of the newly arrived group of settlers, and in the case of the Jews settling in Swarzędź the community leadership in nearby Poznań acted as their representative in the negotiations. Thus Zygmunt Grudziński, the lord of Swarzędź, which itself had been newly established in the early seventeenth century, not long before the issue of this privilege, noted in it that he has concluded 'an everlasting and unalterable agreement with the elder Jews and the entire commonality of the Jews ... of His Majesty's town of Poznań'.[134] The declaration states that the rights of the Jews thus specified originate from the obligations based on the agreement between the two sides. Similarly, elements of obligations based on negotiations are found, for example, in the privilege granted around 1715 by Józef Potocki to the Jews in the newly established town of Kutów.[135]

Very often the efforts of the community council did not cease upon receipt of the privilege, and the community representatives had to resort to renewed activity and efforts to overcome difficulties facing the enjoyment of the rights bestowed. It was in such circumstances that Stanisław Górka, the *voivode* of Poznań, issued an instruction during the *voivodes* and deputy *voivodes* to observe the privileges granted to the Jews by the kings of Poland.[136] A number of proclamations published by King Zygmunt III request that the rights and privileges of the Jews should be honoured.[137] Sometimes, for various reasons, the community was requested to show its privileges in evidence for the rights it enjoyed, for it could not continue to do so if the copy of the document, normally retained by the community elders, had been lost.

Thus the community representatives had to expend great energy to obtain new copies of privileges when the old ones were lost in fires or other circumstances, as frequently occurred. It was especially difficult to obtain copies of privileges issued by the owners of private towns because the documents were rarely lodged in the chancellery records and only in exceptional cases were entered in the municipal records.[138] Copies of privileges granted to Jews in royal towns were much more easily obtained because these were usually lodged in the chancellery records. The receipt of copies of lost privileges was not a simple formality, since the privileges had great significance and legal authority in the contemporary society. They strengthened the position of the individuals and communities that possessed them, and the deprivation or loss of such documents could have serious consequences. The privileges lost their validity and restrictions could be introduced which it was later difficult to have revoked. For this reason, it could happen that during periods of hostility between the peasants and the *starosta* on royal lands, the *starosta* took away by force the privileges held by the peasants, thus making them defenceless and submissive.[139] An occasion is known when a Jewish community was deprived of its privileges.[140]

   The need to possess documents became an especially live issue in the second half of the eighteenth century, when the newly created commissions of public order (Komisje Boni Ordinis) set about verifying the privileges held by royal and certain noble-owned towns. The commissions also took the opportunity to check the privileges of the Jewish communities there. As a result the community elders had to ensure that copies of missing documents were replaced, since they had to be presented on demand to members of the commissions. The emissaries who had been delegated for this purpose evidently did their utmost to secure the copy as quickly as possible. Rare information on such a case is included in a note appended by a member of the Komisje Boni Ordinis to the parchment copy of the privilege of the Jewish community of Kazimierz Dolny, which had been confirmed by Stanisław August in 1765. The member of the commission writes that 'the Jew [*starozakonny*], Leyzor Izraelowicz, a citizen of Kazimierz, having been elected by the entire community of the town of Kazimierz Dolny to go to Warsaw for the confirmation of the privileges, with God's help and his own efforts procured the document and returned within three days'.[141] The speedy settlement of this business in the contemporary conditions, including return journey to Warsaw, probably merited special appreciation and distinction.

Much information may be derived from the preamble, or *arenga*, frequently accompanying the community privileges. This differs in substance from the rest of the document and contains the arguments used to justify the need for issuing a privilege, or confirmation, to the persons concerned. Such reasons may be based on ideological grounds or on factors of a social, economic or religious nature.[142] The direct specific causes leading to the issue of the privilege, such as the need to restore the town, or loss of the document, may figure there. The content of the *arenga* for the privileges of the communities of royal towns are more stereotyped than those for the privileges of communities of noble-owned towns. The royal chancellery rarely showed originality in this matter and normally chose one of the existing variations. The stereotypes were adapted or emended and thus reflect changes in linguistic usage and political, social and economic conditions, as well as in the personnel of the chancellery or resulting from the accession of a new king. Frequently the *arenga* is so general in nature that it does not bear any relation to the specific document to which it is attached. In such cases its contents are linked only loosely to the concrete provisions in the privilege.

A number of privileges of communities or noble-owned towns have an *arenga* which contains no specific reference to those on whom the privilege was bestowed. For justification of the issue of such privileges, it was regarded as sufficient to emphasize the powers emanating from the patrimonial authority of the lord of the town. Accordingly, the lord of the town indicates that he is granting a privilege to the community of Opole 'because the government and the disposal of the town of Opole belongs to us by divine will and law'.[143] The lord of Szamotuły simply states that he is granting the privilege because 'my great wealth is entrusted by God'.[144]

A number of royal privileges in the second half of the seventeenth century include an *arenga* whose contents refer only to the general economic and demographic situation of the locality and not directly to Jewish matters, yet they have some relation to the provisions contained in the document. Similarly a number of privileges reflect the desire of the grantor to repopulate and revive the town as the reason for granting the Jews a privilege. In this way the *arenga* frequently expresses the attitude towards the Jews of the grantor of the privilege and reflects his social milieu, as well as the ideas and prejudices of contemporary society.

Contemporary commentators of the seventeenth and eighteenth centuries often stressed that the privileges granted to the Jews formed a significant element in the social and political structure of the Polish Commonwealth. It was pointed out also that the rights and liberties established by the privileges had been the main factor that enabled the Jews to live for so many centuries in the old multi-national Polish state. The value of these comments is not minimized by the fact that they were often hostile to and critical of the Jews and expressed the view that the Jews were faring much too well in Poland. The noted Polish writer Szymon Starowolski emphasized in the first half of the seventeenth century that 'justice was meted out more quickly to the Jews than to anyone else who had committed a wicked act, and that the Jews got away more easily without a fine than anyone else'.[145] Representatives of the burghers and clergy repeatedly demanded the curtailment of the rights contained in the privileges of the Jews in the Polish Commonwealth.

During his speech to the Diet in 1740 Adam Grabowski, the Bishop of Kujawy, stated that trade would not flourish in Poland 'until the excessive privileges of the Jews were limited'.[146] Protestants also were jealous of the freedom given to Jews in religious matters and attacked this in their writings.[147] Nevertheless the Protestant magnates drew up broad privileges for Jews who settled on their estates, as, for example, Zygmunt Grudziński for the community of Swarzędź in 1621,[148] and Bogusław Radziwiłł for those of Słuck in 1637,[149], Sokołów in 1650,[150] and Węgrów in the same year.[151] The subject of Jewish privileges did not pass without comment from visitors to Poland or foreigners interested in that country who studied the features and peculiarities of the Commonwealth's social and political system. At the end of the seventeenth century Bernard O'Connor, the Irish physician of King Jan III and a man acquainted with internal conditions in the Polilsh Commonwealth, noted in his book on Poland that the Jews there '... enjoy their religion and other privileges, without interruption'.[152]

The Englishman William Coxe, travelling in Eastern Europe in the second half of the eighteenth century, wrote of the Jews that 'this people date their introduction into Poland about the time of Kazimierz the Great, and ... they enjoy privileges which they scarcely possess in any other country except England and Holland'.[153] At the end of the eighteenth century the Alsatian physician F. L. de La Fontaine, long resident in Poland, expressed himself even more emphatically on the subject, claiming of the Jews '... nirgends geniesst er so viel öffentlichen Freyheiten und Sicherheit als hier'.[154]

Note

An extended version of this paper is published in J. Goldberg, *Jewish Privileges in the Polish Commonwealth. Charters of Rights Granted to Jewish Communities in Poland-Lithuania in the Sixteenth to Eighteenth Centuries* (Jerusalem 1985).

4

The implications of Jewish economic activities for Christian–Jewish relations in the Polish Commonwealth

Gershon Hundert

Before the nineteenth century, religious rather than ethnic distinctions were of decisive importance in determining not only legal status but also the quality of relations between people. For this reason I believe that when considering the period of the Polish Commonwealth, it is more appropriate to speak of Christian–Jewish relations than Polish–Jewish relations. An early fifteenth-century royal document, for example, which concerns the exclusion of all merchants from a place, refers to 'nullus mercator, catholicus, ruthenus vel iudeus'.[1] Nevertheless, important as the religious difference was in determining the scope of legal, institutional and social relations beween Christians and Jews, other factors, including nationality or ethnicity, must be considered as well. The notorious and rather ridiculous law of 1643 (which attempted to regulate the profits of various groups) divided merchants into three categories: Poles, foreigners and Jews.[2] It would seem, then, that at least at that point in time, Jews were considered to be neither foreigners nor Poles. However, in discriminatory legislation Jews were grouped most frequently with other non-Christian groups such as Tatars and Turks. But at other times, and usually when commercial considerations, as opposed to social segregation, were primary, Jews were linked with national groups; Scots, Armenians, Italians or Lithuanians.[3] In Polish law then, it would seem that Jews collectively had a special status, the nature of that collectivity usually being defined as non-Christian but also, sometimes, as non-Polish.

In Jewish law and tradition, as well as in communal legislation, distinctions among non-Jews were seldom drawn. The terms *arelim* and *goyyim* are used without further qualification, for example, in the monopolistic legislation of the *kahals*.

If in law each side pictured the other as an undifferentiated monolithic group, the same can certainly be said in terms of religious values as well, but this point requires no elaboration here. It is sufficient to say that the norms of both the church and the synagogue were strongly segregationist in their intent, and that each faith taught that the other was spiritually and morally inferior. Obviously these values, in turn, produced generally negative attitudes.

In terms of the Christian ideology, the oft-repeated contention is correct: that the growing strength of the Counter-Reformation from the end of the sixteenth century, led by the Jesuits who had charge of many of the schools of the Commonwealth, produced an intensification not only of anti-Protestant but also of anti-Jewish animus. This was expressed in the frequent physical attacks and riots on the Jewish streets in urban areas;[4] there were blood libel and host desecration trials;[5] and there arose in that period a genre of bourgeois anti-Jewish literature which was often venomous in tone.[6]

To take one well-known example: Sebastian Petrycy asked, rhetorically, whether Jews should be tolerated in the Commonwealth, or whether they should be expelled forthwith. In their favour he found that they supplied money to people in need; that they served the country's treasury with high taxes; that, as merchants, they paid most of the tolls and duties; and that they were generally peaceful. Weighing heavily against this, however, he found that the Jews were blasphemers, host desecrators, users of Christian blood, bribers of judges and seducers of married women and virgins. Furthermore, the Jews debased coins, stored up gold and carried it to foreign lands, and their scales were rigged. As *arendars* of villages the Jews oppressed Christian peasants, as merchants the Jews stole the livelihood of artisans and merchants of the True Faith. Last, but not least, Jews enticed Christians away from their beliefs.[7] This compendium of anti-Jewish motifs probably reflects as accurately as any other the attitude of Christian burghers toward Jews during the seventeenth century. The juxtaposition of religious, folkloristic and commercial motifs in the writing of the Cracow professor should be noted: these attitudes were quite real, and they resulted in attacks of various kinds which seriously impinged upon the lives of Jews.

The Jews' attitude towards Christians were not more elevated, but were tempered by the Jews' historical experience and by their political situation.[8] Echoing a piece of seventeenth-century Polish doggerel, European opinion came to regard Poland as *paradisus Judaeorum*, and indeed the attitude of the Jews themselves to the land in which they lived was generally positive.[9] Nevertheless, they deemed the world of non-Jews to be full of idolatry, which meant violence and drunkeness, the absence of divinely taught ethics, and ultimately, chaos. The less contact the Jew had with such a world the safer he was in body and soul.[10]

Discussions of laws, of values and of attitudes can be conducted on a rather high level of generalization and abstraction and one can speak of the Jews and the Christians collectively with at least a measure of justification. The analysis of actual behaviour, however, is a much more complex problem.

Any consideration of the economic role of the Jews in Poland-Lithuania must take a variety of factors into account. The number of Jews and the Jewish proportion of the population grew significantly during the entire period under consideration, despite substantial losses in the middle of the seventeenth century. The geographic distribution of the Jewish population shifted eastward so that the greatest proportion was to be found in Ruthenia, the Ukraine, Lithuania and Belorussia. The proportion of Jews in villages also grew and reached its peak in the third quarter of the eighteenth century; thereafter, the proportion diminished. While in the middle of the sixteenth century the majority of the heads of households was engaged in commerce, this proportion diminished with the growing number of *arendators* and artisans. Despite this, during the seventeenth and particularly the eighteenth century, the Jewish share of Polish commerce increased dramatically.

Therefore, when surveying Christian–Jewish relations in the context of the Jewish economic role, chronological and geographical distinctions must be taken into consideration as well as the more obvious differences in the quality of relations between the Jews and the various social groups. Also it must be remembered that the extent and the intensity of economic competition in the towns was much greater in crown cities than it was in private holdings.

In the smaller, newer, private towns Jews were often the only commercial element and therefore they did not face the direct competition of Christian rivals. Even among the artisans there frequently existed a complementary relationship between the trades pursued by Christians and those pursued by Jews.[11] In the larger, older, crown cities, residential segregation tended to be stricter, competition more intense and animosities more dangerous.

Particularly during the sixteenth century but also during the seventeenth and eighteenth centuries, dozens of crown cities and towns, including major centres like Lublin, Warsaw and Wilno, attempted to exclude Jews from residing in their jurisdictions. Other discriminatory (if less extreme) legislation aimed at reducing or eliminating Jewish competition, typically classed Jews as foreign merchants, forbade them to engage in retail trade, limited Jewish wholesale merchants to certain specific goods, or forbade them to lease shops or stores on the marketplace of the town.[12] Frequently guild charters not only excluded Jews from the guild's trade but also limited or prohibited Jewish acquisition of raw materials used by the guild, or forbade them to sell imported products of the same type as those produced by the guild. These varying attempts to circumscribe Jewish commercial activity are known to have been practised before the end of the fifteenth century. Early in the sixteenth century it appears that the largest cities attempted to band together against the Jews. A letter was addressed by the leading burghers of Lwów to their comrades in Poznań in 1521 asking them to join in an effort by the leading cities of the Commonwealth to gain limitations on the Jews' commercial rights at the coming meeting of Sejm.[13] As far as is known, this effort yielded no concrete results, and this was the only time that the towns tried to deal with the Jews collectively. Generally, the burghers of Poland-Lithuania thought of themselves as citizens of single towns, so that the struggles with the Jews were conducted on the local level in each town.[14]

Anti-Jewish policies in the cities, however, were not consistently pursued. Many localities which had the privilege commonly know as *de non tolerandis Judaeis*, made allowance for Jews to enter on market and fair days. Such provisions were made, for example in Toruń, Gdańsk, and Wrocław (Breslau).[15] This ambivalent attitude of the wealthier ruling stratum of the towns was reflected in these and other contradictory policies. Because of the Jews' significance and success in commerce (particularly in their roles as suppliers of goods produced in the countryside and distributors of goods purchased in the towns) their presence was welcomed by certain elements of the municipal population. By the seventeenth century the enforcing of exclusionary policies and their institution became less frequent – a reflection of the devastating population losses and general decline of many towns during that period. The town of Chęciny, for example, severely restricted Jewish residence at the end of the sixteenth century, but by 1661 the survey (*lustracja*) recorded the devout wish of the municipal government that the Jews, the majority of whom had left the town because of a recent plague, would soon return.[16]

As was the case with radical exclusionary measures, less extreme restrictions also lost much of their force in the course of the seventeenth century and this was particularly true in the smaller and the private towns. In some, for example, attempts had been made to keep Jews from renting stores or houses on the *rynek* and from doing business there. Jan Tarnowski forbade Jews to settle on the marketplace in Tarnopol in 1550; there were similar prohibitions in numerous other localities including Parczew (1569), Łuków (1589), and Zaklików (1602).[17] Yet as early as 1625 Jews owned six houses on the *rynek* in Tarnopol; the 1669 privilege to the Jews of Chęciny reversed the prohibition of their residence on the marketplace. An early seventeenth-century prohibition of Jewish settlement on the *rynek* in Żółkiew was being ignored in 1680. In Lublin, where Jews had been forbidden repeatedly to do business on the marketplace, 26 of 46 shops there were in Jewish hands in 1670.[18] Indeed, in many towns in Poland-Lithuania, there was an identifiable tendency for Jews to settle on the *rynek*.[19]

It is striking that another motif among the demands of the Jews' competitors was that the Jews be *required* to conduct their business on the marketplace. A variety of sources from the sixteenth into the eighteenth centuries speak of the Jews' practice of meeting the peasants' carts outside the city walls and buying up the best produce and livestock. City merchants objected and repeatedly forbade the Jews to 'get ahead of the Christians' in this way, demanding that the Jews trade only on the *rynek*.[20] This practice and the apparently ineffectual response of the towns provides one key to understanding the ability of the Jews to compete successfully with the Christian merchants. The latter were inhibited by the archaic and restrictive practices of the urban market place; they would not or could not free themselves from traditional modes. The initiative of others, unbound by this legacy, gradually changed the traditional pattern of urban-rural commercial relations. They were mainly Jewish and Scottish pedlars who wandered in the countryside and the petty merchants and storekeepers who came to supply the needs of the poorer classes in the towns.[21]

In a variety of places, the municipalities and the *kahals* arrived at pacts or agreements which defined such matters as the residence and propination rights of the Jews, their freedom to slaughter animals, the degree to which they would pay taxes to the city, and the extent to which they were subject to municipal jurisdiction. Occasionally the relations between Jews and artisan tradesmen were outlined, as well as matters related to Jewish commercial activity. Pacts which defined the sphere of Jewish commerce are known as early as 1544 (Bełz) and as late as 1778 (Nowe Miasto Korczyn).[22] There is no indication in the agreements of the patriciates of the municipalities allying themselves with the Jewish merchants and defending them against the Christian artisans and the rest of the *pospólstwo*. Indeed, the interests of the artisans seem to have been foremost in the minds of the municipal negotiators in a number of cases. At times these so-called pacts were no more than a means of extortion by the municipality, while at other times they were the result of bribery by the Jewish community. It is true that relations between Jews and Christian merchants soured and the animosity on the artisans' side grew noticeably during the seventeenth century. This occurred not only because of the growing number of Jewish artisans and the increasingly difficult economic situation, but also because of the widening influence of Jewish merchants who increasingly controlled the raw materials which the artisans needed and marketed goods which competed with the artisans' products.[23]

In Lublin, for example, the pewterers complained of 'Armenians, other merchants and Jews' who purchased goods in Lublin to the detriment of the guild. The locksmiths and watchmakers were concerned about Jews, Lithuanians and Scots who were selling merchandise produced elsewhere, and the hatmakers had similar complaints.[24] In most towns, the shoemakers' guild had the right of first refusal on hides brought to town for sale, but complaints were repeatedly voiced by those guilds against Jews 'acquiring the goods of their trade'.[25] Objections were raised in 1636 in Bełżyce, when, after decrying the fact that though the Jews were entitled to only ten houses, 'they already have twenty', the townsmen asked that something be done on behalf of the shoemakers and the furriers who were unable to acquire their furs and hides except from Jews. Their complaints were ignored, for in the next few years the sources record a great many transactions in which Jews sold hides and furs to guild elders 'for their trade' (*do rzemiesła swego*). To obtain their goods, these Jewish merchants could not remain in their own towns.[26]

A substantial part of a merchant's time was spent travelling. Most Jewish merchants usually travelled in groups and this practice served to isolate them from their fellow travellers on the roads.[27] Sometimes though, they travelled alone or with a non-Jewish companion or servant.[28] Authorities in the Jewish community often berated Jews who patronized the inns and taverns of non-Jews where they sat drinking together.[29] Despite prohibitions, it was sometimes the practice of Jewish merchants to dress like non-Jewish merchants.[30] This was not only for their own protection; according to one preacher, some Jews went further than the mere adaptation of the dress of the gentiles and added evil to evil by shaving their beards! 'As a result, sometimes they were not recognizable as Jews, and when asked their names they would reply with a non-Jewish cognomen. And, if sometime one was travelling on the road with some notable non-Jews who did not know he was a Jew, he sinned further by eating forbidden food and drinking unfit wine.'[31] It may well be that this preacher, Sevi Hirsh ben Aaron Samuel Koidonover, was trying to shock his listeners by carrying the consequences of imitating gentile dress to their logical conclusion. More alarmingly he had also warned that drinking in gentile taverns would lead not only to drinking unfit wine, but also to pollution by gentile women.[32] Be that as it may, my contention is that Claude Backvis was not entirely correct in contending that the Jews of Poland formed, 'un monde à part'.[33] Jewish society was indeed insular but there were a great many bridges which were not merely instrumental in nature.[34]

Were these bridges secure enough to support partnerships between Jewish and Christian merchants? There were strong sanctions on both sides against such ventures. They were forbidden by Jewish law, and the *kahals* enacted laws and re-enacted them, even forbidding Jews to enter into temporary agreements, similar to partnerships, with non-Jews.[35] The *kahals'* concern was not only to uphold Jewish law, but also to defend the community which would be likely to be held responsible for losses on the part of the Christian partner. Furthermore, the solidarity of the community was a fundamental part of its security, and there were constant condemnations and bans of excommunication against those who 'reveal the secrets of Israel', to merchants or noblemen and so threaten that solidarity.[36] A Jew who pooled his interests with a Christian defied heaven and the strongest sanctions of his community.

Sebastian Miczynski warned that 'whoever forms partnerships with Jews . . . should know that he will always suffer losses . . . betrayal and fraud await you.'[37] Variations of this attitude, buttressed by canon law and the enthusiasm of the Counter-Reformation, must have been underlined and amplified by the Jesuit teachers in their schools to the extent that a Christian who formed a partnership with a Jew would have suffered sanctions similar to those which the Jew would have incurred in his own community. Still, the urgency and the repetition of the complaints on both sides attest to the existence of such partnerships, though we cannot say with certainty how widespread or numerous they actually were.

Contemporarily, only anecdotal material is available on this subject. Samuel, a Jew from Sandomierz, had a partnership with a Scot named Wilhelm (presumably, William) in the first half of the seventeenth century and together they exported hides on a large scale through Gdańsk.[38] The brothers Israel and Abraham ben Moszko Bogaty of Kraśnik floated grain to Gdańsk in partnership with Stanisław Karfar.[39] There were Jewish–Armenian partnerships in Brody in the 1630s.[40] Such instances, however, tell us only that partnerships between Jews and Christians were not unknown.

The typical alliance between Jewish and Christian merchants was not one of lateral partnership. More commonly Christian merchant bankers provided funds for Jews, purchased raw materials from them or supplied them with imported goods for distribution.[41] Such contacts were frequent and must have served to join, in some measure, the interests of the 'first order' Christian merchants and those of the 'second order' Jewish merchants. Jews, at that time, were an inextricable part of the commercial life of the Commonwealth. Increasingly dominant in small-scale domestic commerce, particularly in the private towns, they played a large, if secondary, role in international commerce at least until the beginning of the eighteenth century, when they came to dominate overland trade with the west. Prior to that time interest and economic dependence linked them to Christians of the same profession, who were often non-Poles themselves. This sharing of interest could therefore have had few political consequences, since it would seem that to the degree that these non-Polish merchants were assimilated they left the commercial field and sought ennoblement and entry to the Polish political elite. The implications of the apparent Jewish alliance with the magnate-aristocrats were more far-reaching.

If we look first at the *szlachta* in general we find that voices were raised frequently in the *sejmiki* on behalf of Christian merchants whose interests were being harmed by Jewish competition. The resolutions adopted in those assemblies were usually worded in a general way, to the effect that Jews were 'exceeding their rights and trading in goods not permitted them, to the detriment of Christian merchants'.[42] Sometimes there were attempts to prohibit Jewish trading in specific items such as wine,[43] oxen and horses,[44] saltpeter,[45] and *potabilia et comestibilia*.[46] These generally anti-Jewish rulings of many of the *szlachta* were mitigated by their conflict of interest with merchants in general. The chief concern of the noblemen was to keep prices low, and the opinion that merchants were raising prices without justification often motivated delegations to the *sejmiki*.[47] Thus the desire to protect the Christian merchants was tempered by the idea that, 'if Jews were admitted to the trade in goods which the merchants unjustly control, this might make everything cheaper'.[48] Thus, the legislative enactments of the nobility reveal fundamentally ambiguous policies and contradictions.

More important still was the two-fold relationship between the Jews and the great landowners. On the one hand, thousands of Jews acted as *arendators* of a variety of monopolies on the holdings of these aristocrats in the villages, the towns and the cities. (This was most common in the eastern and southeastern regions of the commonwealth.) On the other hand, Jews were the primary if not the only commercial population in many of the towns held by the magnates. This led to the development of a symbiotic relationship between the two groups. The Jews found relative security in their dependence for protection and their support from the magnate-aristocrats, while the latter benefited from the financial, managerial and commercial expertise of the Jews.

For much of the period under consideration the *szlachta* would not and the peasants could not compete with the Jews for their place in the Polish economy. The city-dwellers, divided amongst themselves and politically impotent, were the major bearers of anti-Jewish animus. However, as long as there was also a bewildering variety of other national groups pursuing occupations similar to those of the Jews, this animus was somewhat diffused.

By the end of the eighteenth century the other groups had been assimilated and the beginnings of the development of a Catholic bourgeoisie were detectable. That process of urbanization inaugurated a new and different period in the history of relations between Jews and Christians in Poland.

5

A footnote to the history of the integration of converts into the ranks of the *szlachta* in the Polish-Lithuanian Commonwealth

Andrzej Ciechanowiecki

This short article must be taken to be only an extension of the facts already known and recently studied in depth by Professor Jakub Goldberg. It is a footnote to the problem of the integration of christened Jews into the nobility and gentry of the Polish-Lithuanian Commonwealth over the three centuries preceeding the Partitions of that country.

It is a truism that the Polish gentry (*szlachta*) had political, economic and legal rights far wider than their counterparts in Western Europe. Their number was legion – on their votes (often manipulated by the magnates, to whom they owed their allegiance) rested the election of kings (*electio viritim*), the functioning of parliament (the Diet) and of the Tribunals. For better or worse, pre-partition Poland had the largest electorate in Europe, born from this situation. It is therefore obvious that there were many attempts to be admitted (as well as abusive admissions) into the ranks of the gentry, be it from burghers, enriched peasants or converts. Until the end of the 16th century ennoblements were the prerogative of the Crown and later of the King in Parliament. We know of very few documented ennoblements of converts in Poland and the Grand Duchy of Lithuania in the fifteenth and sixteenth centuries, but after the Third Lithuanian Statute of 1588 the situation changed dramatically.

Before taking up this point, I feel obliged to take issue with Professor Goldberg, concerning at least two neophyte families, the Józefowicz-Hlebickis, descendants of the famous Grand Treasurer of Lithuania and possibly (although this has been questioned by geneologists) the Abramowicz[1] (lords of Worniany, at one stage; probably the most important Calvinist centre in Lithuania). Members of both families obtained a major position within the aristocracy of the Grand Duchy. This was not the result of the will of an absolute monarch such as Peter the Great (who could bring a Szafirow into his Council), but of more tolerant, humanistic laws of the Commonwealth, which – for good reasons – brought members of these families to the forefront and gave them a position of eminence.

The Józefowicz-Hlebickis, like many other families, lost some of the power they had held in the sixteenth century, but remained a family of Senatorial rank, connected by marriage with a host of great names, and they continued to hold important positions under the Crown until the fall of the First Republic. The same applied to the Abramowicz family (their arms 'Jastrzębiec' obviously being slightly modified); while very powerful in the sixteenth century and the first half of the seventeenth century, they also lost some of their importance later, but still produced a senator in the eighteenth century (Andrzej, Castellan of Brześć and Knight of the Order of the White Eagle). They remained prominent and wealthy until their extinction towards the middle of the last century. Their marriages were also spectacular.

I would also agree with the late Professor Mieses[2] that in the sixteenth century there were certainly many more converts who, surreptitiously or otherwise, entered the ranks of the *szlachta* in both Poland and Lithuania, than is officially recorded.

The well-known paragraph of the Third Lithuanian Statutes of 1588, which *explicitly* ennobled converts and their descendants, need not be discussed here. Its soundness and legal value have been established sufficiently over the years. Whether it was a product of the humanistically tolerant Renaissance atmosphere pervading the laws of the Commonwealth at the time, or a post-Tridentine example of Catholic missionary expansion – or a combination of both – is of secondary importance. Strengthened by the Constitutional Act of 1601, the Statutes in any case remained in force until 1764.

The resolution of the Constitutional Diet of 1667 and the Pacta Conventa of 1669, the first expressing the concern of the parliamentarians about so many 'new nobles', the second introducing the law about 'scartabellatu', are, to my mind, not primarily a reflection of feelings against converts entering the ranks of the gentry without parliamentary approval, but of the countless irregularities concerning born-Christians within the ruling class. This can also be confirmed by the findings of Nekanda-Trepka's 'Liber Chamorum', a tendentious but valuable source of gossipy information, unfortunately covering only some areas of the Crown (Korona).

Nevertheless, there is an important point to make concerning the territories of South Eastern Poland in the mid-seventeenth century. The facts dealing with the forced abjuration by Jews during the Cossack wars are well documented. Nobody, however, has studied the return to the

Commonwealth of gentile, Jewish or neophyte families after Poland lost to Russia the Ukrainian territories on the left bank of the Dnieper, including the city of Kiev, following the Grzymułtowski treaty of 1668. It is my contention that the clause of the Third Lithuanian Statute concerning converts had been enforced, although perhaps illegally, in those parts of the Grand Duchy which became part of the Crown territories as a result of the Union of Lublin of 1569. After 1668 many of the families considered noble – but devoid of documentary proofs lost in the wars – settled in the Eastern Marches of Poland as members of the gentry.

Because of these factors and above all because of what one might call 'automatic ennoblements', a count of the *szlachta* families of Jewish descent is virtually impossible at the present time. The total is nevertheless substantially higher than the figures so far produced by various scholars.

The situation of the converts would have probably remained unchanged had not Jacob Frank and his disciples appeared in the 1750s – a separate and fascinating subject, but not relevant to the present piece. This mass religious, cultural, and also political phenomenon created fear and uproar among the ruling class of the Polish-Lithuanian Commonwealth for the first time. The possibility of assimilation by the Republic of the Nobles of countless converts, claiming their right to the privileges of the gentry, was difficult to accept.

As is generally known, the Convocation Diet of 1764 revoked the clause of the Third Lithuanian Statute. Nevertheless the (by then) numerous families 'ex gente judeorum' put pressure on the deputies from the Grand Duchy elected for the Coronation Diet of 1764–5, to ratify the rights at least of those who were considered noble as a result of this clause of the Statute. Hence the official ennoblement by 'King in Parliament' (in fact a confirmation of their *statuts quo*) of 48 families of individuals in 1764, with the right for the King to confirm the nobility of ten more families within the year. The Diet of 1768 went even further: it authorized the Monarch to convalidate the nobility of all those who had been christened before 1764. The lists of these so-called ennoblements (in fact confirmations 'per vecchia usanza', as Italian genealogical law would have it) of 1764 and 1765 are known, while we have only fragmentary knowledge of those confirmed in 1768 and less still for 1790. Nevertheless, it would appear certain that they could be counted in hundreds rather than in tens, even without the very late arrival of the 'Frankists'. It is also worth noting that both Z. Belina-Prażmowski and Dr Adam Heymowski, have discovered convert families in Polish Livonia (Inflanty Polskie), who do not appear in these lists, but which produced noble proofs in the Province of Dvina (Prowincja Dźwińska) after the Partitions. We find amongst them two families (Chrzestanowski and Wolski) christened only in 1765, that is, *after* the Parliamentary Acts of

1764, but which still claimed their noble 'status' on the basis of the acts of 1764 and 1768. They were confirmed in this status.[3]

Having repeated these known facts, I will now consider certain problems deriving from them, which to my mind have not been sufficiently studied to date. First of all, I have to admit that the genealogical study of Polish-Lithuanian families, especially of the minor gentry, leaves much to be desired. As a result, the progeny of most families 'ennobled' in 1764 is hardly known, and has created serious problems for genealogists. We can, more or less, trace the descendants of the Jakubowskis, Krzyżanowskis or Przewłockis ennobled during this period, while about other families there is little we can do for the moment. We are equally in the dark about the antecedents, genealogically speaking, of nearly all the ennobled. Secondly, the homonymity of names with other Polish or Lithuanian families (of old, not convert descent), but which bore different arms, makes the task even more difficult (for instance: Bielski, Dobrowolski, Jarmund, Lipski, Michałowski, Orłowski, Pawłowski, Wolański etc.).

To take one detailed example: there exists a well-documented, not unimportant, Lithuanian family named Jeleński, arms Korczak. Their pedigree is impeccable. On the other hand, we know that the brothers Jakub, Mateusz and Stanisław Jeleński, sons of Franciszek 'titled' Treasurer of Zakroczym (I will return to this later), were ennobled 'e gente neophita' in 1764. How are we today to distinguish between two families bearing the same name and the same arms (without even a modification)? The members of the latter (convert) family soon held public office in their provinces, became wealthy, and could easily be mistaken for scions of the certainly much older and distinguished family. To clear this area, we would need, for the sake of historical accuracy, to know how the ex-neophyte families of 1764–5, 1768 and 1790 proved their nobility in Russia or Austria (and in which category) after the partitions of Poland. It is only in these noble proofs that we will find the answer to many of our questions.

One of these questions arises from the phrase in the motion for ennoblement proposed by the Lithuanian deputies in 1764, mentioning that members of the families to be thus honoured had previously held public office. I have tried within my means to verify this assertion. I found that in only *three* cases were members of families 'ex gente judaica' to be ennobled in 1764, office-holders before that date. It is only *after* the ennoblement that we find a large number of members of such families being granted public office in their own region (hence my query about Franciszek Jeleński, 'titled' Treasurer of Zakroczym – particularly as all the known offices held by all the Jelenskis were always in the Grand Duchy of Lithuania, and not in the Crown, that is, the Kingdom of Poland).

A particularly interesting example of what we have discussed above is provided by the Osiecimski family, which is in fact that of my mother. Although Michał Osiecimski is among those ennobled by the Coronation Diet of 1764, and is quoted by all authors as being himself a convert, the existing documentation gives a totally different picture. His son Bonawentura, a rich landowner, already elected by the gentry of the Borysów district in 1800 as a member of its commission of noble proofs (deputacja wywodowa), had of course himself at a certain moment to produce his own pedigree, according to the laws of the Empire introduced by the Ukaz of Catherine II, dated 1782, for all her newly acquired domains. This he did on 12 December 1802 and the necessary diploma confirming his nobility was issued on 21 August 1805. What is striking are the following documents produced in the official proceedings.

Bonawentura establishes first of all that he is proving his descent from four noble generations: In the first generation, *Ignacy*, who in 1675 purchased the estate of Krzywicze Małe in the Palatinate of Mińsk (the act of sale being entered into the books of the Supreme Tribunal of Lithuania) – he ceded this property in 1718 to his son *Kazimierz* (second generation). This act of cession is again entered into the same books. (Kazimierz incidentally also had the life tenancy of another property, Słoniewszczyzna, granted him by the powerful Sapieha family.) In his will of 1749 Kazimierz divides his properties between two sons. *Michał Jan* (third generation), the elder of the two, born in 1727, added during his lifetime to his estates, and in 1757 received from Augustus III the titular dignity of Mostowniczy (praefectus pontium) of the District of Rzeczyca, styled in the grant 'urodzony' (generosus). His further career after the 'ennoblement' of 1764 does not interest us here: two good noble marriages, public service and so on, until his death in 1799. Of his several sons mentioned in his will and in other documents, most held public or court office. We now come to *Bonawentura* (fourth generation), mentioned previously, who died in 1842, having held for many years the highest and very prestigious position of his district, that of marshal of the nobility.

If we use the Kekule system, then Bonawentura establishing his pedigree from the four noble generations would be the *first* one and Ignacy, appearing as the owner of Krzywicze in 1675 the *fourth*, otherwise – like Dr Adam Heymowski[4] – one should consider the father of Ignacy, whose name is unknown, as the first Christian, and therefore *ipso facto* ennobled, forebear. In any case, the change of religion must have occurred some time before 1675 – this date, the first purchase of landed property, being the *terminus ante quem*.

In the official proceedings the act of ennoblement of 1764 is not mentioned at all. The diploma of 1805 shows the arms Lubicz with normal tinctures, without the modifications of the 1765 grant of arms. Nevertheless, in spite of Bonawentura producing a pedigree of four noble generations, he and his family were entered into the I book of nobility of the Government of Minsk, meaning that the family had less than 100 years of nobility. Bonawentura's peers did therefore somehow take into account the act of 1764. But in 1835 the Heraldry Department of the Ruling Senate in St Petersburg, supreme authority in these matters, transferred the Osiecimski family into book VI, covering all families in the Empire which were considered as being always noble (the equivalent of the German Uradel). This took place *after* the well-known Bibikov reforms, which considerably stiffened the rules for noble proofs within the Russian Monarchy. The dates of 1805 and 1835 of the two inscriptions into different books of nobility, particularly the second one, are of great interest. The first seems logical, whilst the second can only be interpreted as the acceptance that the family was officially considered noble as of 1675.

It is also interesting to note from the documents produced, that all – and especially the early ones – were entered into the acts of appropriate institutions of the Grand Duchy, even some which certainly did not require it. One gains the impression of a sense of insecurity in the newly obtained automatic ennoblement and a wish to 'officialize' any act concerning the persons involved.

As a corollary to my subject I would like to mention that all Bonawentura's grandsons took an active part in the Insurrection of 1863, some of them finishing in Siberia (the escape of one being immortalized by Artur Grottger) and that the substantial family estates in White Russia were confiscated. Those who survived settled and prospered in Galicia, where one of Bonawentura's descendants obtained from the Emperor Franz Josef a title of Austrian Count in 1907.

To close this far too long footnote, may I sum up as follows. In the light of the tolerance – extraordinary by the standards of other Western European countries and in the best traditions of Renaissance humanism – which, in the Grand Duchy of Lithuania, allowed the acceptance of converts into the ranks of the ruling class of the Commonwealth, it is absolutely necessary, if one wants to obtain a full picture of the problem, firstly to study the real cultural, political and economic impact of the ennobled converts within the structures of the Commonwealth before the Partitions and after. Secondly, it is necessary to establish the antecedents of those ennobled between 1764–90 (or earlier), and also the ramifications of their descendants until the present time, which I have shown to be a genealogical and historical void. Only then will this particular chapter of Polish–Jewish relations be properly identified – and it is a fascinating one.

6

Polish society and the Jewish problem in the nineteenth century

Stefan Kieniewicz

About half a century ago, the Polish Biographical Dictionary had its beginnings in Cracow. I remember at that time a spirited discussion among people of our profession concerning the attribution of the respective biograms to the most competent authors. It was said that articles in the new Dictionary were being allotted on a partisan basis: nationalist historians were writing about nationalists, freemasons about freemasons, Jesuits about Jesuits, women about women, and, of course, Jewish historians about Polish Jews. Some people argued that such a practice, in contemporary history, does not suit objectivity but fosters an unscholarly and hagiographic approach.

Recalling this old polemic is not inappropriate when speaking of Polish–Jewish historiography. The fact that the history of Polish Jewry was, and is still being, written almost exclusively by authors of Jewish descent, is neither awkward nor misplaced in the present context. It represents a topic important to Jews, above all, and is one that is most familiar to them. It seems that anti-semites, when writing history, are capable only of producing contemptible libels. Non-Jewish authors who are not anti-semites, prefer to eschew the subject, which is a pity.

The exclusivity to which I have just alluded entails some kind of unilateral approach. Jewish authors publishing works written for the Polish market tend to focus mainly on two aspects of their history: the importance of the Jewish contribution to both the Polish culture and economy, and the reprehensible discrimination against Jews by Christians. Both themes are factual and essential; however, they do not embrace the full measure of Polish–Jewish relations in the past.

After the Holocaust and the post-war exodus, research in this field was mostly conducted outside Poland; these findings and publications are hardly available and, in any case, their language is unfamiliar to my country-men. The researchers are hindered, too, I fear, because of an inadequate knowledge of purely Polish affairs. It is indeed unfortunate that there is now in Poland no one who is able to study and revive the history of Polish Jews – a history that is most important to the Polish people, for its own sake and because of Jewish participation in or contribution to our national past.

This article deals with one problem only: that of Polish attitudes towards the Jews in the so-called Partition era, 1795–1918, from the fall of the old Republic to the rebirth of an independent state. These attitudes should be considered within the context of broader transformations undergone by Polish society under foreign rule during the nineteenth century. There are many factors with which to juggle: the necessary abrogation of outlived feudal structures, of peasant compulsory labour, of medieval guilds; the development of the crusade for equal rights for every citizen, independent of birth or creed; and, concurrently, Polish resistance to the foreign yoke, resulting in the stern defence of Polish nationality.

Each of these factors influenced, in varying ways, the fate of the Jewish minority in Poland. It is not necessary here to stress the circumstances of this minority: the growing number of Jews; their persistent cultural distinct ness; their increasing power in the economic domain, and not least, their increasing social differentiation.

It must also be said that a study of Polish–Jewish relations ought to make allowance for the passage of time and the drastic changes of 1831, 1864 and 1905. The study must also take into account the dissimilar features of Russian, Austrian and Prussian rule and the specific conditions of the ten Polish provinces – not forgetting the interactions between Polish and Jewish emigrants. Polish society underwent dramatic changes in the last century. No wonder the Poles' attitudes towards the Jews were highly diversified, according to the social background and political character of various groups or individuals.

I shall not stress the persistent sense of extraneousness felt by the Jew; nor the perennial, insurmountable barrier separating 'the Infidel' from the Christian. Such sentiments prevailed, it would seem, among the rural population, but did not involve a predisposition to mistrust, antipathy or disdain. Here other tendencies seem more important; those which were aimed at modifying and improving both Jewish society and Polish–Jewish relations.

At the root of these tendencies lay the ideology of the Enlightenment – the necessary progress of humanity, a progress which ought to be encour-aged and directed from above. An urgent and beneficial 'Jewish Reform' ranked among other analogous projects, intended or attempted: reform of the peasantry, of the towns, of the Church and so on. Barriers were to be lifted between Jews and Christians; the former had to gain access to fields of activity, at that time closed to them, in agriculture and industry, in the professions, state service and the army. But also the damaging Jewish monopoly in trade and finance ought to be brought to an end. Such concern with a reconstitution of Jewish society met with opposition from both Polish and Jewish conservatives. Two relevant observations may be made in this respect. The state, when directing Jewish reforms, was always more concerned with restrictions than with emancipation. Also, Polish initiatives in this field were hampered, even in semi-independent states (such as the Duchy of Warsaw 1807–12, Congress Poland 1815–30, or the Free State of Cracow 1815–46). A share of the responsibility for the shortcomings of Jewish reform rests, therefore, on the shoulders of the partitioning powers.

Another tendency, different not only in conception but in its degree of applicability, was that of Jewish assimilation, rather than reform. Should this alien population adopt the Polish language, dress, education and way of life; should they resemble the authentic Poles (even while abiding by the Mosaic faith)? Even if that were possible, would there remain any obstacles to a happy symbiosis of the two tribes? None, were it not for one problem. Was the legal emancipation of the Jews a precondition of their assimilation, a question posed by 'enlightened' Jews? Or, on the contrary, was emancipation to be postponed until their eventual assimilation? Most Polish conservatives advocated the second solution, applying the same argument to the timing of the peasants' emancipation. Somebody jested that the Polish nobility would be ready to liberate their serfs as soon as the Polish peasants would recite Homer in Greek – while ploughing! There were other major obstacles to the assimilation of the Jews, most obviously, their civil disabilities. But even after these were removed, only a small fraction of the Jewish upper middle class and the professions crossed over, baptized or not, to the Polish community. Under such circumstances, assimilation for the Polonized Jews meant loss of authority in, and estrangement from, their native milieu.

Some ultra-conservative noblemen feared assimilation, considering Polonized Jews to be a danger to the established order. The influential Frankist coterie was charged with (among other things) conspiring against Polish society and its most valuable traditions. Mistrust of 'Frankism' amounted to persecution mania, and in this context I find it deplorable that the *Un-Divine Comedy*, by Zygmunt Krasinski, which is one of the supreme achievements of European Romanticism, is marred by the grotesque and unseemly theme of the 'Converted Jews'.

Pioneers of social welfare, while campaigning against alcoholism, were eager to attack and condemn the innkeeper, rather than the squire – the then producer of vodka – as the main culprit. In Galicia and on the Eastern

Borders, most innkeepers were Jews who also engaged in petty usury, or practised the sweating system in cottage industry. Temperance associations, well developed in the 1840s and 1850s, and patronized by the clergy, often presented the Jew as the scapegoat, holding him mainly responsible for the dejection of the peasantry.

The Jewish factor was bound to play a role in the struggle led by the Polish patriots against their foreign oppressors, since, generally, any minority held in suspicion tries to remain on good terms with state authorities. In the case of nineteenth-century Poland, this meant foreign authorities. During periods of political crisis, Jews were often accused of and chastised for collaboration with the enemy. Conversely, factions within that minority also sympathized with revolutionaries who challenged the common oppressor of Poles and Jews. Polish democrats discerned the advantage of a Jewish support early in the struggle, and as a result they emphasized their will to grant equal civic rights to Jews – in a liberated country. Progressive Jews responded to the appeal. Two professional Jewish groups happened to be of particular usefulness to the Polish underground movements, booksellers and contrabandists, and both were instrumental in the retail of forbidden literature. None other than Adam Mickiewicz paid a tribute to them in the well-known distich:

> *Hence, notwithstanding Tsarist threats, in spite of publicans,*
> *A Jew smuggles into Lithuania volumes of my works.*

Mickiewicz was not only considered to be the first of Poland's romantic 'Bards'; he also aspired, towards the end of his life, to the role of a spiritual leader of his nation. In this capacity, he stood not only for equal rights for the Jews, but also stressed their unique and under-valued position in Polish society. The Political Declaration of the Polish Legion, proclaimed by Mickiewicz in Rome on 29 March 1848, affirmed in Point Ten: 'To our elder brother, Israel, respect, fraternity and help on his way to eternal and earthly welfare; equal rights in every matter.' In the last stage of the Crimean War, Mickiewicz attempted to enrol some Jewish volunteers to fight under the Polish banner against Tsarist Russia. 'I would not like to see Israelites leaving Poland' was one of the poet's last pronouncements. 'Just as the Union of Lithuania with Poland, despite differences of race and creed, created the political and military power of our Commonwealth, so would Poland's union with Israel, I am sure, increase our force, spiritual and material.'

The apogee of Polish–Jewish friendship was reached in 1861, when the leaders of the Polish patriotic movement put the emancipation of Jews on their agenda. Warsaw rabbis supported the initiative, inviting their co-religionists to collaborate with the Poles and to support their national claims. Polish anthems were sung in synagogues; Jews were to be addressed, henceforth, as 'Poles of Mosaic denomination'. 'The Polish Jews' a poem by Norwid, includes the verses:

> *Homage to you, earnest Nation! In those,*
> *Who did not take fright in the Mongolian tempest,*
> *But fought together with us, the cause of Moses' God,*
> *With a chivalrous glance, and naked breasts . . .*

This Polish–Jewish alliance of 1861 was the single most important factor in forcing the Russian government the following year to proclaim the legal emancipation, postponed for decades, of the Jews in the Congress Kingdom. Another corollary was the participation of numerous Jews in the Polish insurrection of 1863 in the roles of armed volunteers, members of the underground organization or indirect supporters.

However, the insurrection was crushed, and the opportunity for promoting the Polish cause by arms seemed lost for the time being. The emphasis of the struggle of Polish patriots shifted to what was called organic work: the defence and promotion of the Polish economy, culture and education by peaceful and legal means. In this organic programme, the Jewish bourgeoisie played a conspicuous role as did the assimilated intelligentsia of Jewish descent. Bolesław Prus, the well-known journalist and novelist, supported this cause in his columns from the 1870s, campaigning tirelessly against the degradation of Jews. On the contrary, he argued, Poles ought to imitate their orderliness, their thrift and spirit of solidarity; they ought also to collaborate with the Jews in all economic and social enterprises where interests converged. Ideas of this kind were favourably accepted in the last quarter of the nineteenth century: No charitable, educational or cultural institution could be founded in Warsaw at that time without the considerable and freely given support of Jewish financiers. (The Higher Technical School founded by Wawelberg and a Commercial School patronized by Kronenberg are among the best-known of many similar examples.)

The period under consideration can also be envisaged as the culminating phase of assimilation in the large urban centres such as Warsaw, Cracow and Lwów. Advocates of assimilation predominated in the Warsaw *Kahal* and in the main synagogues; numerous intellectuals of Jewish descent achieved prominence in Polish cultural life. It is true that this trend towards the acceptance of assimilation involved only a small percentage of the continually increasing Jewish population. However, relations between enlightened Polish circles and the orthodox Jewish masses, were neither ill-disposed nor embittered. For a Warsaw positivist like Prus, Jews could be laughed at as every minority is laughted at, they ought, even, to be lectured and sermonized – but on no account should they be despised or antagonized *as Jews*. Indeed there were anti-semites in the Warsaw positivist milieu; but on the whole, anti-semitism was considered bad taste and incompatible with progressive views.

Subsequent changes in Polish–Jewish relations were caused, above all, by the impact of capitalist relations which were then predominant in Central Europe. Old communities, Polish and Jewish alike, were rapidly disintegrating as new social classes formed and took shape, and new relationships between these classes radically altered the relationships between the previously conventional groups. Thus, for instance, affluent Polish groups – the aristocracy not excepted – were uninhibited in befriending Jewish millionaires, not only within the parameters of business, but also in social situations. Intermarriages, although not frequent, did not create scandals. Those same Jewish tycoons, on the other hand, were regarded as exploiters by the labouring classes, both Christian and Jewish, and hated accordingly. Scholars, men of letters and artists of Jewish descent were on a friendly basis with their Christian colleagues, but Polish-, German-, Ukrainian- and Jewish-speaking proletarians did not mix as successfully as the educated classes. They tended, however, to consider themselves as components of the same labour class, and the more discerning elements among them collaborated in socialist circles or parties. Early socialist organizations addressed their propaganda to workmen of all creeds and languages alike.

Among the lower middle classes mistrust and ill-feeling was ever-increasing, particularly between Jewish and Christian shopkeepers, pedlars or middlemen. Non-Jewish peasant newcomers, flocking into the cities in the search of a career in trade, were faced with the long-established monopolies of Jewish businessmen. The resulting economic rivalry fuelled anti-semitic resentment.

Polish–Jewish relations were also bound to be influenced by the national problem. How did the Jews behave, in the face of Polish resistance to foreign oppression? In Poznania, under Prussian rule, the Jewish middle class inclined towards German culture and was consequently regarded by Poles with no less hostility than the entire German element. Jews, on the other hand, were not numerous in Prussian Poland and their numbers decreased as a consequence of emigration. In Central Poland, Jews as well as Poles were harassed by the Tsarist reactionary regime – a fact which was the source of solidarity between the two communities, as both became involved in various illegal, antigovernmental activities. Eastern Jews, flocking from the Pale after the wave of pogroms of the 1880s, presented another problem. These Litvaks, as they were called, were Russian-speaking people, and were resented not only as business competitors, but also as a threat to the Polish character of such towns as Warsaw, Lódź or Wilno.

It is appropriate, here, to mention Austrian Galicia, a province which had enjoyed a broad autonomy since the late 1860s, and in which the local administration remained entrusted to conservative Polish landowners. This conservative establishment did not interfere, however, with Jewish affairs. The local administration, on the eve of elections, reached tacit agreements with Jewish orthodox leaders and some Jewish deputies were elected, most often siding with the government. The Jewish population were also represented in municipal self-government. Those in power did not enforce assimilation – although politics of the kind they favoured did assist the same assimilative processes.

Most of the tendencies outlined above seemed, somehow, to die out or, rather, to stagnate towards the end of the century. Hopes for the Polish population as a whole, based on the salutary effects of Jewish legal emancipation, proved ill-founded, since the project did not initiate a marked assimilation trend. Let it be stressed, however, that Jewish emancipation was subject to substantial legislative restrictions under Russian rule.

Yet there were more obstacles to a pacific fusion of the two populations than outlined above, in a country where Jews accounted for ten per cent of the population (almost 40 per cent in Warsaw, up to 90 per cent in more than one *shtetl*). Supporters of the Jewish people considered assimilation to be a unique and infallible panacea; and yet most Jews today envisage it as equivalent to suicide. How could two populations so very dissimilar continue to cohabit on peaceful terms, after having been proclaimed equal before the law?

It is impossible, of course, in this context, to say nothing about the notorious Warsaw Pogrom of 1881, probably initiated by the Tsarist Okhrana. The fact that such provocation succeeded, is in some ways the most disastrous aspect of the affair.

The relationships between national groups of revolutionaries and proletarians were not easy. There had been a period, not long before, when even orthodox Jews forged alliances with Polish patriots to fight against their common oppressor, but after 1864 Polish irredentists could no longer be considered as valuable political partners. The peremptory slogan, 'Proletarians of all lands, unite!' seemed to invite visions of universal fraternity among the labouring classes, yet they took time to materialize in Poland. As late as 1905, under Tsarist rule, socialist parties had only limited influence. In Prussian Poland, socialism was legal, but it was mainly German in character. In Galicia, Polish and Jewish workmen remained united until 1905, when the Labour movement split along nationalist dividing lines and a Jewish Social-Democratic Party had its inception.

I have mentioned, not without reason, the awakening of nationalism. Towards the turn of the century the popular masses of Central Europe became aware of their national identity, for reasons well-known (yet ill-defined), which do not need to be shown here. Such feelings, revealed themselves, among other ways, in national hostility. German, Russian, Polish and Jewish nationalist hostility evolved similarly, being similarly conditioned. Which of these manifestations of aggression should be labelled as offensive or defensive, primordial, or environmental? Who ought to be held responsible for resultant deep divisions? Russian 'Black-Hundreds', Dmowski's National League, or intransigent Zionists? Certainly this is a good subject for a scholarly discussion, and I shall not anticipate its results.

Allow me to end with one disheartening statement of fact. The assimilative trend, which grew noticeably among Polish Jews in the second half of the nineteenth century, slackened, or even came to a halt in later times. Yet, in spite of claims to the contrary, it can be said that this temporary influx of assimilated Jewish elements proved highly beneficial to the Polish economy and culture, and that they featured among the distinguished members of the Polish intelligentsia. It is ironical that a similar statement of the Jewish contribution to Poland's history is more easily justified today, when the phenomenon itself has receded.

A qualitatively new period of Polish–Jewish relations may be dated from 1910, when for propaganda purposes, the National-Democratic Party began to exploit anti-semitic feelings which were dormant among the lower-middle classes. This propaganda began a chain reaction of mutual resentments, the consequences of which are well-known. It is but a poor consolation for Polish people, that infinitely more horrible deeds were perpetrated elsewhere.

7

Polish–Jewish relations in the territories annexed by the Russian Empire in the first half of the nineteenth century

Daniel Beauvois

Most works on the subject of the Jews in Russia take an incorrect approach,[1] since the vast majority of Jews living in the Russian Empire were not inhabitants of Russia proper. Certainly they were administratively subject to Russian law, but they lived in the Western provinces, where the ethnic predominance was Lithuanian, Byelorussian or Ukrainian. However, these three ethnic groups played practically no part in the fate of the Jews, being almost everywhere reduced to serfdom. In fact the Jews found themselves confronted by the former political masters of these provinces, the Poles, who possessing practically all the land, had remained the economic masters.

When, in 1762, Catherine II launched an appeal in Western Europe for settlers to populate her Empire's uninhabited lands, she made it clear this was 'with the exception of the Jews'. This Russian rejection of Jews, confirmed by a law of 1821 completely proscribing the central provinces to them, and, in 1825, the provinces to be colonised (Astrakhan and the Caucasus), explains why they are to be found primarily in the Polish territories annexed in 1772, 1793 and 1795, where high concentrations of Jews had existed since the sixteenth and seventeenth centuries because of Poland's openness, at that period, to the Jews who were being driven from other European countries.

According to I. Levitats, in 1847 in these annexed territories, previously Polish, there were 1,041,363 Jews of both sexes.[2] This population group was thickly clustered, especially in the Ukrainian provinces on the right bank of the Dnieper; indeed, in that area, the Jewish inhabitants outnumbered the Poles. According to the Governor-General D. G. Bibikov's annual report for 1840, the numbers of the three ethnic groups there were as follows (the native Russians counting for only a few units – the administrators and the army in its barracks):[3]

	Volhnyia Province	*Kiev Province*	*Podolia Province*	*Totals*
Jews	177,622	164,782	115,143	457,547
Poles	139,007	129,503	141,702	410,212
Ukrainian serfs	1,453,027	1,394,329	1,435,083	4,282,439

The Jewish population was almost wholly joined with the *mieszczanie* category; that is, it dwelt in the towns and large villages, which belonged to the state or were privately owned and which, commonly, were only insignificant agglomerations. Jews were especially numerous in Berdichev (23,160), Wilno (23,050) and Mińsk (12,976). These inhabitants were poor, even wretched; only a small elite linked to the merchant class could attest to some wealth. Trade was the concern of Jews far more than of Christians. The same statistics of Bibikov give the following figures for the three provinces in the southern part of the Polish section integrated in the Empire:

	Volhynia Province	*Kiev Province*	*Podolia Province*	*Totals*
Jewish merchants	7,223	2,529	2,533	12,285
Christian merchants	215	996	579	1,790

A good idea of the cultural weight of the three ethnic groups represented in Western Ukraine can be gained from the statistics of buildings for religious worship. In 1840, on the eve of the suppression of the Uniate Church, the peasant serfs were almost all Orthodox Christians and naturally the figures for them exceed the others; it is noticeable that the possibilities for the expression of Jewish piety were much greater than those for the expression of the Poles' Roman Catholicism, which between 1831 and 1840 underwent massive confiscations of churches and monasteries:[4]

	Volhynia *Province*	*Kiev* *Province*	*Podolia* *Province*	*Totals*
Synagogues	483	265	360	1,108
Orthodox churches	1,230	1,385	1,556	4,171
Catholic churches	257	59	111	427

If the legal framework within which the Jews of the Russian Empire lived is relatively well-known, given the statutes and successive regulations of 1804, 1825, 1835 and 1844, the living reality of this legislation and especially the inter-ethnic relations have not been adequately studied. An extensive thesis remains to be written based on the abundant material in the Russian archives, notably those in Leningrad and Kiev. The Central Archives of the Ukraine Soviet Republic, for instance, preserve in the collection no. 442 (Governor-General's Chancellery), *opis 1*, numerous files concerning Jews. Having worked in this archive on other research, I was able to make a note of only a few references. Let us hope that some other researcher will be able to exploit these riches. Thus in the collection cited, file (in Russian, *edinica hranienia*) no. 1925 furnishes complete statistics of synagogues, schools and Jewish administration in the three provinces in question for 1835–41. The catalogue (for internal use exclusively!) should be examined methodically for this *opis*. In it there also figure, for example, with reference no. 6189 and no. 6190, thick files (in Russian) so far unexploited (folios 560 and 76 respectively) bearing on the liquidation of the *Kahals* in 1845–9.

Between 1802 and 1832 the nine previously Polish provinces annexed by the Russian Empire were culturally dominated by Wilno, where the Polish university, with the school network it directed, was a veritable *pharos*. As we know, it was from there that Adam Mickiewicz came, who wished, in the final scene of his celebrated poem *Pan Tadeusz*, to present a scene of popular dancing under the sway of the Jewish fiddler Jankiel, a symbol of the true concord existing – or yet to be created? – between the Jewish and Polish peoples.

This ideal vision assuredly does not correspond with the reality of Polish–Jewish relations, which were marked above all by mutual ignorance. Louis Greenberg is not far from the truth when he writes: 'Even authors in the Ukraine and Polish regions who did have opportunity to observe the Jew at closer range, knew virtually nothing of his inner life.'[5]

If it is true that Poland, 'a Jews' paradise' often contented itself with an attitude of hostile ignorance the persistence of which we shall see,[6] one should first draw attention to the Polish efforts to better the lot of the Jewish masses. The cultured Poles at the end of the Enlightenment – which lasted there until nearly 1825 – were persuaded that they were the flag-bearers of 'civilization' and that it behoved them to spread it. The contacts between the *haskalah*, a Jewish enlightenment movement, and the en-lightened Polish world do not seem to have been very numerous although they developed around the same centres, Wilno and Krzemieniec.[7] The ignorance was reciprocal since, as J. M. Delmaire has shown,[8] the *maskilim* (representatives of the Jewish Enlightenment) were, up until the middle of the century, wholly oriented towards Germanic culture.

It is beyond question that it is to Polish influence (notably that of Prince A. J. Czartoryski) on the young Tsar Alexander I that the statute for the Jews of the Empire of 9 December 1804 owes its relative liberalism, and in par-ticular the abandoning, within the 'Jewish committee' formed by the 'young friends' of the Tsar (Kochubey etc.), of the idea of massive deportations to the south that had been put forward by Derzhavin, Paul I's minister of justice.[9] Czartoryski, then the most influential of the Emperor's familiars, was himself inspired, as to the Jewish question, by Polish Enlightenment thought which had been manifested in the Four Year (1788–91) Diet's lengthy discussion of social reforms. On this subject he consulted his com-patriot Count T. Czacki, who, with the help of H. Kołłątaj, initiated at the same time (1803–7) various cultural projects in Volhnyia. There is no doubt that the prince was acquainted with the projects aimed at introducing equal rights for the Jews, proposed during the Polish Four Year Diet,[10] and that he inevitably read the *Rozprawa o Żydach* that T. Czacki had prepared during that period and which Kołłątaj helped him to publish between 1805 and 1807.[11] By this statute the autonomy of the *Kahals* (Hebrew for 'com-munities') was guaranteed on both an administrative and a religious level, and the theoretical tutelage of the Ministry of Public Instruction – altered in 1817 to the Ministry of Public Instruction and Religious Worship, with a special section at the Department of Religious Affairs (Jewish, Moslem, and others) – was relatively light.

On a smaller scale, can one attribute a *rapprochement* between the Jewish and Polish communities to Wilno's intellectual influence? The weakness of attempts to do just this obliges one to be careful. At no time did Polish thought attain the openmindedness existing in France, where in 1791 all civic rights were granted to the Jews. It should nevertheless be emphasized that ostracizing of Jews was not limited to Poland: it was suppressed in Prussia only in 1848, in England in 1858, and in Italy only in 1870.

On the Jewish side, the presence in Wilno of *haskalah* representatives as eminent as M. A. Ginsburg or N. Rosenthal does not seem to have overcome the mistrust felt towards the Polish schools, which had been developing quickly before 1831. The Jews' withdrawal into their ghettoes was very pronounced at the start of the nineteenth century. In accordance with the 1804 statute, elementary lay schools were supposed to be set up for the Jews, alongside the parish schools restricted to Christians, which is why the Wilno university eventually concerned itself with the problem. In April 1808 the Rector, Jan Śniadecki, created a Jewish teachers' training school in Wilno, where reading, writing and arithmetic were taught in Polish. 'Those of this religion, so numerous, are foreigners in our country,' said the Rector. 'I am very hopeful of the benefits when they have become familiar with our language, when they are able to read and understand books in Polish. . . . This institution will last only a few months, in order to form a nest of Jewish elementary school teachers for studying Polish. . . .'[12] It is not known whether the pupils so trained did in fact devote themselves to the elementary schooling of their co-religionists, but it is highly unlikely: a commission bringing together university professors and *Kahal* members met in 1811 in order to induce the Jewish hierarchy to encourage such undertakings, but this came to nothing.[13]

After the Napoleonic upheaval it was again Czartoryski, the Pole, who was in charge of the cultural system in the annexed territories. From 1815 he concerned himself once more with the schooling of Jews, and drew up – but this time in a new key – a memorandum in French for Alexander I entitled *Remarques sur les Israélites*. In a letter of 12/24 July 1817 to the Emperor he summarized the piece thus:

The Jews are a chief cause of the wretchedness of this country. Your Majesty, out of piety and wisdom, has wished to convert them to Christianity. But that notion must be the Government's secret, as is said in a paper I submitted on this subject . . . otherwise this fine, holy idea cannot succeed. It must be hidden from the Jews; a beginning must be made, by administrative directives, on preparing them for conversion; they must first be made Christian culturally. One could not busy oneself enough nor too soon with this, whether it is considered as a matter of humanity or of politics or of religion.[14]

One cannot fail to be struck by this 'civilizing' concept, which necessarily involved emptying Jewish culture of its content and this by means of devious methods, the ultimate goal being conversion! In that year, 1817, the university endowed itself with a Schools Committee; on the committee elected professors were supposed to administer the ensemble of secondary and, incidentally, primary schools. From this committee the Rector requested a fresh plan for the primary schooling of Jews. The *Kahal*, which declared itself unable to act without the governor's orders, called a halt to the project. A plan for a single school, in Wilno, *was* ready on 6 September

1818, but it was only in 1819 that Gordon and Rosensohn were authorized to negotiate on the *Kahal*'s behalf. Eventually the Russian military governor, who looked on this Polish reassertion unfavourably, caused the whole business to fail.[15]

On 12 February 1820 the *adjunkt* Żukowski, who, let it be stressed, taught Hebrew at the university, tried afresh to relaunch the idea; the school would have two classes, one to teach the rudiments of Polish and Hebrew, the other German. The teaching would be funded out of 900 silver roubles yearly. This formula appeared more attractive to the *kahal*, which by that time wished to make schooling compulsory. The schoolmasters would be Christians to begin with, gradually being replaced by Jews. The teaching method would be the Lancaster: that is, the advanced pupils would go over the lessons with the beginners, two to three hours on winter afternoons and two to four hours in the summer.[16] Yet none of these suggestions was finalized. Only the aged Joachim Chreptowicz, who, out of paternalism, maintained a Lancaster school for peasants on his Szczorse estate, accepted a few young Jews, as an example to others. These Jewish students took their prayerbooks to it and studied Polish there from Niemcewicz's *Leibe i Siora*, an eighteenth-century novel preaching Judeo–Christian harmony.

In 1823 the curator Czartoryski returned once more to the objective of harmony; but the days of Polish management were then numbered, and it was only a ritual repetition.[17] The person responsible, in 1830, for education in the formerly Polish territories was the Russian Novosiltsov. Three potential tutors, who had undergone an aptitude examination at the Wilno gymnasium, were given authority to open elementary-level classes for Jews.[18] But this move took place on the eve of the destruction of the university and the Russification of the whole Polish educational system, and therefore was no longer a matter of Jewish–Polish cultural *rapprochement*. After 1832 the *haskalah* representatives, notably Levinsohn, were more desirous of a *rapprochement* with Russian culture. The first Jewish state schools did not appear in Wilno and Żytomierz until 1847, financed by a tax on sabbath candles,[19] and of course under the Russian aegis. It is no exaggeration to say that during the thirty years of the great extension of Polish schooling the two groups, Jewish and Polish, remained almost entirely isolated from one another.

Corresponding to the weakness of the Polish efforts was the Jewish inertia. Everywhere they were content merely to have prayer schools (*chederim*) nearby. Jan Chodźko found the Kiejdany Talmudic school ordinance of 1820 striking. In every district there functioned alongside each Christian parish, one or several small Jewish schools of this type: the *parochs* (Uniate priests) everywhere reported innumerable cases. In the

Wileja district (Mińsk province) alone, Jewish children were learning to read their sacred books in the localities of Krasne Selo, Gródek, Raków, Mołodeczno, Lebediejew, Zaskiewicze, Wileja, Kurzeniec, Illa, Rzeczki, Dolhinów, Krzewicza, Stary Miadzioł, Duniłowicze, Dobszyce, Głebokie, Krajsek. . . .[20]

To allow a Jewish child to attend a Christian school did not always occur naturally to the Kowno Franciscans: they considered this required the university's advice;[21] and, conversely, only a few converts sought such contact. It is not surprising therefore that Jews were rarely to be found in Polish secondary education. In the 13 secondary schools in Wilno province (*gubernija*) in 1824, of 3,319 pupils there were only two who were Jewish. The university, as stated, had in Żukowski a professor of Hebrew who had published a Hebrew manual in 1809. Yet still he did not succeed in attracting Jews, despite his course on biblical archaeology; in 1822–3 of the 825 students enrolled in the *album studiorum* there were only four Jews, all of whom intended to practise medicine.[22]

The difficulty of Polish–Jewish relations was increased by the regulations of 9 July 1804, entrusting censorship to the universities of the Empire. That of Wilno, therefore, in theory had control of the bulk of Hebrew literature and of what was printed by the numerous Jewish presses scattered throughout the formerly Polish territories (even the authorities themselves could not estimate figures for this printed output). On 4 December 1824 Grand Duke Constantine requested the Rector Pelikan to let him have all the available information on this subject: he received an embarrassed reply. Three printing presses in Volhynia were listed, but the university had no information concerning their activities since 1815, when the printers had been requested by the civil governor to send their books regularly for examination. In fact, there were four presses in that province: in Ostróg, Sławuta, Sidełków and Korzec; to which must be added that of Mohylów-on-the-Dniestr in Podolia, those in Mińsk and Grodno, the two in Mohylów province (Kopyść and Szkłow) and finally those in Wilno, owned by Menahem Mannes Romm and Neuman, not to mention Zymel Nachymowicz, a type-caster who was wanting to open his own press in 1826.[23]

Virtually the whole output of these printing works was religious, and Professor Bécu of Wilno, who was responsible for granting an *imprimatur*, entrusted those issued on his behalf from 1808 to the *Kahal*'s delegate, Rosensohn. Later the censor-professors Golański, Bobrowski, and Żukowski enlisted the services of the rare Jewish students; but as soon as a novel initiative appeared – such as the request made in May 1817 by the printer Neuman to publish a newspaper in Yiddish – the project was snuffed out at the highest level. The university refused to undertake the control of the enterprise, as did the curator Czartoryski, on the pretext that the university lacked specialists in the 'Jewish jargon', a very different thing from ancient Hebrew. In 1821, S. Grabowski, the Congress Minister for the Realm, was concerned by the flood of Jewish books printed in the Empire and requested Czartoryski to exercise stricter control over these writings, which were 'divisive of peoples'. The Wilno rector, Malewski, could only invoke the freedom of religious worship and declare himself power-less . . . .[24] The celebrated historian Lelewel, who was, incidentally, of Jewish origin (Loelhöffel), was later for a time official censor of Jewish publications until he was driven away to Warsaw.

After 1826, under Novosiltsov, the university control over Jewish book production took on the dimensions of a repression. Whereas before 1826, according to the Soviet historian G. Ja. Shulkina, 80,000 sacred books came off the Jewish presses annually in the Polish provinces of the Empire (of which 60,000 were exported, particularly to Turkey; until the Turkish market collapsed, and Germany replaced it). In 1828 the censor-professor, Powstański, drew up a plan for prohibiting the reprinting and even the using of sacred commentaries in book form if they had been published before 1826. Under police control a taxed stamp would be affixed on each authorized copy and an additional censor would be employed. These measures were put into effect only in 1836; but the Ostróg printer had already had to shut up shop for circumventing the censorship. In the university's last years, the Hebrew books submitted to censorship became more and more numerous: 18 in 1829, 46 in 1830, 92 in 1831, 107 in 1832.[25] It was not that the volume printed increased, but that control was becoming more and more effective.

A few Jewish book publishers played an extremely important role in the spreading of Polish culture, but not without arousing jealousy and precipitating quarrels. Since its creation the university had had a single official publisher: Zawadzki. About 1821 most of the students were agreed on exposing the exorbitant prices he charged; as a result one of the professors, Groddeck, tried to break this monopoly by favouring another bookseller, the Jew Moritz, a convert to Protestantism. This brought a war in which the xenophobia of the former rector, Śniadecki, was mingled with anti-semitism; but Moritz eventually managed to have himself admitted thanks to support in St Petersburg.[26] Other Jewish bookseller–publishers, already well established in Warsaw, Nathan Glücksberg and his son Teofil, set up in Wilno in 1825, taking advantage of the anti-Polish repression which struck at Zawadzki among others. The Glücksbergs also had a Polish printing-works near the Krzemieniec lycée, which did not suffer because of the closing of Polish schools. After 1832 they prospered in Kiev, in proximity to the Russian university (opened in 1834) where half the student body were Poles.

All these facts show us how difficult Polish–Jewish contacts were to establish. This is less surprising when one becomes acquainted with the mentality and attitudes pervasive in Polish literature and newspapers. Without recourse to Bartoszewicz's or Bałaban's studies, a few Polish publications from the territories annexed by the Empire must nevertheless be mentioned. *Wiadomości Brukowe* (Street News), the satirical newspaper of Wilno during the years 1816–18, continued the 'enlightened' search for an understanding with the Jews or a betterment of their fate. In its issues nos 254, 267, 268, 271 and 272, a series of articles, *O przymnożeniu swobód i wolności żydkom* (on increasing the freedom and liberty of the Jews) was published, in which the notion of 'civilization' and good-neighbourliness is repeated. Christians who do not shy at deceiving Jews, at not paying them, and so on are denounced by mockery. An important Polish work that appeared in 1816, *The General, National and International Economy*, by Waleryan Strojnowski[27] also denounces the old ideas of coercion and deportation to the steppes, and advocates religious toleration. Like the *haskalah* thinkers, the author hopes that the Jewish people will become more radically integrated into society, by means other than keeping a tavern, which, in any case, tarnishes their reputation; he also declares himself in favour of the granting of their full individual liberty and their right to property. On the whole, however, in these regions the tone of literature about the Jews is much more perjorative.

A study by P. Chmielowski at the end of the nineteenth century successfully analysed the deep-seated anti-semitism of numerous Polish *szlachcice* in the Lithuanian-Ruthenian territories.[28] Thus, a long (40-page) article in Ignacy Lachnicki's *Dzieje dobroczynności* (Charity Annals) entitled *Biografia Włościanina nad brzegami Niemna* (Biography of a Niemen Peasant) shows that the Jews constituted a state within a state that no one dared attack, that they blocked all possibility of agrarian reform, and that the serf was exploited by this tribe foreign to his own people. Very curiously, the proprietors of serfs seem always to have wanted to salve their own consciences by holding the Jews responsible for all the misfortunes of their peasants.[29] But the most disturbing ideas are to be found in a work, ostensibly an economic and statistical study, the author of which was a priest, Father Wawrzyniec Marczyński.[30] He wrote that the Jews' internal solidarity, their laws, their 'clergy', aimed only at their avoiding work and living at the expense of the Christians by means of deceit and trickery; at appropriating all the wealth; at cajoling those with power; at corrupting good people by intoxicating them with alcohol. In order to palliate this huge peril, Fr Marczyński collected the written suggestions of Tadeusz Sarnecki, the marshal of the nobility in the Kamieniec district in Podolia, which can be taken to express the thinking of the *szlachta* that had elected him. Sarnecki put forward proposals which he screened with rational arguments, dwelling on the Jewish race's prolific character and the necessity to control this growth and so for this purpose a properly run civil status system had to be set up. But this apparent rationality concealed a purpose which leaves one perplexed: marriage would have to be forbidden to those with under 500 roubles unless they accepted deportation! Furthermore, the very detailed plan made provision for assimilation through instruction, starting with all those in positions of responsibility – rabbis, councillors, merchants – who would have to submit a certificate of studies; for the censoring of books, with the eliminating of whatever was 'contrary to the Government's intentions and to the general good of Christendom' (this, as has been seen, was put into effect a few years later); and for a prohibition on residing within five miles of the frontier – this being in order to prevent smuggling, which was their speciality (such a prohibition was in fact agreed upon by the Russian authorities in 1825; a 50 versts zone along the frontier of the Empire being forbidden).

It is clear that such plans were not conducive to a harmonizing of relations, and the width of the schism separating the two communities can be gauged by analysing the reader, edited for the parish schools (the elementaries intended for peasant-serfs) by Jan Chodźko. Chodźko was a wealthy patron, active, moreover, in propagating Polish schooling and published with Wilno University's official approbation by Zawadzki in 1821: *Pan Jan ze Świsłoczy, kramarz wędrujący* ('John of Swisłocz the Pedlar'). Greeted enthusiastically by the critics, notably K. Kontrym, the book was widely distributed and fed the minds of peasant children for years, being republished in 1824 and 1825, and translated into Lithuanian in 1823; it was still to be in use in 1860. That is to say, generations of children derived from it a few basic principles. The young reader found, in chapter V, a sickening scene in an inn: the dead-drunk bodies lying around on the floor are those of the victims of Jews, the poisoners of the people. There follows a long discourse which teaches the necessity for inkeepers to be Christians, who would never dare to do such a thing as to suck the blood of people nor to bring about the peasant's ruin. The discourse ends with a speech, the effect of which on young minds can be imagined:

'Oh when then,' he exclaimed, 'will the wise prescriptions of our Gracious Monarch, requiring the deportation of the Jews to the southern provinces of the Empire, be fulfilled? Our regions rid of this plague would flourish anew; industry, which in their treacherous hands is degenerating, would if put into the hands of our own townspeople and peasants draw them out of their ignorance and wretchedness . . .'

In this schoolbook, which was deemed also to be inculcating morals, the Jew is presented as the carrier of every evil: a passing tumbler is teaching people to be idle: he must be a Jew! The exhibitors of the performing bears and fortune-tellers in the story are more likely to be gypsies, but they are 'the same bloodsuckers as the Jews'.

The closing of Wilno University and of all Polish schools in 1832 as a result of the rising of 1830–31 marked the end of the Poles' cultural predominance in the western part of the Empire. The intellectual centre of gravity moved towards the University of Kiev, where the number of Jews seems to have been no higher than in Wilno.[31] The Polish landowners remained until 1863, and often after that date provided they were politically submissive (as most of them were) holding a very privileged socio-economic status. Since the intellectual elite lived in France as émigrés and the impoverished nobility left no testimony concerning their relations with the Jews, it is only in the rare writings of the nobility in possession of these regions that the expression of an attitude of mind is found.

In the course of the nineteenth century this attitude appears to have become ossified, hardened. No longer are there to be found even the generous *intentions* discernible here and there at the beginning of the century. This was doubtless due, after 1844, to the Jews' progressive integration into the life of the Empire,[32] whereas the Poles often continued to refuse too conspicuous a collaboration. The Jewish world, despite the Tsarist assimilation methods – military conscription, destruction of internal autonomy – chose increasingly to come to terms with the growing strength of Russia, leaving the Poles to brood on their nostalgia for a power which had declined to nothing. About 1840, one of the intellectual leaders of the Polish *kresy* (border) aristocracy, Henryk Rzewuski, never rises above the most primitive contempt when speaking of the Jews. His *Mieszaniny obyczajowe* (Picture of a Mixture of Customs), published in Wilno in 1841 and 1843, abounds with allusions better left to the oblivion into which his books fell. Here, the references to (to him) displeasing physical features go hand in hand with frustration at seeing Polish properties, whose owners have been ruined in various squanderings, pass into the hands of Jewish usurers. A cluster of memoir writers from the same milieu give vent to the same kind of sentiments which betray between the two communities an irreparable breach. For Count A. Przezdziecki, if Eastern Europe has no town in the Western mould, it is the fault of the Jews, who revel in stagnation and filth, given over as they are to the worst defects and the obstruction of progress. The image of the bloodsuckers consuming the lifeblood of poor people is often repeated,[33] but never do these apologists for serfdom consider the ethics of nor the opportunity to alleviate serfdom, the abolition of which by the Russians in 1861 takes them by surprise. The single contact between the world of landowners and the masses they despised was the yearly fair. It was then that the Polish nobility settled for a few days into the Jews' rooms, freshly whitewashed, while the masters of the house, described as 'a disgusting people' (*sprośny naród*) by the writer, took themselves off to the stables and cowsheds.[34]

Rage at seeing long-standing Polish fortunes crumble away gradually, constitutes for Tytus Szczeniowski an opportunity for the Berdychev Jews to be on the look-out for bankruptcies.

Here many commercial registers bespeak the slavery almost every nobleman has fallen into: registers thick and numerous, Niesiecki's armorials of a new kind, as Count Beyla calls them, which can witness to each family's loss of possessions just as the original attested their nobility.[35]

Even a writer as open-minded on social progress as J. I. Kraszewski, who possessed lands in Volhynia, allowed himself to be won over by this exclusively negative vision of the Jewish world and denounced the disastrous role it played in the countryside.[36]

Perhaps one could not illustrate the Polish landowners' conception of the Jews better than by quoting a Frenchman. H. de Balzac went to visit his dear Evelyne Hańska in 1847 on her Ukrainian estate of Wierzchownia, and what he wrote about Volhynia is most certainly the faithful reflection of what he heard around him. Was not Evelyne Hańska the sister of Henryk Rzewuski whom we cited above?

Everything, starting from Brody, is in Jewish hands. I have not read in any work accurate information on this conquest of Poland by the Hebrews. The Jew reigns and does not govern! That's for sure. The Jews in Germany, in France, are people like you and me ... but in no country in the world is Jewish nationality more brazenly established, like moss in a field, than in Poland; and I understand the loathing people ascribe to the Emperor Nicholas for this usurping power. The Jews gave up nothing in their customs, they made no concession to the way of life of the country where their race was about to spread. They are forbidden to possess and, in Russia, to lease land. They can only trade and be moneylenders. And they do lend at interest and they do trade ....

After an ironic piece about each person's wealth, carried by the women in the form of pearls, 'huge cabbage-heart jewels placed on each frontal lobe', Balzac continues,

Never do Jews marry into Christian families, but they do change religions in order to become ennobled and possess land ... it is always the desire to solidify great wealth that turns a Jew into a Christian; baptism is their 'villein's soap' [*savonnette à vilain*, that is, a title bought by a commoner]. The Jews behave towards one another like convicts in a penal colony, like actors, like every species of outlaw: that is to say they have a faith of their own. Nothing equals their boldness in speculation ... [Balzac here cites the bankers Natanson, Hausener, Halpérine.] The Jews are exceedingly thievish; they are cousins-german of the Chinese in this genus. The number of horses stolen, especially on the frontiers, cannot be imagined. A Jew does not draw back from murder once a large sum is at stake.

Here finally is the memory the writer kept for Berdychev:

A thick cloud of Jews beseiged me, for I counted up to twenty-five of them, all as black as seminarists, with beards that quivered in the sunshine, eyes that shone like carbuncles, and greedy hands that I knocked back with my stick, for they were wanting to handle my watch-chain so as to check its weight and the genuineness of the gold. This riot of cupidity made me shudder.[37]

This hostile irony which the Rzewuski family applied to the Jews was certainly not isolated.

In conclusion we shall say that the historical conditions for a Judeo–Polish *rapprochement* in these three regions were almost never successfully exploited in the nineteenth century. Equally foreign to the native substrata – let us not forget that in 1768, at Humań, the Ukrainian peasants massacred Poles and Jews indiscriminately – these two communities might have been able to meet but never did so. The Polish language was, in places, common to them, but Polish culture, despite the lustre it retained before 1831, had no longer the attraction that Russian culture increasingly acquired. For this reason the squirearchy's gloomy resentment, which fed on anti-semitic cliches succeeded the generous plans of some enlightened Polish leaders proposed at the beginning of the century. Throughout, the Jewish world ignored these 'marginalized' Poles more and more. The end of the century had to arrive for one to see Eliza Orzeszkowa's outstretched hand and a new fraternity uncovered in Wilno between proletarians of the *Proletariat* and the Bund.

8

Jews in the Lublin region prior to the January uprising, 1861–1862

Ryszard Bender

The manifestations of patriotic and religious fervour in 1861 and the pre-uprising conspiracy of 1862 were preceded in Poland by the increasing involvement of youth circles in politics. Young people were engaged in studying the political and military thought of the time, to which they had access in books and publications obtained abroad. They were also developing plans for large-scale political insurrections and for the struggle for independence. These circles consisted mainly of students and secondary school pupils; although young craftsmen, apprentices and shop assistants constituted a considerable part of such groups.

These artisans and shop assistants took part in patriotic activities in Lublin and other towns in the region. Working together with high school students they organized numerous street demonstrations as well as co-ordinating political protests, some of which took place prior to the February unrest in Warsaw.

Archives make no mention of the participation of Jewish youth in the early unrest in Lublin, despite the fact that, in 1860, the population of Lublin was 18,304, of whom 7,891 were Poles and 10,413 Jews (mainly merchants, stall-keepers and craftsmen). Workbenches and trading centres employed mostly young Jews and so it is impossible to claim that Jewish crafts students and shop assistants lived in complete isolation from their Polish counterparts. It is likely that they had some contact with Polish apprentices and shop assistants, although it is difficult to say how far this went. In all probability there would have been little close co-operation since this would have been detected by the authorities and consequently recorded in police documents. Official sources do not, however, make any reference to the patriotic activity of Jews in the cities of the Lublin district any earlier than the unrest of February 1861 in Warsaw.

A large demonstration occurred in Warsaw on 27 February 1861 in the Castle Square. Its aim was to force the Russian authorities to release from detention those arrested two days earlier during political riots in Warsaw. In an attempt to disperse the crowd gathered in the Castle Square and in Krakowskie Przedmieście, the Russians brought in the army. As a result five people were killed.[1]

The news of the bloody events in Warsaw immediately spread across the country and even reached abroad. The whole nation began to protest against the bloody suppression of this manifestation of nationalist feeling on the part of the people of Warsaw. The protest, in which everyone joined, took the form of national mourning, with people from all the social classes wearing mourning dress.[2]

Jews, or as they were then called, 'Poles of the Jewish faith', joined the protest, which became so wide-spread that the French Count, Montalembert, called the Polish nation a nation in mourning.[3] The black clothes of the nation became the symbol of patriotic feelings, expressing the unity of the nation as it protested against the foreign rule,[4] a protest which was met with approval in the republican circles of Europe.

The people of Lublin declared mourning as early as 2 March 1861, and on that day the first service for the dead was held in Warsaw, in the Capuchin Church. Sources tell us nothing of how the Jewish population behaved that day, however, the second service for the dead in Warsaw (held on 6 March 1861 and conducted by the Lublin Bishop Wincenty à Paulo Pieńkowski) was attended by a sizeable Jewish congregation headed by the local rabbi, who sat in an armchair in the porch of the church and stayed till the end of the service.[6] The Jews organized their own services of mourning, one of which was held in Krasnystaw in the local synagogue and in the Jewish school.[7] Soon Jewish synagogues began to host massive religious and patriotic gatherings as did the churches, where the fraternity of both confessions was proclaimed.[8]

In some cases Jews were pre-eminent in mourning. Official sources mention Izaak Etyngier who, in March of 1861, travelled through the towns of the Lublin district and urged people to put on mourning clothes, and in Janów Lubelski Etyngier instructed local clerks how mourning should be worn.[9] At the numerous public meetings in Tyszowce, which took place continually between 28 March and 8 April, Jews always wore mourning garments as did the majority of Poles. At these meetings, speeches were made 'in the republican spirit of Polish national feelings', and it was claimed that a revolution had been initiated with a view to dramatically changing the constitution.[10]

The events in Warsaw and in the towns of the Lublin region brought changes to the social composition of people meeting in the Lublin local club; while before only rich merchants and land owners had attended, now representatives of the poorer population of the town were also welcome, as well as Jews. When, following the example of Warsaw, the population of Lublin established its City Delegation at the beginning of March 1861, a few Jews appeared among its 32 members.[11] This delegation was extremely active both in Lublin itself and in other parts of the country, and the local club building became the site of many public meetings. The meetings which were attended by Poles and Jews alike, were very lively. One day, for example, a Catholic bishop and a Jewish rabbi were solemnly received at a meeting in the local club.[12]

As in Warsaw, the Lublin City Delegation was constituted to maintain law and order in the town, and consisted mainly of rich merchants, and the Jewish members were also from the monied classes. The Delegation was loyal to the Russian authorities and did not support street demonstrations; instead it tried to pacify all the agitators in the town. Its role, therefore, was admirably suited to the needs of the Russian authorities at a time when riots in the city were imminent. Following the example of Warsaw, the Delegation instituted a police force,[13] called, as in the capital, constables or the security guard.[14] With time, the number of constables grew considerably, the Jews making a sizeable proportion of them (one of the units consisted exclusively of Jewish youths.[15]) After the disbanding of the Lublin City Delegation on 2 April 1861, a Committee for Public Security was set up in Lublin on the following day. It was, quite simply, the former City Delegation without its more radical members. This Committee remained active till 15 April 1861, and it too included representatives of the Jewish population.[16]

While some representatives of the Jewish population were active, both in the Delegation and the Committee, others, being more radical, organized anti-state demonstrations in the towns and cities of the Lublin district. The riots in Żółkiewka are particularly interesting in this respect, shedding a lot of light on the attitude of the Jewish community during the period of demonstrations and they point to the degree of involvement by Jews in the events taking place in the country. The riots were minutely described by the mayor of Żółkiewka; on 12 April 1861, in a report to his superiors he spoke of a serious intellectual turmoil in the Jewish population. He also said that they had been conducting secret talks for quite some time, but had recently become openly active, one day arriving at the municipal office to demand the dismissal of wardens (that is, elders in an assembly who were members of the governing body of the Jewish community).[17] They explained their demands by saying that since the Lublin governor Stanisław Mackiewicz had been removed from office, they also could remove their wardens.[18]

At the same time close co-operation was being established in Żółkiewka between the Polish and Jewish community, for example, in the support given by the Jews to the land owner Preszel's plan to oust the mayor of Żółkiewka. This mutual co-operation can also be discerned in the delays in paying taxes, both by the Polish and Jewish community.[19]

Jews demonstrated their support for the Polish patriotic movement by, among other things, joining in the celebrations of the Polish national anniversaries. On 12 August 1861 – the anniversary of the Union of Lublin – all the shops, both Polish and Jewish, in Lublin and in other towns were closed. Windows in the majority of houses and shops (Polish and Jewish) were ingeniously decorated and in the evening brightly illuminated.[20]

On 10 October 1861 – anniversary of the Union of Horodło – among a crowd of several thousand Poles there were Jews who also took part in the celebrations in the fields of Horodło.[21] Marching with such true patriots as Apollon Korzeniowski (father of Joseph Conrad) they arrived there to support the activity of Polish revolutionary circles, the so-called Reds, who were being challenged by the conservative camp of the so-called Whites, a coalition of land owners and rich merchants.

By these means, the Jews of Lublin, just as those in Warsaw, took an active part in the most important demonstrations of political unrest on the part of the Polish population; and this aspect of the Polish national move-ment brought about a *rapprochement* between Poles and Jews.[22] It would seem that the great Polish patriot and rabbi of Warsaw, Dov Ber Meisels, influenced them, at least to some degree.[23] This seems to follow from the fact that leaflets in the Hebrew alphabet, despatched in Warsaw, appeared in Lublin in 1861.[24] That year the Jews of Lublin supported the majority of political initiatives launched by the Polish community, and many of them were to be found in the patriotic and revolutionary Polish camp, fighting for independence.

These times of political unrest caused deep divisions, both in the Polish and Jewish populations. Some of the Jews of Lublin and of other towns in the region joined the conservative and conciliatory political trend, led by rich merchants and land owners. These people wanted to introduce political reforms while postponing the fight for independence until some time in the future. They also wanted to make use of the Tsarist ukase of 26 March 1861, which contained some, admittedly minor, concessions for Polish society, more of an administrative than political nature. The ukase provided for the setting up of councils in cities, districts and guberniyas.[25] But the majority of the population found them quite unsatisfactory.[26]

Among the candidates for city councils in the Lublin district, appeared representatives of Jewish industrial and trading spheres, as well as land-owners, Catholic clergy, Polish industrialists and merchants. The Jews, just like the Poles, participated actively in elections. Elections to the city councils in Lublin, held on 3 October 1861, produced twelve members, among them two Jews.[27] They were the seventy-year-old Lublin merchant Symcha Lichtenfeld and the house owner Natan Miller. Two representatives of the Jewish community were elected deputy members, Natan Szafir and Moilich Zaidenweis;[28] in the election bill they were described as house owners.[29] Representatives of the Jewish community were also members of city councils in Krasnystaw and Hrubieszów.[30]

At its meetings the Lublin city council considered, among other things, Jewish problems. On 30 April 1862, it analysed the question of an elementary school for Jews, showing considerable care about the school and an understanding of its needs. In a resolution the council determined not only the proper level of Polish in the school but also the need for higher levels in the instruction of Hebrew. The requirements that the city council placed before the Jewish school can be summarized as follows: First, the school should have a qualified teacher of the Polish language; second, the teacher of the Hebrew language must see to it that 'the presentation of the Hebrew language and its grammar be carried out with precision since the children learning their prayers in that language do not understand them at all'.[31]

City councils in Lublin, Krasnystaw and Hrubieszów, just as in the remaining parts of the Kingdom of Poland, were active for a relatively short period of time. Eventually councillors became disenchanted with the activities of city councils, constrained as they were by numerous governmental regulations which required that the administration be consulted even in the most trivial of matters. Dependent as they were on the central administration of the councils, of necessity, they occupied themselves with the maintenance of order in their towns. Because of this, councillors grew dispirited and those they were serving lost interest in their work.[32] Meetings were attended by fewer and fewer councillors both Jewish and Polish, reflecting their disappointment with the activities of the city councils. This declining attendance was undoubtedly influenced by, among other things, a decree of the insurrectionary Central National Commmittee of 5 October 1862, calling on the populace to dissolve immediately city and local councils.[33]

The absence of councillors in city council meetings very soon became a permanent state of affairs. However, the outbreak of the January Uprising caused those councils that still existed to be dissolved,[34] as was the case in Lublin. From the middle of January 1863 none of its members, Polish or Jewish, attended the meetings.[35] Jewish councillors adopted a praiseworthy attitude: despite four summonses, issued by the president of Lublin and repeated as late as April 1863, they never reported for meetings.[36] By doing this, Jewish councillors foiled the president's attempts to bring about a split among councillors and to set up, subsequently, a new city council consisting of Jews and some deputy councillors.

In the years 1861–2 massive arrests were made among the city population of the Lublin region, becoming particularly intensive after martial law had been introduced in the Kingdom on 14 October 1861.[37] In that period of repression, terror and police control of the population reached an unheard of level. The massive repressive activities of the Russian authorities affected the Jewish population in an equal measure. Jews from Lublin and from other towns in the region were constantly put under arrest, in the same way as the Poles. The list of people detained in Lublin between 4 and 11 November 1861 includes, among others, Herszek Wajman.[38] Both he and the other people were arrested on charges of vaguely defined 'political offences'. These offences included the singing of banned patriotic songs, the wearing of traditional Polish costumes, having a disrespectful attitude to authorities, and so on. The detention of Szmul Erlich of Biała Podlaska deserves particular mention in this respect. He was detained because his under-age granddaughter played at a service in a Catholic church.[39] This shows that, according to the authorities, a Jew committed a political crime by even attending a Catholic celebration.[40]

There were, of course, Jews in the Lublin region who, just like some Poles, took no part in the patriotic activity of 1861–2, and Russian repression did not extend to them. But cases of Jews openly serving the occupying powers in the years preceding the outbreak of the uprising were generally rare. With reference to towns in the Lublin region, sources mention just a few such cases, the most important being that of the Jewish informer from Puławy, Zajdsznejder, who informed the authorities in Warsaw about weapons brought from abroad by one of the Lublin merchants.[41]

The sources say nothing, however, about the participation of the Jewish residents of the cities of the Lublin region in conspiratorial work.[42] On the basis of research we know that Polish Jews took part in the preparation of the uprising in the Kingdom of Poland, and we can, therefore, presume that Jews in the towns of the Lublin district did not opt out. The degree of their involvement in conspiratorial work remains, regrettably, unknown. On the basis of the attitudes apparent before the uprising, we can assume that the participation of the Jewish population in the various forms of conspiratorial work was not inconsiderable. Names of Jewish conspirators in towns of the Lublin district are not to be found, but neither do we know the names of many Polish conspirators. But this is hardly surprising since conspiracy requires secrecy.

9

Rural anti-semitism in Galicia before World War I

Frank Golczewski

This is not the first time that I have dwelt on the problems of rural anti-semitism in Galicia before the First World War. In a previous work about Polish anti-semitism between 1881 and 1922, I tried to describe the pheno-menon of rural anti-semitism as compared to its urban forms.[1] I tried for the first time to give an idea of the motives of the political propagandists who fostered anti-semitic campaigns. At that time I had access to the mass of pamphlets issued in the Nowy Sącz county by the Union of the Polish Peasant Party (Związek Stronnictwa Chłopskiego), which was founded in 1892 by the clergyman Stanisław Stojałowski and the brothers Jan and Stanisław Potoczek.[2]. As far as I am able to evaluate my findings, their foremost importance lies in the fact that in them I could trace the develop-ment of anti-semitic activity from the form of mass propagation of the idea to the turmoils of 1898 and their aftermath, as documented in the trials of the wrongdoers.

Nevertheless the discussion of this problem is far from exhausted. Even though there seemed not to be too much difference between the Potoczek paper *Związek Chłopski* and the papers of the Stojałowski group we could only suppose a certain degree of representation for the full range of political motives of the populist groups. However, access to Stojałowski's own papers (*Wieniec Polski* and *Pszczółka*) was secured, and it became obvious that, in addition to the motives in the Potoczek paper, there were some new aspects of anti-semitism evident. While in Nowy Sącz political motives were not entirely clear and most anti-Jewish arguments were based on the peasant–inn-keeper relation (and a lot of more or less mysterious legends), a more political or even party political aspect should not be underestimated with Stojałowski. The importance of this lies in the fact that we can easily construct a correlation between this national populism and anti-semitism in Galicia on the one hand and other contemporary forms of pre-Fascist movements in the rest of Europe. It must be borne in mind that both French, Italian and German forms of populism had a leftist (social revolutionary) aspect,[3] were portents of anti-semitism, and led directly to the Fascist or national-socialist parties that had a much greater importance in the course of history than their largely unknown precursors.

Galician poverty is a commonly accepted fact. In the late nineteenth century not only was Galicia the least industrialized part of partitioned Poland, but the agriculture of this kingdom was very under-developed. So, with an agricultural population of 74 per cent (as compared to 60 per cent in the Kingdom of Poland), in all of Europe only Ireland had an equal proportion of dispersed peasants who had only very few contacts with urban centres. It was through urban centres however that modernization both in economic and social terms was initiated.

The only escape from a very low standard of living in a country where sixty people had to support themselves on one square kilometre and where the *per capita* income was one half of that in the Kingdom of Poland (which did not flow with milk and honey either) was emigration, which brought about a drain of the more mobile and enterprising parts of the population. The effects of this on the rural areas (as distinct from the very few 'real' towns) were deleterious as there were neither models of modernization nor the necessary capital to finance reform. The few forms of credit offered were mostly consumers' credits that were unable to increase productivity – on the contrary, the wide acceptance of this form of credit hindered any real effort to change the situation.

In 1888 an industrialist who was a member of the Galician State Council, Stanisław Szczepanowski, described Galician poverty in real terms and tried to form a programme of economic development intended to reform Galicia. Szczepanowski should not be branded as a judeophile, but in his book, which found much acclaim in his time and has until now been regarded as a statistical authority, he showed that the economic situation of Christians and Jews in Galicia varied to only a small degree.[4] Although there was an obvious differentiation in economic activities, there was no visible preponderance of so-called Jewish wealth. Szczepanowski came to the conclusion that both Christians and Jews lived on the brink of economic disaster: 'the average Galician works for half a man and eats for one fourth', he wrote, blaming poverty on the low productivity and poor quality of economic entrepreneurship in the country.[5]

There were two ways to change this situation. One was represented by the rural co-operative movement, which tried to build up capital by exploiting the divergent interests of the Polish peasants and the Jewish intermediaries, using anti-semitic phrases to support their argument. Szczepanowski, on the other hand, argued that even though the ruinous situation of Christians and Jews was basically the same, only with the latter was there a certain prospect of success in accumulating the necessary capital for bringing about a more industrialized and more modern economy.[6] His argument was basically a psychological one: the Pole, no matter if he was a landowner, a civil servant or a lowly peasant, had a certain degree of secure income, and even though it consisted of natural resources he was not forced to save up money as much as his Jewish intermediary, who was totally dependent on the money economy and therefore nearer to the possibility of death by starvation because of changes in his economic situation. This situation encouraged the Jewish people to save money. As a consequence Szczepanowski saw a possibility for economic development only when the country succeeded in combining the efforts of Poles and Jews in order to accumulate the capital necessary to modernize economic life and raise productivity.

I quote these theories only to support the argument that the anti-semitic and populist activity of groups like Stojałowski's was not the only, and certainly not the best, way to escape from the economic dilemma of Galicia. It consumed a lot of economic and political energy developing a religiously motivated class struggle instead of working together towards a common goal.

But there was another dilemma: the different groups that wished to achieve the economic improvement of Galicia were in principle able to co-operate. This conclusion can be drawn from the fact that both the Stojałowski group and the Polish Social Democrats, under Ignacy Daszyński, were in close contact. As late as 5 January 1897 Stojałowski wrote to Daszyński: 'From the Social Democratic Party I am only divided by the gospel – it is the common ownership of land and means of production that I demand. I do not know if I will become a party-member, but I am a Social Democrat.' It was Daszyński who administered Stojałowski's Teschen papers during his detention.[7] All other populist politicians were, at one time or another (together with Stojałowski) members of the same political movement and they left it because of issues that had little or nothing to do with ideological differences.

The fighting between populist groups and the Social Democrats sprang from reasons other than ideological motives. Although it is easy to maintain that party political strife is seldom dominated by issues of ideological differences alone, it is clear that the rivalries between these different groups were essentially power struggles. When examining instances of one group fighting another using Jewish-related problems as ammunition (each claiming that the other has been 'bought by the Jews') it is permissible to conclude that the problems were being used in order to compromise other politicians with whom there were no clear ideological differences.

To illustrate this we could compare this situation to Daszyński's continuing fight against Jewish rival groups that were endangering his own dominant party position. It was at the PPSD-congress of 1913 that he used his famous phrase: 'In the *Polish* lands only the *Polish* proletarian may reign.'[8]

What can be seen is a basic instrumentalization of the Polish–Jewish problem for party political aims. This is a frequent motive as far as the bourgeois groups are concerned, but there is a certain degree of acceptance among scholars that the rural anti-semitism in Galicia was based more in reality, influenced by the existing economic and political system, and therefore not as much to blame as is the case with similar utterances to be heard from the bourgeois milieu. In referring to the justifications expressed in the Stojałowski papers I will try to show that this was not so.

In my opinion anti-semites in modern history are not homogeneous. In order to understand this historical development one has to divide anti-semitic persons into three groups:[9] Firstly, the violent *activist*, a man unable to think independently, who falls prey to slogans and who is driven by a kind of uncontrollable desire to act against people whom he considers to be 'foes'. Anything ranging from a priest's sermon to a well-placed pamphlet will be sufficient to set him into motion. He will accept arguments without question, as long as they confirm the psychological frame of reference into which he has been socialized. The point is that this person is the only active one: he is the one who transforms anti-Jewish slogans into actions. Even though these people are the most visible, to me they are not the real anti-semites. They are those who are able to live peacefully together with the Jews, and even to build up friendly relations, as long as they are not incited to hatred by outside influences.

Those who incite the potential activist, I call *propagators*. They have a certain superiority over the aforementioned activists. They are those who are able to serve as propagandists among the peasants (as far as rural Galicia is concerned). Clergymen, teachers, journalists and others to whom any kind of authority is attached by the lower classes belong to this group. They are more eloquent than the peasants, but still of their world and thus able to influence their activity. I stress this similarity of social background in order to underline the difference between the populist agitators of Galicia and the so-called Narodniki of Tsarist Russia, who were not understood by the countryfolk and were often turned over to the state police. The Galician agitators were close to the peasants, usually former peasants or clergymen who appeared to be 'friends of the people'. The peasants could look up to them, and it was these 'friends' who supplied the motives and gave the sign to act.

The third group is the smallest, but the most important. They are the *politicians*, who need not even be convinced of the sense of anti-semitic theories, but who are fully aware that, with the support of anti-semites they can fulfil their political aims. They co-operate with the Jews if it serves their ambitions (we know of such moves by Roman Dmowski) but they are very quick to profess the most radical opinions as soon as they realize that this is the way to bring about political victory.

As I have shown, Stojałowski was ready to co-operate with Daszyński when they were both hunted by their enemies. On the other hand they could express the utmost hatred for each other as soon as this seemed to be politically opportune.

Here we come to the point of my paper: in reviewing the motives that were professed by the peasants and tracing them back to the populist papers and then to their political authors, we gain an insight into the mechanics of political anti-semitism. It was not the peasants who were interested in this problem, but their political leaders, who could incite them to act violently. This is of very great importance since it provides an opportunity to judge other ways of inciting uneducated masses to act for political ends.

The most effective means of inciting the people of Galicia was the propagation of the idea that the Jews owned fabulous riches. It was not only in these times that the name of Rothschild conjured up a picture of an incredible and mysterious financial empire which is not so easily associated with such names as Getty or Ford. While in Potoczek's paper we find the delightful calculation that a division of only a part of Rothschild's money among the Jews of Galicia would have made each of them an incredibly rich person,[10] in Stojałowski's *Wieniec Polski* we have a similar picture of a Rothschild family that could buy the whole of Cisleithania for their money. This is followed by the prophecy that the Jews would one day buy up Galicia and tell the Poles: 'Take your priests and churches and get off, this is not your country'.[11] The implication is quite clear: the Polish peasants are encouraged to revolt and take the country from those 'rich Jews' – chasing *them* out of Galicia. This argument could easily be explained as a psychological device to induce the rather passive peasantry to action, but in this paper this would lead too far.

Wealth is closely identified with power – a concept which brings us to the point where the links between populism and socialist attitudes must be considered. The manner by which the Jews come into the possession of their wealth is, more often than not, supposed to be criminal. The socialist concept of exploitation is applied to the relation between the Jew and the Polish peasant, the latter serving as an illustration of the former, which supports the case for the acceptance of the populist arguments by modern Marxist interpreters. We know many cases of statements in which Jewish exploitation, the role of the Jew as a capitalist, as an innkeeper and as the destroyer of lower-class morals and finances is described.[12] But we should not take these arguments at face value. Bear in mind the following (about a Catholic capitalist): 'Even if this may be unjust, it is always better a Catholic becomes rich than a Jew'[13] Or 'If you enter a Christian inn on a holiday you do not commit a sin as you do with a Jewish one.'[14]

Here it is possible to detect the 'anti-capitalist' trend of populism. It was not the capitalist or the intermediary or the innkeeper the populists were against, but the Jew who filled those roles – without, of course, thinking of the historical conditions of his entering them. By welcoming a Catholic trader or innkeeper they do nothing except stimulate Christian–Jewish economic competition without any effect on the quality of the economy itself. This can be compared with the National Democrats' statements as they started their boycott movement in 1912. Economic in-fighting is nothing unusual, but on the other hand it is not something that deserves the ennoblement handed out for merit in the economic amelioration of a country.

It was solely because the peasants accepted the notion that a Jewish innkeeper or trader cannot but cheat – as he is ordered by his Talmud to do[15] – that the populist agitators were able to distinguish between Jews and Christian traders: the more you examine their arguments, the less clear their objective economic aims become; only the anti-Jewish aspect remains stable.

But there is a political correlative to this analysis. In the elections of June 1898 there was strong competition between the Stapiński populists and Stojałowski's supporters. It was again on the 'Jewish theme' that Stojałowski fought out his rivalries with fellow populists; this is the new trend found in Stojałowski's papers but not in Potoczek's. There, in fact, were no ideological differences between Stojałowski and Stapiński, but nevertheless Stojałowski had to fight him in order to have his candidate elected. He fell back upon his favourite tactic, stating that Stapiński had been bought by the Jews. In his election paper he wrote about the fight between his own Christian-populist candidate Lewicki and the 'candidate of the Jews', Stapiński.[16] Under the title 'Stapiński and his friends' he described the advocates claiming to be Stapiński's helpers.[17] He stresses the fact that the names of Stapiński's helpers, Nebenzahl, Lewenthal and Tygermann are traditionally Jewish. He continues by suggesting that it was the Jewish communities who called for a Jewish vote for Stapiński (there is good reason to assume that this was correct) and on the basis of this he declares that 'anybody who will now still vote for Stapiński gives cause to consider him as a traitor to the populist cause'.[18] After the elections – in which Stojałowski's candidate was defeated – Stapiński is again described as a 'deputy of the Jews' will',[19] as was Bojko, another more leftist populist politician and deputy whom he called a 'servant of the Jews from the (liberal) paper *Kurjer Lwowski*' (parobek żydów kurjerowych).[20] There are other quotations confirming that anti-Jewish slogans and insinuations were often used as weapons in populist party politics of those days.

What emerges is the first use ever detected of the instrument of anti-semitism in rivalries between groups of exactly the same descent. The lack of ideological differences made it necessary to instrumentalize the 'Jewish question' even when the political adversary was not a Jew at all.

That the situation in 1922 was quite similar should be obvious. As in 1898, the Piłsudski-ite rival of the National Democrat Dmowski's candidate was discredited by opponents who called him 'their president' (Ich prezydent).[21] Similarly with Stapiński, he had nothing to do with the Jews other than that the Minorities' Block had voted for him after the Block's own candidate had to step down from the rostrum. Gabriel Narutowicz was murdered some days later by a painter who believed the politician was indeed the 'Jews' president'. In 1898 there were precedents – shortly after the election, riots took place which precipitated the declaration of a state of emergency in 33 Galician districts. As in 1922 the most vital protagonists of anti-semitism disclaimed any responsibility for the outbreak of the turmoil and tried to blame it on the Jews themselves. There were efforts by many to dissociate themselves from violent anti-semitism and criticism of those who had been incited to violence by the propaganda. Instead of 'force', 'politics' would be used against the Jews. But none of this changes the fact that rural anti-semitism in Galicia was mostly of the same kind as that which became visible in later election campaigns in urban areas. Again it is clear that it had become a well-established political weapon, and that the events of 1898 are to be considered as forerunners of those of 1922.

Stojałowski's journals provide an enormous wealth of material, and in conclusion it seems appropriate to ask what a historian can extrapolate from this source. Indeed is it important and rewarding to concentrate on this rural anti-semitism in Poland? The answer is definitely, yes.

What we are forced to realize is a strict class difference (even though the contrary is stated in the journals themselves) between the political perpetrators of populism in Galicia and the people to whom it is addressed. The division of people involved in acts of anti-semitism into the three groups mentioned above, was not first formulated in relation to the Galician situation, but it is confirmed by the facts established there. Populism was not a purely political movement, but an instrument used by certain politicians to elevate themselves into power – as is nearly every political ideology. With Stojałowski's group there is clear evidence of the exploitation of economic wrongs for private political aims which do not themselves promise an improvement of the economic situation. The elimination of the Jewish intermediaries does not help the economy at all, unless it is combined with an improvement of rural productivity. Szczepanowski said so in 1888, and there is still reason enough to agree.

Also the use of anti-semitic arguments to bring people into political power seemed to be helpful. Anti-Judaism was a long-established sentiment and the rural population that could vote for the first time in the 1890s was more easily won by traditionally established arguments than by appeals for temperance and harder work. It might have been a psychological trick to bring about less drinking and more labour by sponsoring anti-semitic slogans,but it should be clearly stated that while the anti-semitic slogans were accepted, the thinking behind them was not.

The strange application of economic arguments proves that the Stojałowski peasant movement in Galicia was not a 'leftist' one, although it had a social revolutionary quality, certainly. We know that it was directed against Jews as well as land-owners and the upper clergy, but in the context of anti-semitism it had a quality which could be considered right of centre. Gino Germani wrote:

> It is in populist movements that the coexistence of opposite right and left ideologies is most prominent. Populism often becomes a mass movement only in societies where typical Western European leftist ideologies of the working class fail to develop into mass parties. Populism is a multi-class movement. Populism probably defies any comprehensive definition.[23]

Even though Germani wrote about Latin American movements, there are many similarities between his findings and the rural situation in Galicia. However, I would not agree that Galician populism defies definition. Certainly it does not fit into our established patterns of political thinking, but this is only a reason to revise them. As our political culture is mainly one of right/left dichotomy, the investigation into Galician anti-semitism in the 1890s and in 1918–19, when it broke out again in an even more violent form, is cause to ask ourselves if this dichotomy really does describe historical realities, as well as present realities.

There are other ways in which the sources mentioned may be helpful. Historians often find themselves in difficulties when they are forced to work on discrepancies between propagandistic statements and their perception or transformation into historical reality. What we see in Galician rural anti-semitism is that a propagandist structure was transformed into activity. It was Stojałowski himself who accused the peasants, after the outbreak of riots, of acting unwisely. But he was ready to admit that they had done some-thing that was in line with the demands of the current political climate. Again it was a selective realization of these theoretical demands, with only the negative and the destructive being realized since they were in accord with human motivation. It takes more effort to support the positive, innova-tive, productive ways to improve a given position, and they are less easily realized. The lesson is that propaganda must be tailored to the lower instincts if it is to be found attractive. It was the victory of the politician that was the objective; any real improvements that might follow were only of secondary importance. This is a fact any good propagandist knows and will exploit, but one which the more idealistic historian is reluctant to accept. The positive ideals of the populist leaders attract much attention from present-day politicians and historians. When we realize that in those days the more negative traits were more central to historic reality, we should ask ourselves if we should not review this way of looking at the past.

10

Notes on the assimilation and acculturation of Jews in Poland, 1863–1943

Joseph Lichten

This paper has its limits in time and space. There already exists a rich litera-ture on the beginning of the emancipation of Jews in Poland and the active role they played during the uprisings of 1831 and 1863. Jewish assimilation in the last decades of the nineteenth century, however, has been treated by historians from an economic point of view rather than in its cultural and social aspects. Our own century, especially in independent Poland, is still awaiting an objective study. It is true that during that period assimilation developed under difficult conditions and the attention of historians, particularly Jewish historians, was directed more towards the dangerous growth of anti-semitism than to the positive trends of *rapprochement* between segments of the Polish people and the Jewish populace. Hence this paper attempts to present the events of those times in their historical sequence and to arrive at some preliminary conclusions.

My intention was at least to gather together the scattered sources and material regarding that period. However, it would be difficult to pay equal attention to the whole territory of pre-war Poland, and so the present study will be based chiefly on developments in Central Poland, known formerly as the Congress Kingdom, and on the southern part, Galicia (Western and Eastern). In other parts of the country, assimilation developed late as in the east, the so-called Kresy, or the Jewish population was, relatively, too small (as in the former Prussian sector) for an in-depth survey. In addition, sources related to these parts of the country are scanty.

This paper is based on various sources – newspapers of the period, brochures (invaluable material), single proclamations, personal interviews, information and data in several books on similar and even different topics, and my own previous studies.[1] I was handicapped by not being able to examine the appropriate material in the libraries and archives in Poland, although I was provided with some pertinent material.

The existing literature on the subject is a valuable and helpful source, and some of the more outstanding works should be mentioned. Ezra Mendelsohn devoted several important studies to the problems of Jewish assimilation and Polonization.[2] 'The Jews in Polish Culture' by Aleksander Hertz is a classic,[3] and Jacob Shatzky (Szacki), in his monumental *History of Jews in Warsaw* and in a few monographs, considers the assimilation of Jews in Poland.[4] Celia S. Heller,[5] in her sociological study of Jews in Poland during the two World Wars, unfortunately often arrives at conclusions not always based on facts; not as they really occurred but as she would like to see them. In contemporary Poland, three writers, as far as I know, have touched on the issue of assimilation: Artur Eisenbach is interested in the situation of Jews under the legislation of the period in Central Poland;[6] Arthur Sandauer discusses the position of Polish writers of Jewish origin between the two World Wars in the face of growing animosity, if not hatred, on the part of significant factions of the Polish population;[7] and Helena Dattner-Špiewak outlines the main characteristics of Jewish assimilation.[8] In general, Jewish, and to an even greater extent Polish historians pay little, if any, attention to the assimilationist movements. A typical example is Joseph Marcus,[9] who, in 557 pages on the subject of the social and political history of the Jews in independent Poland, devotes two pages to the issue of assimilation.

The very term assimilation, especially under the conditions prevailing in Poland, deserves comment. To formulate a general definition of the term is impossible; it could be used only in a generic way, as a short cut to a deeper and more detailed approach. In order to distinguish assimilation from other similar phenomena or to distinguish between its several forms, scholars often use terms such as acculturation (in Poland, Polonization), cultural acculturation or assimilation, integration, modernization, even accomodation or secularization.[10] But this jargon often confuses the problem even further. In addition, assimilation is not only a programme but a process that undergoes constant fluctuation and which depends on the situation within the group to be assimilated and within the host group. Assimilation is not the sudden manifestation of a *deus ex machina*.

Different authors have different definitions of assimilation, Shatzky, perhaps, being the most demanding. He introduces an additional term: total assimilation, which by his definition is 'the organic identification by an individual with the spiritual and cultural life around him and the kind that cannot be ascribed to careerist designs or utilitarian motives'.[11] Hertz is less rigid; he sees assimilation as 'a process of adopting by a group or its individual members the culture of another group'.[12] Similarly, for Eisenbach assimilation means 'an adoption of models and values of the dominant culture in the domain of customs, attire, way of life, education of children, nourishment, interests, etc. It was evident in the reform of liturgy, rites, religious practices and holidays. It resulted, therefore, in a departure from the traditional norms and models of life of the Jewish community.'[13] Finally, Marcus discusses assimilation only 'as a political movement', and therefore, according to him, the 'assimilants' in question may probably be best defined as people 'standing outside the established parties; who as mostly conscious, non-observant Jews, were politically opposed to a separate Jewish national existence, seeking more or less close association with Polish educated circles and full civil rights for Jews.'[14]

The approach of non-Polish sociologists to the process of assimilation creates difficulties when an attempt is made to apply it to the Polish situation. The definition of Arnold M. Rose is a good example: he insisted that assimilation be understood as 'the adaption by a person or group of the culture of another social group to such a complete extent that the person or group no longer has any particular loyalties to his former culture'.[15] Such an approach could be applied only to a very small number of assimilated Polish Jews; as we will see later, the majority of them retained conscious ties with their Jewish origin.

All these definitions, thoughtful as they are, are lacking one basic element. Assimilation does not mean only a formal, almost technical, submission to the other culture. The decisive element in the process is the attitude, the feeling, affection and desire of the assimilants to merge, not only with the basic elements of the other culture, but also with the aims, plans, even dreams of the other group or nation. There are expressions illustrating that attitude throughout the history of Jewish assimilation in Poland. Wilhelm Feldman, one of the spokesmen of the movement at the turn of the nineteenth century, exclaimed:

Not you, doubtful *quiriti* (citizens), to pass judgement about my rights to Polishness, and I will not ask anybody at all for such rights. I took them, as I take Polish air, Polish culture and above all, Polish duties.[16]

On the eve of Polish independence, Maurycy Karniol, well-known assimilationist leader of the following generation, spoke on behalf of Polish-Jewish youth, which in 'spirit and culture' belonged to the Polish nation:

We do not ask anyone for certification of our Polishness, because it is already proven by the beating of our hearts and the rhythm of our feelings; nor do we ask from anyone for proof of our Jewishness, since we are rooted in it by the strength of our blood, by the faith of our forefathers, and by the love of our brothers.[17]

Precisely without this emotional element, the vast majority of Zionists in Poland and Zionist sympathizers – who adopted the Polish language, attire and way of life – nevertheless belonged to the Jewish nationality and combatted assimilation.

At the end of the eighteenth century Jewish emancipation in Poland was already being swiftly transformed into patriotism and attachment to the native land. Naturally these were the first steps of a small minority; the rest of the Jewish population was closed in the old religious orthodox tradition and paid little attention to the changes in the world around them. Nevertheless, sincere patriotism and a desire to draw closer to the Polish community were making inroads on these traditions, though not without difficulty, particularly in obtaining the right to live in the cities or choosing a trade or employment. As early as the sixteenth century Moses Isserles proclaimed his attachment to 'this land of refuge'.[18] And three hundred years later Ber Meisels, the patriot of the national uprisings, referred to Isserles in the following words:

> Our greatest religious authority, Moses Isserles, on whose rulings the whole house of Israel is based, showed us in his decisions regarding the relations of Jews to nations of other religions, that we should love the Polish nation more than any other, because the Poles have been our brothers for centuries.[19]

Polish feeling among Jews increased in the face of dangers threatening the state and later during the uprisings. The Kościuszko insurrection and the regiment of Berek Joselewicz, and the events of 1831, 1846, 1848 and 1863 clearly left their mark on growing assimilationist trends; it was more than simply a matter of patriotic sentiments. In their new approaches the Jews did not, however, forget their centuries-old traditions, comparing Poland to the Biblical Zion. When King Frederic August visited Cracow on 3 May 1810 (a day not without significance), the Jews from the Casimir Synagogue handed him a welcoming letter entitled 'A Psalm of the Daughters of Sion', which claimed that 'Poland is for the Jews a fertile Palestine'.[20] While a sizeable part of Jewish Warsaw began to adopt the Polish language and some aspects of Polish culture, and the Jews of Cracow had already manifested their affection for Polish revolutionary efforts, the Jews in Lwów started to show interest in Polish aspirations much later. Their Enlightenment expressed itself at first in the intermediate period, devoted to German culture, and they established their own organization, Guardian of Israel (Shomer Yisrael) in the 1860s.

Almost twenty years later a new society, the Covenant of Brothers (Agudas Achim), came into being and advocated Jewish assimilation to the Polish community. Leading personalities of this new trend were Wilhelm Feldman and Alfred Nossig. Simultaneously in Lwów an assimilationist periodical written in Polish appeared under the name 'Ojczyzna' ('Fatherland'). The editor was Nathan Loewenstein, another leader of the movement, one of the founders of the Covenant of Brothers and later the chairman of the Association of Folk Schools named after Bernard Goldman, an insurgent in the 1863 uprising, who, after its collapse, settled in Lwów. Loewenstein was also one of the founders of the 'Unity' group ('Zjednoczenie') established in 1907, a movement which will be discussed later.

Publications devoted to the assimilationist ideals played a very important role in the progress of the movement in the Polish Kingdom and in Galicia.[21] The first was a weekly *Dostrzegacz Nadwiślański — Der Beobachter an der Weichsel*, published in Warsaw in both Polish and Yiddish. This pioneering initiative was taken by Antoni Eisenbaum (Ajzenbaum), who was called the 'commander-in-chief' of Jewish assimilationists. Well-educated, Eisenbaum was in charge of the famous School of Rabbbis for some time, which graduated very few rabbis but several future leaders of assimilation. Agaton Giller recalled that,

He taught the Jews to love the land on which they were born and to fulfil towards that land the duties of a grateful son. He was convinced that the Jewish community could expect freedom of religion and equal rights only from the Poles . . . propagated the freedom of the Mosaic tradition together with faithfulness towards Poland and the use of the Polish language among the Jews.[22]

Almost ten years after Eisenbaum's death, during the unforgettable days of 1861, a patriotic manifestation took place at his grave, with singing, speeches and embraces between Jews and Poles.[23]

Thirty seven years after *Dostrzegacz Nadwiślański* closed, a new weekly for Polish Israelites, this time in Polish only, was founded in Warsaw, *Jutrzenka* (*The Dawn*). The editor was Daniel Neufeld. The publication was widely supported by the assimilationist segments of the Jewish community and the progressive Jewish intelligentsia. *Jutrzenka* paid close attention not only to Polish–Jewish friendship but also the importance of Christian–Jewish understanding. It was closed by the Russian censors after the failure of the 1863 uprising, and its editor was sent to Siberia, accused of being a 'Jewish revolutionary'.

Less than three years later, another Polish-language weekly made its appearance, *Izraelita* and was published for almost half a century,[24] most of the time by Samuel Cwi Peltyn, a well-known journalist and educator. Peltyn stressed the importance of the education of the Jewish masses in Polish culture. At the outset he also advocated religious reforms, but later abandoned those efforts. From time to time *Izraelita* published articles and items of a religious nature. To signal the importance of Jewish attachment to the land of their sojourn, the paper even quoted Jeremiah's words to the Jews of Babylon:

Build houses and live in them, plant gardens and eat their fruit ... And seek the welfare of the city to which I have exiled you and pray to the Lord in its behalf; for in its prosperity you shall prosper.[25]   (Jeremiah 29:5,7)

The intellectual level of *Izraelita* was high and the contributors included not only Jews but also such writers as Eliza Orzeszkowa and Maria Konopnicka. During the long period of its publication it gave a profile of changes in Polish–Jewish relations and growing anti-semitism. It also described disagreements within the Jewish community, the arrival of a large number of Jews from Russia, the so-called Litwaks, the increase in Jewish nationalism with the advent of Zionism, the growth of Jewish socialism of all shades, the difficult economic situation which forced Jews to mass emigration, and orthodox Jews rigorously attached to religious tradition. *Izraelita*, struggling for the education of the Jewish masses in the Polish language and culture, definitely opposed and discouraged the use of Yiddish (called 'jargon'), although the paper very often considered it worthwhile to publish assimilationist sentiments in that language. Yiddish was to remain an educational tool as long as large segments of the Jewish community used it in daily life.[26]

The publication relied on the support of Jewish industrial leaders, who were becoming more powerful under the banner of positivism and 'organic accomplishments', because many of them realized how deeply the nation suffered after the failure of the romantic dreams of the 1863 uprising. But a better-educated Jewish intelligentsia was also leaning more and more toward the assimilationist movement.

The thorny problem of Polish–Jewish relations was very often discussed in the columns of the weekly. Anti-semitism was growing, and around the turn of the century there were even violent incidents in the streets. In many cases they were provoked by the Tsarist police, and a sizeable number of the Polish community opposed these outbreaks. Nevertheless, there was overt animosity if not hostility. The adherents of assimilation often faced the dilemma of how to continue their activities in the face of growing Polish prejudices and discrimination against the Jewish people. They concluded that assimilation could not depend on the attitudes of the other side. Assimilation was a process that must go on, regardless of adverse conditions:

Can we, veterans of adversity and most experienced masters of the art of perseverance, apply the principle: my country is only where we are happy? No! A thousand times no! Our country is the land where we were born and have grown up, our nation is the one in which we live, the one we wanted to become a part of in better times. And whatever happens let it come, let volcanos erupt here and there out of the womb of this earth, let the scum of this nation in moments of madness act with hostility against us – we have no right to abandon our position, we have no right in such moments to be disloyal to this land, to this nation and to ourselves! To renounce unity with the nation in order to look for a place that exists only in dreams would be a thoughtless act, and it would bring not positive but only negative results.[27]

A similar approach was later adopted by assimilationist youth in independent Poland, when conditions started to be even worse than before.

In the fervour of discussion among various sectors within the assimilationist movement, *Izraelita* represented only one faction. At the turn of the century some were of the opinion that the weekly was not Polish enough, its policies being too Jewish; they represented the point of view that assimilation should mean a total break with the Jewish origin, including conversion to Catholicism in their scheme. Not many were ready to take such a step. On the other hand, another segment was of the opinion that *Izraelita* had isolated itself from too many Jewish people, that it was not Jewish enough in its outlook, and therefore could not gain the confidence of the masses.

The problem of conversion was widely discussed in the periodical and in public and private gatherings. The attitude towards it was different under the partitions and later during the independence of Poland, and the motives for conversion were different during these two periods. During the partitions, assimilated Jews, with rare exceptions in some professions, did not convert for financial or career reasons. Comparably, the decision to assimilate into the Polish language, culture and people was not motivated by pragmatism. It demanded personal sacrifice, and in the nineteenth and early twentieth century conversion meant a final step toward unity with the Polish people. At that time Catholicism was already so linked with Polishness that some people hoped to become even better Poles by adopting the majority faith, their own faith being, in most cases, more symbolic than deep. In the decision, therefore, to change one symbol for another, love of country was a decisive factor. As Shatzky stated:

Under the political conditions of the time assimilation did not mean merely embracing Polish culture. The Roman Catholic Church played too important a role in the preservation of Polish culture to make it possible to separate Catholicism from Polonism.[28]

Intermarriage was not a rare phenomenon, and this too was motivated by a desire to hasten the assimilation process rather than by materialistic reasons. Such decisive steps seemed successful, at least in the pursuit of a personal career, but in most cases, even the most illustrious individuals who converted to Catholicism and intermarried, expressed a continuous desire to retain ties with their Jewish origin and to be active on behalf of the Jewish community.

Undoubtedly, the growing hostility of sections of the Polish community toward the Jews revived their feelings of solidarity. Examples are abundant, one of the most outstanding being that of Jan Bogumił Bloch, one of the greatest financial and industrial potentates in the Polish Kingdom and Tsarist Russia. When the Tsarist authorities intended to extend the laws restricting the rights of the Jewish population in Russia to the territory of the Polish Kingdom, Bloch, together with Henryk Natanson (another prominent assimilationist leader), convinced the Warsaw Stock Exchange to prepare a lengthy document describing the important and necessary role the Jewish community played in agriculture, trade and craft artisanship. As a matter of fact, according to some, the material in it was so intensely pro-Jewish that it even overestimated their role in those fields. The document was officially presented to the Russian authorities in 1886. As a result restrictive laws were not introduced.[29] Bloch converted at the age of fifteen, but his will opened with the pronouncement: 'I was my whole life a Jew, and I die as a Jew.'[30]

Antoni Lange, a prominent poet and literary critic, born a Jew, son of an insurgent in the 1831 uprising, published a pamphlet in which he stated:

> To be a Pole is tied so closely to Catholicism that the two things seem to be inseparable. If you are not a Catholic, you are not a Pole. It is one of the falsehoods which are inculcated so deeply that it is difficult above every difficulty to combat it . . .

> Turning to our previous reflections, we shall answer the question, is it possible for Jews in Poland to convert to Catholicism, with the question, is this really much desired? Catholicism has been and is a misfortune for Poland: what sense therefore would there be to increase and to deepen that misfortune?[31]

Lange converted nevertheless. It is not clear if he did so before or after publishing his pamphlet.[32]

Assimilators of various shades of opinion had ambitious plans for the Jewish community in the fields of education and religion. They were concerned with growing Jewish nationalism and the popularity of Zionism, and they had to respond to the nationalism and anti-semitism of the Polish community. Nevertheless, they did not establish any overall organization devoted to these purposes. There were many explanations for these phenomena. Poland was partitioned, each part had different local problems to solve: many supporters of assimilation refused to take part in any political movement; others were of the opinion that merely belonging to such an organization would be inconsistent with their beliefs since it would separate them from the rest of the community; and still others thought that not Jews but their Polish compatriots should introduce their Jewish brethren into the stream of Polish culture and way of life. Others preferred not to be publicly exposed to the accusations of Jewish nationalists, who slowly but surely were becoming more belligerent toward them, and to the attacks of Polish nationalists, who were fast moving from verbal anti-semitism to street violence and a demand for an economic boycott against the Jews.

This does not mean that the assimilated Jews were not in touch with each other. The romantic spirit that prevailed during and immediately after the nineteenth-century uprisings gradually gave way to the 'positivist patriotism' of the organic pursuit of economic reconstruction of the country. The illegal circles of the previous period continued, but they followed the new trends. As before and during the last decades of the nineteenth century, these clandestine circles educated a number of young people in the spirit of assimilation, and they later became leaders of the movement. They included not only sons and daughters of the wealthy and highly educated, but also employees of medium-sized businesses, salesmen and artisans. The assimilationists took part in community activities and played leading roles. For several decades the upper class sat on the boards of the Jewish Religious Community (*Gmina Wyznaniowa Żydowska*) and the Grand Synagogue in Warsaw. The assimilationist middle and lower classes were active, among others, in the Association of Salesmen of the Mosaic Faith in the capital, which soon became their ideological fortress. Two trends emerged in the association, one more conservative and favouring the classic principles of positivism, and the other more progressive, demanding democratization of the economy and greater attention to the condition of the lower classes, but both followed assimilationist trends.

An army of soldiers is growing – white collar workers – who make a social jump and become standard bearers of radical assimilation, social and cultural. The more progressive this sector becomes, the more converts it creates.[33]

The majority of the members were strongly opposed to speaking Yiddish at their meetings, and this initiated a long and sometimes violent struggle between the assimilationists and nationalists. *Izraelita* reported often and at length on these events.

The press continued to play a prominent role as a forum for discussion and exchange of views. Despite wistful pronouncements in the hostile Jewish press that assimilation was bankrupt, as late as 1906 there came into being *Nowa Gazeta* (*New Newspaper*), this time a daily paper representing a classic assimilation position. It did not depend exclusively on Jewish readership and Jews were not its only contributors; but it followed the assimilationist ideology and paid close attention and devoted a lot of space to Jewish problems in general. *Nowa Gazeta* opposed Zionism as a separatist movement and espoused the view that in the face of the worsening Polish–Jewish relations, the only solution was equality of rights for the Jewish population and complete unity with Poland and Polish culture. *Nowa Gazeta* was published until the rebirth of independent Poland.[34]

At the same time, individual leaders interested in the so-called 'Jewish question' published pamphlets attempting to present their views on the general political situation and especially on the present and future of Polish–Jewish relations. Antoni Lange,[35] mentioned above, arrived at the conclusion that there were two major reasons for the Polish–Jewish conflict. One was that the Jews were 'strangers' in the community. What was responsible for this situation, in his opinion, were those elements that criticized this enstrangement, yet, at the first sign the barriers were coming down, they stoutly defended the walls of the ghetto, seeing to it that the people remained in physical and cultural seclusion. The other reason he gave was the 'provisional' character of the Jewish sojourn in Poland which was advocated by some segments of the Jewish community who turned their attention to another land.

Many years later, on the eve of World War I, Anatol Muhlstein, a prominent diplomat in independent Poland, deplored the inertia of the assimilationist movement. He complained that the movement neglected the education of the Jewish masses. Their own language should be used, since they did not understand Polish; all this despite the fact that he opposed the use of Yiddish in general. Muhlstein accused the movement of leaving the education of the masses in the hands of the Hasidim and Hedarim, who 'deformed the soul of the child' and did not oppose the propaganda of Litwaks and Jewish nationalists.

A pronounced aversion to the so-called 'Litwaks' was evident throughout the history of the assimilationist process. They were accused of antipathy to Polish culture, being in favour of Russian culture and language, and of promoting Jewish nationalism and Zionism. It must be added, however, that while the first generation of Jews coming from Russia to the Kingdom of Poland were indeed educated in Russian culture, the subsequent 'Unity' movement frequently counted among its members second-generation Litwaks born in Poland. Muhlstein concluded that the assimilationist movement should conduct educational activities among those it wanted to assimilate, instead of trying to convince those it intended to be assimilated.

Arguing that assimilation is possible and even necessary, recalling naturally the age-old examples of Berek Joselewicz, Henryk Wohl and Leopold Meyet as *the merits of these men of action should glorify them also as men of words* [my italics]. Speaking truthfully, it was an assimilation for export, condemned *a priori* to a defeat.[36]

Another brochure published by a non-Jew, J. Baudouin de Courtenay, introduced the theory of multi-nationality and dual nationality, which aroused considerable interest among a group of Jewish youth; but that was much later, in independent Poland, when they tried to reconcile their attachment to Polish culture with their Jewish origin. Some of Baudouin's views were strongly criticized, some praised. A contemporary of Lange, he also opposed the identification of Catholicism with Polishness (and Protestantism with the German character).[37]

Kazimierz Sterling, a prominent lawyer, was active in the assimilationist movement from his early youth until his death (1933). He published a pamphlet with his views on the responsibility of Polish Jews toward their country,[38] taking a diametrically opposite position from that of Anatol Muhlstein. Sterling was of the opinion that assimilated Jews should be totally integrated into the Polish nation and no longer engage in the assimilationist process. He was not always consistent in his views.

Famous was his defence of Jacob Klotz, a volunteer soldier during the Russo–Polish war of 1920–21, who refused to be sent to an internment camp established for Jewish soldiers and officers. Jews were distrusted, since they allegedly sympathized with the enemy (!). Against orders, Klotz left the army and was accused of desertion. In his defence of Klotz, Sterling went beyond his professional duty, performing a demonstration on behalf of a Polish volunteer soldier, deeply hurt by the distrust and suspicion expressed by his superiors. Many soldiers were in Klotz's situation.[39]

During his long and active life, he changed or adjusted his views more than once, but only as far as tactics were concerned, basically remaining faithful to the ideals of his youth. He participated until the end of his life in every assimilationist initiative, also in those advocating educational activities among the Yiddish-speaking segments of the Jewish community, which he had originally opposed.

With the war of 1914 drawing near, hopes for Polish independence grew as the country readied itself to take an active part in the forthcoming events. The same spirit which prevailed half a century earlier, on the eve of the uprisings, reappeared. Organic positivism gave way to a new romanticism and a new period in the history of assimilation among Polish Jews began. An urgent desire was reborn to stand up and fight side by side with their Polish fellow-citizens.

The outbreak of World War I brought with it the realization that a decisive moment for Poland had arrived. Two leaders of the assimilationist movement, Loewenstein and Steinhaus, signed the manifesto of the *Polish Circle* (*Koło Polskie*) in Vienna (August 1914), which expressed the sincere hope that Poland would soon become independent, since 'the Polish nation lives and wants to live', and called for the creation of the Legions.[40] Many Jewish students studying abroad, some from Galicia and others from the

Russian sector of partitioned Poland, joined the Legions. This does not mean that all of them were convinced assimilationists; nevertheless, judging by their previous and post-war affiliations, the number was sizeable. Assimilationist youth rapidly assembled in the former Polish Kingdom. Only a few weeks after the Germans entered Warsaw the decision was taken to set up a 'philanthropic union' with an assimilationist section to oppose the 'nationalist-Zionist agitation'. On 5 October 1915, there appeared the Association of Polish Youth of Jewish Origin – 'The Torch' (Związek Młodzieży Polskiej Pochodzenia Żydowskiego – 'Żagiew'). The name 'Żagiew', alongside the later popular 'Unity', became a sign of identification for assimilationist youth in independent Poland.[41]

Żagiew reacted immediately to the proclamation of the German and Austrian monarchs announcing the birth of independent Poland (although as a constitutional monarchy), and in a special manifesto addressed to the Polish Jews, declared that 'beginning today they will prove by their behaviour and actions, their sincere sentiments of gratefulness and attachment to the land which for centuries fed their forebears and where they are buried.'[42]

On New Year's Day 1917, Żagiew issued an appeal, this time addressed to its own ranks, for the establishment of regional organizations and scouting units, under the name of Berek Joselewicz (Drużyny Skautowe im Berka Joselewicza). The plan called for the formation of 'one large organization of Polish youth of Jewish origin, strong enough to make Jewish nationalists tremble, an organization which would be helpful to the Polish Government when it began to solve the Jewish question.'[43]

The first regional group of Żagiew was established in Łòdż and also published a similar proclamation. Shortly thereafter, more groups were founded in other cities. German occupying authorities became alarmed by a movement that was blatantly anti-German and which advocated Polish independence; several members of the National Board were arrested and sentenced.

On 15 August 1915, Żagiew started to publish its own periodical under the same name, which survived for seven years until new assimilationist publications appeared. The editors were prominent leaders of the younger generation, Stefan Lubliner and Jan Ruff. Ruff, in particular, played a crucial role in these eventful times and deserves special attention.

Zjednoczenie in Lwów and Żagiew in Warsaw – which subsequently also called itself 'Zjednoczenie' ('Unity') – both attempted to educate high school students in the assimilationist spirit. Zjednoczenie formed scouting circles of young people and Żagiew scouting teams, both in the name of Berek Joselewicz, a hero who was generally considered a spiritual father of Jewish assimilation. Not much is known about how successful and widespread this initiative was, but both groups issued fiery proclamations to Jewish youth:

Standing on guard for a Polish idea among Jews, we Polish youth of Jewish religion intend to inculcate in the Jewish masses, to which we are tied and to which we will irresolvably be tied (in the future), by mutual origin, faith and tradition of our fathers, sincere love and affection for Poland and sentiments of real citizenship in the Polish Republic.[44]

The proclamation also said that assimilationist Jews would combat Jewish separatism but would also demand equal rights for the whole Jewish community. The manifesto of the Warsaw group was even more outspoken:

... dissatisfaction and hatred of Poland and the Polish people, inflamed by Jewish nationalists among Israelite masses, reach the youth who study in the atmosphere of Polish culture ... The Jewish scouting movement represents anti-Polish trends. It was organized and well cared for by nationalists of the worst and most inexorable kind.[45]

Several Jewish scouting teams trained future pioneers for Palestine and its members declared themselves Jewish by nationality, while Polish scouting troops with few exceptions were anti-semitic and refused to accept Jewish youth. Hence the decision to form special units for young assimilationist members. Moreover, the German occupying powers looked askance at the movement and finally declared it illegal.[46] The scouting teams had no alternative but to protest and suspend their activity.

This is how the academic assimilationist youth was organized until 1924. The main centres were Warsaw and Lwów, but there were several regional branches. Their aims were almost identical, but there was one major difference: the Lwów group was in sympathy with moderate socialist ideas, while the orientation in Warsaw was generally democratic middle class.

With the idea of uniting all these groups and tendencies in a single compact organization, delegates were invited to a conference in Lwów from centres of Polish youth of the Mosaic faith from all of Poland. This congress (in 1924) founded the Związek Akademickiej Młodzieży Zjednoczeniowej (ZAMZ) (Association of Unity Academic Youth), with headquarters in Warsaw. Its 'Ideological Declaration' eliminated the emphasis on 'assimilation' and replaced it with 'unity' maintaining that, 'Jews have been settled in Poland for more than 800 years ... thus Poland is the only homeland of Polish Jews ... So one must abandon all thought of a concerted, obligatory, mass emigration of Jews from Poland to any destination whatsoever ... The democratic impulse will build a political, cultural, and sentimental union of Jews with the State and the Polish nation.'[47] As did the younger generation, veterans of Warsaw's Żagiew and Lwów's Zjednoczenie joined the nationwide general congress of ZAMZ.

This was a period of impressive developments of all kinds. ZAMZ took in centres from Warsaw, Lwów, Cracow, Wilno, and Gdańsk as well as provincial circles from Łódź, Lublin, Częstochowa, Kielce, and Przemyśl, not to mention smaller towns. Membership lists did not survive, so we do not know how many people were enrolled in the new organization. It is likely that, including sympathizers, they must have numbered between three and four thousand. It is known that at one of the Warsaw chapter meetings there were upwards of 400 members.[48]

Then a School Youth Section was set up which became popular in self-taught groups of school youth. It started up as an autonomic part of ZAMZ and was immensely useful in a period of economic depression. The self-taught groups included only a small number of children of rich families. Membership included sons and daughters of the intelligentsia – professional people, journalists, and businessmen – but also tradesmen, shopkeepers, and artisans. In a word, the whole range of the Jewish middle and lower-class population. Often they were the first generation born in Poland, and their fathers, who sometimes still had Russian first names, belonged to the so-called Russian Jews (Litwaks) who had settled in the Congress Kingdom in the late nineteenth or early twentieth centuries. The Polish school had raised them all in the spirit of Polish patriotism. There were others who came from homes where their parents and grandparents had reared them in traditions of attachment to Poland, while others did not have these family traditions. Not all of 'Unity' youth were even moderately well off; they asked for relief from university fees or summer colonies, they applied for cheap meal coupons, short-term loans and discounts on purchasing mimeographed lectures (scripts). Nevertheless, the myth still persists of the well-off children of the old assimilation, who allegedly were supposed to make up a majority of ZAMZ membership, and even scholarly work often suffers the ill effects of this assumption.

Związek Akademickiej Młodzieży Zjednoczeniowej had its own modest publishing house and issued several periodicals in the course of its existence. *Rozwaga* (Reflection), founded in 1918, was a monthly dedicated to the idea of the unity of Jews with the state and the nation of Poland. In 1924, *Rozwaga* became the mouthpiece of the main board of ZAMZ, but it stopped publishing in 1928, when *Zjednoczenie*, a monthly with the same sub-title, moved from Lwów to Warsaw and replaced it, becoming the official organ of ZAMZ. At about the same time *Dzwon* (*The Bell*) began to appear three times a month under the slogan 'political and social democracy is the solution to the Jewish question'. *Dzwon* had socialist sympathies and modelled itself on the ideology of the Lwów *Zjednoczenie* milieu.[49]

Of course, other periodicals appeared before and after 1924, apart from aforementioned *Żagiew*. They included *Zgoda* (*Concord*; Cracow); *Uwagi*

(*Observations* – writings devoted to Polish work among the Jews; Łódź); *Głos Młodzieży* (*The Voice of Youth*; Warsaw); *Nasza Jutrzenka* (*Our Dawn*), an illustrated magazine for children and young people (Lwów), but these publications were not widely circulated and, except for *Nasza Jutrzenka*, they were all short-lived.

The older generation of assimilationists, the leaders of the assimilationist movement and trends, had been very active and effective in the late nineteenth and early twentieth centuries in strengthening bonds of co-operation and understanding with the progressive sectors of Polish society by working through joint organizations and in their own socio-political circles. But when World War I broke out, they did not immediately begin setting up an organizational framework of their own, in the manner of the youth. There were many reasons for this. There were various political orientations, both Austrian and Russian, already active in Poland-wide structures, especially economic organizations, and some of their leaders had changed religion and no longer wanted to concern themselves with Jewish affairs. Others were still mentally tied to their beloved principles of positivist 'organic work' of the recent past, which had done much service to the so-called Jewish question but which had already made room for the youthful romanticism of ideas of independence and defending it by all means. Of course, there were small groups and worthy individuals who had not forgotten the ideals of their youth. They included politicians, professors, lawyers, editors, industrialists – leaders of great significance and influence.

However, late in 1917 a formation with a broader outlook was estab-lished. It was the Towarzystwo Pracy Społecznej wśród żydów w Polsce (Association for Social Work among Jews in Poland) the first association in the territory of the Congress Kingdom of citizens espousing the assimilation program.[50] Barely a year later, in what had been the Austrian Partition, a regional Związek Polaków Wyznania Mojżeszowego (ZPWM) (Association of Poles of the Mosaic Faith) was founded, and soon after there was Związek Równości Obywatelskiej Żydow-Polaków (ZR) (Association of Equality for Polish-Jewish Citizenry). The ideological basis of both organizations were the same, but they acted independently and not jointly, only because of personal differences between the leaders of the two groups.

ZPWM concerned itself with cultural activities, founding Polish schools for Jewish children, and publishing *Nowa Jutrzenka* (*New Dawn*) for young people. ZR issued its own newspaper, first under the name *Dzień* (*Day*) and later as *Goniec Wieczorny* (*Evening Courier*). The paper appeared for almost two years until the General Congress in mid-1919 changed the structure of the 'Unity' movement which was active throughout Poland. All of these organizational efforts were disbanded, however, and henceforth their influence was not very great.

For several months there were attempts to consolidate all these sectorial groupings, until 10–12 May 1919, when a general congress was called in Warsaw for the Zjednoczenie Polaków Wyznania Mojżeszowego Wszystkich Ziem Polskich (Association of Poles of Mosaic Faith of All the Polish Lands). There were 438 registered delegates representing 23 cities.[51] The congress stipulated that:

> Without abandoning the faith of our fathers nor renouncing its tradition and history, we take our stand unreservedly in favor of Polish nationality; we give ourselves wholeheartedly to the Polish homeland and desire to serve it and co-operate in its growth and development. At the same time we demand full and real equality of rights and the elimination of any economic or political discrimination. We want to be Polish citizens with full rights and duties, and not second-class citizens.[52]

A national board was elected. It seems, however, that this association was not active for a very long time either.

Later on, the Stowarzyszenie Przyjaciòł Młodzieży Akademickiej 'Zjednoczenie' (Association of Friends of Academic Youth 'Unity') was also established which was more active and prominent leaders of the 'Unity' movement took part. As already stated, 'Unity' did not have sufficient funds to be of great financial help to its student members, and the new Association took upon itself this responsibility, at least in part. It also saw the possibility and the need to take on larger projects, including building an academic house for students of limited means. The Association of Friends hoped to handle such matters even though it was not large, but the influence of its members made it respected in the community.

It is extremely difficult to establish how many Jews in Poland, in precise numbers, belonged to or sympathized with the assimilationist movement. Usually infallible sources, such as census lists, are not particularly helpful here.

There were two censuses in free Poland, in 1921 and 1931. According to the first census, there were 2,846,000 Jews in Poland, while the second census gave a figure of 3,114,000. The first census carried a heading 'nationality' and 707,400 Jews gave their nationality as Polish. One can assume that a Jew whose native tongue was Polish and who was raised in Polish culture belonged to this group. In this first census, then, about 25 per cent of the Jews said they were of Polish nationality.

The census of 1931 had the heading 'native language' instead of 'nationality'. Only 381,000 Jewish citizens gave Polish as their native tongue in this census. This number, however, does not reflect the actual state of things. Rather, the situation should have been the reverse; the number should have been higher. There should have been more than in the 1921 census, because even Zionists (and they were the largest group), with few exceptions, spoke Polish as their native language, even though they considered themselves Jewish in nationality. But under the increasing influence of anti-semitism, it was they who vigorously urged *all* Jews to give Jewish as their native tongue as a sign of protest, although this was not actually the case.

Moreover, closer analysis of the results of the 1931 census shows that the drop in the number of Jews who gave Polish as their native tongue from the number who had given Polish as their nationality in the previous census was most drastic in the Eastern territories. The Jewish population of those *voivodes* was in a difficult situation. The Jews there were afraid to opt for the Polish language for fear of angering the territorial minority that was ill-disposed to things in Polish.

Hertz understood all these difficulties:

Given that approach, an attempt to use a statistical test to determine the dimensions of the assimilation of Polish Jews would have been a thankless and fruitless task. There were different degrees and shades of assimilation, and there were contradictory attitudes in the people themselves.[53]

The mid-1920s also saw the appearance of the Związek Żydów Uczestników Walk o Niepodległość Polski (ZZUWNP) (Association of Jews Participating in the Struggle for Independence of Poland).[54] This was an organization of ex-combatants, and it also included former members of Żagiew and Zjednoczenie. But not all members of this association adhered to the ideology of 'Unity'. This ideology was not uniform. The leadership realized that changed conditions in the world and in Poland, in particular, called for a different approach, not the classic one that prevailed before the war and during Poland's first years of independence.

There were constant deliberations with a single theme: the achievement and future of the assimilation of Polish Jews as a social phenomenon. 'Unity' organizations were aware that the process of emancipation, acculturation and even Polonization (chiefly linguistic) was advanced among the Jewish masses, but they also realized it was not something they thought about, or to which they had aspirations.'Unity' youth had a deeper and broader understanding of assimilation. They went beyond the external sphere of dress, life in the separate sections of the city and even the language, and spoke of feelings and convictions, links integrating Jews with Polish culture and society.

Subsequent 'Unity' generations shifted the programme from a negative to a positive key; although they were attacked, they chose not to be attackers themselves. They did not want to 'renounce' anything or 'abandon' the traditions of their forefathers. Gradually, the problem of nationality stopped being the fundamental question. The stronger Polish nationalism grew, the more the Jewish community stressed its Jewish nationality and the higher rose the wall separating both nationalist feelings. And the more tragic incidents occurred, the more the 'Unity' people wanted to talk of democracy and the rights of the individual citizen. They avoided sharp distinctions, they tried to get close to the mass of Jews and they demanded full citizenship rights for them. The 'Unity' movement went through several difficult periods of internal controversies, one of which was the problem of conversion. For this reason the Second Congress of ZAMZ (in 1928) took the following decision: 'The 'Unity' camp will condemn the corruption of social ethics by insincere conversion for opportunistic reasons to this or any other faith.'[55]

The 'Unity' idea made a distinction between the notion of a 'community' and the idea of 'nation' (and even 'nationality'). Some were ready to consider even the possibility of 'dual nationality', a suggestion advanced years earlier by J. Baudouin de Courtenay. 'Unity' people felt that they came from the Jewish community and felt duty-bound to it, one of the reasons their testimony so often speaks of their bond with 'the Jewish mass'. They realized that the Jewish community as a whole comprised the historical, traditional, and religious elements that were bound up with it. These elements turned to the past but also existed in the present and would continue to do so in the future. In that sense, the term community should not be confused with the nation. In the vocabulary of the 'Unity' movement, nation meant an element of the state, and the movement felt bound to and fought for only one state – the Polish state.

In the 1930s the international situation and conditions inside Poland made the work of academic 'Unity' youth very difficult, and the older generation had memories of a different situation in the past and was even more disheartened. Anti-semitism grew rampant during the last years of independence. Although there was no real possibility of a large Jewish emigration to Palestine, the Zionist orientation nevertheless made headway in the community. Anti-Jewish excesses in the Jewish sections of towns and cities as well as in institutions of higher learning became daily occurrences even though democratic segments of the Polish community tried hard to mitigate anti-Jewish hostility. Nevertheless, ZAMZ made every effort to continue its ideological and educational activities and self-help (medical and medicinal assistance, loans, libraries etc.). *Zjednoczenie* continued to appear fairly regularly, though not without financial difficulties.

Against this background, a number of prominent Jewish citizens who were attached to Polish culture and who did not look to a Jewish state in

Palestine as a solution to the 'Jewish question' in Poland, founded first in Wilno and later in other regions the Żydowski Klub Myśli Państwowej (The Jewish Club of National Thought). This new organization was considered 'neo-assimilationist', since it differed from the classical movement in two particulars: it considered itself to be a political association (classical assimilation was apolitical, at least in principle) and it did not pay much attention to the differentiation between Polish and Jewish nationalities (as had been the case in the past). The accent was on the proper education of a Jew as a 'conscientious and true citizen of the Polish state'.

This neo-assimilationist movement was strengthened by a new association Wszechstanowy Blok Żydów Polskich (Bloc of Polish Jews of All Classes). It was legalized in Lwów in 1936, with branches in Cracow and Warsaw.

On the 9 and 10 September 1937, all existing branches and sections of the Bloc were called to Warsaw for a national congress. The congress elected a national board and a president, Salomon Ruff from Lwów. Most significant was the change of the previous name to the Association to Work for Unity (Związek Pracy Zjednoczeniowej). The new association returned to the traditional name, stressing again the word 'Zjednoczeniowy' ('Unity').

In its 'Ideological Declaration', the Congress declared Poland to be the only Fatherland of its members and demanded that the State treat its citizens according to their personal accomplishments and merits, regardless of their religion or national origin. The 'Declaration' opposed emigration of Jews from Poland, unless it was necessary for economic reasons and expressed sincere thanks to the democratic segments of the Polish-Christian community, which nobly defended the rights of the Jewish populace. Several postulates dealing with the current political and social situation were adopted. The approaching armed conflict did not give the neo-Unity movement enough time to put its plans into practice.[56]

From the day that Hitler invaded Poland, both ZAMZ and ZZUWNP, whose membership and leadership included older exponents of the 'Unity' movement, made very strong appeals describing the grimness of the moment. There was a call from former combatants to the Jewish population, 'To combat! To fight! To work!' Deeply affected by the approaching storm of war, in which they were to take active part, they harked back to the glorious past:

Polish Jews! In this historic moment it must be understood that we are fighting for our most sacred concern, for the Fatherland, for Honor, for our glorious future, for the freedom of all peoples, and the Rebirth of Humanity

Conscious of this responsibility and mindful of those heroes who are dear to us:

Col. Berek Joselewicz, Henryk Wohl, Rabbi Majzels, legionaries Manspeerl and Sternschuss, Corporal Storch and their many comrades who gave their blood for love of the land of Poland – we all vow to fight this battle until we win.[57]

The war obviously made any kind of overt organizational activity impossible. Many 'Unity' supporters remained in Poland, and under the German occupation they were shut up in ghettos, from which they fought the invader with deeds, words, and pen. It was the fate of others to find themselves in the USSR, and those who stayed alive joined the Polish army units that were then being formed there. Others still, after the defeat of September, made their way across to Hungary, Romania, or Lithuania and reached France, and they fought in the French, Norwegian, Libyan and Italian compaigns.

Jerzy Stanisław Flaum was one of the founders of Żagiew and one of the most gifted proponents of 'Unity' ideas. While in the Polish army in France, he was sent a Declaration of the Związek Żydów Uczestników Walk o Niepodległość Polski issued under the German occupation on 1 March 1940. It declared, among other things:

A condition of International Justice, a foundation for Lasting Peace and amicable co-existence of nations *is the building of a strong and great Poland*.

To achieve this goal Polish Jews will be unsparing in offering their blood and their possessions – in the belief that they are fighting for Something Great and Just – their homeland, which will be a thoughtful Mother to all her children, and for the reconstruction of a country in which there will be no place for religious or national discrimination.

Jewish combatants – mindful of the glorious tradition of Jews who have taken part in every struggle for the Freedom and Independence of Poland, from the Kościuszko Insurrection through the January and November uprisings, the Legions, and the wars of 1920 and 1939 – *vow* all their strength to help rebuild Poland, warmly welcoming the formation of the Polish Army in allied France, in which all would wish to serve who hold dear the idea of Independent Poland.[58]

In an article written for the Jewish New Year and Yom Kippur, Jerzy Stanisław Flaum greatly expanded the thought of the above Declaration:

There is a centuries-old tradition of Jewish participation in the struggles for Polish freedom and independence. As sons of the same Motherland, the Polish Jews have written a glorious page in the history of the struggles for the Independence of Poland ... We shall celebrate together the day of victory – the day we return to our country. All this generates a feeling of brotherhood and union among us ... Poland will guarantee all its citizens equal rights to a free and happy life. We Polish soldiers will fight for that immortal Poland, that proverbial Mother who is good to all.[59]

At about the same time, another Declaration by the same association reached Belgium by a complicated route; it had been written in the USSR. It is known that the authorities traced the authors of this Declaration, and all of them were arrested.

The members of ZAMZ also took an active part in underground work during the occupation, and a lot of information is available concerning the work in Warsaw. The 'Unity' people had their own group in the ghetto, and they were in contact with activitists on the other side of the ghetto walls, some of whom hid out and as far as possible worked on the 'Aryan side'. The names of pre-war members of 'Zjednoczenie' crop up often in memoirs, battle descriptions and accounts of the struggles.

One incident connected with the work of the underground press in the Warsaw ghetto deserves special mention. A periodical entitled *Żagiew* (*The Torch*) began coming out, and the editor, according to existing reports, was Stefan Lubliner, who had founded the original *Żagiew* 27 years earlier as the organ of the Związku Młodzieży Polskiej Pochodzenia Żydowskiego (Association of Polish Youth of Jewish Origin). Three issues from the first half of 1942 survive and only a single copy of each: an issue from January (unnumbered), one from March (no. 3), and one from May (no. 5); each running to 12–16 pages. All three issues took a verse by Jerzy Żuławski as a motto: 'My children, may God soon take these shackles from our legs'.[60]

The January issue, which seems to be the first, begins with a brief declaration, 'Instead of a Foreword'. It reads:

Despite all of Hitler's special laws and persecutions, despite the walls and fences the Germans hope will cut the Jews off from the rest of the Polish people, the Jews have been, are, and will continue to be members of the Great Polish Community, they are citizens of the Polish Fatherland and nation, they are *Poles*.

Therefore:

A free, independent, and strong Poland is our highest Ideal and our most important task.[61]

An analysis of the three surviving issues leads one to conclude that the wartime *Żagiew* espoused assimilationist ('Unity') ideas as well. It supported the Polish government in exile, the government's Delegation in Poland, and the Home Army, it reverently commemorated Józef Piłsudski, and enthusiastically described the journeys of General Sikorski and cited his statements. The publication took a stand for Poland as a whole and maintained that Jews were members of the 'Polish national community' that 'the Jewish community must understand and defend the position that Jews in Poland are first of all citizens of the Polish Fatherland and Nation (and only then Jews)'. *Żagiew* had to combat indifference, obtuseness and passivity among wide sectors of the community under occupation. *Żagiew* fought all out against several gangs of Jewish collaborators who served as lackeys to the occupying powers. The three surviving issues singled out and made a special attack on a gang known as 'Trzynastka' (so-called for the street number, thirteen, of its headquarters), with a certain Abraham Gancwajch as leader. The publication also carried the names of single informers in the ghetto on a black list, and warned self-respecting people to have no contact with them.

One of the books written about the ghetto in occupied Warsaw mentions *Żagiew* several times. One of the editors, together with several people who wrote for it, proposed at a meeting of the Co-ordinating Committee of the underground press on the 'Aryan side', that *Żagiew* be taken into 'the community of publications fighting for freedom'. The motion was defeated by the votes of the right-wing press. The Jewish journalists suffered deeply and took the decision hard.

Żagiew was not concerned about material aid, as they had said themselves, it simply wanted to have a feeling of fellowship and a sense of equal standing in the joint struggle for human rights. For the small group that rallied around the paper, *Żagiew* was a banner. This banner was scorned and treated as if it were not as good as other banners, even though, like all the others, it was a symbol of the struggle for freedom, which is a single struggle.[62]

It would seem that the May 1942 issue was the last. But in the autumn of the same year *Żagiew* appeared again; it was, however, a different publication. This time it was published by 'Trzynastka' for its own diversionary ends while hiding behind a highly respected name.[63] The editor of the seemingly 'illegal' but actually Gestapo-financed publication was soon executed as a traitor and provocateur by Żydowska Organizacja Bojowa (The Jewish Battle Organization).

There is evidence that Stefan Lubliner, the editor of the original *Żagiew* lost his life with several colleagues during the first liquidation of the ghetto (July 1942). But some ex-combatants who survived made an armed attack on the 'Trzynastka' leaders who were responsible for the *Żagiew* provocateur action. They too perished.

Thus, the organized 'Unity' movement had its beginning and its end with *Żagiew*. Only a few individuals survived the catastrophe of war, and these former members and supporters of the movement are scattered around the world. It is possible that their private archives may yield additional material concerning their experience and the history of the movement.

This study of Jewish assimilation in Poland in modern times has aimed to present one aspect, and one aspect only, of Polish–Jewish relations. It was not my intention to discuss either the totality of those relations from every political and social angle, or the history of Polish anti-semitism. Likewise, the attitudes of those segments of the Polish community and prominent individuals who, throughout the whole period, bravely, honestly and idealistically manifested determined friendship and deep solidarity with their Jewish brethren were given only marginal consideration.

The positive and negative reaction of different strata of the Polish populace to the issue of Jewish assimilation will need to remain the subject of a separate study, but I hoped here to demonstrate that Jewish assimilationist trends emerged fairly soon after the *Haskalah* appeared on the cultural horizon of Western Jewish life, although somewhat later in Poland. The important fact is not so much the question of how many people were engaged in the movement at the beginning or later, but that the movement continued without interruption throughout the whole historical period until the tragic end. The assessment of its magnitude will always be subjective; for some it was very small, for others it was significantly large considering the degree of isolation of the centuries-old, traditionally orthodox Jewish community of Poland. What is far more important is the depth of feeling and the devotion to the cause.

Indeed, Jewish assimilation in Poland was never a mass movement and always faced difficulties, finding itself attacked from both sides. These difficulties became almost insurmountable during the last years before the Nazi invasion. But it was a historical phenomenon of political and social significance, and as such it deserves attention; it was undoubtedly a memorable and remarkable occurrence in Polish and Jewish life.

Since assimilation was not a mass movement and its future was not decided in democratic elections (where numbers testify to the importance of a movement) it relied heavily on individual leadership rather than on numbers. My plan to draw a series of profiles of Polish assimilationist leaders will have to wait for a special study.

As I pointed out at the outset, assimilation was not a uniform phenomenon. It was different in various historical periods and developed differently in the various territories of partitioned Poland, and later in independent Poland. Nor was it uniformly intense in its approach to the problems and goals of the Jewish community at large. The most dramatic and contentious issues were nationality (narodowość) and conversion to Catholicism.

There were so many shades of assimilation, and some of them could barely be considered as such, so it is important to distinguish assimilation from acculturation, or even Polonization. At the same time it is appropriate to recognize that, with some exceptions, the classic assimilationists were not ready to break all of their spiritual ties with the rest of the Jewish community. Indeed, although highly critical of the backwardness of the way of life of the Jewish masses, they also appreciated that stubborn Jewish traditionalism contained some prime Jewish values that should not be lost.

Despite claims to the contrary, assimilationists included rich and poor alike (there were more wealthy people until the outbreak of the First World War and more poor people in independent Poland), sons and daughters of old and well-established families, as well as the children of later arrivals, the so-called 'Litwaks'. The assimilation process depended in large measure upon internal conditions in the Jewish community and outside, in the country at large, so it was a constantly changing conglomeration of issues and problems, but all aiming at the constant goal of unity with the nation of Poland and its culture.

The pressure of Jewish nationalist, Zionist and other movements, could already be seen in Jewish life in Poland at the end of the nineteenth century and it gained in strength later. The result was that many people began looking at assimilation processes as a negative trend, as something contrary to Jewish ideals and interests, a movement of which decent Jews should almost be ashamed. A very significant incident occurred in connection with the publication of a classic and praiseworthy two-volume work, *Żydzi w Polsce Odrodzonej* (1928). The first volume simply 'forgot' to mention that the 'Unity' movement existed during the period when 'Unity' was quite active. It was only in the second volume that a note from the editors appeared; an item in small print explaining the omission as a 'technical oversight'. The item was fifteen lines long (vol. II, p. 285) and treated the subject of the movement harshly and not without factual errors.

It is not the purpose of the present paper to become involved in generalizations or political judgements; the facts are important and I have tried to present them as objectively as possible. The essence and the nature of my theme was not to argue or to debate a triumphant 'I told you so' by those who were lucky to see the realization of their dreams. Suffice it to remember that the internal differences among Jews at that time were unfortunately not resolved in a normal sequence of ideological debates and sensitive reasoning; they were settled by the sword of a mortal enemy. Thus there is no reason at all to applaud the fact that Jewish assimilation in Poland ceased to exist as an organized community movement, together with many other social and political aspirations. One can feel only deep sadness that its adherents perished together with their other Jewish brethren.

This does not mean, however, that assimilation disappeared in other corners of the world and even among Polish Jews, individuals still exist who follow the 'Unity' ideology. They are active and are writing in Poland and in the world at large. In Poland, some of them do so for pragmatic reasons, those outside Poland continue as a part of their previous upbringing and deep convictions. Surprisingly enough they can be found even among the younger post-war generation. But that is a different subject.

11

Interwar Poland: good for the Jews or bad for the Jews?

Ezra Mendelsohn

The title of this paper is in the form of a joke, but the question it poses is a serious one. I might not have phrased the title in this way had it not been for the appearance of a number of new studies dealing with the fate of the Jews in interwar Poland, and there follows a very brief survey of the ways in which these various scholars have looked at this subject.

If one looks at the historiography dealing with interwar Polish Jewry – and by now there *is* a historiography – two basic points of view, or even two 'camps' of thought can be detected. One, not surprisingly, is the 'Jewish camp' (though not all Jewish scholars belong to it), the other the 'Polish camp' (though not all its adherents are Poles). The attitude of most Jewish scholars has been, and continues to be, that interwar Poland was an extremely anti-semitic country, perhaps even uniquely anti-semitic. They claim that Polish Jewry during the 1920s and 1930s was in a state of constant and alarming decline, and that by the 1930s both the Polish regime and Polish society were waging a bitter and increasingly successful war against the Jewish population. The impression sometimes gained from reading the works of these authors is that Jewish life in Poland was a nightmare of almost daily pogroms, degradation and growing misery. This is the message received from reading the publications of the older generation of East European Jewish scholars, such as Lestchinsky, Mahler, Trunk and Linder. A similar point of view is put forward by a representative of a new generation of Polish Jewish scholars, Pawel Korzec. The YIVO publication *Studies on Polish Jewry, 1919–1939* (in Yiddish and English, 1974), and Korzec's book *Juifs en Pologne* (1980), are good examples of the attitude of the Jewish camp, as is the excellent book by the Israeli historian Imanuel Meltser, *Maavak medini be-malkodet. Yehude Polin 1935–1939* (1982). The most influential work of this kind is Celia Heller's *On the Edge of Destruction* (1977), now available in paperback and required reading in many courses on Jewish history in the United States. The title of this book expresses very clearly the author's belief that interwar Poland was a disaster area for the Jews. She believes, and so do other adherents of this camp, that the years 1919–39 were a rehearsal for the Holocaust period. The Poles pushed the Jews to the 'edge of destruction', and the Nazis (with Polish help) destroyed them.

One can, of course, detect in the writings of this camp the long-established Jewish point of view that most, if not all, gentile states (and gentiles in general) are anti-semitic, particularly East European states and East European gentiles. To cite just one relevant example, consider the comments of Nahum Sokolow, who came to Poland in late 1933 to establish a local pro-Palestine committee. The man he wanted to head this committee was Zdzisław Lubomirski, an enemy of the Endecja, an opponent of economic anti-semitism, and a supporter of the national aspirations of the Jewish minority. Despite this, Sokolow believed that even this finest representative of the liberal aristocracy was probably an anti-semite, and that all Poles 'were anti-semites to one degree or another'.[1] Sokolow was a far more sophisticated observer of the Polish scene than Celia Heller, but the roots of her analysis are to be found in the perception of Polish reality as depicted by Sokolow and others.

The basic attitudes expressed by Heller and other members of the Jewish camp have recently been challenged by a number of scholars. An example is the recently published book by Joseph Marcus, a Polish Jew, which is certainly the best single-volume treatment of Jewish history in interwar Poland.[2] Marcus's book is, among other things, a long diatribe against a group of Jewish economists and sociologists whom he calls 'reformers'. Among the many sins of these 'reformers' was their considerable exaggeration of the economic decline of Polish Jewry, itself the result of their having been blinded by Zionist ideology. In fact, Marcus tells us, the Jews in Poland were not poverty-stricken, and even in the late 1930s the Jewish middle and lower middle classes were holding their own, with the majority of Jews being more comfortable than most Poles. Polish efforts to strike at the Jews' economic wellbeing through such means as the Sunday rest law, etatism, numerus clausus, boycotts and so on, were ineffective. Jewish strikes against Jewish-owned enterprises were more damaging to the Jewish economy than Polish state-sponsored measures. The real problem, he concludes, was Polish poverty and Jewish over-population: 'The Jews in Poland were poor because they lived in a poor, underdeveloped country. Discrimination added only marginally to their poverty.'[3]

Marcus's position, which is mirrored in the work of some young Western historians of Jewish Eastern Europe,[4] is shared by the distinguished Polish historian Jerzy Tomaszewski. He, like Marcus, complains that the Jewish question in interwar Poland has been studied too much in isolation, and he, too, emphasizes that much of Jewish suffering was the result of Polish poverty and backwardness. Only the rapid economic development of the Polish state could have helped to solve the Jewish question, which was in essence an economic and social question. This did not happen, and so the Jews, as everyone else, continued to suffer. Professor Tomaszewski also thinks that the Jews have tended to paint far too lurid a picture of their grievances, and he suggests that some of these grievances were more or less self-inflicted since many Jews did not, for understandable reasons, favour an independent Polish state. The pogrom in Lwów in 1918 was not such a serious affair, and the Polish state successfully resisted Endek pressure further to oppress the Jewish population. Even in the late 1930s Poland tried to ameliorate the condition of Polish Jews residing in Germany.[5] All this is a far cry from *On the Edge of Destruction*.

Another work worth mentioning in this context is the rewarding dissertation by Władysław T. Bartoszewski on the image of the Jew in the mind of the Polish peasant.[6] Bartoszewski suggests that the Polish peasant basically saw the Jew as a stranger, more or less as he saw the German, the Polish burgher, or even the peasant from another village. He maintains that it is completely wrong to believe that the Polish peasant was an anti-semite, a modern term which he says is connected with the rise of modern nationalism and foreign to the peasant mentality. Indeed, the author tells us that 'I do not find much use for anti-semitism as an analytical concept because it is unworkable and confusing.'[7] True, the peasants did think of the Jews as Christ killers and as users of Christian blood for baking their matzos, but these beliefs, we are told, 'did not influence the behaviour of the peasants'.[8] Here, surely, is a revisionist point of view, though by no means a novel one.

To conclude this short review Norman Davies' brilliant history of Poland should be mentioned.[9] Here, I think, some of the trends I have noted in the works of Marcus, Tomaszewski and Bartoszewski are expressed in the sharpest and most extreme fashion. Davies insists that 'the condition of Polish Jewry in the interwar period is often described out of context', for which he blames the Zionists, who were hostile, so he thinks, to the establishment of the Polish state.[10] The Jewish question, he thinks, was so intractable chiefly because of an 'unprecedented demographic explosion' which 'countermanded all attempts to alleviate social conditions'.[11] Davies, too, suggests that the Jews were not living on the breadline in Poland, that the Endecja hated not only Jews but also Germans, Ukrainians, Socialists and gypsies. Further, he maintains that in fact the Jews had many allies, including the socialists, the communists, and the liberal intelligentsia. The pogroms of Lwów and Pińsk were 'so-called pogroms'. As might be expected, Professor Davies denies any similarity between the 1919–39 period and the years of German occupation, claiming that 'the destruction of Polish Jewry during the Second World War was . . . in no way connected to their earlier tribulations.'[12] The author of *God's Playground* also addresses himself to another issue which is directly relevant here: If things were so bad for Polish Jews then how can we explain why they were so creative and so vital a community? As he so eloquently puts it, 'Anyone who has seen the remarkable records which these people left behind them, and which have been collected in YIVO's post-war headquarters in New York, cannot fail to note the essential dynamism of Polish Jewry at this juncture. All was not well: but neither was it unrelieved gloom.'[13]

Just as the approach of the Jewish camp has deep roots in Jewish attitudes, so the approach of the Polish camp has a venerable tradition behind it. Polish writers have long claimed that anti-semitism in the Polish lands was a foreign import, coming from either Germany or Russia, or even caused by the celebrated influx of 'Litvaks' in the late nineteenth century.[14] As will be demonstrated this was not an exclusively Polish point of view.

Before expressing my own attitude towards the Jewish fate in interwar Poland, I would like to emphasize something which is surely apparent to every student of the subject, namely that the subject is beset with an extremely complex set of problems. Bartoszewski may not be right to discard the term anti-semitism altogether, but the fact is that no one really knows *how* to define this phenomenon. Similarly, there are grave difficulties in defining such terms as fascism, totalitarianism and assimilation. One man's anti-semite is another man's nationalist, just as one man's pogrom is another man's social revolution. Was the Sunday rest law a piece of anti-semitic legislation or, as the Polish left believed, a progressive law greatly benefiting the working class? Another example, with reference to a different but important minority in Poland; was the effort to force the Orthodox Church to adopt the modern calendar progressive or anti-Ukrainian? It all depends on who you are and where you stand. The Polish Jews themselves could not always decide what was anti-semitic and what was not, just as American Jews cannot decide if Jesse Jackson is another Haman or a well-meaning but clumsy politician. Not infrequently they accused each other of being Jewish anti-semites. Let me cite a few examples of Jewish disagreement over this issue in Poland of the mid-1930s. As is well known, after Piłsudski's death the Polish government lent its support to emigration, seeing it as a desirable solution to the Jewish question. All Jews believed that this was an anti-semitic policy. But what about the leaders of Polish Zionism, who also believed that Jewish emigration would solve the Jewish question? In 1927, Grünbaum announced that there were one million

too many Jews in Poland and he repeated these sentiments at a press conference in Warsaw in 1936. The views of this celebrated Zionist, hitherto
extremely unpopular in Polish government circles, were greeted with
approval by Senator Rostworowski and Prince Radziwiłł, advocates of
Jewish emigration, both of whom denied vehemently that they were tainted
with anti-semitism. (Indeed, they used Grünbaum's statement in order to
exonerate themselves from such a charge.)[15] Grünbaum was accused by
Jewish anti-Zionists of being a wicked anti-semite and even his allies
deplored his 'unfortunate declaration'.[16] He defended himself by drawing
attention to the exceedingly fine distinction between Endek anti-semitism,
which spoke of emigration but meant expulsion, and the Zionist conception
of the historical inevitability of Jewish emigration to Palestine.[17] His
enemies were not convinced, accusing him of having carried out 'an act of
hatred towards Jews', while he insisted that his only sin was the sin of
'realism'.[18]

A much greater furore was stirred up, of course, by Jabotinsky's 'evacua-
tion' plan, applauded by the Endek press and denounced by Grünbaum and
his allies, who detected in it extremely dangerous anti-semitic elements.[19]
Sholem Asch wrote that Jabotinsky had 'placed the most dangerous weapon
in the hands of those who hate us'.[20] To give just one further example, in
1936 the PPS member J. Borski wrote a pamphlet entitled *Sprawa Żydowska
a socjalizm. Polemika z Bundem* (*The Jewish Question and Socialism. A Polemic with
the Bund*). Here the Polish socialist rejects the Bund's belief that anti-
semitism will disappear with the emergence of a new socialist order, and
approves of the Zionist prognosis. For his pains he was denounced by
Bundists as an anti-semite, and defended by the Zionists.[21] The issue
became increasingly clouded. Moshe Kleinbaum (Sneh) tried to clarify and
pacify in an article called 'Zionist Anti-semites and Anti-semitic Zionists',
but of course the controversy continued to rage.[22]

Not only was there no agreement among Polish Jews as to who was an
anti-semite and who was not, but often it seems that some Jews held views
on the general issue of Polish anti-semitism which differed little from the
Polish notion, cited above: that anti-semitism was foreign to Poland. Many
found it convenient to argue that in fact the Polish people were free of the
anti-semitic disease, which was being artificially spread by the wicked
regime or by 'outside agitators'. In 1937 the General Zionist Apolinary
Hartglas reminded his readers that Russia, and not Poland, was the scene of
the most terrible pogroms of the prewar years and that the current anti-
semitic terror was the work of a few men of ill will.[23] It was often said that
before agitators of the Endecja came to do their dirty work the relations
between Jews and peasants in the *shtetl* and village were truly idyllic; a point
of view which dovetails neatly with Bartoszewski's anthropological study.[24]

This point of view however, coexists uneasily with the notion mentioned above, that all gentiles are anti-semites.

Having made a short detour, I shall now return to the main theme of this paper, the question posed at the outset. First, a few concessions to the Polish camp. It is true, Jews do often exaggerate their suffering, as, on occasion, do all minorities (including the Poles). It is a fact that the number of victims of the Lwów pogrom was greatly exaggerated in the Jewish press, and that there are many other examples of this, as Professor Golczewski has demonstrated.[25] I would certainly agree with Professor Tomaszewski that the Jewish question should not be regarded in isolation from other problems. It may be difficult for Jews to admit it, but other groups had problems too – the other minorities, Polish peasants, Polish workers and so forth. After reading Marcus's book I have little doubt that most Jews were in fact better off than most peasants. And it should be admitted, too, that Polish Jewry after 1933 was in a happier situation than German Jewry, and perhaps, even, Romanian Jewry. Finally, I certainly think that Professor Davies's remarks concerning the creativity of Polish Jewry have a great deal of credence, and I shall return to this point later on. Having said that, it cannot be denied that external events, which cannot be blamed on the Polish state or on Polish society, had a tremendous impact upon the condition of Polish Jews – the great depression, for example, and the rise of Hitler in Germany.

Some of the points made by the Polish camp, beginning with the claim that the Jewish question in Poland was chiefly a social and economic one (a position, by the way, taken by both Foreign Minister Beck and by Jabotinsky) need examination.[26] No one can deny that the large number of Polish Jews and their peculiar economic structure and role in the Polish economy had influenced attitudes towards them, just as no one can deny that Polish backwardness must be taken into account in any effort to understand the Polish state's Jewish policy. But it is surely misleading to assume that the condition of Polish Jewry and the backwardness of the Polish state rendered *inevitable* the state's policies and society's attitudes towards the Jewish minority. Pre-World War I Hungary was also a backward country with a poor Jewish population, but its leaders, instead of urging Jews to emigrate and supporting boycotts of their stores, preached the integration of the Jewish community into Magyardom and welcomed the Jews as modernizers of the Hungarian economy. On the other hand, Germany's wealth, and the wealth of its Jewish community, did not prevent the German people from taking an extreme anti-semitic stance from 1933 onwards. In 1917 Russia was a poor country, but Soviet Russian policy towards the Jews (who were more or less identical to the Polish Jews) was certainly entirely different from Polish policy.[27]

In Poland itself there is evidence that the Western regions, where there were very few Jews, and where the economic situation was relatively good, were marked by a particularly strong anti-semitic tradition, while Jewish–gentile relations were better in the economically primitive Kresy. This short excursion into comparative history teaches us, I think, that the kind of economic determinism to be found in the writings of some Polish scholars does not really supply us with the key to an understanding of the situation in the interwar years.

Nor do I find it possible to believe that the Polish peasantry, brought up in the Church and believing in Jewish guilt for the crucifixion, really thought of the Jews as just another category of 'strangers'. Certainly their attitude towards the Jews was ambivalent, but is not this always the case in majority/minority relations? The attitudes of whites towards blacks in the American south was also ambivalent, but ambivalence does not rule out hostility. To be sure, Endek agitators helped to bring to the surface anti-Jewish sentiments, but surely such sentiments were very much in existence before these agitators arrived in the village? They were not working in a vacuum. I would therefore call into question both Dr Bartoszewski's conclusion and the Jewish view of the 'good peasant' corrupted by the evil anti-semite. The latter view is obviously the product of an understandable reluctance on the part of some Polish Jews, many of whom were sincere Polish patriots, to admit that anti-semitism had roots in the Polish countryside. It is also a product of a no less understandable, desire to romanticize the 'good old days' (of the old Polish state, or of 1861–3) as opposed to the harsh realities of the interwar years. It should be treated by historians as a myth, not a reflection of reality.

As for the creativity of the Jews in independent Poland, Prof. Davies is obviously right. We have only to compare the flourishing of autonomous Jewish culture, religion and politics in Poland with the situation in Germany, the Soviet Union or America, to see this. But, as we all know, such creativity is linked with oppression, with anti-semitism, with the refusal of Polish society to allow for Jewish integration. After all, the American blacks created their autonomous culture in times of slavery and apartheid. A degree of oppression may be good for minorities in the collective sense, though it is bad for them as individuals: the Jews of Germany after 1933, and the Jews of Hungary from 1938 on, became more creative in a Jewish sense. The Polish Jews who went to America abandoned Yiddish for English, while many who stayed behind continued to speak and write in the traditional Jewish language. Does this mean that Poland was better for the Jews than was America? Or does it mean that Poland was an anti-semitic country, and America was not.?

My own point of view is as follows: I cannot imagine anyone seriously denying that interwar Poland was an anti-semitic country, both in its policies and in the attitudes of large sections of the Polish population. The depth of Polish anti-semitic feeling fluctuated, and historians will continue to argue both over its extent and its impact on the Jewish population. Jewish sources in the 1920s and the 1930s spoke of a Polish economic policy of 'extermination', in the twenties they were exaggerating by a great deal, in the thirties they were exaggerating much less.[28] In 1937 Senator Moses Schorr declared that the Jews in Poland were 'ex lex', again an exaggeration (perhaps) but how much of an exaggeration at a time when the inheritors of the Sanacja were adopting the Jewish policy of the Endecja?[29]

I do not believe that this anti-semitic policy was inevitable. Anti-semitic attitudes, like other prejudices, exist everywhere; but policies are the result of conscious decisions. Poland inherited a 'Jewish problem'. For various reasons the new Polish state rejected the assimilationist Jewish policy of pre-war Hungary or interwar Soviet Russia. I believe that the crucial factor here was the belief among the governing Polish elite that Poland had re-emerged as a nation state, the main mission of which was to advance the interests of the Polish nation – when being a 'nation' was defined as being able to absorb certain non-Polish elements but not being able, or not desiring, to absorb the Jews. This self-definition inevitably led to anti-Ukrainian policies (but did, theoretically, allow for assimilation of the Ukrainian element) and to anti-Jewish policies and attitudes. Israelis are in a good position to understand that any state which defines itself as a mono-ethnic entity, but which in fact includes within its borders members of other ethnic groups that cannot be absorbed, must act in a way which is deleterious to the interests of these other groups. Again, exactly how adversely the interests of the unassimilable minority will be affected depends on various local factors – the Jews of independent Lithuania suffered less, I think, than the Jews of independent Poland. But the definition of Poland as an exclusivist (at least so far as the Jews were concerned) nation-state rendered impossible the kind of situation which may have prevailed in the medieval Polish state or even during the period of the second revolt against Russia (when the idea a 'Polish–Jewish alliance' against Tsarism gained popularity in some circles).

It is worth mentioning that some interwar Jewish leaders emphasized this very point. Yitshak Grünbaum and his allies insisted that Poland must become a 'state of nationalities' and thus fulfil its historic mission to offer freedom to the small national groups of Eastern Europe threatened by forced Russification. Thus the 'minorities' bloc' of 1922 and 1928, which he invested with great ideological significance.[30] In 1936 Rabbi Rubinstein, Sejm deputy from Wilno, mourned the death of the old Polish ideals of federalism. He had hoped, he said, that the Wilno region would become a kind of 'Eastern Switzerland', an example of 'ex oriente lux'. This, he claimed, was the authentic vision of the great Piłsudski, who had spoken in the same vein at the opening of the University of Wilno. Instead, Polish chauvinism had taken over, transforming Wilno into an arena of ethnic hatred directed against all non-Poles, and especially against Jews.[31] Sholem Asch also believed that the Polish decision 'not to recognize the three and one-half million Jews as an organic part of the Polish population' was responsible for Jewish suffering.[32]

Of course we could say (and it *has* been said, by Marcus and many others) that Grünbaum, Rubinstein and other Jewish leaders, were hopeless romantics, out of touch with reality, not aware of what the twentieth century and twentieth-century nationalism was all about. Grünbaum, the Polish patriot, stood for a Poland which no longer existed . The 'state of nationalities', the 'Switzerland of the East', was not to be, and this proved fatal to the Jewish interest.

In conclusion, I would like to offer a few 'proposals' to both the Polish and the Jewish camps. I see no reason why the Polish historians should not admit that interwar Poland was an anti-semitic state, in the sense that it acted, in many ways, against the Jewish interest. Few, if any, American intellectuals would deny that America was (and still is) an anti-black country. Possibly one reason why Polish scholars are reluctant to state that Poland was an anti-Jewish country is that they are accustomed to regard Poland as a victim, and victims are extremely reluctant to admit that they have victimized others. But such things are possible.

As for the Jewish side, we should admit that we owe the Poles a good deal. Above all, we owe a debt of gratitutde to Polish freedom, which allowed the Jews in the 1920s and 1930s to participate in politics, open schools, and write as they pleased. In interwar Poland the Gerer Hasidim could remain Gerer Hasidim, and the pioneers could organize vocational training in anticipation of aliya to Palestine. Polish freedom, allied with Polish anti-semitism and Jewish modernization, made possible the emergence and popularization of the new Jewish politics, which, among other things, helped to build the state of Israel. Those of us who define ourselves as Jewish nationalists should add that we owe a debt of gratitude to the interwar Polish state for offering its Jewish citizens a model of a heroic, and successful, national struggle, which so inspired young Jewish members of the Bund, of Hashomer ha-tsair and of Betar. Interwar Poland was a relatively free country, a highly nationalistic country, and an anti-Jewish country. The experience of Polish Jews between the wars was a combination of suffering, some of which was caused by anti-semitism, and of achievement, made possible by

Polish freedom, pluralism and tolerance. Modern Polish nationalism led, inevitably, to anti-semitism, but it also inspired Polish Jewish youth to raise the banner of Jewish nationalism. Our gratitude to the Poles is, to a degree, reminiscent of the gratitude owed by America to England for having persecuted the pilgrims, but it is nonetheless something we should keep in mind.

Interwar Poland was therefore bad for the Jews, in the sense that it excluded them from first-class membership in the state. This had led, by the late 1930s, to a widespread feeling among Polish Jews, and especially among the youth, that they had no future in Poland, and that they were trapped. Interwar Poland was good for the Jews because, among other things, it provided an environment in which forces were unleashed in the Jewish world which many Jews regarded then, and today, as extremely positive. This is not to give an ambiguous answer to the question posed at the outset, but to show that more than one answer is possible. Indeed, more than one answer is necessary. I think we can say of Jewish history in interwar Poland that it was 'the best of times and the worst of times': The best of times in the sense of the extraordinary creativity of Polish Jewry, the worst of times in the sense of the fulfilment of the bleakest prophecies, made mostly by Zionists, concerning the imminent fate of the East European Jewish diaspora. With this I rest my case.

12

Relations between Polish and Jewish left wing groups in interwar Poland

Jerzy Holzer

The problem of the relationship between Polish and Jewish left wing groups has been discussed on many occasions, though only in a marginal and fragmented way. It suffices here to mention the two articles, one by the present author and the other by Jacek Majchrowski, published in the 1983 special issue of *Znak*,[1] as well as the writings by Ezra Mendelsohn. I do not claim to present the matter in an exhaustive and comprehensive way here – that would call for some in-depth research – I shall do no more than inspire a discussion on this occasion. I deal here with Jewish affairs only in the context of the political history of Poland, and it is to my disadvantage that I do not know the literature in Hebrew and Yiddish.

I consider the socialists and the communists as the political left. Regardless of fundamental differences in their outlook, they stemmed from the same, or at least very similar, ideological traditions.

Within the Polish socialist parties active before 1918 the view prevailed that putting forward separate political postulates on the Jewish question was not appropriate for socialism. At first, tendencies unequivocally oriented toward assimilation were dominant. Despite the fact that there was a considerable number of socialist activists of Jewish origin (though Polonized and intolerant towards Jewishness), the separate character of the language and culture of Jews was treated reluctantly by socialists, the majority of whom regarded it as the foundation of mental backwardness, while the Jewish religion was considered virtually no more than a superstition. It may sound like a joke, but the PPS (Polish Socialist Party) journal in Yiddish was first edited by the only Jewish intellectual in the PPS at that time (1898) who was familiar, though vaguely, with Yiddish, Max Horwitz, and then later by Leon Wasilewski, who personally had nothing to do with Jewishness, and who for this purpose took up a few lessons in Yiddish.[2] In the PPSD (Polish

Social Democratic Party) of Galicia, the most radical opponent of all tendencies towards granting autonomy to Jewish socialist communities was Herman Diamand.[3]

The unequivocal assimilation-oriented tendencies gradually gave way to a more flexible stand, by which the linguistic and, to a certain extent, the cultural separateness of Jews was recognized. This separateness, however, was actually seen as a practical problem, revolving around such questions as whether to have more numerous publications in Yiddish, or to have Jewish party cells or, even a PPS Jewish Organization or a PPSD Jewish Section. Within the PPS and PPSD there was, nonetheless, a clear opposition to the separate organization of Jewish socialists into their own parties, regarding not only the socialist Zionist movement (since in this case opposition could be justified as a rejection of the concept of Zionism and not merely opposition to Jewish separateness) but also the Bund. After the rift in the PPS certain new tendencies appeared in both factions. The PPS Revolutionary Faction managed only to attract a small group of assimilated activists; the PPS Jewish Organization joined the PPS-Left almost *in corpore*. For the Revolutionary Faction, one of the ways to account for this course of events was to explain it by alluding to the impact of Russian culture on Lithuanian Jewry, that is the Jews of the eastern borderland. One consequence of Russification and the migration of Litwaks (Lithuanian Jews) into the territory of the Polish Kingdom, it was claimed, was the development, among Jews there, of a more reserved attitude towards the Polish demand for independence. It would be an exaggeration to see anti-semitism in such arguments; their leading spokesman was Julian Unszlicht. Pressured on the one hand by Social Democrats, and on the other by 'the Faction boys', the PPS-Left tended towards the Bund and started to take a more sympathetic view of its basic position, though still retaining a critical attitude, especially, of its separate activity.[4]

The stand of the SDKPIL (the Social Democracy of the Polish Kingdom and Lithuania) did not differ much from the later positions of the PPS-Left; it accepted the Bund (though not the Zionists) as a comrade in struggle. The SDKPIL regarded the former – regardless of the Bund's own intentions – as a messenger of assimilation, that is, of the unification of Jewish and non-Jewish workers' interests, always in a given territory. But this meant nothing but the negation of a Jewish ethnic nationhood divided by state borders. 'That such an assimilation, which is, anyway, unavoidable, takes place through the Jewish "jargon" [i.e. Yiddish], does not alter the matter in the least.'[5] It was argued that 'Jews do not constitute a separate nationality and do not possess a culture of their own', but for tactical reasons it was decided not to assert this in quite such a provocative manner.[6]

In their pre-1918 position, the Jewish socialist parties refrained from

giving answers to questions about their attitude towards Poland and Polish
nationalism. Both Bund and Poale-Sion (and indeed all Jewish territorial-
ists) appealed to Jews over the entire area of the Russian empire. There was
no doubt that should Poland eventually re-emerge and gain independence,
it would be a bitter blow to the Jewish socialist parties because the largest
Jewish community located in one state anywhere in the world would split in
two. Hence not only doctrinal positions but also profound differences in
political interests inclined Jewish socialists to criticize the nationalism of the
PPS. On the other hand, the national autonomy postulated by the SDKPiL
and of the PPS-Left somewhat later, were more easily matched with another
vision of autonomy (though it differed in that it was founded on concepts of
culture and nationhood, not on territory): that presented by Bund and by the
territorialist trends among Jewish socialists (it should be stressed, however,
that the SDKPil and PPS-Left viewed autonomy only as an emergency or
provisional solution).[7]

The recollection of these fundamental differences in approach before
1918 requires some further explanation. Regardless of their differences
and antagonisms, the socialists, whether Polish or Jewish, were the only
political group that rejected all national prejudice (a small exception may
be made for minor and unimportant groups of liberals open to assimilated
Jews). In this framework mutual charges of being influenced by nationalism were nonsense, unless we consider nationalism to be the inability to
understand specific foreign ethnic problems – but should we then call the
SDKPiL nationalist since it did not recognize foreign ethnic problems as a
fact?

With the formation of an independent Polish state in 1918 the situation
for both sides, Polish and Jewish, changed radically. Of fundamental significance was not only their attitude to the independent Polish state but also to
the Bolshevik revolution and a possible European revolution on the same
pattern. Only in 1918 and a few subsequent years did it become possible to
set up the first party of which Jews and Poles could become members
without renouncing their nationality (or perhaps mutually resigning, to
some extent, some of their attributes?). This, of course, was the Communist
Workers' Party of Poland, later known as the KPP, which we are entitled to
regard as equally part of the Jewish and Polish political left.

The KPP continued, in some measure, the traditional attitude towards
the Jewish question. Indeed, it embraced the faction groups from Poale-
Sion and the Bund (the latter only after a temporary operation between 1922
and 1923 as a separate Jewish communist party in Poland, the so-called
Kombund); it tolerated linguistic and, to some extent, cultural Jewish
autonomy, but this always stemmed from practical needs rather than
comprehension of the Jewish national problems. There were voices calling

for autonomy for the Jewish communists, but such tendencies were rejected as incompatible with the fundamental principles of communism.[8]

On the one hand, the solution of the Jewish question was seen as possible only through revolution and proletarian dictatorship; on the other, nationalist and separatist tendencies were condemned as heading towards organizational and political separateness.[9] The positive programme for Jews, apart from the equality of rights, included only empty phrases concerning the unhindered development of Jewish education and culture. In view of the fact that there were not separate Jewish political and self-governing institutions, and given the negative attitude to the cornerstone of Jewish cultural separateness – religion – this meant only an extension of the period within which the assimilation would be accomplished on the principle of the melting pot.

A very controversial statement, in the light of this, is Majchrowski's view that the numerous participation of persons of Jewish origin in the communist movement and their prominent role in the movement led to the fact that 'fundamentals of the ideology' created by this group 'could not present the Jewish question in a manner running counter to it. (sic)'.[10] In essence, the communist concepts boiled down to eliminating the Jewish question by doing away with Jewish separateness and, in effect, melding the Jews with the rest of the population. It is possible, from the Jewish viewpoint, that this must have stirred emotions similar (*toutes proportions gardées*) to those raised by propositions formulated by Kazimierz Krzywicki, in 1870, on the dilution of the Poles in the Russian sea for their good – emotions that had angered the national-minded Poles.

The KPP had its own specific mode for the continuation of the views on the attitude towards Poland and the Poles which had been formulated by its leaders before 1914. At first the need for Polish independence was actually denied, but then it was verbally recognized, together with the perception of the 'homeland of the world proletariat' in the Soviet Union, and it was assumed that the best prospect for Poland in a Communist revolution was joining the multi-national Communist state. Such views were, of course, cherished equally by both Polish and Jewish members of KPP. Nevertheless, it was Jewish communists who perceived in the USSR a confirmation of the abolition of the Jewish question in a multi-national communist state. It would have been hard to expect from them any greater sensitivity to Polish national problems than to the specific ethnic Jewish cause.

The Polish Socialist Party, united and composed of parties previously operating in particular areas, avoided making a clear-cut stand of its own on the prospects of solving the Jewish question in Poland. Its attitude towards the Zionist solution as proposed by both factions of Poale-Sion, and also to the proposed national-cultural autonomy, was rather hesitant. On the other hand, however, the interwar PPS did not make any serious effort to secure influence in Jewish milieux (except for the assimilated Poles of Jewish origin) and, in a way, tacitly recognized the autonomy of the Jewish socialist movement. Jewish socialist parties were encouraged to establish closer co-operation. It seems Ezra Mendelsohn is mistaken in burdening PPS with responsibility for the noticeable lack of such co-operation. It was rather the reverse: the Jewish socialist parties took to criticizing the PPS sharply, charging it with nationalism and reformism, and tried to place themselves somewhere midway between PPS and KPP.

It is necessary to recall that even though it avoided any programmatic delineation of the prospects of the Jewish question in the contemporary political life of Poland, the PPS determinedly opposed anti-semitism and all forms of discrimination against the Jewish population. This, of course, did not mean that the PPS grass roots were totally free of such sentiments. It is typical, for example, that during the 1918 elections it was decided not to put forward the candidacy of Feliks Perl (in Warsaw) in the top position on the ballot, while placing his name in the second position met with strong criticism from the Warsaw PPS leaders, who feared a loss of votes.[11] At the same time, Perl continued to be a member of the party caucus until his death and he also was the editor-in-chief of *Robotnik*, the central party organ. Among top party people and deputies, those of Jewish origin abounded.

It seems that the content of the programmes of the PPS concerning the Jewish question derived from a contradiction between emotions (still close to the assimilation tendencies) and realism (which excluded the assimilation of those three million Polish Jews and more, even though it was difficult to find another solution). It was not until the decline of the Second Polish Republic that one of the top journalists of the PPS, Jan Maurycy Borski, had the courage to publish a brochure supporting the concept of Jewish emigration, explaining that the Jewish question in Poland was impossible to solve and that anti-semitism was lasting by nature.[12] Although Borski did not clearly support Zionist concepts, it is more likely than not that he was close to them. Thus he came under fire not only from the Bund (directly hit in this case), but also from other PPS activists). Zygmunt Zaremba charged Borski with nationalism and, in accord with Marxist doctrine, argued that under socialism anti-semitism would die down the moment the Jewish population became productive.

Immediately after 1918 the fascination of the Jewish socialist movement with the Russian revolution and communism led to an explicit negation of the positive restoration of Polish statehood and to a conflict with Polish national aspirations. The fascination with communism sprang from a belief that it effectively liquidated ethnic oppression, including all forms of discrimination against Jews, an outcome anticipated in a socialist future. Evidence of this was to be found in, among other things, the very broad and often exaggerated involvement of leaders of Jewish origin in Red Russia. These views do not demand further analysis since they brought a considerable proportion of its spokesmen in Bund and Poale-Sion, via factions, to the communist movement (and the communist views have already been discussed above).

We are more interested here in the attitudes of those who remained in the socialist parties, particularly in the two factions of Poale-Sion, the Right and the Left, and in the Bund. From the formal point of view all these parties recognized independent Polish statehood and voiced their support for it, as well as declaring the need to co-operate with Polish communists and (occasionally) socialists in the political struggle in Poland. The most extreme position in this respect was taken by the Poale-Sion-Left, which declared its unequivocal support for Soviet Russia and endeavoured to convince communists to combine their concepts with the Zionist version of solving the Jewish question.[13]

As already mentioned, the Bund and Poale-Sion-Left charged the PPS with nationalism, and shunned co-operation with the party because of this. The search for an accord with communists and the reservations about Polish socialists who had favoured independence, created, in the final outcome, an ambiguity as to the real attitude of the two parties towards Polish sovereignty. In this respect, the situation did not change until the 1930s, and then as the result of a number of developments: the victory of Nazism in Germany and the consequent upsurge of anti-semitism in Poland on the one hand, and an ever more apparent development of the Soviet Union and the international communist movement that did not coincide with the expectations of Jewish socialists. It was then that co-operation on the part of the Jewish socialist parties with Polish socialists ceased to be an exclusively programmatic slogan and turned into a (more or less) frequently realized and implemented form of action.

In the final analysis it seems appropriate to comment that both the Polish and the Jewish political left, though tolerant towards the other national group and devoid of the xenophobia which permeated almost all other political camps, found it difficult to understand their respective national problems. The Polish and the Jewish communists arrived at mutually shared beliefs, but the price was the cessation of all attempts to solve Polish and Jewish questions in a manner that would secure the lasting foundations of national autonomy. Polish as well as Jewish socialists viewed their respective national problem through the prism of their own needs. For the Polish socialists these needs boiled down to bringing the Jewish socialist movement into the orbit of Polish problems, thus winning an ally. Offering no more than warm-hearted tolerance of the Jews and opposition to anti-semitism, the PPS was unable to propose anything concrete for the future of the Jewish national existence. For the Jewish socialist, Polish problems played a secondary role since they felt that the conditions necessary for a solution of the Jewish question were only marginally dependent upon the existence of an independent Polish state – however, nothing much changed in the Bund or the Poale-Sion programmes after 1918. The Jewish socialist movement drew its strength (and a relative strength, at that) from its separateness, and not from the identification of Jews with Poles. Moreover, the negative or at least indifferent attitude of the Jewish socialists to religion – the cultural foundation of Jewry – inclined them even more strongly towards 'separatism'.

13

Polish–Jewish relations in occupied Poland, 1939–1945

Władysław Bartoszewski

Serious shortcomings beset much of the research into the problems faced by the population of Poland, subjugated and occupied since September 1939, for whether that research be purely scholarly or its findings intended for a more general public, it seems to be either fragmentary or ill-defined: it concentrates solely or principally on the circumstances common to just one national group, Polish or Jewish for example, or else it concentrates on only one section of society, either urban or rural, or it deals with only one professional group. However, in order to come close to a real and reasonably full representation of the circumstances common to both the Poles and the Jews in an occupied country, it seems right to throw a many-sided light on their situation in order to consider the social, political and psychological factors inherent in both national groups, whatever their creed, who, in 1939, were placed in specific historical circumstances.

The Jewish minority in Poland constituted approximately ten per cent of the total population and in fact, this proportion seems to be an underestimation in the light of the criteria set by Germany in the Nuremburg Laws. More than 75 per cent of the Jewish population in Poland was concentrated in urban areas whilst only 25 per cent lived in rural regions. There was, therefore, a marked concentration of Jews in specific areas of the country

The economic situation of Jews in Poland was no different from that of Christian Poles. The world crisis at the end of the 1920s and the beginning of the 1930s contributed to a widespread pauperization of hundreds of thousands of families in Poland, regardless of creed or origin. Furthermore, it must be remembered that until the First World War, a large part of Poland had belonged to Tsarist Russia for 120–140 years and was underdeveloped both socially and economically. Similarly, the economic situation in Southern Poland, which had been seized by the Habsburgs in the eighteenth century and remained under Austrian jurisdiction right up to the end of the First World War, was very unfavourable. This contributed to the well-known phenomenon, seen mainly in the United States, of the emigration of poor Jewish and Polish immigrants in search of a living. The development of social and civilizing influences among both Jewish and Polish communities was almost impossible, given the cultural and educational levels that existed in those Polish territories which had been a part of the Russian Empire for over seven generations. In comparison with most other European countries a large part of the population lived in a state of complete backwardness. Within the sphere of nationalistic politics, successive invaders instigated and exacerbated political conflicts between various religious and national groups, conflicts caused by religious and ideological intolerance as well as economic rivalry.

The official political policy of anti-semitism, so characteristic of the last decades of Tsarist Russia, had a particularly harmful effect on the population of Poland, although it never assumed the same proportions in Poland as it did in Russia or the Ukraine. It is also characteristic that in the urban areas and among the intelligentsia, where anti-semitism had already begun to develop before the First World War, the political climate was pro-Russian, while social attitudes tended towards conservativism.

Nationalistic conflicts between Poles and Ukrainians, Poles and Germans, Poles and Jews, were characteristic of the difficult problems that existed in the social and political life of the Polish nation, although each conflict had its own basis and justification, with varying individual effects. It is indisputable that before 1939 anti-semitic attitudes existed in Poland, as did political organizations with anti-semitic programmes. However, the real scope and social effect of these kinds of activities and attitudes, which have been both exaggerated and underplayed in various writings, is debatable. A most relevant aspect seems to be the isolationist tendency of both groups, that is, an inadequate integration and lack of openness on the part of both communities living, in essence, *beside* one another but not together. One must also remember that Poland, and particularly her eastern territories, was an especially important centre for orthodox Jews – with all the accompanying attitudes and social consequences.

Polish Jews had a very strong sense of their own separate national identity as was demonstrated in the last census of 1931, when approximately 85 per cent of Jews who were Polish citizens put down Yiddish or Hebrew as their mother tongue. This attitude was distinct from the self-determination of Jews in contemporary Germany, France and England. At the outbreak of World War II Poland was tolerant of Jewish autonomy in religious, political and social life, and this included education and cultural activities. However, only a certain number of the intelligentsia and some Polish and Jewish labour activists recognized the need to oppose the stereotyped attitudes and prejudices which resulted from the differences between each group and from the mutual sense of alienation. Simultaneously with these events, a very important role was being played by many thousands of Jews in Polish academic, cultural and professional life, for they were the co-creators of what then constituted contemporary Polish civilization.

The events of 1939 brought about the division of Poland, so that in terms of actual acreage the country was split almost equally between the Third Reich and the USSR. As a result, 48.4 per cent of the territory with 62.9 per cent of the total population was under German occupation, while the USSR had 51.6 per cent of the land (after incorporating the Lithuanian Republic) together with 37.1 per cent of the total population. 61.2 per cent of Polish Jews lived under German occupation and 38.8 per cent under that of the USSR, according to the eminent statistician, Ludwig Landau, who based this estimate on pre-war statistics. In the course of 1939, however, there was a shift in the population from west to east and we can therefore assume that, at the beginning of the occupation, the number of Poles, as well as Jews, who found themselves in the eastern half of Poland was somewhat larger whilst the number in the west was smaller than shown in pre-war statistics, which were based on permanent domiciles.

Throughout occupied Poland both the German and Soviet occupying authorities made every effort to differentiate between the nationalities, and different tactics were used when dealing with the various national groups. It is characteristic, however, that as early as 30 October 1939 Himmler ordered the removal, over a four-month period, of all Jews and 'any particularly undesirable Poles' from the western territories incorporated into the Reich. In real terms, by the end of February 1940 this resulted, in Warthegau alone, in the forcible removal, of 200,000 Poles and 100,000 Jews. Although politically the Nazis had various reasons for these activities, it meant that the fates of both the Polish and Jewish populations had merged.

In accordance with the so-called 'Unternehmen Tannenberg', mass executions of Poles were carried out along the coast (Pomorze), in Great Poland (Wielkopolska) and Silesia (Śląsk); this meant that as early as the autumn of 1939, 50,000 people had died. In central Poland – Warsaw, Cracow, Częstochowa, Lublin and many other towns – the Germans had managed to make mass arrests within the first few weeks of occupation. The insidious arrest, on 6 September 1939, in Cracow, of 183 academics – professors and lecturers of the Jagiellonian University and the Mining Academy – had particularly severe repercussions. Twenty of them were made to pay with their lives. In December 1939 the Germans carried out two mass executions in Bochnia near Cracow and in the Wawer settlement near Warsaw; the death toll was 170. At the end of April 1940, Reichsführer SS Heinrich Himmler ordered the removal of 20,000 Poles to concentration camps. In May 1940, the beginning of the German offensive in the west, a grand design of exterminating the Polish intelligentsia within German-occupied Poland began, known as AB (Ausserordentliche Befriedungs-aktion). This extraordinary campaign of pacification was to entrap above all (according to the SS) 'the spiritual and political leaders of the Polish resistance movement.' (SS Brigadeführer Bruno Szreckenbach.) On 14 June 1940 the first transport of Polish political prisoners was taken to a newly opened camp in Auschwitz, which, during the next year, was inhabited almost exclusively by Poles. Amongst them were a few thousand people rounded up in the course of raids on streets and houses, while later in the summer of 1941 Soviet prisoners were also sent there. The listing, if only in a very general way, of the events which marked Hitler's policy towards the Poles seems relevant since in the same period (that is, until mid-1940) the repressive and racially discriminating measures carried out against Polish Jews branded them as a racial group (or more accurately a national religious group), but did not suggest that the entire Jewish population might be exterminated. In the face of the mass executions, the introduction of compulsory labour for Jews from the age of fourteen, the necessity to wear armbands bearing the Star of David; the limiting of free movement; the creation of the first ghettos (in Piotrków and Lódź), fiscal pressure and the confiscation of property, did not then appear either to Poles or Jews to be a greater or less bearable hardship. It must be made clear that at this stage the Polish and Jewish communities were equally, though erroneously, confident that the war with Germany would soon be over and that victory would go to the allies.

Similarly, the situation east of the demarcation line, as set down in the August and September agreements of 1939 between the Germans and the Soviets, gave no warning of the impending threat of extermination of Jewish nationals. The mass deportations of people into the depths of the USSR affected the Poles most of all, although repressions did occur against pre-war Jewish social and political activists who had worked in Zionist organizations as well as in the Bund. This period of the occupation is not well researched or chronicled in the annals of history. There is also a lack of accurate sociological records and statistics concerning individual national groups who became part of the administration and machinery of oppression set up by the new Soviet authority in the delineated territories. It is maintained in various tales and reminiscences that collaboration with Soviet authorities on the part of the Jewish proletariat against the Poles was widespread, but such stories should be treated with great caution. It certainly seems to be true, however, in the opinion of Poles living in the eastern provinces of pre-war Poland, that the fall of Poland and the tragedies which accompanied the occupation were less keenly felt by the Jewish population than they were by their Polish neighbours. Naturally such circumstances can be explained in various ways: for example, there was a section of Jews domiciled in that particular region who, although they were Polish citizens, had Russian or Jewish orthodox cultural roots. There was also a sense of relief that the rule of Nazi Germany had not spread to these areas. But above all there was perhaps a greater sympathy with communist ideology and the USSR than there had been with Poland and its pre-war political system. One also cannot discount the fact that over the ensuing months attitudes in this part of Poland developed quickly under Soviet rule. Facts, however, are always facts, and according to a great number of Poles the national minorities in eight of the provinces of eastern Poland were engaged in anti-Polish and pro-Soviet activities.

With Hitler's invasion of the USSR in June 1941 and the relatively fast progress of the Nazi offensive, all the territories of pre-war Poland were soon under German rule. This included among other sections of the population, the Jews who were Polish citizens, or at least those who still remained because they had not yet been deported or had not succeeded in fleeing to the USSR at the last minute. Only small areas, the pre-war provinces of Lwów, Stanisławów and Tarnopol came within the orbit of the Government General. Other Polish provinces were now administered by a new creation: the Reichskomisariat of Ukraine and Ostland. As is well known, it was on these newly conquered territories that the systematic extermination of the Jewish population began even before the proposals for the 'final solution' were passed at the Wannsee conference a few months later. Despite the difficulties of communication, news from the eastern territories did reach central Poland, and it was reported in the Polish and the Jewish underground press, the latter being distributed in the Warsaw ghetto. Only a few weeks later, at the beginning of December 1941, the first extermination camp on Polish soil was set in motion by the Germans, situated in Chełmno beside the Ner. News of this appeared in the Polish underground press within a matter of weeks and it also reached Jewish social and political activists in the Warsaw ghetto at least; it is a fact, too, that no practical conclusions were drawn as a result. Marek Edelman described the situation in 1945:

The Warsaw ghetto did not believe the news, all those who clung to life could not believe that life could be taken from them in this way, only organized youth movements which were carefully monitoring the rise of German terror accepted these events as probable and real and decided to embark on a large scale propaganda campaign which would inform the community.

It certainly was no accident that even before the mass exterminations began in central Poland orders had been issued forbidding Jews, under threat of death, to leave their designated areas; anyone found deliberately or indirectly helping fugitives from the ghettos would also suffer the death penalty and it was further stated that an attempt to help would be 'punished in the same way as an accomplished deed'. In the wake of this order of Hans Frank, individual district chiefs and even those in the lower echelons of the Nazi administration published a series of warnings and prohibitions regarding the ever-increasing number of cases of Poles harbouring and helping Jews who had escaped from the ghettos. Fischer, the Governor-General of Warsaw and its outlying areas, who was formally and actively in charge of the largest Jewish community in Poland, the Warsaw ghetto, made it known in his proclamation of 10 November 1941 that the death penalty would be meted out to all who 'provide refuge or any other kind of help' to Jews in hiding. Anyone who informed the German police about Jews living outside the ghetto and anyone informing on those actively helping such Jews was rewarded commensurately. This certainly created an incentive to the criminal class but obviously did not produce the desired results, since it was not long before various warnings and directives from the Germans began to reappear, demonstrating that in spite of everything the Polish population was still helping those who were being persecuted. Thus, for example, the piece in the *Lwów Journal*, an organ of the Nazis printed in the Polish language in Galicia:

Unfortunately the fact remains that the inhabitants of the rural areas secretly persist in helping Jews, this disloyal attitude harms the community as a whole and thus people involved in such action. Through various illegal routes, the rural community by using all the cunning at its disposal, evades express orders, delivering foodstuffs to the local Jewish population . . . Country people must, once and for all, sever all contacts with and disassociate themselves from all Jewry, they must break the seriously anti-social habit of aiding the Jews.

The year 1942 brought the destruction, staggered over various months, of the ghettos which currently existed in the Government General, large numbers of their inhabitants being sent to extermination camps in Bełżec, Sobibór and Treblinka and later to Auschwitz. This was the realization of the general plan of extermination passed and accepted in Berlin in 1942.

It is not my aim to give a detailed account of the way in which the extermination of Jews progressed in various parts of Poland throughout 1942. The basic facts were already apparent on 10 December 1942 in a note written by the Minister of Foreign Affairs of the Polish Government in London, Edward Raczyński, to the Allied Governments. What is relevant to the topic in hand, however, is to establish the degree, if any, to which the tragic deterioration in the situation of Jews in Poland, now threatened with mass extermination, influenced the attitude of the Polish community towards the victims. It is also relevant to establish the degree, if any, to which the Jews were helped either individually or collectively, what form that help took and how successful it was; what possibility there was of mutual contact and how it worked in practice; whether the problems involved in this kind of contact existed in the corporate consciousness of the Polish and Jewish communities; and if they did exist, how they were overcome.

In the first months of setting up enclosed residential areas on Polish territory which would be allocated only to Jews, opinion regarding the future of the ghettos was divided. In principle, however, there was a general belief within the Jewish community that this form of isolation would not make it impossible to survive the war, even though it was coupled with oppression and exploitation. There was also the theory that survival might be possible if people paid the price of passively adapting themselves to their circumstances. It was well known throughout Poland that conditions in the poverty-stricken, disease-ridden ghettos gradually killed the physically weak and the poor, and these factors were discussed in the reports that were sent out to the Polish Government exiled in London and by the Polish underground press, which had a wide circulation. Even before the famous letter of 11 May 1942, written by the Polish Bund to the Polish Government in London, the regular waves of terror intended as preventive measures and practised against the Poles throughout the country between 1941 and 1942, and the particularly intense campaign of terror raging in Warsaw (since here the concentration of Poles was more numerous than in any other single area), meant that people had grown accustomed to the dramatic hardships that had become a part of everyday life. Regular arrests, overflowing Gestapo prisons, the constant transportation of prisoners to various concentration camps, resulting in the Poles constituting the largest single group in each of the Nazi camps – all this took the focus of people's attention away from what was happening behind the walls of the ghettos.

There exists no real research as to the level of awareness, if indeed there was any at all, within the closed ghetto communities, of the real intensity of German terror against the Poles, and especially of the carefully planned campaign to exterminate the Polish intelligentsia. In 1942 the majority of the Polish population in the urban areas of central Poland lived in conditions of abject poverty, and although one cannot compare the subsistence levels and standard of living of the people in the ghettos with that of the people living outside, nevertheless we cannot totally disregard the fact that the Polish population was totally absorbed in the day-to-day battle for the most basic means of survival.

In such circumstances how can one define Polish–Jewish relations in German-occupied Poland?

The mutual threat posed by the Germans during their military operations and the anti-German feelings of the majority of the Jewish population helped to bring the two groups closer together in some areas as early as the beginning of the military campaign. One positive experience of this was the unequivocal solidarity shown by a great number of Jews in Warsaw during the city's siege. Various orders issued by the Nazis and the initial excesses committed against the Jews meant that during the very first weeks of the occupation the groups of Poles who had been ill-disposed and hostile towards the Jews began to review their attitudes and even to show sympathy. This has been well chronicled by the Jews, the Poles and by the Germans.

With the creation of the ghettos (and this *was* the intention of the occupying forces) a strong sense of grievance, a feeling of being unjustly treated, came to both Jews and Poles alike, for they had been rehoused by force. It must be remembered that within the huge Warsaw community alone 138,000 Jews were forced into the ghetto from various districts around the city, whilst 113,000 Poles were forced to leave the area assigned to them to live in so-called 'Aryan' districts. Consequently a huge number of people who fell victim to these compulsory measures felt discontented and wronged. This enforced change of domicile, like all mass activity, was undoubtedly accompanied by various abuses, including the exploitation of people's misfortunes, but generally speaking both sides were aware that they had become objects to be manipulated by the policies of the invaders.

Real contact of a private nature between the Poles and the Jews existed in Poland on a large scale among the culturally integrated Jewish intelligentsia and to some extent among the richer urban dwellers, as well as among a small number of intellectuals and those involved in industry and finance. The usual situation, however, was that people simply lived side by side, certainly there was an absence of mutual contact, and particularly contact of a personal nature. The exceptions prove the rule. Among the people whom the Nazis regarded as Jews (regardless of their actual cultural or even religious status) there were those who managed to escape the ghettos created in 1940–41, but more often than not these were the people who already had personal ties with the Polish community. Amongst the fugitives from the ghettos, especially during the early days of slum creation, there was a preponderance of people who had friends in the Polish community.

Since Nazi terror reigned throughout the Aryan districts, the chances of remaining successfully hidden undoubtedly depended on a fluent knowledge of the language and on having close ties with the community. In practice, therefore, such chances did not exist for people who had, for long years, been practising very different customs in their behaviour, their dress, their manner; people who not only did not know the language or the environment but who were also deprived, by their own community, of the opportunity to adapt. In the circumstances that prevailed in Poland at that time, this affected if not the majority, then certainly a large percentage of Jews. Wanda Grosman-Jedlicka, for example, recollects:

We belong, it seems, to a small group of people of Jewish origin who did not allow themselves to be confined to a ghetto. Together with my husband, at the end of the summer of 1940, we took the decision to change our name and embark on an illegal existence, the very moment that the German authorities in Warsaw announced that the time had come for the Jews to be forcibly resettled to specially assigned districts. I did not know then that we would have to stay in hiding for four years: when I was told that the chances of survival within the ghetto walls was greater than outside, I replied that the Germans had not built the walls merely to pull them down at a later date and courteously set all the inhabitants free.

My decision turned out to have been the right one. My husband, it's true, did not survive the war – but that was not because of our particular situation – he, together with thousands of inhabitants from the Bielany district, was transported in the second week of the uprising and died in a prison camp. I survived with my two sons, staying in Warsaw or its environs. Moreover since I was now installed on the Aryan side I could help in the rescue of my more distant relatives and particularly their children, during the ghastly month of July and after.

We belonged to a family who had been polonized many generations ago, we were thus fully assimilated and we were Christians. All this greatly helped our chances of survival (there were no glaring external differences, nothing to distinguish us either culturally or in matters of religion).

And now it must be stated that survival would have been absolutely impossible were it not for the generous disinterested help which often defied all limits of self-sacrifice and bravery on the part of many people, friends and strangers alike. Most often it was given by those who had no moral duty, on a personal level, toward me and my family.

One of the people who helped, Regina Zakrewska, writes: 'My whole family, being members of the progressive Polish intelligentsia, were friendly before the war with the Jewish intelligentsia which was more or less polonized. It is not surprising, therefore, that during the tragic period of the occupation we remained loyal to our friends, all of whom probably survived the war and the occupation because of that.'

The decision not to go into the ghetto had, in each individual case, a series of economic as well as professional and family consequences. We must also remember that the idea of solidarity and the nature of one's contact with the community were interpreted in various ways. For example, one characteristic problem was that of mixed marriages between Jews and Poles. On this subject, Emmanuel Ringelblum writes (in *Polish—Jewish Relations During the Second World War*):

The Germans' anti-Jewish regulations were not successful in disturbing stable Polish–Jewish unions. 'Aryan' families made every effort to protect their Jewish members by securing suitable 'Aryan' papers for them or simply by hiding them or moving them to other districts and cities so as to wipe out any trace of them. It was almost axiomatic that if a Jew had Polish relatives in his family he could count on their help, even when the entire familiy was anti-semitic.

Apart from the personal ties already mentioned, material interests also created certain bonds that led to contact being maintained between the independent groups. Besides the extreme cases of abuse which took place everywhere, the ties between businessmen and industrialists often had a positive part to play. They were a contributory factor in the traffic, which the Germans declared to be illegal, of foodstuffs and other goods in which both sides were involved.

The commencement of the extermination programme against the Jews filled most of the population not only with horror but also with fear that a similar fate might be awaiting them. The criminal ruthlessness of the Germans towards the Jews, regardless of sex or age, was accompanied by the very same ruthlessness towards the Poles who helped them, no matter for what reasons. Research on this subject is still incomplete and it is doubtful whether it could ever be completed, but we can certainly say that many hundreds of Polish families died as a result of helping the Jews. Individual victims, therefore, can doubtlessly be counted in thousands, not hundreds. This was bound to influence people's readiness to take risks. In continuing to analyse, in any given context, the issues of help and co-operation within the concrete circumstances described here, we could pose the question (to which there probably is no answer): would any other community as a whole and in analogous circumstances be willing to go further in a wholesale sacrifice to save others?

Obviously the motives for helping Jews were varied. Besides family links, the ties of friendship or professional bonds, a recurrent motive which appears in many eye-witness accounts, was simple human empathy. Christian motives amongst religious people for whom the concept of neighbourly love had a deep meaning must also be taken into account, as must the feeling of solidarity with victims who had been hit even harder than the Poles themselves by the criminal activities of the invaders. Another fairly common motive for helping and hiding Jews was avarice. There is no reason to keep silent about this particular phenonemon. If we discount the cases of exploitation and abuse which took place, usually, only in extreme situations, then we have to accept that paid help was often long-lasting and successful, since in the last analysis it contributed to the saving of many lives. The poor material conditions of the Polish population, and particularly the urban population in wartime, bring into question the very possibility of giving systematic aid without having the necessary material means.

In this context the material help which the Polish Government in London allocated from its budget and the sums sent, through its mediation, by Jewish organizations in the USA made a very real difference, and in fact from mid-1942 this became a critical factor. Individual organizations, whether they were political or social – that is, socialist, liberal or Catholic – gave aid within their own sphere of activity and to the best of their ability to small groups of people mainly in the big city areas such as Warsaw, Cracow and Lwów.

In 1942 circumstances changed radically; the number of fugitives from the ghettos rose as a result of deportations and the Jewish underground movement now became more structured – all this contributed to developing and extending an institutionalized form of aid. During the summer and autumn of 1942 the groups the activities of which preceded the creation of the Council for Aid to Jews (code-named 'Żegota') were of the conviction that their paramount aim must be the saving of the greatest possible number of lives currently under threat, with particular regard to children, whilst ensuring that as far as possible these people would survive the war; secondly, they aimed to systematically and simultaneously inform and warn the governments and communities in the so-called 'Free World', the allies, about the extensive extermination of the Jews.

However, in line with the general policies of the Polish underground movement, which did not envisage mass armed and open combat, it was believed that, until a realistic possibility presented itself of such a conflict being successful (perhaps in the last stages of the war) most of the money should be used to aid the Jews in keeping themselves alive rather than in arming themselves. Those among the widespread Jewish and Polish communities who thought realistically, believed in a pragmatic assessment of the possibilities, especially since the extent of the aid was inadequate anyway. The fact that it could never be adequate and that there was no real possibility of saving even a couple of hundred thousand people, not to mention millions, from a tragic fate did not, of course, bring any comfort whatsoever to the victims, nor should it soothe the consciences of passive eye-witnesses. After all, from a moral viewpoint, the first dictate of many creeds and philosophies is to sacrifice one's own life for that of a neighbour. In reality this ideal is very seldom practiced.

In analysing the extent of the aid given to Jews, a tendency among many scholars is to look only at the final results. Psychologically this may be understandable. However, anyone who has researched the problems inherent in trying to save the Jews in Poland during the period of their extermination, especially if they took part in any way, knows that a great deal of energy and effort was spent in aiding those who were in hiding on the Aryan side, or in extricating from the ghettos and camps people who finally, in spite of everything, could only be saved for a short period. And this, surely, is the reason for the great discrepancy when we come to assess in numbers the extent of the aid given (the problem is the number of people being saved set against the number who were actually saved).

Although to experts this will appear a truism, we must remember the conditions and the extent of the impending menace which existed in German-occupied Poland, just as it existed in the areas east of the Bug and San between 1942 and 1944. In no other occupied European country, nor in Germany itself, were there such large-scale round-ups, searches and blockades of whole districts in all the larger cities, in an effort to find Jewish fugitives. There were many reasons why the Nazis had grown particularly suspicious: the mass participation of the younger and middle generation of Poles in secret organizations alone worried them. The scope for activity was therefore very limited. By the second half of the war some hundred thousand Poles were either in prison or in concentration camps. When we include their families, who were also affected, we are speaking of roughly two million people living in particularly difficult circumstances. Neither the generally accepted policy of passive resistance in occupied Poland nor the force of armed resistance – which on a European scale was unique and perhaps only comparable to Yugoslavia – alter the fact that even the Home Army, then the largest and most effective organization of Polish activists, was not after all a regular army fighting in regularized circumstances. There was no undertaking, nor any possibility of a serious or effective undertaking, to free one's own colleagues and leaders if they had been arrested by the Gestapo and were now either in prison or in concentration camps. (Sporadic attempts of this kind had minimal success and brought dispro-portionately large losses in their wake.) And no one felt any surprise although, for many, it was a painful process.

Historians who study the opposition movement, as well as some diarists, had and still have a tendency to idealize and monumentalize the part they played, while underestimating the efficiency and perfidy of the methods used by the huge, highly-specialized intelligence and police machinery of the Nazis. With the help of a network which included informers of various nationalities, individual and mass arrests could be systematically prepared and carried out many times throughout each year of the occupation. People as well-protected as the Home Army's high command and leading activists fell victim to the informers, as did the leaders of various political parties. The commander-in-chief of the Home Army, Stefan Rowecki, and the Delegate of the Government in Exile, Jan Piekałkiewicz, fell into the hands of the Gestapo in this way, to mention the most spectacular examples.

The fight against these informers was well organized, with the death sentence being meted out on a scale unknown in the occupied countries of Western Europe, but still it was impossible to stamp out this phenomenon completely, for nowhere has it ever been possible completely to ward off even the worst forms of criminal behaviour when it is commonplace. Jewish fugitives also fell victim to the informers, as did the people who aided them.

There were relatively frequent instances of blackmail and extortion for material gain, often involving the most helpless victims. It was difficult to fight this type of criminality but nevertheless the fight was waged. There are no well-researched statistics at our disposal showing the exact number of Jews and gentiles who throughout Poland and in over five years of occupation fell victim to the informers and paid with their lives, or at least with their freedom and health. It must be stated, however, that the situation was generally accepted as a grave and sensitive one, hence the ruthless attitude of the Polish secret organizations and the organized militant groups within the ghettos towards the informer. Emanuel Ringelblum when stating that, 'the life of a Pole harbouring a Jew is not an easy one', was motivated, among other things by the 'extreme terror' which reigned in Poland. He wrote:

The best elements in our society, the most high-minded and self-sacrificing are being deported in droves to concentration camps or to prisons. Spying and denunciation blossoms in Poland and we can largely thank the mass of authentic and phoney Volksdeutsche for this. There are arrests and raids at every turn. On the trains there are continual searches for arms and smuggled goods, it is no different on the city streets.

Moreover, Ringelblum also notes that 'the people are poisoned daily with the venom of anti-semitism in the press, the radio etc.'

This statement by an esteemed historian and social activist, working with the Jewish underground movement in Warsaw, is undoubtedly just in its assessment of the aims and intentions of the Nazi propaganda machine in occupied Poland. It must, however, give rise to serious doubts once the real social effects of Nazi propaganda are analysed. The Poles did not have any radio sets and only a small percentage of the population listened to the official Nazi news bulletins which were transmitted by loudspeakers in the streets. The German-controlled Polish language press was regarded with the greatest distrust and one should not overestimate its power to shape attitudes. Anti-Jewish articles urging people to adopt an attitude of indifference towards the Jews had a far greater influence; these *were* read, having been published in the clandestine press by extreme Polish right-wing groups. Particular reference is made here to a couple of periodicals produced by two factions of the prewar Radical Nationalist Group (Obóz Narodowo-Radykalny, ONR), known as the 'Szaniec' Group, and the National Armed Force (Narodowe Siły Zbrojne); there was also the National Confederation (Konfederacja Narodu) which was led by Bolesław Piasecki and to a lesser degree the publications brought out by the Nationalist Party (Stronnictwo Narodowe). A small group, calling itself 'The Sword and the Plough' (Miecz i Pług) also played a highly suspect role. It must be said, however, that the leading press controlled by the main Polish political parties, and above all the papers published by the Home Army and by the Delegate Office of the Government-in-exile, informed their readers about the situation of the Jews in Poland in a tone befitting the tragic circumstances and in a spirit of solidarity with the victims, giving an unequivocal assessment of the crimes which were being perpetrated. It is undisputed that the press of the Home Army and of the Delegate Office of the Government-in-exile commanded the highest respect and trust among that section of the population which actually read underground journals and papers.

In Western writings, and hence in the public opinion of many countries, the general view seems to be that the extermination of the Jews by the Germans on Polish soil was carried out in an atmosphere of hostility on the part of the Poles towards the victims. This view, is expressed, among others, by writers who are not directly involved in the study of the problems which existed during the Holocaust and who did not witness the events but who base their arguments on analyses of the anti-semitic tendencies in Poland before 1939 (for example, the world-famous sociologist, Professor Alexander Hertz).

I believe that as far as the period of occupation is concerned these views are unjust. In the conditions which prevailed in occupied Poland and which have been described here, the stand taken by the majority of the population towards those who were being persecuted was more humane than one might have expected, taking into consideration, for example, the contents of prewar and anti-semitic publications, or people's recollections of anti-semitic demonstrations in Polish colleges of further education during the thirties, or the boycotts staged of Jewish citizens in some professional circles, or even the misunderstandings that occurred prior to 1939 regarding the competitiveness that existed in financial areas. On the whole, one can say that the attitudes adopted by the Polish intelligentsia and by the Catholic Church, which was such an infuential element in Polish life, were quite principled and indeed sometimes highly principled. One observation that comes to mind here is that a great many Poles wanted to help the Jews, having first conquered an understandable fear, but they could not achieve the proportionately desired effects and thus felt helpless. One can also accept that fear led people to isolate themselves from events and consequently they became passive. One can finally ask the question whether it would have been possible to achieve more and save more lives in the attempt to rescue the Jews in Poland whilst progressive extermination was being carried out. Theoretically undoubtedly, it was as if, in those particular circumstances, the ways and means had existed of successfully hiding not thousands but hundreds of thousands of people over a period of two or three years, but no expert specializing in the affairs of occupied Poland could ever suggest or prove the existence of such a possibility.

The moral issue still remains. From a moral point of view it must be stated clearly that not enough was done either in Poland or anywhere else in occupied Europe. 'Enough' was done only by those who died whilst giving aid.

14

The Relief Council for Jews in Poland, 1942–1945

Teresa Prekerowa

The Relief Council for Jews (Rada Pomocy Żydom, RPŻ) was neither the first nor the only Polish underground organization which extended its aid to Jews in hiding outside the ghetto, on the so-called 'Aryan side'. More elementary forms of aid, based on personal acquaintances came before. It has been the rule that in periods of historic cataclysms people's conduct, particularly that of whole groups resisting violence, frequently imitates traditional patterns, verified by the past experience. Some time has to pass before new organizational forms that take account of the current and specific circumstances start to emerge. This is true of Poland, where underground charity work in 1940 and even in 1941 was organized along the lines reminiscent of the first decades of the twentieth century. This meant that political, trade union and professional organizations took their members, both Jews and Poles, with their families, under care. The political parties maintaining links with the Polish Government-in-exile in London and its Delegatura for the homeland that ranked among the most active in the relief work were: the Polish Socialist Party 'Freedom–Equality–Independence' (Polska Partia Socjalistyczna 'Wolność–Równość–Niepodległość', PPS-WRN); the Democratic Party (Stronnictwo Demokratyczne, SD); the Union of Polish Syndicalists (Związek Syndykalistów Polskich) and the social Catholic organization, the 'Front for Polish Re-Birth' (Front Odrod zenia Polski, FOP). Various communist groups were also active in organizing help, and they combined efforts after their unification in January 1942 into the Polish Workers' Party, whose numerous members could be found both inside the ghettos and among Jews in hiding. Guidelines of the Department for Work and Social Security of the Delegatura issued in 1941 stipulated that help for Jews should be organized by the organs of the 'Underground State'.[1] But subsequently these rules had to be abandoned since the system of financial inspection adopted by the department was inconsistent with the situation of the people in hiding.

It is obvious that no underground relief action, no matter how generous and substantial, could meet even the most essential needs of the people exposed to the extermination policy of the invader. For Jews in particular, the gap between their needs and the relief available opened wider from month to month, reaching truly dramatic dimensions in the summer of 1942. For that reason more and more people from underground circles came to the conclusion that the amount of aid had to be increased considerably and the forms it took expanded and differentiated. Growing pressure was exercised on the Delegatura to secure adequate organizational and financial means for that purpose; no other major source of finance was available for the relief action since all Polish public institutions were banned by the Nazis and the Polish population were becoming rapidly impoverished.

The Delegatura responded to the public demand by setting up the Aid Committee for Jews on 27 September 1942. It was headed jointly by a famous Catholic novelist, the President of FOP, Zofia Kossak-Szczucka, and by Wanda Krahelska-Filipowiczowa, linked to the Democratic Party. Other leading personalities who had already been engaged in a relief action for the Jews were also recruited from those two circles. A certain expansion of their activities was possible when the Delegatura made some extra funds, although modest in the beginning, available to the Committee, and in Autumn 1942, help was extended to 180 persons.[2] Funding of the committee was only the first step. While its day-to-day activities were gathering momentum, endeavours were made to restructure the relief work in such a way as to gain a broader social backing. Two large, clandestine Polish parties, the WRN and the Peasant Party (Stronnictwo Ludowe, SL), as well as the Jewish parties, the Bund and the Jewish National Committee (Żydowski Komitet Narodowy, ZKN) joined the relief action.

The Aid Committee to Jews was eventually disbanded on 4 December 1942 and the Council for Aid to Jews (RPŻ, cryptonym 'Zegota') was founded on the same day. Its presidium consisted of the representatives of the co-operating parties, Julian Grobelny of the WRN (the president[3]), Tadeusz Rek of the SL and Leon Feiner of the Bund (the two vice-presidents) Adolf Berman of the ŻKN (the Secretary) and 'Ferdinand' Marck Arczynski of the SD (the treasurer). Other members of the presidium were Emilia Hizowa of the SD and Władysław Bartoszewski of the FOP. The secretary's office was run by Zofia Rudnicka of the SD, her support (and simultaneously the main liaison officer of the council on the lines Warsaw–Cracow and Warsaw–Lwów) being Janina Raabe-Wąsowiczowa of the SD. Witold Bieńkowski of the FOP, President of the Jewish Affairs

Division in the Delegatura, was delegated by the underground authorities to the council.

This organizational pattern was to be followed by the local branches of the council in some bigger towns, where they were to be linked to the respective district offices of the Delegatura. Implementation of that project encountered enormous problems; for example, in Łódź the embryo local branch of the council was destroyed by arrests, incidentally for reasons other than the relief action for Jews. Eventually, local branches of the Council were set up only in Cracow in April 1943 and in Lwów, presumably in May 1943.

In Cracow, Stanisław Wincenty Dobrowolski of the WRN became the President of the Council, Władysław Wójcik of the WRN its secretary, Anna Dobrowolska of the SD its treasurer and Maria Hochberg-Mariańska (after the war Miriam Peleg, resident in Israel) represented the Jewish community on the council. Other members of the presidium were Jerzy Matus of the SL and Janusz Strzalecki of the SD. The underground government authorities were represented by Tadeusz Seweryn, the Commander-in-Chief of the Civilian Struggle in the Cracow district.

The Lwów Council was set up in particularly difficult circumstances. The course of the wartime events was that from September 1939 up till June 1941 Lwów was under Soviet rule, then subject to the rigours of the Nazi occupation. Consequently social stuctures in existence prior to 1939, both Polish and Jewish, disintegrated more completely than elsewhere and fewer members of the politically active intelligentsia remained. Moreover, any clandestine Polish action was rendered even more difficult and dangerous by the threat from the local Ukrainian nationalists. From the few documents preserved concerning the region in that period it is impossible to reconstruct the organization of the Lwów Council, its fate and activities. What is known is that the council's president was Laryssa Chomsowa of the SD and that the treasurer was Przemysław Ogrodziński of the WRN, both of them closely co-operating with the district Government Delegate Adam Ostrowski as far as the relief action for Jews was concerned. It is uncertain, however, if other co-workers of the Council, whose names appear in the documents, were also its members, or if they co-operated with it on an irregular basis.

The RPŻ's aim consisted in extending help to the Jews in hiding on the 'Aryan side', irrespective of their social status or political membership, and its action was guided only by the existing needs and possibilities of relief. A precondition of this activity was getting subsidies granted by the Delegatura. Initially the amounts granted were not large, ranging from 150,000 to 300,000 zlotys a month, so the council made determined and systematic efforts to raise funds. In its numerous memoranda and at the audiences with the Government Delegate the enormous needs of the fugitives from the ghetto were presented – they were homeless, stripped of even personal effects and without any means of survival. Their case was presented in letters sent to the Government-in-exile in London, on which the budget of the Delegatura depended. All these efforts proved to be fruitful: the amount of the subsidy was revised several times and amounted to 2,000,000 zlotys a month in the summer of 1944, and the amounts alotted to the Relief Council for Jews by the State Treasury eventually totalled 28,750,000 zlotys. A contribution of 5,300,000 zlotys to the sum at the council's disposal was made by the International Union of Jews in America, the Bund and the ŻKN. All in all, the RPŻ raised and distributed funds amounting to about 34,000,000 zlotys.

Was that amount big or small as compared to the funds at the disposal of other relief organizations? Beside the council, the only organization subsidized regularly by the Delegatura was the Social Organization for Self-defence (Społeczna Organizacja Samoobrony, SOS). Zofia Kossak was responsible for its relief action for the persecuted. It should be remembered that among the people in SOS's charge there were many Jews, particularly children. If we compare grants to these two organizations we can see that a monthly subsidy to the RPŻ was six times that granted to the SOS. However, each of the two underground Jewish organizations (the ŻKN and the Bund) raised and distributed funds comparable to those at the RPŻ's disposal, that is about 30,000,000 zlotys each. These sums were contributed by the international Jewish organizations through the intermediary of the Polish Government-in-exile in London.

Given the Council's revenues, it could afford to pay individual monthly grants of the order of 500 zlotys, and yet, financial problems arose at times, either because of a sudden increase in the number of people under the Council's care, for example during the Ghetto Uprising, or when the Delegatura failed to receive the expected money. It reached the country by way of air drops, but it must be remembered that only 56 per cent of the air missions ended with a full success. If payments to the RPŻ happened to be smaller than usual, or, more often, delayed, the Council temporarily had to cut down its grants to 350–400 zlotys, or even as little as 250–300 zlotys a month. Cases occurred of relief payments being stopped altogether to recipients in a better financial situation, while those in greater need received unchanged amounts. From time to time a person in need of winter clothes, of money for the increased rent or for some other extraordinary purpose was paid a considerably higher amount of 1,000 to 1,500, or even 2,000 zlotys.

The most common rate of 500 zlotys a month, although not high, was in fact sufficient for a modest living. Industrial and communication workers, as well as those employed in the municipal service sector, received even smaller incomes. As a matter of fact, relief payments made by such a 'well-to-do' organization as the Home Army did not exceed the above-quoted figures. If a member happened to be killed or imprisoned as a direct result of his service to the underground organization, the Home Army only granted aid to his family if he had been the sole bread-winner and if, as a consequence, the family was left in an extremely difficult position, without any opportunity to earn its living. The maximum relief amount for an adult could not exceed 900 zlotys, and the amount paid for a child was 240 zlotys. For Warsaw those rates were subsequently revised to 1,100 and 300 zlotys respectively. And yet figures found in the preserved lists of payments of the Home Army never reach even half the amounts of the permissible maximum rate levels.[4] Conversely, individual reliefs paid by the Bund and the ŻKN were higher than those of the RPŻ. Each of the organizations distributed a total amount of a size comparable to that which was at the council's disposal, but over a considerably shorter time.

The RPŻ did not have its own network to distribute money but resorted to the organizational links of the political parties represented on the Council. Nevertheless, it controlled the financial operations of each of its sections with precision. Control was particularly difficult since the rules of clandestine work had to be observed. Clearing of the accounts was based on the acknowledgments signed by the recipients with their original, but currently unused family names, or with their first names only, and it was the handwriting which was the main proof of authenticity of the 'receipts' which were used by persons distributing the money for settling their accounts with the local branch of the Council. Then, after periodical inspections by the Revisory Commission – in Warsaw it consisted of Rek and Feiner, in Cracow of Hochberg-Mariańska and Seweryn – the acknowledgments had to be destroyed for security reasons. But in both local branches of the council some workers preserved the receipts and hid them carefully in order to be able to give at any moment an account of their properly fulfilled duties. Those acknowledgments, brought to the light of day after the war, are valuable archival sources.

To estimate exactly how many people received the financial relief from the council is not a simple task, due to the fragmented character of the records. In the middle of 1944 the number of persons who benefitted from the council's financial relief amounted to 3,000–4,000 (out of this number there were about 600 in Cracow, and at least 120 in Lwów). According to the estimates made by the ŻKN workers, financial aid of the three organizations, the RPŻ, the ŻKN and the Bund, reached about 12,000 people.

Another line of the council's activity apart from the financial relief, was the procuring of forged personal documents for the people in its charge. A Jew or a Pole of Jewish origin while in hiding on the so-called 'Aryan side' had to be equipped with papers and certificates acceptable to the Germans who would control him, so that they remained convinced that he was fully authorized to live in the Polish quarter of the town. In all, he should possess an identity card (the so-called Kennkarte) issued by the German authorities and certifying his Polish nationality; a work certificate (the so-called Arbeitskarte); a residence certificate, a baptism certificate and, if applicable, a marriage certificate, the two latter issued by the Church. Only such a set of documents could transform a former fugitive from the ghetto into an 'Aryan'.

Catholic priests rendered an enormous service to the Jews in hiding by supplying them with authentic baptismal and marriage certificates of the people who, by that time, were dead, or had vanished or were absent from the country (before and during World War II, church parishes in Poland performed functions of Registries). Officers of the municipal administration, for their part, helped to obtain the right certificate of residence. But soon all these possibilities were exhausted and when the number of people in hiding ran into tens of thousands, their needs could be met only by forged documents.

Each local branch of the Relief Council for Jews from the start had to procure such documents for people under its care. The Warsaw Council initially collaborated with some clandestine presses turning out forged documents, which were run by the Home Army, and provided for the military underground. Later on, the council collaborated mainly with two privately owned presses, which after a period became so closely involved in the council's affairs that they could almost pass for its own. One of them operated until Autumn 1943, when its leader was arrested and perished at the hands of the Gestapo, the other was started soon afterwards. Each of them produced several sets of documents daily, and orders from the council were executed within a period of one to three days. The number of sets of documents supplied by both shops totalled about 50,000 according to the estimates made by Arczyński, the council's officer responsible for that line of its activity.

The Cracow branch of the council encountered fewer problems in that area. By coincidence, some of its workers (members of the PPS-WRN, the SD and the SL), were in close contact with the shops working for those organizations. Thanks to that close collaboration, the demands for forged documents of the people under care of the Cracow council could be entirely satisfied. The Lwów branch of the council depended, presumably totally, on the forged documents procured by the Home Army.

The RPZ not only faced all the problems involved in procurement and delivery of the documents to people in its care, but did so free of charge while other organizations were normally charging their customers sums equal to their prime cost. At that time 'black marketeers' demanded from 2,000 to 5,000 zlotys for a forged 'Kennkarte' or a baptismal certificate. It should be remembered that some needs of the people in the ZKN's and the Bund's charge were served by the forged documents procured by the RPZ. 'Legalization' was a large-scale, systematic and uninterrupted procedure, in the absence of which, hiding Jews on the 'Aryan side' would be impossible, and for that reason it is one of the greatest achievements of the council.

Another formidable task facing the council consisted in finding accommodation for people in its charge. All contacts with a Jew carried the death penalty, to say nothing of harbouring him under one's roof. 'A Jew living in the flat of an intellectual or a worker or in the hut of a peasant, is dynamite liable to explode at any moment and blow the whole place up', wrote Emanuel Ringelblum.[5] When the Germans discovered a person of Jewish origin hidden on the premises all its occupants were killed – including children and the aged. People were scared, they shrank from risk. 'Zegota's' workers did not ignore danger and they felt fear, but they were conscious of a moral obligation to hide people hounded and murdered by the invader. They persuaded people to act, endeavouring to lower their mental barriers and putting forward arguments helpful in combatting fear. Everyone on the council was in search of accommodation: members of the presidium, women active as liaison officers, representatives of the collaborating parties. None of the accounts given by the people linked in one way or the other to 'Zegota' fails to make a reference to a persistent hunt for a room, for a corner in a room, for some place to hide.

The council made it a matter of principle that all dealings with owners of premises should be entirely honest, and that Jews must not be introduced as 'Aryans' since it would mean exposing people's lives to risk. If, in case of a give-away the owner of the premises attempted to explain to the Germans that he did not know about the Jewish origin of his lodger, they would certainly not accept it; perhaps under similar conditions all owners of premises would exploit that argument. However, several accounts given by the council's workers testify, that, under unusually stringent conditions, some of them came to break that rule in order to rescue people in their charge.

Even more risk than letting rooms to persons of Jewish origin attended the organization of the so-called 'premises-to-pass-along' and 'hide-outs'. 'Premises-to-pass-along' served the people newly conducted out of the ghetto; some of them could not regain their equilibrium after painful experience of the 'closed quarter' of the town. Fugitives used to pass some days or even weeks in these places, before documents were procured for them, contacts established, permanent accommodation found and so on. Frequently they were offered instruction meant to facilitate their adaptation to life under changed conditions. Premises of that sort were the easiest to disclose; they had no excuse in case of a give-away. Only the very strong, and the very committed people working for the council had the wherewithal to run them.

'Hide-outs' were arranged either inside flats or on larger premises. Some were used in moments of danger only, others were permanently occupied by the illicit lodgers. The security offered by a 'hide-out' depended on the ingenuity of its construction: it had to remain unnoticed even during a search. The person on the Warsaw Council who excelled in designing such 'hide-outs' was the architectural engineer, Emilia Hizowa. One of the biggest structures of the kind was made by the two market-gardeners, Mieczysław Wolski and Władysław Marczak in 84 Grojecka Street, Warsaw. Thirty Jews lived there in hiding, Emanuel Ringelblum with his family among their number, and financial responsibility for their upkeep rested largely with the RPŻ and ŻKN. Unfortunately on 7 March 1944 the 'hide-out' was disclosed: those in hiding and those hiding them were shot.

Finding accommodation meant hiring premises and paying rents and there was a diversity of conditions pertaining in this respect. Some owners of premises put them at the council's disposal for no material reward, doing it for moral reasons, provided their financial situation was good enough. Other owners, irrespective of their lodgers being Jews or non-Jews, demanded rents of an equal amount. A third group demanded higher rents from Jews than from other lodgers. This extra amount was considered to be the cost of the complication in the lives of the owners of the premises arising from the presence of dangerous lodgers. The owners could no longer receive their customers at home or run some kind of semi-legal market production on which a part of the population relied for their living. The extra amount demanded by the owners of the 'hide-outs' was partly an equivalent of the extra attention required, but first and foremost was linked to the risk-bearing. Moderate rent increases did not incapacitate either fugitives or the council; problems notwithstanding, it was easier to get some extra money than to find other suitable accommodation. The RPŻ opposed the transformation of room-hiring into a lucrative trade in which some owners of premises speculated, demanding exorbitant rents and cashing them ruthlessly. The extent of this behaviour is hard to assess, but perhaps it was infrequent since the number of people able to afford such payments was limited.

The council's accommodation needs were great, several times more than the number of people under its care. Blackmail, unfortunate coincidences by which the presence of illicit lodgers was disclosed, or, occasionally, their own imprudence, rendered the immediate change of place unavoidable. It is possible that any Jew who survived the occupation in hiding stayed in more than one place during that period; many had to move a few times, or even as often as a dozen or so. The council's workers played a considerable part in finding new accommodation, always in great demand.

The brutality and ruthlessness of the Nazi occupation regime did not spare the weakest and most vulnerable – the children. In spring 1942, according to the data of the Municipal Administration passed to the underground, 4,000 children were begging for their bread in the streets of Warsaw, half of them Jews. So, 2,000 Jewish children were risking their lives by digging their way under the wall enclosing the ghetto, sneaking through holes to the 'Aryan side' to beg for money for bread, cereals or potatoes and coming back to the ghetto to feed their hungry families. Those who already had nobody to return to used to squat in great numbers in the debris of buildings until they met people who were willing and able to take care of them, or the Germans who raided and killed them systematically.

Before the RPŻ was funded, the relief for Jewish children had been organized in secrecy by a certain number of the workers of the social security departments of the Municipal Boards, by workers of the Central Council for Social Aid (Rada Główna Opiekuńcza, RGO), orphanages and other charitable institutions. Since the lack of funds was the limiting factor of their charity, these people contacted the RPŻ immediately after its funding. Initially the council financially supported their work from its own coffers, but subsequently the council set up its Children's Division, headed from the autumn of 1943 by Irena Sendlerowa. Henceforth it was the main underground organization working for the protection of Jewish children; it also co-ordinated the work of the groups who had previously been active in providing relief and who had no direct or indirect contacts with the RPŻ's members. In Cracow, where no Children's Division was set up, the lot of the Jewish children became of special concern to all members of the council's presidium,

The group in the RPŻ's charge consisted in part of the street children (it was they who should be given priority, insisted Julian Grobelny, the President of the RPŻ) and in part of children carried or led out of the ghetto, usually by members of the Bund and the ŻKN.

There were two possible means of further action, one or the other of which was followed as circumstance permitted. About 50 per cent of the children were placed with Polish families, the so-called foster families, the other half was enrolled in orphanages or similar homes. Foster-families generally took those children whose features were not typically semitic, as they were to pass for the members of the family. Younger children, with no memories of the ghetto, were taken more willingly than older ones, since they were less likely to speak out of turn, in the presence of undesirable listeners, of names and terms or events which only could have happened inside the ghetto, such as travelling by horse-driven tram.

Since the children in foster-families were loved and cared for, they were able to become one of them very quickly. The council did not receive any reports on children being badly treated by their foster-families; quite the reverse, with many foster-parents declaring after a time their intention to make a legal adoption. But that tendency ran counter to the policies of the RPŻ: it had forcefully stressed that its activity was not intended to de-nationalize Jewish children and to re-root them in the Polish environment, but merely to harbour them for the perilous period of the occupation, later returning them to their parents or to the Jewish organizations which might be ready to take care of them.

The families of some fostered children benefited from relief payments, the amount for a child being equal to that for an adult. Others were helped by the council's collaborators who were employed in the legal institutions of social security and who secretly arranged for those children to become eligible for the relief payments of a similar amount. The remaining children benefited only from the money occasionally earmarked for specific purposes, to buy clothes for example; sometimes the aid was given to them in kind, in the form of milk coupons or clothes parcels, and so on. Con-current with this was the council's regular aid to children which involved procuring suitable documents and moving a child immediately from one place to another in case of a give-away or blackmail.

The children for whom foster-families could not be found were placed in orphanages or homes run by convents (the RGO) or those run under the management of the Warsaw or the Cracow Municipal Boards. The council's role ended when the institution concerned took the child in and when finan-cial responsibility for his upkeep was accepted by a higher-rank institution. The children who had the most semitic features tended to be taken in by the convent orphanages, since it was less probable that the presence of the Jewish, that is non-Catholic, children would be expected and spotted there by Germans conducting a search. Behind the convent walls, beyond the reach of blackmailers and informers Jewish children could at least play freely with other children of their age – a vital need to be satisfied.

Jewish parents made the frequent objection that if their children were brought up by the Catholic families, and even more so in homes run by convents, they would not adhere to the faith of their forefathers and would finally become Catholics. But the identification of children with the Catholic community was a security precaution, for they merged with the environment they lived in. At the slightest cause for suspicion the Germans employed a test to check if a child had undergone a religious training – by ordering him to make a sign of the cross or say a prayer.

Statistical data on children under the council's protection, as with other data of this kind, are only tentative. According to Irena Sendlerowa some 2,500 harboured children were registered by the Warsaw branch of the council and a considerable proportion of them were traced after the war.[6] They were returned to their parents or taken to Israel by the Central Committee of Jews in Poland. The lot of children rescued by the Cracow Council was similar. Since no special register was in existence, even most approximate figures are hard to quote.

In the case of a Jew who had semitic features and who consequently could not go out, happened to be ill and in need of medical aid, drastic action took place. People under whose care they remained could not approach an unknown, untested medical doctor, for the obvious reason that not all members of that profession were equally reliable; some of them were even Volksdeutschen. Conversely, a doctor guided by even the most genuine feelings of humanity could construe a request made by a stranger to help a Jew in hiding as in fact a provocation.

The RPŻ facilitated contacts between Jews in hiding and doctors. The grass-root level sections of that organization kept in touch with doctors and nurses who were acquaintances either of the RPŻ's members or of the people in hiding. In Cracow no organization other than this simple one was necessary, but in Warsaw, where the number of people in hiding was much greater, a special health service section was implemented. In autumn 1943 Dr Ludwik Rostkowski, the representative of the clandestine Conciliatory Committee of Medical Doctors (Democrats and Socialists) joined the section and promised his honorary services as well as those of his colleagues.

The system was well organized. Secret post boxes were set up where addresses of the sick persons and the descriptions of their ailments were deposited by the heads of the sections. The RPŻ's liaison worker made a round of these post boxes a few times a week to collect calls and to pass them on to Dr Rostkowski. He then decided what specialized help was necessary in each case and which doctors should be asked to see particular patients. Notes with their addresses were passed to the respective doctors by Dr Rostowski's son, a medical student himself. The work of nurses was organized in a similar manner. Medical examinations and procedures were free of charge and medicines were purchased by the council. This section functioned until the beginning of the Warsaw Insurrection in August 1944. Many dozens of doctors contributed to its work and the number of home visits by a single doctor varied between a few to several dozen per month. It can be concluded from various accounts that the RPZ's effective health service was able to relieve people from the panic and fear of illness, for they knew that if in need they could count on a generous and competent medical aid.

That the Warsaw Council establish contacts with the forced labour camps was demanded by the representatives of the Jewish political parties. Both the Bund and the ŻKN were intensely interested in getting news from the camps and in keeping in touch with their own members there. At the time railway journeys were particularly dangerous to Jews hiding their identity because of frequent inspections on the trains and in the stations. Initially the RPŻ's emissaries' journeyed to the provinces only from time to time, but later they travelled so frequently that in the summer of 1943 the council set up a section for organizing these missions and appointed Stefan Sendlak to be its head. He was the PPS activist in Zamość, from where he had to escape. It was then, while hiding himself in Warsaw, that he set up the Zamość-Lublin Relief Committee for Jews, its activities mainly financed by the RPŻ. The permanent staff of the council's section for organization of the couriers' missions consisted of the writer Tadeusz Sarnecki and his future wife, Ewa. Numerous couriers co-operated with the section (some of them known only by their pseudonyms) travelling to places in every district of the General Government except in its southern part which was encompassed by the Cracow Council activity.

The Council's emissaries aided camp prisoners by bringing them money, drugs, and letters from the political parties and from their own families and friends. The couriers maintained contacts with the forced labour camps at Budzyń (a branch of Majdanek concentration camp), Trawniki, Zamość, Częstochowa, Piotrków, Radom, Pionki and Skarzysko-Kamienna as well as with the ghettos in Łódź, Białystok and Vilna. One of the most outstanding achievements in the couriers' work was getting Emanuel Ringelblum out of the camp at Trawniki and organizing his flight to Warsaw, which was accomplished in autumn 1943, after a series of unsuccessful attempts, by a railwayman – the Home Army officer Teodor Pajewski. Other actions of that kind, both complicated and risky, were not always successful. Moreover, escapes undertaken by the prisoners themselves were substantially supported by the council, which supplied money and forged documents as well as facilitating their safe passage after leaving the camp.

Equally, if not more significant in this respect were the achievements of the Cracow RPŻ. Regular help was extended to the prisoners, consisting mainly of the Cracow Jews, of the nearby Plaszów camp. The liaison was maintained through the employees of the German firms operating in the camp which used the slave work of the prisoners. For example, transport workers managed to smuggle in such products as flour, beans, cereals and other foodstuffs.

Courageous men and women who were the liaison officers of the RPŻ – amongst their number were Józefa Rysińska, Ada Próchnicka, Tadeusz Bilewicz, Mieczyslaw Kurz – reached labour camps at Putków, Szebnie, Skarzysko-Kamienna and other localities. They also helped prisoners who had the courage to attempt an escape from Auschwitz. There were frequent contacts with Lwów, particularly with the labour camp in Janowska Street, from where several prisoners were extricated, Maksymilian Boruchewicz (after the war, Michal Borwicz) being among them. Those couriers' missions were heavily paid for: Ada Próchnicka lost her life, Jósefa Rysińska was submitted to a very severe interrogation and then kept for a long period in the Plaszów camp, and there were other activists from the provinces who lost their lives.[7]

The RPŻ people were aware that neither the council's activists alone, nor a much bigger group including its collaborators, would be able to achieve any meaningful results without broad social support. Therefore efforts were made to create a climate which was favourable to the actions of the relief groups. Members of the presidium in the first instance pressed the underground authorities and the Government-in-exile to appeal to Polish society to help the hounded Jews in every possible way. They also demanded from the underground press of the political parties to which they themselves belonged information to be published on the martyrdom of Jews and their acts of resistance, and to exhort the Polish community to stand by them even at the expense of its own security. These were attempts to offset the opinions of the clandestine nationalistic periodicals which persuaded their public that the lot of the Jewish minority 'is not our affair'. In order to supply editorial boards of the clandestine periodicals with edited materials in the autumn of 1943 the council published three issues of the *Komunikaty Prasowe* (*The Press Service News*) which reported the liquidation of the Jewish camps in the Lublin region and the uprising in the ghetto of Białystok, along with other important events. The underground press failed to react in any significant way to the information published, which perhaps, contributed to the closing down of the title.

Unaided, the council published and distributed three leaflets in May, August and September 1943, their total edition being 25,000. They quoted the pronouncements of the Polish Prime Minister, the Commander-in-Chief General Władysław Sikorski (of May 1943) and one of the Government Delegates for the Homeland, Stanisław Jańkowski (of 30 April 1943) calling on the Poles to give the Jews support and proclaimed punishment for extortionists and informers. Both leaflets were signed by the 'Polish Independence Organizations'. Moreover, in September 1943 the council edited 5,000 copies of a leaflet, written in German, which contained an alleged proclamation of the German resistance movement warning against crimes against Jews. It was circulated among German soldiers and administration officers.

The council also participated in distribution of pamphlets concerning the tragic fate of the Jewish population, edited by the Information and Propaganda Office of the Home Army, as well as those edited by the ŻKN and the Bund, all of which deeply moved the readers both in Poland and abroad.

From its inception the council demanded severe and immediate punishment for extortionists and denunciators whose criminal acts brought about the death of many people in hiding and, frequently, of their protectors as well. Criminals were generally organized in strong gangs and not only did they go unpunished but, on the contrary, they were backed by the police authorities of the invader. But to prove an informer's guilt was extremely difficult, since the underground administration of justice in Poland had very limited opportunities to conduct inquiries. The victims of blackmail could offer very little information; terrified at the time of the blackmailing, subsequently they were often unable to give any description of the blackmailer which would be useful in tracing him down. Since the only punishment at the disposal of underground organizations was a death penalty, its application was avoided in all dubious cases.

Although the council made several independent efforts to collect adequate evidence material, for the most part they failed, and the Command in Charge of Underground Struggle refused to rely on them for its judgement since 'they were of an accusing and not of an evidential nature'.

The council managed to collect the admissible materials only in a single case of the blackmailing of Adolf Berman. Thanks to the experience he got, he was able to act in such a way as to bring about liquidation of the gang, but this was as late as January 1944. Some time earlier, in 1943, on many occasions, the Council exhorted the Delegatura to combat blackmailers with more determination. On 6 April of that year, for lack of other measures, it even suggested some fictitious sentences to be passed against the *schmalcownicy* to intimidate others, but the proposal was rejected by the Delegatura, which did not want to expose the credibility of its statements to doubt, even if that fiction could have brought a temporary relief to the blackmailed.

Notwithstanding the problems which faced the underground administration of justice, 150 Gestapo informers of Polish nationality had been put to death by the end of April 1943. Blackmailing Jews was not explicitly mentioned in substantiation of the death sentences, but carrying them out resulted in a decline in the numbers of Jews blackmailed by the scum of society.

The first death sentence was carried out in Cracow on 17 July 1943 and was announced in the *Biuletyn Informacyjny* (the Information Bulletin) on 2 September; Jan Grabiec, a tailor, was sentenced to death for blackmailing both Poles and Jews. Two weeks later the same source communicated that Borys vel Bogusław Jan Pilnik was shot for blackmailing and for denouncing Jews to the Germans – only Jewish victims on this occasion. Then similar announcements concerning Warsaw, Cracow and other Polish towns started to appear in the press, although still more death sentences than reported were carried out. Although punishments for extortionists did not wipe out the plague of blackmailing, they reduced it so much that it ceased to be of primary importance to the council.

The main lines of the council's activity already described, were accompanied by occasional relief actions intended to be an immediate and flexible response to changes in the position of the Jewish population, the council being ready to take every opportunity to come to its rescue. To give some examples, one may quote the council's financial support to the fighting in the Warsaw ghetto in April 1943, the rudiments of a military training as well as the purchase of the simple technical means of defence (the two latter actions organized individually by some RPŻ members). Other actions involved the conduct of several people, by a secret passage, over the borders to Hungary by the workers of the Cracow Council, who took people from one town to another in search of a safer place to hide, as well as other similar actions.

How big was the group active in all the relief measures listed above? It is impossible to give an answer. The number of activists informed of the council's existence and fully aware of their membership of it was limited to but several dozen at the central branch and to even less at the two local branches combined. The relief money, forged documents and other relief they procured were distributed (as mentioned above) through channels of political and social organizations by their members, convinced that they were executing orders of their respective organizations. Very often, people who did not belong to any political party became engaged in the council's activity, but they neither knew nor wished to know what the sources of aid were. As a matter of fact, all those people were the associates of 'Żegota' who learned about the organization as late as post-1945. As the council's network merged with the networks of other underground organizations, it is impossible to assess, even crudely, the numbers of the council's taskforce.

Similar difficulties occur with an assessment of the number of people in hiding who benefited from the council's protection. Statistics concerning the recipients of financial aid and the numbers of rescued children have already been examined. But it must be remembered that several times more people benefited from other forms of aid as vital as forged documents and accommodation. And yet, it is impossible to quote any definite figures, particularly since not all those people who were under the care of 'Żegota' managed to survive the war. Of those who did, not everyone – for the reasons mentioned above – realized that it was that organization which extended its help to him.

Finally, I should mention that the Polish Government-in-exile in London set up there on 20 April 1944 the Council for Matters concerning the Rescue of the Jewish Population in Poland (Rada do Spraw Ratowania Ludności Żydowskiej w Polsce), which was an organizational counterpart of the home-based RPŻ, and which began to operate on 25 May that year. Adam Ciołkosz of the PPS was its president, Emanuel Scherer of the Bund its secretary, and its members were Rabbi A. Babad, the representative of the Agudat Israel, Anzelm Reiss, a member of the presidium of the Representation of Polish Jewry with its seat in Palestine (Reprezentacja Żydostwa Polskiego z siedziba w Palestynie), Witold Kulerski and Stanisław Sopicki. The Polish Government-in-exile set the budget of the council at £100,000 sterling annually. Out of that sum the council instantly earmarked £80,000 sterling to the RPŻ in Poland, but the outbreak of the Warsaw uprising made the transfer impracticable. The help extended by the council in London reached Bergen-Belsen and attempts were made to establish contact with other camps as well as co-operation to that end with the Jewish organizations in the Allied Nations' countries; but soon afterwards the final events of the war put an end to that tardy initiative.

Representatives of both Polish and Jewish organizations were members of all the Council for Aid to Jews branches, set up either by the Government-in-exile or by the Delegatura. Each of the two national groupings was far from being ideologically and politically uniform, but that did not preclude harmonious co-operation and mutual trust within the council. The work of the Warsaw and Cracow councils was carried out in the course of two years both in great harmony and a sound moral climate, in spite of the permanently imminent danger. The courage, energy and ingenuity of the workers permitted them to make the most of the means they commanded for the benefit of people in their charge.

In no other country of Europe under the Nazi occupation was a similar council created to attempt to rescue the Jewish population, within which such a wide spectrum of socio-political convictions would be represented, which would be attached to the central underground authorities, whose activities would be financed by the state budget and which would manage to continue for so long.

15

Polish and Jewish historiography on the question of Polish–Jewish relations during World War II

Yisrael Gutman

For many years now, there has been a sharp debate between Jews and Poles about the character and quality of Polish–Jewish relations during World War II. One has the impression that this polemic is growing increasingly acerbic, and that the views and charges raised by the opposing sides resemble parallel lines in that they hold no hope of ever converging and enabling thereby a genuine dialogue of encounter. This apparently insoluble divergence is, it would seem, the reason for the intensity of the controversy, which has reached the point of mutual reprobation. In the view of some Jews – especially Jews of Polish origin – the Poles are incorrigible anti-semites, while there are Poles who claim that the Jewish complaint against them is totally unfounded and is a malicious assault on the good name of the Polish nation.

This conspicuous confrontation might be interpreted by the generous spirit of as a means of emotional release for people who have endured years of suffering, violence and humiliation. But no excuse can be made for historians and public figures, from whom we are entitled to expect a measure of dignified restraint and the ability to scrutinize events and complex problems in the spirit of scholarly detachment, for behaving in this manner.

Regrettably, many books and publications dealing with the overall issue of Polish–Jewish relations or its specific aspects are marked by fixed *a priori* conceptions or have actually been written in the service of one or the other schools of thought in the public debate. Consequently, a Jewish historian who, on the basis of meticulous research, dared to be critical of certain Polish political circles and institutions was immediately labelled anti-Polish, and more or less the same situation pertains in respect of

Polish historians who offend the sensibilities (and what is often the hyper-sensitivity) of the Jews.

Under such conditions, it is obviously impossible to create an atmosphere congenial to objective and thoroughgoing research. By way of contrast, Robert Paxton and Stanley Hoffman, American writers who were critical of Vichy France and broad segments of the French population during the war, are not regarded as distinctively anti-French but as scholars who produced an illuminating analysis of this dark chapter in history. Similarly, Fritz Fischer and his disciples are not considered anti-German because they shed light on the highly controversial subject of German proclivities and intentions before World War I.

As a rule we are inclined to give a fair hearing only to arguments that are congruent with our tastes and outlook, and we tend to credit a line of reasoning that is favourable to our views. What is more, it is quite natural that Jews and Poles, peoples who have experienced generations of collective suffering, should manifest a strong sense of patriotism – which in this case finds expression as a vigorously defensive response to any hint of censure. Nevertheless, the need to face the truth – an act that calls for civil courage and objectivity – is, in the final analysis, both the test of true devotion and lasting values and the moral responsibility of the historian.

One example may be cited to illustrate the issue under consideration. In 1983 a Polish translation of a volume of writings by the Polish-Jewish historian Emmanuel Ringelblum appeared in Warsaw. The title of the volume is *The Chronicle of the Warsaw Ghetto*,[1] and the author's notes on the ghetto period, as well as the essays written during the final period of his life, indeed proved Ringelblum to be more a chronicler than a historian. The Polish version includes all the works Ringelblum wrote during the war and is almost identical in content to the original Yiddish edition, published in 1961 and 1963,[2] with one glaring exception: the section on Polish–Jewish relations during World War II.[3] Why all the notes and articles about the ghetto's inhabitants and ghetto life were sanctioned as suitable for the Polish reader but the material directly relating to the Poles was excised is a highly intriguing question. The answer is not provided in the book's introduction, and we can only assume that a definitive decision was made to suppress the full truth about this subject.

The purpose of this paper is to draw attention to a few critical aspects of Polish–Jewish relations during the war and briefly to examine the points of view adopted by historians regarding each point, as well as the selective documentation and evidence cited to support their assumptions.

The point of departure for any comprehensive study of this subject must be the elucidation of a basic question: did the collapse of the independent Polish state, the occupation of the country by Poland's traditional enemy, and the brutal oppression suffered under the Nazis change the attitude of the Poles toward the Jewish minority in their midst? And if such a change did occur, how can it be characterized and how did it affect mutual relations in everyday life?

Professor Władysław Bartoszewski, in his introduction to the book *Righteous Among the Nations* (p. lxxxiv) offered a decisive reply to this question:

> The conditions of the German occupation led in general to a marked decline in anti-semitic sentiments which had existed in pre-war Poland. The common fate of the persecuted, suffering, fighting people helped to awaken a sense of solidarity and a will to help those who were dying. And although the views and prejudices formed before the war could not but affect the attitudes of people, on the whole they under-went considerable modification. There are many examples to indicate that the behaviour of individuals was determined then mainly by character and moral attitude and not by association with a specific political programme or party before the war.[4]

I am quite sure that this judgment is an accurate reflection of Władysław Bartoszewski's personal will and feelings. I also agree that noble human instincts moved many individual Poles to actions that were not necessarily consonant with – and may even have been contradictory to – their known political views. Nevertheless, I cannot agree that the views and actions of the Polish people underwent a general process of modification born of the con-ditions and bitter experience of the times. Our study of the Nazi era as a whole has taught us that the common suffering of people under occupation or of prisoners in camps did not always lead to better mutual understanding or to an awareness of the necessary conditions for self-defence. Often a slight difference in standing or privilege, deliberately highlighted by the Nazis, was a source of considerable tension and even contention between individuals or groups within the oppressed population.

I believe – and Professor Bartoszewski has made reference to this aspect of the situation in the passage quoted – that we cannot detach or dissociate the period of the war from the broader historical framework, especially as ideological trends and deep-seated prejudices proved to have a lasting vitality. Certainly I reject the notion of everlasting Polish anti-semitism as nonsense. On the other hand, it would be equally senseless not to acknow-ledge that anti-semitism constituted an important factor in the forging of Polish national policy and public opinion for a span of fifty years, from 1918 to 1968. In any case, Professor Bartoszewski's views are not corroborated by the first-hand Jewish or Polish sources relating to this subject.

One of the chroniclers of the Warsaw ghetto, Abraham Levin, noted in his diary on 7 June 1942:

Very often the question arises whether there is a moderation or mitigation of the deep-rooted Polish anti-semitism. As is true regarding most questions, the contrasting opinions and views [about this one] are poles apart. Many Jews held that under the impact of the war and the stunning blows that have affected the country's entire population, Jews and Poles alike, a considerable change has taken place in the attitude of the Poles toward the Jews, and a majority of Poles have ascribed to the 'philo-semitic' spirit. those who advance this view base themselves or rely on a number of incidents to prove that as far back as the first days of the war, the Poles displayed feelings of compassion and goodwill toward the poor Jews, and especially toward the Jewish child beggars. These feelings are still valid . . . It is well known that our beggar children wandering by the dozens and the hundreds along the Christian streets receive generous [handouts of] bread and potatoes and are thus able to feed themselves and their relatives in the ghetto. This is the viewpoint of the optimists. The pessimists, on the other hand, held that the Poles had received an instructive lesson in anti-semitism. Hatred of Jews [translated into] the concrete form of the ghetto and confiscation of property, penetrated deep into their bones. These pessimists find support for their views in various statements about the Jewish question that have been made by Poles. In conversation many Poles have expressed the opinion that once the Germans are driven out, the expropriated Jewish property will be a difficult problem to handle. By no means are they prepared to relinquish the Jewish property that the government has handed over to them . . . I myself am inclined to accept the former view. I see the relations between Poles and Jews in a positive light and believe that the present war will cleanse our globe of much dirt and savagery. The benevolent winds of liberty and brotherhood will blow from the east and the west. Moreover, after this war Poland will adhere to the ideals that have guided the Russians, the British, the Americans, the Free French and the Polish legions in their common struggle. There will be no shelter here for anti-semitism, at least not for public anti-semitism.[5]

Emmanuel Ringelblum, in his above-mentioned *Polish—Jewish Relations*, contended that:

It must be admitted with shame and sorrow that the 'Judas' press [the legal press published under German control], supported by the anti-semitic illegal press, have aroused a predictable response among the population. Under the influence of the anti-semitic hue and cry in the *Nowy Kurier Warszawski* in April and May of this year [1943], the campaign initiated by the Germans against the Jews on the 'Aryan' side elicited a response from broad segments of the population. When they crossed over to work on the 'Aryan' side, Jews employed in places of work [outside the ghetto] knew in advance that after an anti-Jewish article in the press, or even a 'reader's comment', an exasperating day of provocations, stone-throwing by the mob, and the like awaited them.[6]

In his concluding remarks, Ringelblum was even more outspoken in contending that 'Polish Fascism and its ally, anti-semitism, have won over the majority of the Polish people'.[7]

The Polish literary scholar Kazimierz Wyka wrote in his highly acclaimed book *Życie na niby*:

Even if I am alone in my pronouncement and I can find no one to follow me, I will repeat again and again: No, a hundred times no! The methods and aims are shameful, the result of demoralization and degradation. In short, the morals and economic outlook of the average Pole vis-à-vis the Jewish tragedy is as follows: the Germans who murdered the Jews committed a crime. We are incapable of doing anything like that. The Germans will be punished for their crime. They have sullied their consciences; but we – we have already profited and will continue to profit in the future without disturbing our consciences and without having blood on our hands.[8]

Let us now listen to the voice of the Polish underground. From time to time, the regular reports sent by the Delegate's Office to the Polish Government-in-exile in England contained information about the condition of the Jews and included remarks about the attitude of the Polish population and the underground authorities towards the Jewish question. Incidentally, the information conveyed to London constituted the raw material of several appeals that the Polish Government-in-exile addressed to the free world on behalf of the Jews being murdered on Polish soil. A report by the Interior Department of the Delegate's Office covering the period 15 August to 15 November 1941 stated:

The tide of anti-semitism that had previously been aroused by word of how the Jews behaved under Soviet occupation has recently declined in response to the ordeal being endured by this nation. But the latent anti-semitism that lingers on in Polish society is being exploited by German propaganda and by the underground press of various right-wing persuasions. The issue is exceptionally sensitive; it may even divide society in two, each segment having contrary political attitudes. The prevailing viewpoint is that the Jewish problem can be solved only through a massive, inernationally co-ordinated emigration of Jews from Poland. Once Jewish supremacy in economic life is a thing of the past, mutual relations must be guided by a compromise predicated on the total loyalty of Jews to the Polish state.[9]

Another memo from the Delegate's Office dated 31 December 1940, stated:

The boldest dreams of the staunchest anti-semites have already been surpassed by what the occupier has managed to accomplish in the sphere of the anti-Jewish struggle. But the delicate structure they have erected may easily collapse after the victory of the democratic states. Our reactionary anti-semites are haunted by this prospect; it is a fear that disturbs their dreams. They realize that German policies are not permanent. In private many Poles express satisfaction upon seeing the Jews being removed from Polish suburbs, offices, professions, industry, and commerce in [Warsaw] and other cities. But under no circumstances will they demonstrate their satisfaction in public. . . . At the same time, only a fraction of the Poles openly display favourable attitudes toward the Jews . . .[10]

Another document written by an official of the Delegate's Office on 8 November 1941, stated:

Human compassion for Jewish suffering notwithstanding, there is hardly a person in Poland who would fail to demand a definite policy on the Jewish question, and particularly regarding the Poles' appropriation of Jewish positions in [the country's] economic life. Without at least a minimal programme leading toward this objective, no government will be able to stay in power.[11]

Finally, a quotation from a memo written by Roman Knoll, head of the Foreign Affairs Office attached to the Delegate's Staff for the Homeland, and sent in August 1943:

In the Homeland as a whole – regardless of the general psychological situation at any given moment – the position is such that the return of the Jews to their jobs and workshops is quite out of the question, even if the number of Jews were greatly reduced. The non-Jewish population has filled their places in the towns and cities; in much of Poland this is a fundamental change and final in character. The return of masses of Jews would be perceived by the population not as an act of restitution but as an invasion against which they would have to defend themselves, even by physical means ... The Government is correct in assuring world opinion that anti-semitism will no longer exist in Poland; but it will no longer exist only if the surviving Jews do not endeavour to return to Poland's cities and towns *en masse*. Considering the difficult situation, the Homeland sees only one way out: the Polish Government must take the initiative – immediately, if possible – with the aim of creating a national centre for the Jews of Eastern Europe. This project should be drawn up in co-operation with Jewish Zionist circles; [it] should focus on an East European territory for the future Jewish state, in preference to Palestine – which is too small for the purpose, too exotic, and has aroused conflict with the Arab world – and in preference to some tropical colony to which the Jews will refuse to emigrate. It may be too early to decide precisely what territory should be considered. Our attitude in this matter should be philo-Jewish rather than anti-Jewish.[12]

Historical conclusions and generalizations should not be drawn on the basis of political or ideological considerations, even if they are engendered by the best intentions. The task of an historian is to study the facts and events of the past and to interpret them in their historical context. It seems to us, a small group of Israeli historians who have examined an appreciable number of Polish and Jewish sources, that anti-semitism played an important role in forging both Polish public opinion and the country's political prospects during the war. A certain sector of the Polish population, appalled by the Nazi atrocities and inspired by sincerely patriotic motives, fought against anti-semitism and, despite the danger to their own safety, became involved in help and rescue actions. But another segment of the population (the size of which is difficult to estimate) played a major role in exacerbating the plight of the Jews. Influenced by the Nazis' anti-Jewish policy, they not only supported the Nazi programme being executed in Poland but actually abetted it by exposing Jews in hiding or those who tried to change their identity. Many of the Jews who escaped and took shelter among the Poles were first blackmailed and then handed over to the Germans by the gangs of *szmalcownicy* or extortionists.[13]

In fact, added to the anti-Jewish sentiments of the pre-war period were a host of new contentions that served to further poison the already negative atmosphere. The first of the new claims derived from the charges that the Jews had accorded the Soviet invaders a warm welcome in the Eastern territories and had exhibited hostile behaviour toward the Poles for as long as these areas remained under Soviet control. In the limited framework of this article I cannot do justice to this thorny problem. For the issue essentially constituted a major clash of interests that divided Jews and Poles. On the face of it, the decisive majority of the Poles perceived themselves as confronting two invading enemies. For the Jews, there was only one deadly enemy – the Nazis – since the Soviets (objectionable as their ideological system may have been) provided a means of escape and salvation.

The other focal issue related to the Jews was their collective expulsion from various positions in the Polish economy and the confiscation of Jewish property. Without doubt, the majority of the Polish people were overtly or covertly satisfied with the ejection of the Jews from the country's economic life, and the same majority shared the opinion that the reinstatement of the Jews in their jobs and the restoration of Jewish property was entirely out of the question. Moreover, this definitive stand on the part of so large a sector of the population largely determined the views of the political parties (with the exception of the Socialists and certain Liberal circles). Consequently, the representatives of the various political factions continued to press for the mass emigration of the Jews, and the search for a territorial solution to the Jewish problem gave rise to some very strange ideas about prospective destinations for the Jewish people.

Let me now turn to the second object of scrutiny in our discussion: the Polish underground and its relation with the Jews. In this context I do not intend to refer to individuals or single political groups. The subject under review is the Delegate and his staff, who were the official representation of the Polish regime in the underground during the occupation. The Nazi subjected the Poles to an oppressive regime and deprived them of autonomy and national rights. As a result, the Polish nation was unable to protest against the German atrocities perpetrated on its soil or aid the Jews in any way on an official level. The Germans did not consult with the Poles about

how to deal with the Jews, and the Poles, as a rule, did not participate in the
Nazis' anti-Jewish actions.

On the other hand, the Poles did exhibit a large measure of internal
solidarity and put up a united stand against the enemy. The profound moral
and political influence of the Polish underground, coupled with the efficient
organization of the clandestine cells, amounted to a formidable authority
that was often referred to as the 'underground state'.[14]

Thus we are obliged to ask what means of contact and co-operation
existed between the Poles and the Jews within the framework of this
underground state. The answer is that until the final months of 1942 there
was no contact, no assistance, no co-operation; just total segregation and
alienation.

Kazimierz Iranek-Osmecki opened the chapter entitled 'Organized
Civilian Help' of his book *He Who Saves One Life* by saying that, 'during the
early years of the occupation, no official link existed between the Polish
underground movement and the Jews. Because the Jews had not, at that
time, evolved an underground organization of their own, the Polish underground authorities had to contact Jews unofficially.'[15]

This explanation of why the Polish underground did not establish contact
with the Jews 'during the early years of the occupation' simply cannot be
accepted. For it is neither correct nor honest to cite the lack of parallel
Jewish underground organs as a justification for not having approached the
Jews. The fact is that the Jewish underground parties and youth movements
in Warsaw were organized almost immediately at the start of the occupation,
and very soon thereafter a body was established to co-ordinate the Jewish
underground and self-help activities. The connection between Poles and
Jews did not exist because the Polish underground subscribed to the view
that the Jews were an alien body whose fate neither concerned the Polish
nation nor required any special action. The Polish Government-in-exile
claimed to represent the entire Polish population – minorities included –
and from the start one representative of a Jewish political faction, and subsequently two, were members of the Polish National Council, a sort of
parliamentary body formed in exile. Yet no Jewish representative was
included in the broad clandestine organization established in Poland by the
Delegate, despite the fact that he was the official executor of the exiled
government's policy on Polish soil.

In May 1944, at a time when no Jewish community or ghetto (other than
the remnant of the Jews of Łódź) remained in Poland, a secret report on the
Jews and the Jewish problem during the Holocaust was sent out of Poland. It
was addressed exclusively to the Prime Minister of the Polish Government-
in-exile, Stanislaw Mikołajczyk. The author of the document, Witold
Bieńkowski ('Witold', 'Kalski'), was well versed in the Jewish tragedy, hav-

ing been one of the founders of 'Żegota', the Provisional Committee to Aid the Jews, and from the early part of 1943 onward head of the section for Jewish Affairs in the Delegate's Office. Bieńkowski's report states that '. . . If during the first stage of the war (until the end of 1941) there was no Jewish problem, either in the political or the visceral sense, beginning with the establishment of the ghettos and the steadily rising Jewish martyrdom, there emerged a sense of understanding and partnership in suffering and struggle of the entire population of the Polish Nation.'[16]

In point of fact, the complete segregation and alienation continued until the last month of 1942, not 1941. But the crucial point here is to expose the reason for this 'block' and the total indifference of the Polish underground when it came to the Jews. Obviously the Polish nation was enduring a period of oppression and suffering, and it is quite natural that the focus of attention was on the condition of the Poles. The Jews themselves have a saying that the fate of the poor in your own town is closer to your heart than the fate of the poor far away. Nevertheless, the martyrdom, or the special treatment that the Nazis accorded the Jews, did not start at the end of 1941, just as the establishment of the ghettos did not begin then but went back to the end of 1939. In 1941 alone, 43,000 Jews died of starvation and epidemics in the Warsaw ghetto, meaning that ten per cent of the ghetto's population succumbed to inhuman conditions. So that the disturbing question is inevitably why, for the extended period of three whole years, no help in the field of welfare, no support of either a material or moral kind, was ever extended to the Jews – citizens of Poland in every way – by the official Polish underground.

Can the developments that occurred during the last months of 1942 be considered a substantive change in the general Polish attitude towards the Jews? Prior to that time, a few concrete steps had been taken by individuals and groups of Poles, but the involvement of the underground marked a new phase in Polish–Jewish relations. The activities of 'Żegota', a clandestine organization founded by Poles with the declared aim of aiding and saving Jews, were unique in all of Europe. The impetus to create 'Żegota' came from two quarters, but credit is due primarily to a small group of truly noble people whose feelings were expressed in an appeal drafted by the prime mover behind the organization, the Polish-Catholic writer Zofia Kossak-Szczucka: 'Whoever remains silent in the face of murder becomes an accomplice to that murder.'[17] From the end of September 1942 onward, in the light of the harrowing expulsion and mass murder in the Warsaw ghetto, the Provisional 'Żegota' Committee initiated its operations.

The other impulse came from the political parties and their activists in the underground. The Delegate's Office took 'Żegota' under its wing, and from the beginning of 1943 onward the organization was officially affiliated with the Office. The Delegate was guided in this decision primarily by political considerations, namely, Poland's interest and image throughout the free world both at the present time and in the future. But the activists of 'Żegota', the people who actually bore the taxing and perilous task of rescue, were among the bravest heroes of the war, truly 'the righteous among nations'. I will not go into the various aspects of this heroic humane struggle during those terrible times of indifference in the face of cruelty. The effectiveness of the aid rendered by 'Żegota' has been and continues to be the subject of a debate in which I have taken part. But here I will only state in brief that 'it was very little considering the dimensions of the tragedy, and it was considerable in the light of the conditions and spirit of the times'.

In tribute to these people, I would like to quote the closing passage of the chapter entitled 'The Idealist' in Ringelblum's *Polish—Jewish Relations*:

There are thousands of idealists like these in Warsaw and throughout the country, both in the intelligentsia and the working class, who help Jews very devotedly at the risk of their lives. Every Jew snatched from the clutches of the bloodthirsty Nazi monster had to have an idealist like this watching over him day after day like a guardian angel. The great majority of these people helped the Jews in return for remuneration, but is there in fact money enough in the world to pay for their self-sacrifice? People who hid Jews for money alone and lacked a strong moral motivation rid themselves of their dangerous ballast sooner or later by turning the Jews out of their flats. The ones who kept the Jews in their flats were those who did so not only for Jewish money. This gallery of Polish heroes could provide subjects for wonderful novels about the noblest idealists who feared neither the enemy's threats on his red posters nor the obtuseness and stupidity of Polish Fascists and anti-semites who deem it an anti-national act to hide Jews.[18]

From this encouraging subject, I turn to the final point of my argument: Polish–Jewish relations in connection with the armed resistance of the Jews. We are not free to avoid the *sine qua non* that largely informed this issue: the Jews lacked the tradition, the proper training, and the means to mount an effective armed resistance. In the eyes of the Poles, and of the European peoples as a whole, Jews were generally considered unfit for military service and were often viewed as a cowardly people incapable of acting or reacting as fighters. Certainly no less important was the concern of many AK officers that the Jews were being guided by communists and served as a tool of the communist movement and Soviet aims. In fact, the influence of the communists over the Jewish population in general and the Jewish resistance movements in particular was very limited.

The chief obstacle among Jews was a certain scepticism about the efficacy of resistance. After all, the portrayal of the European resistance movement as ever-ready and ever-resolute in its determination to fight under any conditions is more legend than historical fact. The armed organizations in the occupied countries entered into armed confrontation only when they stood a reasonable chance of bringing about a modicum of relief in the oppressive situation or achieving some gain in the future. These prospects were not open to the Jews, who could not hope to achieve any gains by fighting. Their fate was sealed. The prospect of aid and rescue could come only from outside. Regardless of what they might do, the Jews could not rescue themselves.

Yet despite these reservations, faced with the prospect of final, total annihilation, the Jews in many of the ghettos established Fighting Organizations peopled by members of the Zionist and Socialist youth movements. From the foundation of the very first cell, a constant effort was made to establish contact and enter into co-operation with the Polish armed underground. For the Jews living in the General Government and the territories annexed by Germany, the Polish underground was the only source of arms, intelligence and training. From Wilno, Białystok, Częstochowa, Cracow and other ghettos, the Jewish fighters urgently appealed to the officers and commanders of the AK. In each case the response was evasive or lacking altogether. A few reports and orders of the AK's high command went so far as to describe Jewish partisans as 'criminal gangs established by fugitive Jews and mainly by young Jewish women'.[19] And in a number of instances, Jews who had escaped the ghettos were pursued and killed by units of the NSZ.

I prefer to focus my remarks on Warsaw where, once contact was established, a limited quantity of arms was transferred to the ghetto and the Jewish Fighting Organization ultimately acquired the formal recognition of the AK. Much has been written about the Warsaw ghetto uprising and the link between the ŻOB and the AK. Yet only a few of the many books and articles are based on credible material and have delved into the complex process of approach or elucidated the positions of the two sides. More astonishing still is the role played by people who were themselves involved in the events and, who have tried, in retrospect, to create a new, subjective and ultimately fictional version of the affair.

The example of General Tadeusz Bor-Komorowski is typical in this respect because of his high level of responsibility and the scope of his fantasy. In his memoirs, *The Secret Army*, Komorowski wrote about the Jewish connection at length:

As early as July 29th we had learned from the reports of railroad workers that the transports were being sent [from Warsaw] to the concentration camp at Treblinka and that there the Jews disappeared without trace. There could be no further doubt this time that the deportations were but a prelude to extermination.

General Rowecki, swift in his decision as always, made up his mind that we could not remain passive, and that at all costs we must help the Jews so far as it lay in our power. He called a conference, at which, however, some doubts were expressed. The argument ran: 'If America and Great Britain, with powerful armies and air forces behind them and equipped with all the means of modern warfare, are not able to stop this crime and must look on impotently while the Germans perpetrate every kind of horror in the occupied countries, how can we hope to stop them?' Rowecki's opinion was that failure to show active resistance would only encourage the Germans to further mass extermination on the same lines.

We had a department in our organization which arranged protection and help for escaped Jews and the distribution of money to them which had been sent to us from London for the purpose. A certain 'Waclaw' was chief of the department, and he was now instructed by Rowecki to get through to the Ghetto and establish contact with the Jewish leaders. He was to tell them that the Home Army was ready to come to the assistance of the Jews with supplies of arms and ammunition and to co-ordinate their attacks outside with Jewish resistance from within.

The Jewish leaders, however, rejected the offer, arguing that if they kept quiet the Germans might deport and murder 20,000 or 30,000 and perhaps even 60,000 of them, but it was inconceivable that they should destroy the lot; while if they resisted, the Germans would certainly do so. When 'Waclaw' reported this to Rowecki, the General decided to intensify the sabotage of German lines of communication in such a way as to hamper and delay the deportations.[20]

Not a single one of the details in Komorowski's description – the meeting, the decisions, the offer of aid, or the independet actions by the AK – is based upon fact. Komorowski, who penned his memoirs in exile, evidently wished to present a more positive picture of the Poles' behaviour during the war. The truth of the matter is that the alleged meeting and the decisions adopted on Rowecki's initiative are pure fiction. Moreover, the civil and military branches of the Polish underground did not make approaches to the Jews at that time, and neither was there any department for providing beleagured Jews with aid. It is true that an AK officer, whom Komorowski refers to as 'a certain "Waclaw"' and whose real name was Henryk Woliński, was assigned to handle 'Jewish affairs'. But during the period under consideration, Woliński's task was limited to gathering information on what was happening on the Jewish front for the benefit of the AK and the Delegate's Office. Indeed, Woliński wrote a detailed report on his ties and work with the Jews, but it contains no reference to Rowecki's alleged order, or the negative reply supposedly received from the Jews, or to any independent action decided upon by the Poles, as Komorowski would have us believe.[21]

I should note that, as a rule, the Polish scholars have not adopted Komorowski's curious version of events, and Professor Bartoszewski has made a very positive contribution toward achieving a reconstruction of the truth. On the other hand, writers and historians further removed from the sources and atmosphere of the time are inclined to believe a man who bears a famous name or appears to have been a reliable commander. Thus so outstanding a scholar as Raul Hilberg accepted Komorowski's version without reservation or doubt.[22]

The fact is that the aid extended in Warsaw – and we must emphasize that aid eventually was provided to the Jews – was a classic instance of too little too late. Due to a few obstacles, contact between the AK and the ŻOB was broken for a time, and when Yitzchak Zuckerman arrived on the 'Aryan' side of Warsaw a few weeks before the outbreak of the ghetto uprising, the AK pressured him to have the revolt cancelled.[23] In its place they suggested smuggling the Jewish fighters out of the ghetto and attaching them to partisan units outside the city. This plan was a corollary of the AK's own political considerations and tactics. According to the organization's long-range strategy, the time was not yet ripe for a revolt, and fighting in the ghetto would only engender an even more repressive atmosphere. This is yet another example of the attempts to protect political interests during this period. In the end, units of the AK and the AL mounted a few modest actions during the ghetto uprising, but their outcome was of marginal importance to the broader battle.

In concluding this paper, I wish to state my belief that we historians bear a heavy responsibility as witnesses to an epoch of bestiality. The challenge we face is difficult and sometimes even painful, but silence is tantamount to denying or avoiding the truth. I do not know whether the writing and study of history is an effective way of preventing future human disasters. After all, mankind has been contemplating history and pondering the mistakes of its forebears for generations, but the reality of our lives has continued to be one long chain of wars and oppression of our fellow men. Nevertheless, I believe we must give every new lesson a chance to check the spread of evil. This demands of us, first of all, the courage to admit the truth to ourselves, to overcome many obstacles, and to confront challenges boldly. Such a course is almost a mission, and we are merely mortals plagued by all the weaknesses of our kind. But we are obliged to try.

16

Polish–Jewish relations, 1944–1947

Michal Borwicz

The Jews who survived the Nazi occupation in Poland had behind them five years of daily confrontation with death, mass slaughter and the loss of their closest relatives. The vast majority of Jews who had survived in the Soviet Union found themselves there as a result of mass deportation or imprisonment with hard labour. Both groups were deprived of their families. Whole communities disappeared, age-old organizations and institutions amounting to a heritage.

In this situation the move towards emigration began immediately. The motivation was simple: to leave this huge graveyard where every step revived memories of individual and mass tragedy. Meanwhile, Zionist organizations continued to realize their own emigration programme; the events of the preceding years may have served to strengthen the movement, but they had certainly not created it. There was also another category of emigrant (both at the beginning and later): those Jews who, having spent the war in the Soviet Union had come to know its system, wished to put as much distance as possible between it and themselves.

However, there were also many survivors who wished to stay; those who felt particularly strong ties with Polish language and culture, and also the many who felt that their mission or sometimes even the whole meaning of the lives they had been spared lay in continuing the age-old history of the Jews in Poland. From the first, institutions sprang up, inspired by this desire for renewal. The Central Committee of Jews and its branches were not, in fact, free of the so-called 'party key' which had been imposed upon them, and it was effectively only an umbrella for the many remaining institutions. Firstly, the political parties with their agendas for the new political order allowed (as was also the case with Polish organizations) the functioning of most political parties. Thus, though the revisionists were banned, organizations such as Poale-Sion (right and left), the General Zionists and the Bund were re-established, not to speak of the Jewish

Section of the Polish Workers' Party (PPR). In addition there were religious groups, co-operatives and social welfare organizations, mainly orphanages and doctors' surgeries. There were Jewish theatre groups and a dynamic Jewish Historical Commission which was tackling one of the most urgent tasks of the movement: the gathering, editing and publication of material, documents and chronicles recording the truth about the fate of the Jews under the Nazi occupation. There were also newspapers in both Polish and Yiddish, a Union of Jewish Writers, and a Jewish publishing house. Funds for all these organizations came from Jewish organizations based abroad, the Joint among others; the fact that money was given with these particular aims in mind is a clear indication of the desire to build anew upon the ruins left by the war.

Unfortunately, all this so-called 'organic' work was carried out in a climate of intense anti-semitism and of violent crimes being perpetrated against the Jews. Let us leave aside for the moment the crushing legacy of the last few years preceding the war, painstakingly maintained during the years of occupation not only by fringe organizations such as the Falanga or Confederation, but also by the Endecja which formed part of the coalition supporting the government in London, and by the press representing all these movements. Let us ignore also the questions which invariably arise in every discussion concerning the various types of informer and blackmailer that sprang up, for despite their widespread activities and the great grief and havoc they caused, this behaviour was ultimately restricted to a band of individuals.

A central question of course was the disposition of former Jewish property. There is no truth in the generalizations about its appropriation following the deportation and death of the owners or tenants. However, when houses and shops were left empty there was nothing to prevent others from moving in. There were hundreds of apartments in the larger cities and towns and dozens in smaller towns (of which there were, after all, a great many throughout the country). Together with the shops, they represented a step up the social ladder and even if they had been seized without official authorization, the return of their original owners was bound to cause problems.

It must be added, and emphasized, that the process of martyrdom in general or in particular detailed instances, was most certainly not photogenic. I use this shocking term deliberately. Emaciated, starving, bruised bodies in rags, crowded together in ghettos or with shaved heads and striped uniforms in the camps evoke pity and anger. It is only natural, unless automatic mental correctives come into play. The Germans were well aware of this and did all they could to prevent such correctives from arising and sympathy for their Jewish victims being aroused.

Another factor was also significant: during the occupation, the Jews, cut off from the rest of the population, became something distant and alien. Attitudes towards them were not those of people reacting to other people, but to a concept. It is easy for any propaganda machine to manipulate a concept with its own aims in mind.

The paramount prevailing traditional stereotype was that of 'Żydo-komuna' (Jewish communism), the association of the Jewish intellectual with communist tendencies, but this impression appeared to have a concrete base. From the time of the Red Army's invasion of the Eastern regions in September 1939 this popular rumour spread over the country, exaggerating the role of the Jews in the Russian advance. Towards the end of the war, the fact that Stalin's tactics aimed to overcome and Sovietize Poland became quite evident. The severing of diplomatic relations with the Polish Government-in-exile (using Katyn as a pretext!), the introduction of the Union of Polish Patriots and the PKWN into the political arena, the creation of the Berling division, the appointment of the National Home Council and, finally, the halting of the Red Army offensive at the outbreak of the Warsaw uprising – all these, while the Germans were still occupying the country, brought the feelings of hostility towards the Soviet Union to boiling point. On 1 January 1945 the 'Provisional Government of the Polish Republic' proclaimed by the Polish Committee of National Liberation came into being; it was without doubt a Soviet pawn. On 4 February the Conference of the Big Three began in Yalta. Six weeks later, the 27–28 March saw the abduction and arrest of sixteen representatives of the Polish opposition movement and – beginning on 18 June – a show trial was held before the Highest Military Court of the Red Army. At each successive stage of these events, hostility towards the new regime deepened, together with the conviction that one occupation had merely been replaced by another.

The dignitaries of the newly-imposed government included many who were of Jewish descent. I shall disregard here the problem raised in the writings of former communists like Chęcinski,[1] Hersz Smolar,[2] Gronowski-Brunot[3] and others, suggesting this was a deliberate tactic on the part of Stalin. Similarly, a related hypothesis was that the number of Jews was not as great as commonly thought, but that they were pushed into spectacular posts which evoked particular enmity. It is a fact that their presence and function within the State apparatus seemed completely to bear out slogans about the 'Żydo-komuna'. (To substantiate this theory, rumour-mongers suggested that almost all the dignitaries were of Jewish descent; fantastic family trees were concocted for many non-Jews, including Radkiewicz, the Minister of Internal Affairs, controlling the police.)

The animosity felt by many towards the 'Żydo-komuna' (a threat apparently now supported by concrete and easily exploited evidence) in many cases veiled an anti-semitism born of and nurtured by base interests originating elsewhere – that is, among those who, as a result of the extermination of the Jews, had made a fortune, large or small. These were the numerous tenants of previously Jewish-owned apartments, or the 'treuhanders' (German trustees), particularly those set up in the larger and more profitable enterprises. One should not generalize unduly as all these categories also included honest people who simply took advantage of the state of affairs in which they found themselves, and from whose actions no general ideology can be derived. In any case, strengthened by a multitude of other motives which were not admitted aloud, the climate was steeped in anti-semitism. By way of illustration I once noted a phenomenon which for readers unfamiliar with the atmosphere of that time was difficult to envisage.[4] The Provincial Jewish Historical Commission in Cracow, of which I was then Director, was collecting, among other things, accounts concerning the numerous Poles who had helped the Jews during the Nazi occupation, very often at the risk of their own lives. Within the context of the experiences of our witnesses, we began to publish these in our journals quite early on. Many of those mentioned by name (and portrayed in especially good light) came to us with the accusation that by naming them we were exposing them to unpleasant situations and even revenge. (In later publications, if clearly requested by the concerned parties, that is, the former protectors, several of these names had to be omitted or indicated by initials only.) It must be emphasized that many Polish circles were very firmly against anti-semitism and expressed this as far as it was possible. I shall return to these groups later and to the difficulties of the struggle in this area.

Concerning the murder of Jews, the *Encyclopedia Judaica* states that in 1945 alone there were 353; the victims had nothing to do with communism. They were usually victims of random violence, pulled out of trains and buses and in certain cases Jews who, on returning to their previous homes, fell into the hands of neighbours who had in the meantime appropriated their possessions.

The pogroms followed: in July 1945 in Rzeszów; in Cracow on 11 August of the same year; on 4 July 1946 in Kielce, where 42 Jews, men and women, were murdered and several dozen injured. I will not elaborate on these as the details are widely known. It is evident that in all three cases there was provocation in the shape of accusations of Jewish ritual murders and the same methods were employed everywhere. But who master-minded these provocations?

According to Tadeusz Żenczykowski, 'the instigator behind the Rzeszów anti-semitic outbursts was the Chief of the Regional Security Service, Major Władysław Sobczyński'. According to Żenczykowski, a year later 'he

organized similar events in Kielce'.[5] Other names were also mentioned, and
with regard to Kielce stories of Soviet manipulation had been circulating for
some time. Krystyna Kersten gave voice to them, citing a body of circumstantial evidence.[6] It should merely be noted here, however, that in Kielce
there was a court case, a hearing and sentences were imposed, but the
central instigators never became unduly alarmed. Even at that time, the
behaviour of certain local dignitaries and members of the militia and army
was already suspicious. In Poland itself, of course, the press did not pay any
attention to this, but in reading the reports of foreign journalists a whole
series of details compel consideration.

According to one thesis, the aim of the secret Soviet provocateurs was to
deprive Poland of the sympathy of Western nations immediately before the
elections intended to confirm and ensure the Soviet takeover. The
secondary consequence (perhaps not forseen, but exploited nevertheless)
was that an even greater number of Soviet 'specialists' was employed in the
Security Service under the pretext that the organization was unable to deal
with its tasks. (It should be noted that a nine-year-old boy, Henryk
Blaszczyk, who was the main instrument of the Kielce provocation is now in
his forties and lives in Poland, but over these few decades no one seems to
have questioned him closely about his instructors at the time and today
journalists seem unable to gain access to him.)

All these incidents are being widely researched now, not only in Poland
but particularly in Western Europe and America, and it is noteworthy that
there were many foreign journalists present in Poland during the first days
following the end of the war. The annihilation of Jews and the fact that the
largest German extermination camps were situated in Poland drew both
Jewish and non-Jewish journalists to the country. Other political developments – the enforced system of a so-called people's democracy, the 'satelli-
zation' of Poland, despite the existence of the Polish government in London
and the earlier obligations of the Allies – made the changes in Poland highly
topical, so there were many witnesses to the events of 1945. Whatever is
unearthed about the degree of Soviet involvement, there is no doubt that in
order for the provocation to succeed, there had to be conditions for such an
'outburst'. Unfortunately, these conditions did exist and, to make things
worse, were at an inflammatory level. Where did the Church stand in all
this, the only legal institution, which 'held sway over souls'?

In May 1946, Rabbi Dr David Kahane and the Secretary General of the
Jewish religious associations, Professor Michal Silberberg, went to the
residence of Primate Hlond (then still in Poznań), in order to gain an
audience and request that a pastoral letter be issued on the subject of the
murders which were occurring almost daily. They also submitted a memorandum in which they warned of the dangers of a violent outburst if the

Church did not raise its voice on the matter. Primate Hlond returned the memorandum immediately via his secretary and declined to give an audience to these delegates of religious organizations.

On 3 June 1946, a month before the Kielce pogrom, Dr Joseph Tennenbaum, President of the World Union of Polish Jews who had come from the United States (their headquarters were in New York) succeeded after repeated endeavours in being received by Primate Hlond. To all Dr Tennenbaum's arguments, based on a list of the murdered, Primate Hlond consistently responded with references to the presence of Jews in authority 'endeavouring to enforce a system inimical to the majority of the nation'.[7] The concept of the 'Żydo-komuna' and of common responsibility was thus clarified in full. A similar chain of events (without going into rhetorical details) occurred during the interview Cardinal Hlond granted to a large group of foreign journalists on 11 July, a week after the Kielce pogrom.[8]

In Kielce itself, three weeks before the pogrom, Bishop Kaczmarek received a delegation of local Jews who were alarmed at the unambiguous threat of an outburst of violence. He refused their request to issue a pastoral letter and the content of his answer was analogous to the Primate's declaration. On the day of the pogrom, when the crowd was attacking the building housing the Jewish Committee, the chairman tried to telephone the Bishop's residence to ask for intervention. The Bishop's office refused to grant him a connection. After the pogrom, Bishop Kaczmarek declined to add his name to a joint declaration – signed, among others, by the opposition Peasant Party (PSL). Instead he made a separate declaration. Without specifically mentioning the occurrence in a single sentence he speaks generally about the 'bloody drama provoked by a tangle of events' and 'a misfortune has occurred, particularly because it happened before the eyes of the young and of children'. As a result, the curia called upon the people to maintain peace and to consider their actions.[9]

Bishop Wyszyński of Lublin (who in later years as Primate of Poland protested, in Moczar's era, with great courage against organized anti-Jewish onslaughts) after the Kielce pogrom, only repeated the general opinion that enmity was felt towards Jews because they 'took an active part in the political life of the country'. But there was more. In the same declaration made to the Jewish delegation in Lublin the following statement appears: 'The Germans murdered the Jewish nation because the Jews were the propagators of communism.' In reply to questions posed by the delegates regarding his position on the accusations of ritual murder the Bishop said: 'At the trial of Beilis many old and contemporary Jewish books were gathered, but the question of the use of blood by Jews was never completely clarified.' In short, Vatican II was still long-distant.

If, as much of the circumstantial evidence seems to suggest, the post-war pogroms, with the Kielce incident at their head, were the consequence of Soviet provocation, intended to turn Western opinion against Poland during these crucial and difficult years, then it must be admitted that the provocations succeeded, and beyond the hopes of the provocateurs. Not only because they encountered impassioned and willing executors on the spot among the crowds whom nobody (either in Poland or abroad) could accuse of pro-Soviet sympathies, but also (and maybe even more so) because they gained what amounted to a positive echo of sentiment from the direction of the Church hierarchy. It should be noted that the churchmen's interviews were given under the specific condition that they would be published abroad. Each pronouncement included a stereotyped statement to the effect that there was no reason to issue pastoral letters because the Church obviously condemned all killing. In such a context, if the Western reader noticed it, the sentence must have seemed a bloody irony.

However, the Bishop of Częstochowa, Dr Teodor Kubina, spoke out openly and firmly against the rumours of ritual murder, and indeed, despite advanced provocation, there was no pogrom in Częstochowa. Individual priests, such as Father Henryk Weryński in Cracow, also worked to counteract anti-semitic propaganda, while the leaders of the Evangelical church unequivocally and movingly condemned the Kielce pogrom.

The Cracow newspaper *Tygodnik Powszechny*, which was close to the curia and under the editorship of Jerzy Turowicz, took a consistently humanitarian stance, challenging the propaganda of hate not only in its editorials but in all its writing. Bearing in mind its high standards and the popularity it enjoyed, the paper's influence was undoubtedly beneficial: the Archbishop of Cracow, Cardinal Sapieha, took part, as a honorary patron, in a celebration marking the third anniversary of the Warsaw Ghetto uprising in April 1946; this gesture was very positively received.

I have mentioned that many Polish circles were decidedly against anti-semitism and they gave expression to this as far as was possible. I say as far as was possible because such action was rather complicated. In the first place, none of the four official parties had retained either their traditional form or social basis. The Communist Party changed not only its name (to the PPR), but driven by the desire to acquire as many members as possible and at any cost (so its membership would be greater than the PPS), gathered elements which, on its own terms, were suspect. The PPS, despite the attempts of the PPR to break it up, had already experienced deep divisions, having been granted legal status in July 1944. Mistrust of the Democratic Movement, which, after all, counted members of the progressive intelligentsia among its ranks, sprang from the conviction that the movement contained many communist 'plants'. Finally, we come to the Peasant Party

(PSL), which was then at the height of its popularity: contrary to the opinion of the emigration, Stanisław Mikołajczyk became the saviour of the moment for Polish society at that time. According to prevailing popular opinion he had arrived bearing the pledge of England and America. Consequently, he was enthusiastically supported by large sections of the population, who had nothing in common with the Peasant Party, and by the extreme right: not as the leader of his party, but as the legal head of the opposition, a man who enjoyed the confidence of the West, and thus the guarantor of radical changes. On the other hand, Mikołajczyk and his party, counting on free elections controlled by the Allies wished, if only by means of this last, to convey that the whole nation stood behind the Peasant Party. Not wishing to alienate anyone, including right-wing elements, the Peasant Party and its organ *Gazeta Ludowa* avoided making any clear condemnations. For this reason the reactions of *Gazeta Ludowa* to the pogroms were rather luke-warm.

Finally, because of censorship, in no open article against anti-semitism nor in any open discussion, could the concept of the 'Żydo-komuna' be debated since communism itself was not open to discussion – it was to be presented positively.[10] This was the most important motif of the time.

The Jewish population was concentrated mainly in the large towns except in the Reclaimed Territories, that is to say the regions of Lower Silesia, since there the new administration directed the majority of those repatriated from the Soviet Union and there greater opportunities to establish oneself than elsewhere. From the outset a large proportion of Jews worked in positions where no Jews had worked before the war; down mines, at steelworks, on farms. There were Jews in towns like Wałbrzych, Wrocław, Richbach, Bielawa, but also in the surrounding villages where many Jews had wealthy farms.[11] This grouping of Jews in large towns in central Poland and Silesia temporarily had a positive side as far as culture was concerned. Plays were performed to full houses in two Jewish theatres, one in Łódź and the other in Silesia.[12] The appearances of well-known actors at poetry readings and the like were equally well attended. This interest and support made it possible to establish schools where Yiddish and Hebrew were on the curriculum and the ORT, in accordance with its mission, established and maintained technical schools.

The feeling of shock which followed the pogrom in Kielce caused another sudden wave of emigration, both legal and illegal.[13] As mass repatriation from the Soviet Union had come to an end, the Jewish population now stood at less than half its previous size.[14] Essential changes were to come in the near future with the wholesale Stalinization of the country.

I would like to conclude with a few general remarks. As elsewhere, the

Communist Party attempted to pressurize the Jewish sector politically by means of its representatives. The object of this pressure – not without cause – was the Jewish Historical Commission's publishing activities. I can now say, not without pride, that the Commission was able to systematically withstand and oppose all these pressures. Today, after 38 years and after all the changes these years have seen, one experiences no sense of shame or embarrassment on reading any of the numerous publications issued by the Jewish Historical Commission.

Regarding the Polish population, it was, as before, a society made up of many groups who not only avoided becoming subject to any kind of anti-Jewish psychosis but – according to their strength and possibilities – bravely fought against it. It was the combination of the prevailing conflicts, the methods used by the regime and the official censorship, coupled with the promotion of official propaganda, that paralyzed their efforts.[15] The future was also to bring basic changes to the position of the Church on a world-wide scale, as a result of Vatican II, as well as in Poland.

Political constellations in Poland were to change, but always within the limits of the existing system. As far as the Jewish question is concerned, the first post-war years already held all the ominous portents for the future. With each recurring wave of anti-semitism and anti-semitic activity, the Jews were to suffer but Poland itself also suffered, practically, morally and in the opinion of the world. Organically tied as I was to both Polish and Jewish culture and to the Polish struggle for liberation, I felt, on being confronted with all these incidents, not only outrage at the great wrongs being inflicted upon the Jews, but an equally deep concern for the wrongs inflicted by anti-semitism on the Polish nation. I know that many non-Jewish Poles reacted in a similar way.

17

The Jewish issue in post-war communist politics

Lukasz Hirszowicz

The issues of continuity and change must loom large in any discussion of the Jewish question in the ideology and politics of post-war Poland, particularly in the eyes of scholars familiar with the history of Polish–Jewish relations. In the presentation I will mention only marginally the issue of the continuity of anti-Jewish prejudice in the public mind. The communist establishment, which emerged as a political force and as the rulers of the country under the banner of revolutionary change, is the main bearer of continuity in this respect. This is not an unfamiliar paradox: after seizing power many a revolutionary movement has come to emphasize the continuity of national interests and ideologies. The true paradox is the perseverance of the Jewish theme in the ideology and politics of Poland in spite of the enormous change in the strength and character of Poland's Jewish community.

Although no published official statistics exist, the numerical decline – almost the disappearance – of the Polish Jewish community is indisputable. Following World War II, this community was subject to an extraordinary instability. The still numerically significant community of the first post-war years was reduced by emigration as a result of the Holocaust trauma, post-war conditions and the emergence of the State of Israel. The remainder of roughly 50,000 Jews was halved by the post-October 1956 emigration, in spite of the fact that a certain number of the Jews repatriated from the USSR at that time remained in Poland. Those who decided to remain were again considerably reduced, and perhaps more than halved, by emigration in the wake of the 1968 anti-semitic campaign.[1]

Whether the Jews in Poland after, say, 1950 were truly a community is debatable. Only a fraction of the numbers mentioned above declared themselves Jewish in their personal documents or took the step of joining Jewish organizations, secular or religious. Nevertheless, perhaps a great majority of them were identified as Jews by the population and by the authorities.

This fact is of the greatest importance because it rendered the Jews – whatever they may have felt about themselves or how they identified themselves – subject to the authorities' Jewish policies. This became especially clear in 1968. The fact that the Jews were so few did not mean that their position was unimportant. A large number of the Jews lived in Warsaw and other big cities. Many belonged to the intelligentsia, and of these quite a number were engaged in intellectual pursuits as writers, film-makers, journalists and academics. Perhaps most of this group were party members. Until 1968 most of this group believed, to varying degrees, that the new regime in Poland would liberate them completely from their Jewish predicament and facilitate their full assimilation into Polish society.

Prominent among these Jews were leading communist activists, including some who occupied top positions in the party-state. They came to constitute the cornerstone of the political use of the Jewish issue in post-war Poland. In this respect, there has been an amazing element of continuity: in the early post-war years it was the regime's enemies who used the Jews as an argument to show the un-Polish character of the new dispensation;[2] subsequently, particularly in 1968 and afterwards, the Jews were denounced by the communist establishment as aliens responsible for all Poland's difficulties and as the spiritual fathers, and indeed members, of the anti-socialist opposition. Their Jewish ethnic origin was invariably either hinted at or emphasized.

For Poland's communist rulers the Jewish question appeared in a number of different guises, emerging consecutively during the various stages of Poland's post-war history. In the first stage, which coincided with Gomułka's first tenure, the communist regime – imposed as it was on an unwilling nation – sought to present itself as being genuinely Polish and to avoid being identified with the Jews. Gomułka and his team regarded the Jewish question as a function of the mood of the population and as an obstacle to their attempt to shed the image of being stooges of a foreign power and thus acquire Polish legitimacy. Gomułka's policies, especially his cadres policy, were conceived accordingly, but many of them were destined to remain only intentions on account of the dearth of qualified and reliable cadres. Hence the Jewish question appeared as part of the complex of illegitimacy and, since this complex continues to haunt the communist regime to this day, so too does the Jewish question, although its role varies according to circumstances.

In its next manifestation, the Jewish question arose as an element in the power struggle within the party. This occurred in two stages, firstly in the period of Stalinism, which was relatively short in Poland but nevertheless very important, and then during the build-up to the Polish October of 1956. At the beginning of the struggle against the so-called right-wing nationalist deviation – that of Gomułka and his closest friends – the charge of being soft on anti-semitism and, therefore, of not making appropriate use of reliable old communist Jewish cadres played a certain role.[3] Soon this began to give place to another set of arguments about Jewish unreliability, arguments which were a pale replica of the Soviet campaign against 'cosmopolitism', the Slánský trial and the 'Doctors' Plot'.[4] In contradistinction to the attitude to the Jews during Gomułka's first tenure (an attitude which had its roots in the Polish situation) the new attitudes and policies were introduced because they were in line with those which were being established throughout the Soviet bloc. Measures were taken against a few high-ranking Jewish cadres as a repercussion of the Field affair,[5] and in 1952–3 an anti-Jewish purge was initiated, which was stopped only after Stalin's death. These developments were of considerable ideological importance since they made anti-Jewish attitudes and policies acceptable in the party.

During the build-up to the October 1956 crisis, the Jewish question acquired a major role in the internal party struggle and retained much of this role for well over a decade. The internal party struggle unfolded against the background of a major crisis of communist rule in Poland at a time when a major power struggle was going on in the USSR. The political gimmicks used in the power struggle in Poland were the demand that personal responsibility for Stalinist terror be exacted, primarily for the repression and demotion of communist leaders and activists, and the demand that the system, which was a fertile ground for abuses of power and economic mismanagement, be reformed – without, however, jeopardizing the regime. Top party leaders were under attack and, after Bierut's death in March 1956 the supreme position of party First Secretary was at stake.

The above is a very rough and schematic presentation of the claims put forward by the Natolin and Puławska factions which crystallized in the party in 1956. The Jewish issue entered the factional rivalry through the attempt by the Natolin faction to make the Jewish comrades, or some Jewish comrades, scapegoats – to 'Judaize' the issue of personal responsibility, as well as to gain an edge in the struggle for power positions by introducing the principle of national regulation of cadres. The Puławska faction retorted by accusing its opponents of anti-semitism and invoking the connection between anti-semitism and political and social reaction, a connection well-established in the minds of the Polish liberal intelligentsia. It should be realized that the Natolin faction was composed of communist leaders of pure Aryan blood, while the Puławska faction included a considerable contingent of Jewish communists.[6]

Both the Natolin and Puławska factions played to an audience much wider than the party Central Committee or even the Party *actif*. While the addressees of the Puławska faction were reform-minded groups in the *apparat* and population – at a moment of crisis in October 1956 they even implicitly appealed to the prevalent anti-Soviet sentiments – the Natolin faction addressed itself to those in the *apparat* who desired as little change as possible, to the anti-Jewish feelings in the party and the population in general, and to the Soviet leaders.

Although in October 1956 the Natolin faction was defeated, it can be seen from the above that the Puławska faction had little chance of maintaining its strong position in the PUWP. Indeed, its position was gradually undermined. The way in which this occurred was again connected with the use of the Jewish question in the power struggle within the party.[7]

First of all, the personnel policy adopted by the new Gomułka regime towards the Jewish cadres was aimed at gradually removing them from the *apparat*, without, however, resorting to spectacular purges. This was probably in accordance with Gomułka's own inclinations and with the discriminatory practices prevalent in the USSR and the Soviet bloc. Simultaneously, there emerged a faction in the party under General Moczar which transformed the Jewish issue into an instrument for gathering support in the party *apparat* and among the public.[8] Moczar aimed at supreme power – that is, – at replacing Gomułka – and harping on the Jewish issue and arranging limited purges of Jewish personnel was a way of both strengthening his faction and undermining the position of the Gomułka leadership which, in this context, could be presented as 'soft on the Jews', linked with the Jews (real and imaginary), and even as almost Jewish. In a wider context, the issue of the Jews in the party and in the life of the country in general was a useful element in the political philosophy propagated by Moczar himself and by other spokesmen of his faction. This philosophy was, in fact, a variation of the mainstream party political philosophy of national communism which was becoming established under the Gomułka regime.[9] It should be emphasized that, in practice, Gomułka's policy in the matter of the Jewish cadres and that of Moczar had opposite aims. Gomułka saw in his Jewish policy a contribution to stabilizing the situation in the establishment and the country, while Moczar wished to destabilize the situation by using the Jewish issue. An analogy comes to mind with Endecja tactics in their struggle against Piłsudski and his successors.[10]

In its third manifestation, the Jewish question arose in the context of the regime's struggle against the opposition. This emerged in 1968 in a more or less complete form. The use of the Jewish issue was well prepared and well rehearsed in the course of the systematic efforts to bolster the position of the

Moczar faction in the party and the country. Indeed, an important feature of the struggle against the opposition was to present them as a direct continuation of a defeated party faction, emphasizing the Jewish genealogy and connections of both.

The historical circumstances of the 1968 anti-Jewish campaign should not be forgotten. These were not only the Six-day War of 1967 and the prolonged Middle East crisis. Even more important was the emergence of dissident, opposition and reform movements, stronger and more difficult to deal with than before, in Czechoslovakia, Poland and the USSR itself. In the USSR the emergence of a Jewish nationalist movement concurrently with other kinds of dissent should be noted. Hence the Jewish preoccupation of Polish communism linked up with those of other countries in the Soviet bloc which were also faced by the exigencies of the struggle against unwelcome trends.

The chain of events in Poland began in 1967 with an accelerated purge, first of all, but not exclusively, of Jewish cadres from the party *apparat* and the army. Gomułka himself gave the purge a green light in his 'Fifth Column' speech to the trades union congress on 19 June 1967. This was, in a sense, an escalation of the smaller purges which had been going on since 1963–4, when Zambrowski was removed from the Politburo and Moczar became Minister of the Interior.[11] The purge bore all the hallmarks of a Moczar-inspired action, being directed against individuals connected with or sympathetic to the Puławska faction, and concentrating on institutions in which Moczarites had difficulties in penetrating and taking control, such as the Party Higher School of Social Science (WSNS), some military institutions and some publishing houses. The purge was accompanied by intensified anti-Zionist and anti-semitic propaganda, but this was kept within certain limits, at least in the propaganda in the media.[12]

The next stage of the events began early in 1968, ostensibly in connection with the protest against taking off the stage Adam Mickiewicz's romantic nationalist drama, *Dziady*. The developments in Czechoslovakia no doubt loomed large in the minds of both the student protesters and the communist authorities.[13] The students' movement, which in March 1968 spread to higher education establishments throughout the country, was used as a pretext for a vicious campaign in the media and the usual non-media channels. It was here that the Jewish theme appeared in its third, anti-opposition role. The purge was further escalated to cover almost all fields of public life: the state apparatus, the economic institutions, higher education, and so on. Gomułka's reasons were no doubt rooted in his efforts to defend his position in the party and in his impatience with the revisionist and liberal views of the students and their real and alleged supporters. He also, presumably, took into account possible reactions to the events in Poland in the USSR and the Soviet bloc countries. A numerous *actif* of old Moczar supporters and new recruits carried out the task, but again it was Gomułka who approved the measures and added momentum to the campaign in a speech on 19 March to party *apparatchiks* from all over the country.[14]

In this phase, the purge was strongly linked to the onslaught on the students' movement. Professors and junior university staff were sacked, accused of having inspired the movement ideologically and of sympathizing with the students. High officials were purged because their offspring participated in the student protest, or were said to have done so. Others were purged simply because they were connected by a common Jewish origin with some of the student leaders and other purged officials. All were suspected and accused of serving the same foreign masters who were allegedly pulling the strings of the student protest in Poland.[15]

The purpose of the propaganda campaign which began on 11 March was to link as closely as possible the leaders and activists of the student movement and their supporters with the state and party officials purged during the present campaign or earlier; that is, to place genuine dissenters and oppositionists in one basket with individuals who were part of the establishment but had become *personae non gratae* for one reason or another and usually through no fault of their own. This entire group – rebels and those expelled from the establishment alike – was presented as mostly non-Polish and always anti-Polish. They were accused of seeking to topple the existing leadership and to replace it by another (under Roman Zambrowski, it was strongly suggested) and of seeking to restore the position of the ousted Stalinist Jewish leaders in order to serve interests inimical to Poland. The Polish rebels and those purged from the establishment were said to be acting on behalf of Israel, international Zionism, world Jewry and imperialism, in particular US imperialism and West German revanchism.

As can be seen, the propaganda campaign had two foci – Polish internal affairs and the international interests of the Soviet bloc. The propagandists dinned into the heads of the population that the Polish national interest and the Polish ethnic element had finally to establish their dominance in the country's government by removing the Jewish Stalinists and their heirs. The international interests of the Soviet bloc and its Middle Eastern preoccupations did not always find a response in Polish hearts and minds. There had, however, been a Polish–Soviet nexus since 1945 – the bogey of German revanchism – and it was to this nexus that the effort to publicize and denounce the alleged alliance between Israel and world Jewry with the German Federal Republic was related. This campaign had been going on before the events of 1967–8, with the active participation of leading Moczarite lights such as Kazimierz Kąkol and Tadeusz Walichnowski.[16]

An anti-semitic campaign aimed at the Jews' international links and alleged service to causes alien to the nation was no novelty in Poland. In its traditional, right-wing variety, which was not only anti-communist but was also opposed to socialist and libertarian ideas, it was primarily the communist Soviet Union which was allegedly served by the Jews.[17] The new, communist variety, as practised in Poland and elsewhere in the Soviet bloc, was obliged to attack different bogeys and to assume a different name, that of anti-Zionism. Another Soviet characteristic is also apparent. There has always existed in the USSR and other communist countries an inclination to present dissent as a product of foreign and inimical machinations. This argument was used not only in Poland and not only in 1968: it was the line taken by Soviet propaganda about the Czechoslovak 'Spring' of 1968 – in this case, a resolution of a Plenum of the Central Committee of the Czechoslovak Communist Party included 'opposition from Zionist positions' among the reasons for the crisis of communist rule in Czechoslovakia.[18] The Soviet dissident movement since the late 1960s until this day has also been linked by the Soviet media with Jewish ethnic origin and Zionism.

The anti-semitic campaign and purge of 1968 played on existing anti-Jewish prejudices – prejudices which, it seems, had been on the decline since 1956, and were particularly weak among university students. The campaign and the purge were aimed at sowing confusion and deceiving the public; the most immediate aim was, probably, to intimidate Polish society. These two aims were indeed achieved. The conviction that the events were little more than an internal party affair was shared by many Poles, including, it seems, important elements in the Catholic Church.[19] Some even thought that all this might be beneficial from the national point of view: it would make Poland 'more Polish'.[20] Many may have felt disgusted by the anti-semitic campaign but were led to believe that the Jews were the intended victims and that ethnic Poles were safe if they behaved, and might even benefit if they joined. An intimidated society did not react to the new oppressive laws and practices introduced after the events of March 1968 – laws which had met with a strong opposition and could not be enacted earlier. More important still, the participation of Polish forces in the invasion of Czechoslovakia passed virtually without protest. Dissent was isolated and temporarily crushed. The other side of this development was the invigoration of the party which, at grass-roots level, had led a rather subdued existence under the Gomułka regime.

Such were the historical circumstances in which the Jewish question arose as an instrument in the struggle against dissent and opposition. At the time, this was blurred by the fact that 1967–8 was the final act in the internal party struggle which began in 1955–6. Since 1968 the anti-Jewish theme has become an established component in communist propaganda. It is used more sparingly in relatively peaceful times and more widely and with greater emphasis in times of crisis. This was clearly noticeable in 1975-7 – especially after the workers' riot of June 1976 and the establishment of KOR – and in 1980-2, during the period of Solidarity and after the establishment of the military regime.[21]

After 1968 the Jewish question lost its direct significance in internal party rivalries since there were virtually no Jews to be dislodged from the power structure of the party state. This is not to say that there have been no such rivalries, or that Jewish themes have disappeared entirely from the internal party scene. First, it is noticeable during the entire period after the 1968 campaign that these themes have been used in a relatively subdued way by the mainstream party element and in a more explicit manner by certain groups which have usually been described as hardliners. Further, since the principal target of the anti-Jewish propaganda was the opposition to communist autocracy, there existed differences of inclination or opinion – sincere or simulated, genuine or assumed for inner-party political purposes – with regard to the treatment of the opposition. This included whether and to what extent anti-semitic/anti-Zionist propaganda should be resorted to, and these differences have sometimes been a component of a power struggle in the party. Nevertheless, the struggle against the opposition has been the primary objective in the pursuit of which the anti-Jewish propaganda was used. The times of Solidarity as well as the period after the military *coup* of 13 December 1981 are instructive in this respect.

In 1980-1 much was said in the offically controlled media, as well as through non-media channels (whether openly or thinly disguised) about the Jewish character of the opposition, its origins and activities, and the allegedly pernicious role played by the Jews in Poland's history. In the main, the themes of the 1968 propaganda were used and extended. A novum was, on the one hand, the appearance of organizations with an outspoken anti-semitic ideology, such as Grunwald and the hard-line Katowice party forum and, on the other hand, a resolute and vocal opposition within society to the anti-semitic propaganda and anti-semitism in general.[22] The anti-semitic groupings were sponsored by important elements in the party and its central leadership who either sympathized with their views and/or regarded them as helpful in stemming the tide of Solidarity. The opposition to these opinions was motivated not only by the rejection of racialism and xenophobia but also, and probably mainly, by awareness of the harm done to Poland's image in the world and an understanding that anti-semitism was part of a package which included oppressive aims and hard-line policies.[23] Significantly, the view that the anti-semitic propaganda was an internal party affair was not repeated.

In the first weeks after the military *coup* a considerable amount of anti-semitic propaganda appeared. This was soon soft-pedalled, but remarks about the Jewish affiliation of the leaders of the opposition and references to the 1968 events continue to appear in the Polish press, and the anti-semitic Grunwald Patriotic Union maintains a twilight existence. However, at the same time that anti-semitic propaganda was rampant, in December 1981 and January 1982, the authorities took steps to placate the Jews by signing an agreement with the American Joint Distribution Committee which had been expelled from Poland in 1968, and by reassuring the leaders of the Social and Cultural Society of Polish Jews,[24] one of the ethnic minority bodies which operate in Poland. In 1982–3 the authorities embarked on a major exercise to generate Jewish goodwill by celebrating the 40th anniversary of the Warsaw ghetto uprising with much publicity in the country and abroad. Initiatives, with a distinctly pro-Jewish colouring, which originated among parts of the Polish public, have been tolerated and even supported by the authorities. All this has clearly demonstrated the motive of expediency in the communist use of the Jewish question: as long as the military regime was unsure of the extent of active resistance, it did not hesitate to resort to intense anti-semitic propaganda and still uses it against its opponents; yet the regime exploits the long Polish–Jewish historical connection in order to embellish its image. Some probably hope to ease Poland's way in the world of international finance through cultivating the Jews.

It should be kept in mind that in 'real socialism' expediency and ideology are intimate bedfellows. One of the functions of official party history, which is the embodiment of this relationship, is to explain and justify current policies by endowing them with historical context and perspective. It is therefore not out of character that the role the Jewish question has played in communist politics should be reflected in the portrayal of the party's past to the *apparatchiks*, the *actif* and the general public too.

In the first years of People's Poland, when the Jewish question was seen mainly in connection with the party's efforts to acquire Polish legitimacy, Gomułka sought to present the Polish Workers' Party (PPR) as a virtually new creation which has distanced itself from the incorrect, or at least irresolute, positions of the pre-war Communist Party of Poland (KPP) on the Polish national question. The new Polish state, unlike interwar Poland with its high percentage of national minorities, was a national state and the composition of the party should be national too.[25]

The opposition of the ethnic Polish element in the party and the alien Jewish one was implicit in these views, and it became more and more explicit in the course of the inner party struggle in the 1950s and 1960s. The participation of the former KPP Jewish activists in the organs of the party and the state and the role they acquired in the leadership, were said to be at the expense of the ethnic Polish cadres and to have subverted the Polish ways of the party. It was these Jews who practised Stalinism, and later became revisionists and even embraced Jewish nationalism and Zionism. In June 1968, Andrzej Werblan, a high-ranking Central Committee member, published a piece in which these views were codified.[26] Werblan depicted the role of the Jews in Polish communism, in interwar and People's Poland, as the real reason for the 1968 events which, from this perspective, were the culmination of a long-standing conflict in the party between the Polish and the Jewish elements.

In 1980–1, with the general preoccupation with the reasons and roots of Poland's crises, party ideologists, historians and propagandists claimed that the turn in the party's policies in 1948 – when Gomułka was removed from the leadership – was the origin of the later crisis-ridden development of the People's Republic. According to these views, the Jews, who at that time assumed leading positions in the party, were not removed in 1956, and they were burdened with the responsibility for the return to 'bureaucratic centralism' – another neat word used in these debates. They were decisively defeated and eliminated in 1968. The implication, and this was often stated explicitly in words and print, was that the physical and spiritual heirs of these leaders were the evil spirit behind Solidarity and all the anti-socialist activities against the party and the state.

This presentation of the history of Poland's ruling party was given in a number of variations: milder versions appeared in the party's central organs, *Trybuna Ludu* for instance,[27] and much more extreme ones in *Żolnierz Wolności*, *Za Wolność i Lud* and other organs.[28] In the free conditions of the Solidarity period polemics appeared against this view, in particular against the thesis of the Jewish character of Stalinism in Poland, and against the view of the responsibility of Jewish leaders for the developments since October 1956.[29]

However, as far as the party press is concerned, only *Polityka* has opposed these anti-semitic versions of Poland's recent history. But these versions continue to be circulated and, as mentioned above, the media often carry explicit references or veiled hints regarding the Jewish origin of the regime's opponents and the non-Polish and Jewish origins of the opposition. Zionist circles – a euphemism for Western Jewry and Israel – are occasionally mentioned as Poland's enemies who initiate all kinds of anti-Polish slander in an attempt to damage the reputation of Poland and the Polish nation. It seems that the communist regime, even when showing interest in correct relations with Jewry and Israel, still feels that political expediency demands the retention of the Jewish bogey in its gallery of Poland's internal and foreign foes.

Notes

INTRODUCTION

1 *Polin*, the Hebrew word for Poland was obviously derived from the German *Polen*. But its etymology was also explained as deriving from the Hebrew words *po lin* – there find rest (or haven).
2 '*Cum ira et studio*'. A Polish version of this article appeared in *Puls* 24 (winter 1984–5 London). The English language version quoted here is to appear in the first issue of *POLIN. A Journal of Polish—Jewish Studies.*.
3 p.160
4 The report, which is in the Hoover Institution Archives, Polish Government Documents Collection, box 921, was published by David Engel in *Jewish Social Studies* I, Vol. XLV.
5 L. Dobroszycki, 'Restoring Jewish Life in Post-war Poland', *Soviet Jewish Affairs*, 2 (1973), p. 59.
6 '*Cum ira et studio*', *Puls*, 24 (winter 1984–5).
7 Marek Leski, 'Glossa do "Żydów Polskich" Normana Daviesa' ('Gloss on Norman Davies' "Polish Jews") *Arka*, 10 (1985).
8 J. Ficowski, *Odczytanie popiołów* (A Reading of Ashes, London, 1979).
9 A. Slonimski.

CHAPTER 1   BEGINNINGS OF JEWISH SETTLEMENT IN POLAND

1 See for example M. Weinreich, *History of the Yiddish Language*, tr. S. Noble (Chicago, 1980), p. 90.
2 Cf. *Gli Ebrei nell alto medioevo* (2 vols, Spoleto, 1980) Settimane di studio XXVI, with contributions by T. Lewicki, A Gieysztor et al.; S. W. Baron, A. Kahan, N. Gross, *Economic History of the Jews* (New York, 1975) especially the bibliography, p. 290 ff.
3 M. Lombard, *L'Islam dans sa première grandeur VIIe-XIe s.* (Paris, 1977); M. Lombard, *Espaces et réseaux du haut Moyen Age* (Paris, 1972); H. Łowmiański,

210 *Notes to pp. 16—18*

Początki Polski. Z dziejów Słowian w I tysiącleciu n.e. (The beginnings of Poland. On the history of the Slavs in the first millennium of our era) vols I–VI 1/2 (Warsaw, 1964–85); T. Lewicki, 'Il commercio arabe con la Russia e con i paesi slavi d'Occidente nei secoli IX–X' in *Annali dell Instituto univ. orientale di Napoli*, vol. 8 (1959), p. 47 ff.

4 N. Golb and O. Pritsak, *Khazarian Hebrew Documents of the Tenth Century*, 2 vols (Ithaca, 1982); P. B.Golden, *Khazar Studies: An Historico-Philological Inquiry into the Origins of the Khazars*, 2 vols (Budapest, 1980); O. Pritsak, 'The Khazar Kingdom's Conversion to Judaism' in *Harvard Ukrainian Studies, vol. II/3 (1978), p. 261 ff*; D. M. Dunlop, *The History of the Jewish Khazars* (New York, 1967); M. I. Artamonov, *Istoriia Khazar* (Leningrad, 1962).

5 T. Lewicki, *Źródla arabskie do dziejów Słowiańszczyzny* (Arab sources on the history of the Slavs), vol. I (Wrocław, 1956); Ibn-Hurdadbih, p. 43 ff.

6 Golb and Pritsak, *Khazarian Hebrew Documents*.

7 T. Kowalski, 'Relacja Ibrahima ibn Jakuba' (The account of Ibrahim ibn Jakub) in *Mon. Poloniae Hist.*, s. II, vol. I (Cracow, 1946); T. Lewicki, 'Certaines routes commerciales de la Hongrie du haut Moyen Age', *Slavia Antiqua*, vol. 14 (1967), p. 15 ff.

8 F. Rörig, 'Magdeburg und die ältere Handelsgeschichte' in *Wirtschaftskräfte im Mittelalter* (Vienna, 1971), p. 612 ff; F. Kupfer and T. Lewicki, *Źródła hebrajskie do dziejów Słowian i niektórych innych ludow środkowej i wschodniej Europy* (Hebrew sources on the history of the Slavs and some other peoples of central and eastern Europe) (Wrocław, 1956), p. 43 f; *Passio sancti Adalberti* J. Karwasińska (ed.) *Mon. Pol. Hist.*, n.s., vol. 431 (Warsaw, 1962), p. 76.

9 A. Zaki *Archeologia Małpolóski wczesnośredniowieczenego* (The archaeology of Malo – Polska in the early middle ages) (Cracow, 1974).

10 The work of Iehuda ben Meir ha-Kohen is preserved in later rabbinical writings; cf. Kupfer and Lewicki, *Źródla hebrajskie*, p. 33; I. A. Agus, *Urban Civilization in Pre-Crusade Europe* (Leiden, 1965), vol. I, p. 93.

11 Kupfer and Lewicki, *Źródla hebrajskie*, p. 41 ff; B. Weinryb, *The Jews of Poland: A Social and Economic History of the Jewish Community in Poland from 1100 to 1800* (Philadelphia, 1973), p. 21, does not accept the identification with Przemysl.

12 W. Swoboda in *Słownik Starożytności Słowiańskich* (A dictionary of Slavic antiquities) (1980) vol. VI, p. 537 ff.

13 M. K. Karger, *Drevnii Kiev* (Kiev, 1958), vol. I, p. 13; *Słownik geograficzny Królestwa Polskiego i innych krajów slowiańskich* (A geographic dictionary of the kingdom of Poland and other Slav countries) (1883), vol. IV, p. 537 ff.

14 D. S. Likhačev (ed.) *Povest vremmennykh let* (Moscow, 1950), vol. I, p. 196.

15 S. Suchodolski, *Początki mennictwa w Europie środkowej, wschodniej i pół nocnej* (The beginnings of coinage in central, eastern and northern Europe) Wrocław, 1971; Gieysztor in *Gli Ebrei*.

16 Kupfer and Lewicki, *Źródła hebrajskie*, p. 56 ff.

17 R. Kiersnowski, *Wstęp do numizmatyki polskiej wieków średnich* (An introduction to Polish numismatics of the middle ages) (Warsaw, 1964), p. 71.

18 *Codex diplomaticus necnon epistolaris Silesiae* (Wrocław, 1956), vol. I, 103/1203, 107/1204 (Iozeph et Chazkel Iudei).

19 *Słownik geograficzny*, vol. XIV, p. 883 ff.

20 Weinreich, *History of the Yiddish Language*, p. 45 ff.

21 Ibid., p. 61: 'a separate language of Jews, however similar to Greek'.

22 A. Asher, *The Itinerary of Rabbi Benjamin of Tudela* (London, 1840), vol. I, pp. 111 and 164.

23 J. Hoffman, 'Die Östliche Adriaküste als Hauptnachschubbasis für den venezianschen Sklavenhandel bis zum Ausgang des 11. Jah.', *Vierteljahrschrift für Sozial- u. Wirtschaftsgeschichte*, vol. 55 (1968), pp. 165 ff; S. W. Baron, *A Social and Religious History of the Jews*, 2nd edn (New York, 1957), vol. 3, p. 1220 f; A. Bruckner, *Słownik etymologiczny języka polskiego* (Etymological dictionary of the Polish language) (Cracow, 1927), pp. 669.

24 Weinreich, *History of the Yiddish Language*, p. 83.

25 Kupfer and Lewicki, *Źródła hebrajskie*, p. 269.

26 Weinreich, *History of the Yiddish Language*, 'there was the Slavic determinant encountered in western Knaan.'

27 Ibid., p. 90.

28 Agus, *Urban Civilization*, p. 220.

29 E. Ashton, *A Social and Economic History of the Near East in the Middle Ages* (London, 1976), p. 36 ff; H. L. Misbach, 'The Balanced Economic Growth of Carolingian Europe', *Journal of Interdisciplinary History*, vol. 3 (1972), p. 261 f; D. Herlihy, 'Three Patterns of Social Mobility in Medieval History', ibid., vol. 4 (1973), p. 263 ff.

30 Suchodolski, *Początki mennictwa*, p. 97.

31 K. Maleczynski (ed.) *Galli Anonymi Cronicae*, *Mon. Pol. Hist.* (Cracow, 1952), s. II, vol. II, p. 63.

32 S. Suchodolski, *Mennictwo polskie w XI i XII wieku* (Polish mints of the eleventh and twelfth centuries) (Wrocław, 1973), p. 105 ff.

CHAPTER 2 MERCHANTS AND BUSINESSMEN IN POZNAŃ & CRACOW

1 A. Mączak, 'La Pologne et l'Europe', in *Dzieje gospodarcze Polski do r. 1939* (Economic History of Poland to 1939), ed. B. Zientara (Warsaw, 1973), pp. 241–4. See too J. Topolski, 'La reféodalisation dans l'économie des grandes domaines en Europe Centrale aux XVIe et XVIIe siècles', in *Studia historiae oeconomicae* (Poznań, 1971), vol. 6, pp. 51–63. Finally, obligatory reading, A. Wyczański, 'Le XVIe siècle, époque d'une crise de la paysannerie polonaise?' in *Studia hist. oecon.* (Poznan, 1978), vol. 13, pp. 113–18.

2 A. Mączak, *Między Gdańskiem a Sundem* (Between Gdansk and Sund) (Warsaw, 1972), p. 139. The author dates the decline to the first half of the seventeenth century.

3 See in G. Labica (ed.) *Dictionnaire critique du marxisme* (Paris, 1983) the articles *Mode de production* and *Féodalisme*.

4 M. Horn, 'Rzemieślnicy żydowscy na Rusi Czerwonej na Przelomie XVI i XVII w' (Jewish craftsmen in Red Russia at the turn of the 17th century) in *Biul. Żyd. Inst. Hist.* 91 (1960), pp. 28–70.

5 Y. Renouard, *Les marchands et les hommes d'affaires italiens au Moyen Age* (Paris, 1968), p. 7.

6 M. Horn, 'Majer Bałaban, historyk żydów w Polsce i pedagog' (Majer Bałaban, Historian of the Polish Jews and Pedagogue) in *Biul. Zyd. Inst. Hist.* 3–4 (1982), pp. 3–16.

7 K. Bartoszewicz, *Antysemityzm w literaturze polskiej, XVI—XVII w.* (Anti-semitism in Polish literature) (Cracow, 1914).

8 I am referring to the *Mémoires de maitrise*, the originals of which are now held in the Jewish History Institute in Poland (Warsaw).

9 'La Pologne et la Hongrie aux XVIe–XVIIe siècles' in *Actes du colloque polono—hongrois de Budapest 1976?*, ed. V. Zimanyi (Budapest, 1981).

10 M. Grycz, *Handel Poznania, 1550—1655* (Poznań Trade) (Poznań, 1964).

11 S. W. Baron *A Social and Religious History of the Jews, Poland and Lithuania 1550—1650* (New York, 1976), vol. XVI, pp. 182–4.

12 D. Tollet, 'Marchands et hommes d'affaires juifs dans la Pologne des Wasa, 1588–1668'. Thesis for the Doctorat d'Etat, 628 p. + X p, submitted 17 March 1984, in the University of Paris I – Panthéon-Sorbonne. Cf. pp. 52–128.

13 S. Hoszowski, 'Klęski elementarne w Polsce w latach 1587–1648' (Natural Catastrophes in Poland from 1587 to 1648) in *Prace z dziejów Polski feudalnej ofiarowane Romanowi Grodeckiemu na 70 rocznicę urodzin* (Warsaw, 1960), pp. 453–66. The author considers that the bad harvests and the epidemics only rarely affected the whole of Poland and that they did not cause price rises because of the lack of means of transport. The author however points to some difficult periods for the ensemble of the Confederation, in 1589–90, 1598–1602, 1621–5 and 1628–31, when the epidemics coincided with bad harvests.

14 On this question cf. A. Jobert, *De Luther à Mohila, la Pologne dans la crise de la Chrétienté, 1517—1648* (Paris, 1974), pp. 37–40 and 185–207.

15 D. Tollet, 'La Littérature antisémite polonaise de 1588 à 1668', in *Revue francaise d'Histoire du Livre* (Bordeaux, 1977). 14, pp. 1–35.

16 In this connection, anti-semitism in Poland had penetrated less than in Spain. Cf. in *Les problèmes de l'exclusion en Espagne, XIVe—XVIe siècle*, studies brought together by A. Redondo (Paris, 1983), pp. 51–75, Josette Riandière la Roche's study, 'Du discours d'exclusion des Juifs, anti-judaisme ou anti-sémitisme?'.

17 D. Tollet, 'Marchands et hommes d'affaires juifs', pp. 332–92.

18 Y. M. Bercé, in *Révoltes et Révolutions dans l'Europe moderne* (Paris, 1980), p. 174, points out that in Eastern Europe 'les seigneurs n'étaient plus des rentiers mais des entrepreneurs'. This explains at once the relatively moderate taxation and the absence of popular uprisings. Moreover, the nobility tried to counter absolutism by refusing to pay excessive state taxes at least until the wars in the middle of the seventeenth century.

19 J. Bieniarzówna, *Mieszczaństwo krakowskie XVII w.* (The Cracow bourgeoisie in 17th century) (Cracow, 1969), pp. 9–102; D. Tollet 'Les gens au pouvoir dans les villes royales dans de la Pologne des Wasa (1588–1668)' in *Społeczeństwo Staropolskie* (Warsaw), T. IV, forthcoming.

20 Relevant here is one of the *Maitrises* kept in the Ż.I.H.: H. Giejzer, *Życie żydów w*

Polsce XVI i XVII w. na podstawie responsów (Maitrise No. 51) (The life of Jews in Poland in the 16th and 17th centuries according to the *Responsa*).

CHAPTER 3 PRIVILEGES GRANTED TO JEWISH COMMUNITIES

1 See M. Bobrzyński, *Szkice i studja historyczne* (Sketches and historical studies) (Cracow, 1922), vol. I, p. 187; K. Maleczyński, *Zarys dyplomatyki polskiej wieków średnich* (An outline of the Polish charters in the Middle Ages) (Wrocław, 1951), p. 19; W. Sobociński, 'Historia rządów opiekuńczych w Polsce' (A history of tutelary authorities in Poland), in *Czasopismo Prawno — Historyczne* (1949), vol. II, pp. 310–312; H. Grajewski, *Granice czasowe mocy obowiązującej norm dawnego prawa polskiego* (Time limits in the validity of the norms of old Polish law) (Łódź, 1970), pp. 19–20; S. Kuraś, *Przywileje prawa niemieckiego miast i wsi małopolskich XIV–XV wieku* (The privileges of German towns and villages in Małopolska in the fourteenth and fifteenth centuries) (Wrocław-Warsaw-Cracow-Gdańsk, 1971), pp. 20–1; T. Opas, 'Miasta prywatne a Rzeczpospolita' (Private towns and the Republic) in *Kwartalnik Historyczny* (1971), vol. XXVIII, p. 32. As a result, to secure themselves against the danger of losing their rights, the Jewish communities made a point of having their privileges frequently confirmed, and throughout the period of the Polish Commonwealth, 'up to and including the reign of Stanisław August, it was considered that a document issued by the reigning king had greater legal force than the documents of his predecessors', see, Kuraś *Przywileje prawa niemieckiego*, p. 21.

2 See Bobrzyński, *Szkice i studja*, vol. I, p. 182.

3 S. Kutrzeba, *Historia źródeł dawnego prawa polskiego* (A history of the sources of old Polish law) (Lwów-Warsaw-Cracow, 1926), vol. II, pp. 297–317; S. Bershadsky, *Litovskie Evrei* (Lithuanian Jews) (St. Petersburg, 1883), vol. I, pp. 74–6; I. Lewin, 'The Protection of Jewish Religious Rights by Royal Edicts in Ancient Poland', in *The Quarterly Bulletin of the Polish Institute of Arts and Sciences in America* (1943), pp. 3–23. The source analysis of privileges and similar documents in Poland has so far mostly covered the medieval period. An attempt has been made recently to widen this scope to include the Renaissance; see A. Tomczak, 'Kilka uwag o kancelarii królewskiej w drugiej połowie XVI w.' (Some remarks on the royal chancellory in the second half of the sixteenth century) in *Archeion* (1962), vol. XXXVII, pp. 236–252. On privileges as one of the most important kinds of medieval documents, see Maleczyński, *Zarys dyplomatyki*, p. 26; S. Kętrzyński, *Zarys nauki o dokumencie polskim wieków średnich* (An outline of the knowledge of Polish medieval documents) (Warsaw, 1934). The concept of the privilege underwent changes in the Middle Ages, see H. Breslau, *Handbuch der Urkundenlehre für Deutschland und Italien* (Leipzig, 1912), vol. I, pp. 57–8, 62–3, 77.

4 See S. Grodziski, 'O nową syntezę historii źródeł dawnego prawa polskiego' (For a new synthesis of the history of the sources of old Polish law), in *Czasopismo Prawno — Historyczne* (1974), vol. XXVI, 1, pp. 1–20.

5 A. Prochaska,'Przywileje dla starszyzny cygańskiej w Polsce (Privileges of the

Gypsy elders in Poland), in *Kwartalnik Historyczny* (1900), vol. XIV, pp. 83–9; J. Broda, 'Przywileje nominacyjne na króla cygańskiego w Polsce z 1731 r. i na wójtostwo (The privilege of nominating the Gypsy king in Poland in 1731 and the Gypsy elders in 1732), in *Czasopismo Prawno — Historyczne* (1951), vol. III, pp. 346–56.

6 See Grodziski, 'O nową syntezę historii źródeł dawnego prawa polskiego', p. 14.

7 See A. F. Stewart (ed.) *Papers Relating to the Scots in Poland, 1576—1793* (Edinburgh, 1915).

8 See J. Kazimierski, 'Z dziejów Węgrowa w XV–XVII wieku' (On the history of Węgrow from the fifteenth to the eighteenth century), in *Rocznik Mazowiecki* (1970), vol. III, pp. 275–6.

9 See J. Bardach, *Historia państwa i prawa Polski* (A history of the state and law of Poland) (Warsaw, 1964), vol. I, p. 160.

10 See J. Morgensztern, 'Regesty z Metryki Koronnej do historii Żydów w Polsce (Abstracts from the Royal registers dealing with the history of the Jews in Poland, 1574–1587), in *Biuletyn Żydowskiego Instytutu Historycznego* (196), vol. XLVII–XLVIII, pp. 70, 110, 112–13, 121; J. Morgensztern, 'Regesty dokumentów z Metryki Koronnej i Sigillat do historii Żydów w Polsce (1668–1696) (Abstracts of documents from the Royal registry and the office of the Seal dealing with the history of the Jews in Poland, 1668–1696), in *Biuletyn Żydowskiego Instytutu Historycznego* (1969), vol. LXIX, pp. 78–80; M. Horn, *Regesty dokumentów i ekscerpty z Metryki Koronnej do historii Żydów w Polsce 1697—1795* (Abstracts of documents in excerpts from the royal registers dealing with the history of the Jews in Poland, 1697–1795) (Wrocław-Warsaw-Cracow-Gdańsk-Łódź, 1984), vol. I, pp. 3–17 and vol. II, pp. 49–55.

11 See G. Rolbiecki, *Prawo przemysłowe miasta Wschowy w XVIII w.* (The industrial law of the town of Wschowa in the eighteenth century) (Poznań, 1951), p.500; R. Gawiński, *'Reforma cechów rzemieślniczych w Polsce w okresie rozkładu feudalizmu'* (Reform of the artisan guilds in Poland in the period of the collapse of feudalism), in *Zeszyty Naukowe Wyższej Szkoły Ekonomicznej* (Łódź, 1959), vol. V, p. 50.

12 Morgensztern, *'Regesty dokumentów z Metryki Koronnej i Sigillat do historii Żydów w Polsce (1668—1696)',* pp. 78–80.

13 See ibid.; Horn, *Regesty dokumentów i ekscerpty z Metryki Koronnej,* vol. I, pp. 13–17; vol. II, pp. 49–55.

14 In 1566 King Zygmunt August issued a privilege to Benedykt Lewith granting him the monopoly of importing Hebrew books and trading them in in the Polish Commonwealth, cf. M. Bersohn (ed.) *Dyplomataryusz dotyczący Żydów w dawnej Polsce na źródłach archiwalnych osnuty (1388—1782)* (A list of charters dealing with Jews in former Poland taken from archival sources, 1388–1782) (Warsaw, 1910), pp. 76–7; Morgensztern, 'Regesty z Metryki Koronnej do historii Żydów w Polsce (1574–1587)', p. 119. The Yiddish translation of the Bible made by Jekutiel ben Isaac Blitz, published in Amsterdam between 1676 and 1678, includes the privilege of King Jan III allowing the circulation and sale of this book in Poland.

15 On privileges granting the monopoly of publishing newspapers in Poland in the eighteenth century, see J. Łojek, *Gazeta Warszawska księ Łuskiny (1774– 1793)* (The *Gazeta Warszawska* of Father Łuskina, 1774–1793) (Warsaw, 1959), p. 18; J. Szczepaniec, 'Monopol prasowy Tadeusza Włodka w Polsce w latach 1793–1796' (Tadeusz Włodek's press monopoly in Poland in the years 1793– 96), in *Ze skarbca kultury* (From the treasure house of culture) (Wrocław, 1964), pp. 5–115; J. Łojek, 'Likwidacja monopolu prasowego Tadeusza Włodka (1796)' (The liquidation of Tadeusz Włodek's press monopoly in 1796), in *Rocznik Historii Czasopiśmiennictwa Polskiego* (1967), vol. VI, 10, p. 10.

16 On the privilege granted by the leaders of the Targowica Confederation to the ennobled townsman Dangel in 1793, see K. Zienkowska, '"Urodzony" majster Dangel i jego spór z cechami warszwawskimi (Z dziejów manufaktur mieszczańskich XVIII w.)' (Master Dangel and his dispute with the Warsaw guilds –on the history of bourgeois manufacturing in the eighteenth century) in *Warszawa XVIII wieku* (Warsaw in the eighteenth century) (1972), vol. I, pp. 267–9. In Austria, however, manufacturers of luxury goods received privileges from the kings freeing them from the limitations imposed by the guild regulations, see G. Otruba, 'Von der "Fabriksprivilegien" des 17. und 18. Jahrhunderts zum "Osterreichischen Fabrikenrecht" 1838', in *Scripta Mercatura* (1976), vol. II. See also K. Wierzbicka-Michalska, 'Monopol czy wolna konkurencja (Z dziejów teatru warszawskiego w latach 1791–1793)' (Monopoly or free competition – on the history of the theatre in Warsaw in the years 1791– 1793), in *Warszawa XVIII wieku* (1975), vol. III on a different type of individual privileges. Bujak writes of the Jews of the period that they 'did not achieve anything outstanding (in commerce). At least we do not hear of any great Jewish merchant and financiers in the eighteenth century', see F. Bujak, 'Siły gospodarcze – czynnik gospodarczy w upadku dawnego państwa polskiego' (Economic forces – the economic factor in the collapse of the old Polish state), in H. Madurowicz-Urbańska (ed.), F. Bujak, *Wybór pism* (Collected works) (Warsaw, 1976), vol. II, p. 258.

17 See J. Kalisch, 'Sächsisch-polnische Pläne zur Gründung einer See und Handelskompanie am Ausgang des 17. Jh.', in J. Kalisch and J. Gierowski (eds) *Um die polnische Krone Sachsen und Polen während des Nordischen Krieges 1700–1721* (Berlin, 1962), pp. 48–9, 53–6, 59–60, 65–6, 69.

18 See W. Pohorille, 'Dostawy wojskowe Szmula Jakubowicza Zbytkowera' (The military supplies of Szmul Jakubowicz Zbytkower), in *Księga ku czci Berka Joselewicza* (A book in honour of Berek Joselewicz) (Warsaw, 1934), pp. 125–7; E. Ringelblum, 'Samuel Zbytkower – An Economic and Social Leader in Poland at the Time of the Partition', in *Zion* (1938), vol. III (in Hebrew); A. Eisenbach and J. Kosim, 'Akt masy spadkowej Judyty Jakubowiczej' (The will of Judith Jakubowicz), in *Biuletyn Żydowskiego Instytutu Historycznego* (1961), vol. XXXIX, p. 89.

19 Archiwum Główne Akt Dawnych in Warsaw (AGAD), Archiwum Radziwiłłowskie, XXIII, 132, fo. 26r–26v.

20 AGAD, Księga kanclerska, 25, pp. 22–3.

21 Archiwum Państwowe Lublin, Księga Miejska Opola, 6, fo. 292v.

22 Kutrzeba, *Historia źródeł*, vol. II, p. 307: '... the most numerous group, numerically much larger and more significant than the other two [groups, of general and regional privileges], consists of privileges issued by the kings to individual Jewish communities.'

23 For the causal nexus between the two, see M. Schorr, *Rechtsstellung und innere Verfassung der Juden in Polen. Ein geschichtlicher Rundblick* (Berlin-Vienna, 1917), p. 9.

24 Cf. Volumina Legum, vol. I, p. 550; M. Bałaban, 'Ze studiów nad ustrojem prawnym Żydów w Polsce. Sędzia żydowski i jego kompetencje' (Studies on the legal situation of Jews in Poland. The Jewish judge and his competence), in *Pamiętnik ku czci Prof. Przemysława Dąbkowskiego* (A memorial to honour Professor Przemyslaw Dąbrowski) (Lwów, 1927), p. 49.

25 Previous constitutions of the Diet limiting the power of the burghers were promulgated in 1496, 1507 and 1508, cf. *Volumina Legum*, vol. I, pp. 371, 533, 544; these, however, did not directly affect the privately owned towns.

26 Cf. *Volumina Legum*, vol. I, p. 282; vol. II, pp. 124, 252, 367, 368; see Opas, 'Miasta prywatne a Rzeczypospolita', p. 30; A. Wyrobisz, 'Rola miast prywat-nych w Polsce w XVI i XVII wieku' (The role of private towns in Poland in the sixteenth and seventeenth centuries), in *Przegląd Historyczny* (1974), vol. LXV, p. 33.

27 See Bałaban, *Ze studiów nad ustrojem prawnym Żydów w Polsce*, p. 249.

28 Wyrobisz, 'Rola miast prywatnych w Polsce', p. 33; A. Wyrobisz, 'Materiały do dziejów handlu w miasteczkach polskich na początku XVIII wieku' (Materials on the history of trade in Polish small towns at the beginning of the eighteenth century), in *Przegląd Historyczny* (1971), vol. LXII, p. 715.

29 Beginning in 1518 the royal courts refused to adjudicate cases concerning peasants in *szlachta* villages, see Bobrzyński, *Szkice i studja*, vol. II, p. 213. The competence of the referendary courts was limited in 1538 to cases involving royal lands, see J. Rafacz, *Sąd Referendarski Koronny. Z dziejów obrony prawnej chłopów w dawnej Polsce* (The royal referendary court. On the history of the legal rights of peasants in former Poland) (Poznań, 1948), p. 10.

30 J. Bardach, 'Statuty Wielkiego Księstwa Litewskiego – pomniki prawa doby Odrodzenia' (The statutes of the Grand Duchy of Lithuania – memorials to the law of the Renaissance epoch), in *Kwartalnik Historyczny* (1974), vol. LXXXI, pp. 755–65.

31 AGAD, Archiwum Radziwiłłowskie, XXIII, 132, fo. 26v.

32 Ossolineum, II (1431), p. 95.

33 S. Ettinger, 'The Legal and Social Status of the Jews in the Ukraine from the Fifteenth to the Seventeenth Centuries', in *Zion*, vol. XX, 3–4 (1955), pp. 134–8 (in Hebrew); J. Bardach, 'Sądy i postępek sądowy na lewobrzeżnej Ukrainie w XVII–XVIII wieku' (Courts and court procedure in left-bank Ukraine in the seventeeth and eighteenth centuries), in *Czasopismo Prawno — Historyczne* (1968), vol. XX, 2, p. 131; idem, 'Statuty Wielkiego Księstwa Litewskiego', pp. 773–4.

34 See Central Zionist Archives, Jerusalem, Sokolow Archives, A (1855). Independently of this, the community of Łuck also owned a privilege granted

by King Zygmunt August on 30 June 1556, cf. *Russko—Evreisky Archiv. Dokumenty y regesty k'istorii litovskich Evreev (1550—1569)* (Russian–Jewish Archive. Documents and abstracts on the history of Lithuanian Jews 1550–1569) (St. Petersburg, 1882), pp. 52–4. In 1506 and 1527 the Jews in Łuck were granted certain tax concessions, cf. *Russko—Evreisky Archiv. Dokumenty y regesty k'istorii litovskich Eevreev (1388—1550)* (St. Petersburg, 1882), pp. 68–9, 148–9.

35 The privilege granted by King Stefan Bathory is also mentioned in the inspection report of the Łuck *starostwo* of 1628, cf. A. Jabłonowski (ed.) *Lustracje królewszczyzn ziem ruskich, Wołynia, Podola i Ukrainy z pierwszej połowy XVII wieku* (Inspections of the royal lands in Rus, Volynia, Podolia and the Ukraine in the first half of the seventeenth century) (Warsaw, 1877), pp. 167–8. The privilege granted by King Stefan Bathory was confirmed in 1589 by King Zygmunt III, cf. Dyplomataryusz, pp. 113–14; in a special document of 1626 King Zygmunt III permitted the construction of a synagogue in Łuck, cf. ibid., pp. 127–9. For the construction of a fortified synagogue there, see M. Horn, *Powinności wojenne Żydów w Rzeczypospolitej w XVI i XVII wieku* (Military obligations of the Jews in the Republic in the sixteenth and seventeenth centuries) (Warsaw, 1978), pp. 56–8.

36 Cf. Central Zionist Archives, Jerusalem, Sokolow Archives, A (1855).

37 Copy of a letter concerning Jewish residence sent by Karol Kobyliński to the Burgomaster of Sokołów, AGAD, Komisja Rządowa Spraw Wewnętrznych, 185, fos. 112r–113r. The authority and the powers of the lords of privately owned towns are discussed in greater detail by S. Kutrzeba, 'Autonomia miast i władza ustawodawcza panów miast w dawnej Rzeczypospolitej Polskiej' (The autonomy of towns and the legal authority of the lords of towns in the former Republic of Poland), in *Księga Pamiątkowa ku czci Oswalda Balzera* (Memorial book in honour of Oswald Balzer) (Lwów, 1925), vol. II, pp. 91, 93; Z. Kulejewska-Topolska, *Nowe lokacje miejskie w Wielkopolsce od XVI do końca XVIII wieku. Studium historyczno-prawne* (New urban locations in Wielkopolska from the sixteenth to the end of the eighteenth centuries. A historico-legal study) (Poznań, 1964), pp. 62–70; Opas, 'Miasta prywatne a Rzeczypospolita', pp. 28–33. Sometimes the *voivodes* granted privileges to Jewish communities in royal towns, see W. Chomętowski, 'Wiadomości o życiu i pismach Jana Ostroga wojewody poznańskiego' (Information on the life and writings of Jan Ostroga, *voivode* of Poznań), in *Materiały do dziejów rolnictwa w Polsce w XVI i XVII wieku* (Materials on the history of agriculture in Poland in the sixteenth and seventeenth centuries), ed. W. Chomętowski (Warsaw, 1876), pp. 27–32.

38 AGAD, Księga Kanclerska, 25, pp. 840–4.

39 AGAD, Księga Kanclerska, 30, pp. 1052–8.

40 Ossolineum, II/1431, p. 97.

41 AGAD, Księga Kanclerska, 34, p. 150.

42 AGAD, Księga Kanclerska, 25, pp. 35–8.

43 Ossolineum, 1431/II, pp. 56–8.

44 AGAD, Księga Kanclerska, 27, pp. 667–71.

45 AGAD, Księga Kanclerska, 27, pp. 510–16.

46 AGAD, Księga Kanclerska, 27, pp. 112–14.
47 Ossolineum, II/1431, p. 97.
48 Cf. *Volumina Legum*, vol. V, p. 192.
49 Cf. ibid., p. 288. The privilege granted to the Jews of Parczew is mentioned by Morgensztern, 'Regesty z Metryki Koronnej do historii Żydów w Polsce 1588–1632', p. 69; eadem, 'Regesty dokumentów z Metryki Koronnej i Sigillat do historii Żydow w Polsce 1668–1696', p. 75. This privilege is omitted by M. Zakrzewska-Dubasowa, *Parczew w XV—XVIII wieku* (Parczew from the fifteenth to the eighteenth century) (Lublin, 1962).
50 Cf. *Volumina Legum*, vol. VII, pp. 26–9, 81–3, 352; vol. VIII, pp. 95, 147–8; vol. IX, p. 404, mentioning other constitutions having only temporary or local significance.
51 Cf. *Volumina Legum*, vol. VII, p. 352.
52 Kuraś, *Przywileje prawa niemieckiego*, p. 48.
53 S. Estreicher, *Kultura prawnicza w Polsce XVI w* (Legal culture in sixteenth century Poland) (Cracow, 1931), p. 15.
54 AGAD, Księga Kanclerska, 28, pp. 439–43.
55 Cf. Biblioteka Polskiej Akademii Nauk w Kórniku, nos 2063, 2064.
56 See Ł. Charewiczowa, *Dzieje miasta Złoczowa* (The history of the town of Złoczów) (Złoczów, 1929), p. 64); E. Horn, 'Położenie prawno-ekonomiczne Żydów w miastach ziemi halickiej na przełomie XVI i XVII w.' (The legal and economic position of Jews in the towns of the Halicz region at the turn of the sixteenth and seventeenth centuries), in *Biuletyn Żydowskiego Instytutu Historycznego* (1961), vol. XL, pp. 21–2, 24. On the conflict of privileges issued to Jews in Poland and other European countries with other laws, see Kuraś, *Przywileje prawa niemieckiego*, pp. 46–7.
57 Cf. *Volumina Legum*, vol. II, p. 295. Serious gaps appeared in the fifteenth century and at the beginning of the sixteenth in documents issued by the Lithuanian Chancellery as well as the Chancellery of the Lands of the Crown of Poland, see I. Sułkowska-Kurasiowa, *Polska kancelaria królewska w latach 1447—1506* (The Polish royal chancellery in the years 1447–1506) (Wrocław-Warsaw-Cracow, 1967), p. 103; J. Bardach, *Studia z ustroju i prawa Wielkiego Księstwa Litewskiego XIV—XVII w.* (Studies on the constitution and law of the Grand Duchy of Lithuania from the fourteenth to the seventeenth century) (Warsaw, 1970), pp. 361–2. After 1538 entries made in the records of the Land Registry of the Lands of the Crown of Poland became more precise, see Kutrzeba, *Historia źródeł*, vol. I, pp. 113, 116. The standard of work of King Stanisław August's chancellery, which recorded the privileges issued by that king, was greatly improved in the 1780s, see M. Rymszyna, *Gabinet Stanisława Augusta* (The Cabinet of Stanisław August) (Warsaw, 1962), pp. 68–9, 113, 139.
58 See Kuraś, *Przywileje prawa niemieckiego*, pp. 46–7; M. Trojanowska, *Dokument miejski lubelski od XIV do XVIII wieku. Studium dyplomatyczne* (The urban document in Lublin from the fourteenth to the seventeenth century. A study in diplomacy) (Warsaw, 1977), p. 44.
59 Cf. *Volumina Legum*, vol. II, pp. 51, 68, 94.

60 W. Skrzetuski, *Prawo polityczne narodu polskiego* (The political law of the Polish nation) (Warsaw, 1784), vol. II, p. 77. The other work on law published in this period also emphasizes that the Jews 'are to practise trade in towns in accordance with agreements and pacts. Where such contracts have disappeared, or have not been hitherto concluded, they should be concluded following the example of other towns', cf. T. Ostrowski, *Prawo cywilne albo szczególne narodu polskiego* (The civil or particular law of the Polish nation) (Warsaw, 1784), vol. I, p. 36. This was also indicated by T. Czacki, *Rozprawa o Żydach* (A discussion on the Jews) (Vilna, 1807), p. 89.

61 See *Volumina Legum*, vol. VII, p. 352.

62 See W. Smoleński, *Stan i sprawa Żydów polskich w XVIII wieku* (The position and question of Polish Jews in the eighteenth century) (Warsaw, 1876), p. 1.

63 See T. Opas, 'Sytuacja ludności żydowskiej w miastach szlacheckich województwa lubelskiego w XVIII wieku' (The situation of Jews in noble towns in the Lublin province in the eighteenth century), in *Biuletyn Żydowskiego Instytutu Historycznego* (1968), vol. LXVII, p. 21.

64 See Bałaban, 'Ze studiów nad ustrojem prawnym Żydów w Polsce', pp. 250–1. For the proclamation of King Jan Kazimierz on a similar issue, on 13 July 1660, see Morgensztern, 'Regesty z Metryki Koronnej do historii Żydów w Polsce (1633–1660)', pp. 115–16.

65 See W. Ćwik, 'Ludność żydowska w miastach królewskich Lubelszczyzny w drugiej połowie XVIII w.' (The Jews in royal towns in the Lublin province in the second half of the eighteenth century), in *Biuletyn Żydowskiego Instytutu Historycznego* (1966), vol. LIX, p. 34.

66 See Opas, 'Sytuacja ludności żydowskiej w miastach szlacheckich województwa lubelskiego', p. 21.

67 Archiwum Państwowe, Lublin, Księga Miejska Opola, 6, fo. 291v.

68 See Opas, 'Sytuacja ludności żydowskiej w miastach szlacheckich województwa lubelskiego', p. 21.

69 Central Archives for the History of the Jewish People, Jerusalem, PL/Wr, p. 4.

70 L. Lewin (ed.) 'Neue Materialen zur Geschichte der Vierländersynode', in: *Jahrbuch der Jüdisch-Literarischen Gesellschaft in Frankfurt-am-Main* (1905), vol. III, pp. 119–20, 80; I. Halperin (ed.) *Acta Congressus Generalis Judaeorum Regni Poloniae (1580—1764)* (Jerusalem, 1945), pp. 309, 473 (in Hebrew).

71 See Opas, 'Sytuacja ludności żydowskiej w miastach szlacheckich województwa lubelskiego', p. 21.

72 See J. Michalski, *Studia nad reformą sądownictwa i prawa sądowego w XVIII w.* (Studies in the reform of the courts and the law of the courts in the eighteenth century) (Wrocław-Warsaw, 1958), p. 162.

73 During the process of reform in the state in the second half of the eighteenth century attempts were made to limit the independence of the municipal and noble courts of justice. Several reform projects were also put forward in the period to introduce basic changes in the Jewish judicature, see J. Michalski, 'Problem ius agratiandi i kary smierci w Polsce w latach siedemdziesiątych XVIII w.' (The problem of *ius agratiandi* and the death penalty in Poland in the 1770s), in *Czasopismo Prawno — Historyczne* (1958), vol. X, 2, p. 176; A. Eisen-

bach, J. Michalski, E. Rostworowski and J. Woliński (eds), *Materiały do dziejów Sejmu Czteroletniego* (Materials on the history of the Four Year Sejm) (Wrocław-Warsaw-Cracow, 1969), vol. VI.

74 See S. Gierszewski, *Obywatele miast Polski przedrozbiorowej. Studium źródło-nawcze* (The citizens of the towns of pre-partition Poland. A study of the sources) (Warsaw, 1973), pp. 37, 68.

75 See ibid.

76 See ibid., pp. 31–2.

77 Cf. *Volumina Legum*, vol. VII, p. 352. In the editing of this law, the privileges of the Jewish communities are given parity with the privileges granting permission for the foundation of towns; hence the erroneous statement of the constitution, which refers to the Jews '... in their own Jewish towns, which have been established by privileges ...'.

78 See also Gierszewski, *Obywatele miast Polski przedrozbiorowej*, p. 38.

79 Cf. Z. Kędzierska (ed.) *Lustracja województwa rawskiego 1789* (The inspection of the province of Rawa 1789) (Wrocław-Warsaw-Cracow-Gdańsk, 1971), p. 58.

80 Cf. H. Madurowicz-Urbańska (ed.) *Lustracja województwa sandomierskiego 1789* (The inspection of the province of Sandomierz 1789) (Wrocław-Warsaw-Cracow, 1965), vol. I, p. 164.

81 Cf. *Dyplomataryusz*, p. 261.

82 Cf. ibid., p. 77; Opas, 'Sytuacja ludności żydowskiej w miastach szlacheckich województwa lubelskiego', p. 32.

83 See B. Groicki in *Porządek sądów i spraw miejskich prawa magdeburskiego* (The ordering of courts and urban matters in accordance with Magdeburg law) ed. K. Koranyi (Warsaw, 1953), p. 59; J. Goldberg, 'Poles and Jews in the Seventeenth and Eighteenth Centuries – Rejection or Acceptance', in *Jahrbücher für Geschichte Osteuropas* (1974), vol. XXII, p. 271.

84 See J. Mazurkiewicz, 'O niektórych problemach prawno-ustrojowych miast prywatnych w dawnej Polsce' (On some legal-constitutional problems of private towns in old Poland), in *Annales Universitatis Mariae Curie – Skłodowska* (1964), Section G, vol. XI, 4, pp. 110–11; Opas, 'Sytuacja ludności żydowskiej w miastach szlacheckich województwa lubelskiego', pp. 25–6; R. Mahler, 'Z dziejów Żydów w Nowym Sączu w XVII i w XVIII w' (On the history of the Jews in Nowy Sącz), in *Biuletyn Żydowskiego Instytutu Historycznego* (1965), vol. LVI, pp. 39–40; J. Ptaśnik, *Miasta i mieszczaństwo w dawnej Polsce* (Towns and burgers in old Poland) (Warsaw, 1949), pp. 246–7.

85 See Mazurkiewicz, 'O niektórych problemach prawno-ustrojowych miast prywatnych w dawnej Polsce', p. 110.

86 Biblioteka Polskiej Akademii Nauk, Cracow, 439, fo. 186v.

87 See 'Ordynacja miasta dziedzicznego Łasku' (The ordinance of the private town of Łask) (25 October 1795), in S. Rodkiewicz, *Z przeszłości miast polskich* (On the past of Polish towns) (Warsaw, 1926).

88 Archiwum Państwowe Lublin, Księga Miejska Opola, 6, fo. 291v.

89 Archiwum Państwowe Lublin, Chełm Castrensia, 95/20422, fo. 209r.

90 This occurred more rarely in royal- than in noble-owned towns; see Goldberg, 'Poles and Jews in the Seventeenth and Eighteenth Centuries', p. 271;

Charewiczowa, *Dzieje miasta Złoczowa, p. 67;* Opas, 'Sytuacja ludności żydowskiej w miastach szlacheckich województwa lubelskiego', pp. 25–6. In the town of Bochnia some individual Jews received municipal citizenship even in the sixteenth and seventeenth centuries, see F. Kiryk (ed.) *Księgą przyjęć do prawa miejskiego w Bochni 1531—1656* (The book of acceptance to municipal citizenships in Bochnia 1531–1656) (Wrocław-Warsaw-Cracow-Gdańsk, 1979), pp. 14,27, 39, 45, 58, 59.

91 See Mazurkiewicz,'O niektórych problemach prawno-ustrojowych miast prywatnych w dawnej Polsce', pp. 117–18; J. Goldberg, 'Between Freedom and Bondage – Forms of Feudal Dependency of the Jews in Poland in the Sixteenth–Eighteenth Centuries', in *Proceedings of the Fifth Congress of Jewish Studies* (Jerusalem, 1972), vol. II, pp. 111–12 (in Hebrew). The few works that mention this problem do not amplify our knowledge of Jewish rights to full ownership of immovable property in noble-owned and royal towns, see A. Leszczyński, 'Sytuacja prawna Żydów ziemi bielskiej od końca XV w. do 1795 r.' (The legal situation of the Jews of the Bielsk region from the end of the fifteenth century to 1795), in *Biuletyn Żydowskiego Instytutu Historycznego* (1975), vol. XCVI, p. 5.

92 For a source analysis of such regulations issued on Jewish matters, see Kutrzeba, *Historia źródeł,* vol. II, pp. 310–13.

93 See Mazurkiewicz, 'O niektórych problemach prawno-ustrojowych miast prywatnych w dawnej Polsce', p. 110; idem, *Jurydyki lubelskie* (Lublin rulings) (Wrocław, 1956), p. 78.

94 It is clear from the privileges that the right to hold land did not operate in the sixteenth to eighteenth centuries as Grodecki claims it did in earlier periods. Grodecki even claims that in Poland the Jews 'had the right to acquire full ownership of land, just as the nobles or clergy', see R. Grodecki, 'Dzieje Żydów w Polsce do końca XIV w.' (The history of Jews in Poland until the end of the fifteenth century), in R. Grodecki, *Polska piastowska* (Poland of the Piasts) ed. J. Wyrozumski (Warsaw, 1969), p. 629. Elsewhere, however, he notes limitations in this sphere introduced by the privilege of Bolesław the Pious in 1264, see, ibid., pp. 658–9.

95 Central Archives for the History of the Jewish People, Jerusalem, PL/Wr-19, p. 3.

96 Ossolineum, 2224, fo.3v.

97 AGAD, Dokument Papierowy, IV, 5, 4e, p. 3.

98 See Goldberg, 'Between Freedom and Bondage', p. 111; Leszczyński, 'Sytuacja prawna Żydów ziemi bielskiej', pp. 6–7.

99 A. Codello, 'Zbiegostwo mieszczań rzeszowskich w pierwszej połowie XVIII w.' (Urban fugitives in the Rzeszow province in the first half of the eighteenth century), in *Małopolskie Studia Historyczne* (1958), vol. I, p. 25; T. Opas, 'Wolność osobista mieszczań miast szlacheckich województwa lubelskiego w drugiej połowie XVII i w XVIII wieku' (The personal freedom of the burghers of noble towns in the Lublin province in the second half of the seventeenth and the eighteenth centuries), in *Przegląd Historyczny* (1970), vol. LXI, pp. 619, 627.

100 AGAD, Zbiór Czołowskiego, Judaica Generalia, 3101, fos 20r, 20v.

101 Ibid.
102 Central Archives for the History of the Jewish People, Jerusalem, PL 357, p. 8.
103 Ossolineum, 2224, fo. 3v.
104 Central Archives for the History of the Jewish People, Jerusalem, PL/SW, p. 5.
    The situation in some royal towns was different. For example, in the first half of
    the seventeenth century the *starosta* of Chełm required the duty of the corvěe
    not from the Jewish house-owners in the town but only from the Jews occupied
    rented accommodation, cf. M. Horn, *Żydzi na Rusi Czerwonej w XVI i pierwszej
    połowie XVII w.* (Jews in Red Rus in the sixteenth and first half of the
    seventeenth centuries) (Warsaw, 1975), p. 266.
105 The public notary of Lwów, Felicjan Kubiński, claimed in 1644 that Jews did
    not want to perform the corvěe, cf. W. Łoziński, *Patrycjat i mieszczaństwo lwow-
    skie w XVI i XVII wieku* (Patriciate and burgers in Lwów in the sixteenth and
    seventeenth centuries) (Lwów, 1902), p. 194: 'bo gdzie trzeba pańszczyznę
    robić, tedy się oni (Żydzi) od tego ochraniają i ukrywają' (for where it is
    obligatory to perform the corveé, they [the Jews] avoid it and hide themselves).
106 See AGAD, Archiwum Publiczne Potockich, 132, p. 239.
107 See ibid., p. 240.
108 AGAD, Zbiór Czołowskiego, Judaica Generalia, 3101, fo. 20r. On the attitude
    of Stanisław Poniatowski to the Jews, see K. Kantecki, *Stanisław Poniatowski
    kasztelan krakowski, ojciec Stanisława Augusta* (Stanisław Poniatowski, the
    castellan of Cracow, father of Stanisław August) (Poznań, 1880), vol. II, p. 137.
    This benevolence does not accord with Stanisław Poniatowski's known
    negative attitude towards the Jews. On the project for social and political
    reforms in the Polish Commonwealth, he states: '. . . it is clear to everyone how
    this nation [the Jews], numerous in the entire kingdom, is happier than our
    burghers and our subjects, and that someone has written aptly "Polonia
    Paradisus Iudaeorum". How they find protection everywhere, how through
    their tricks, swindles and solicitations they have deprived the Christians of all
    trade and means of livelihood, and how little they pay to the Commonwealth',
    see ibid., p. XCIII, 'List ziemianina do pewnego przyjaciela z innego woje-
    wództwa'.
109 Central Archives for the History of the Jewish People, Jerusalem, PL/Wr-19,
    p. 3. The involvement in the choice of the Jewish elders by the lords resulted
    from the nature of their authority over the inhabitants of their towns and
    villages, see Kutrzeba, *Autonomia miast i władza ustawodawcza panów miast w
    dawnej Rzeczypospolitej Polskiej* (Urban autonomy and the legislative power of the
    lords of towns in the former Republic of Poland), pp. 93–4. This involvement
    stemmed from the whole gamut of social, legal and economic relationships in
    the Polish Commonwealth. It extended beyond the explanation of Katz that it
    was because the Jewish leaders 'were responsible to the authorities for the
    community's financial obligations, such as the payment of taxes and the
    sending of gifts', see J. Katz, *Tradition and Crisis — Jewish Society at the End of the
    Middle Ages* (Glencoe, 1961), p. 92.
110 Ossolineum, 2224, fo. 4.
111 AGAD, Komisja Rządowa Spraw Wewnętrznych, 185, fo. 90v.

112 Central Archives for the History of the Jewish People, Jerusalem, PL/Wr-19, pp. 4–5.

113 The rights of village self-government in old Poland were similar in character, see J. Rafacz, *Ustrój wsi samorządnej małopolskiej w XVIII wieku* (The constitution of rural self government in Małopolska in the eighteenth century) (Lublin, 1922), p. 191. The view has recently been expressed that the administrative rights received the jurisdiction of the state authorities in the Polish Common-wealth, see Opas, 'Miasta prywatne a Rzeczypospolita', p. 36.

114 Ossolineum, 1431/II, p. 61. Stefan Czarniecki granted this privilege in 1661 when he was *starosta* of Ratno; he became *starosta* of Ratno in 1657 and acquired the town as his hereditary property in 1659, see A. Kersten, *Stefan Czarniecki 1599—1655* (Warsaw, 1963), p. 416.

115 This difference is also discussed by Katz, *Tradition and Crisis*, p. 89.

116 W. Pałucki, *Studia nad uposażeniem urzędników ziemskich w Koronie do schyłku XVI w.* (Studies on the payment of local officials in Poland until the turn of the sixteenth century) (Warsaw, 1969), pp. 7–8, 45, 275; T. Zielińska, 'Mechanizm sejmikowy i klientela radziwiłłowska za Sasów' (The operation of dietines and the clients of the Radzwiłłs under the Saxons), in *Przegląd Historyczny* (1971), vol. LXII, p. 31.

117 The Jews were able to gain the support of such an eminent and influential statesman as Chancellor Jan Zamoyski, and through his personal intercession King Stefan Bathory granted certain rights to the Jewish community of Augustów in 1578, cf. Dyplomataryusz, p. 104. The *szlachta* assembled at the Dietine in Łęczyca on 26 January 1658 decided that its elected deputies should demand in the Diet that 'the Jews of Łęczyca . . . should retain their privileges', cf. AGAD, Łęczyca Castrensia Relationum, 442, fo. 498. See I. Lewin, 'Udział Żydów w wyborach sejmowych w dawnej Polsce' (The role of Jews in Sejm elections in former Poland), in *Miesięcznik Żydowski* (1932), vol. II, pp. 46–65; Zielińska, 'Mechanizm sejmikowy i klientela radziwiłłowska za Sasów', p. 416; J. Kitowicz, *Pamiętniki czyli historia polska* (A memoir on the history of Poland) ed. P. Matuszewska and Z. Lewinówna (Warsaw, 1971), p. 442; *Materiały do dziejów Sejmu Czteroletniego*, vol. VI, pp. 276–8, 376–7, 387–98, 515–16. The *szlachta* in the *voivodeship* of Kujawy criticized such instances of protection relating to the Jews at the Dietine on 8 January 1685, cf. A. Pawiński (ed.), *Dzieje ziemi kujawskiej* (The history of Kujawy territory) (Warsaw, 1888), vol. III, pp. 93–4.

118 A reflection of this co-ordinated activity in Poland is seen in a petition sent to Stanisław August in 1766, signed by 'His Most Illustrious King's and Merciful Lord's faithful Jewish subjects residing in the Lands of His Crown' ('Najja-śniejszego Króla Pana Miłościwego wierni poddani Żydzi w Koronie będący'), cf. Muzeum Narodowe w Krakowie, Zbiory Czartoryskich, 806, p. 163.

119 Petrycy, Sebastian *Polityki arystotelesowej to jest rządu Rzeczypospolitej* (The Politics of Aristotle and the government of the Republic) (Cracow, 1605), vol. I, p. 75.

120 Piotr Kmita, *voivode* of Cracow in the first half of the sixteenth century, used to accept gifts of silver, gold and other precious objects from the Jews yet at the

same time did not refuse money from their opponents, the merchants and craftsmen of Cracow, see Pałucki, *Studia nad uposażeniem urzędników ziemskich*, pp. 7–8, 275. See also R. Szczygieł, *Konflikty społeczne w Lublinie w pierwszej połowie XVI wieku* (Social conflicts in Lublin in the first half of the seventeenth century) (Warsaw, 1977), p. 133. There are reasons to assume that analogous practices also continued in the eighteenth century, see T. Zielińska, *Magnateria polska epoki saskiej. Funkcje urzędów i królewszczyzn w procesie przeobrażen warstwy społecznej* (Polish Magnates in the Saxon era. The role of officials and the royal demesne in the process of tansforming social strata) (Wrocław-Warsaw-Cracow-Gdańsk, 1977), p. 31.

121 S. Miczyński, *Zwierciadło Korony Polskiej* (The Mirror of the Polish Crown) (Cracow, 1648), p. 94.

122 S. Starowolski, *Stacje żołnierskie* (Soldierly stations) (Cracow, 1936); see S. Kot 'Polska rajem dla Żydów, piekłem dla chłopów, niebem dla szlachty' (Poland – paradise for the Jews, hell for the peasants, heaven for the nobility), in *Kultura i Nauka. Praca zbiorowa* (Culture and knowledge. A collective work) (Warsaw, 1937), p. 7; S. Starowolski, *Wady staropolskie. Robak złego sumienia człowieka neibogobojnego i o zbawienie swego niedbałego* (Old Polish faults. The worm of bad conscience and of a non-God fearing man and his neglect of his salvation (Cracow, 1853), p. 87.)

123 Information about the activity of the state treasurers in the first half of the eighteenth century is given by M. Nycz, *Geneza reform Sejmu Niemego* (The genesis of the reforms of the Dumb Sejm) (Poznań, 1938), pp. 105–8, 258; Zielińska, *Magnateria polska*, p. 32.

124 See J. S. Jabłonowski, *Skrupuł bez skrupułu w Polszcze albo oświecenie grzechów narodowi naszemu polskiemu zwyczajniejszych ... przez pewnego Polaka* (A scruple without scruples in Poland or the revelation of the most common sins of our Polish nation by a certain Pole) (n.p., 1730), 'I na nich [podskarbich] się to prawdzi co o Żydach mówią: kto za Żydami mówi to już wziął, a kto przeciwko Żydom, to chce wziąć.

125 Central Archives for the History of the Jewish People, Jerusalem, PL 160 (Parchment Document).

126 AGAD, Księga Kanclerska, 25, p. 297.

127 AGAD, Księga Kanclerska, 25, p. b562.

128 Goldberg, 'Poles and Jews in the Seventeenth and Eighteenth Centuries', p. 258.

129 In the sixteenth century the personnel of the royal chancellery supported themselves only by the contributions and fees received from the parties interested in preparing or sealing the documents, see A. Tomczak, *Walenty Dembiński kanclerz egzekucji (około 1504—1584)* (Walenty Dembinski, executive chancellor (approx. 1504–84) (Toruń, 1963), p. 128.

130 Kuraś, *Przywileje prawa niemieckiego*, p. 38. Occasionally the community elders forged privileges, see S. Rosiak, 'Rzekomy przywilej Kazimierza Jana Sapiehy dla Żydów w Lubczu w 1690 r.' (The alleged privilege granted by Kazimierz Jan Sapieta to the Jews of Lubiec in 1690), in *Ateneum Wileńskie* (1938), vol. XIII, pp. 32–44.

131 See Trojanowska, *Dokument miejski*, p. 12.
132 A. Warschauer, 'Die Entstehung einer jüdischen Gemeinde', in *Zeitschrift für die Geschichte der Juden in Deutschland* (1890), vol. IV, pp. 170–81.
133 R. Koebner, 'Locatio – zur Begrifssprache und Geschichte der deutschen Kolonisation', in *Zeitschrift des Vereins für Geschichte Schlesiens* (1929), vol LXIII, pp. 1–32; I. T. Baranowski, 'Wsie holenderskie na ziemiach polskich' (Dutch villages on Polish territory), in *Przegląd Historyczny* (1915), vol. XIX, pp. 64–82; W. Rusiński, 'Osady tzw. "Olędrów" w dawnym województwie poznańskim' ('Olendry' settlements in the province of Poznań) (Poznań, 1939) (Cracow, 1947); J. Goldberg, 'Osadnictwo olęderskie w dawnym województwie łęczyckim i sieradzkim' (Dutch settlements in the former provinces of Łęczyca and Sieradz), in *Zeszyty Naukowe Uniwersytetu Łódzkiego* (1957), Seria I, vol. V, pp. 67–110; K. Ciesielska, 'Osadnictwo "olęderskie" w Prusach Królewskich i na Kujawach w świetle kontraktów osadniczych' (Dutch settlements in Royal Prussia and Kujawy on the basis of settlement contracts), in *Studia i Materiały do Dziejów Wielkopolski i Pomorza* (1958), vol. VI, 2, pp. 220–55.
134 Central Archives for the History of the Jewish People, Jerusalem, PL 357, p. 11.
135 AGAD, Księga Kanclerska, 27, pp. 593–4.
136 Bałaban, 'Ze studiów nad ustrojem prawnym Żydów w Polsce', p. 252.
137 Morgensztern, 'Regesty z Metryki Koronnej do historii Żydów w Polsce (1588–1632)', p. 60; 'Regesty z Metryki Koronnej do historii Żydów w Polsce (1633–1660)', p. 115; 'Regesty dokumentów z Metryki Koronnej i Sigillat do historii Żydów w Polsce (1660–1668)', p. 68–88.
138 See Kętrzyński, *Zarys nauki o dokumencie polskim*, p. 455.
139 J. Bieniarzówna, *O chłopskie prawa* (On peasant law) (Cracow, 1954), pp. 26–30; I. Rychlikowa, 'Sytuacja społeczno-ekonomiczna i walka klasowa chłopów w dobrach Wodzickich Poręba Wielka (The socio-economic situation and the class struggle of the peasants on Poręba wielka, the estate of the Wodzickis), in *Studia z dziejów wsi małopolskiej w drugiej połowie XVII w.* (Studies on the history of the countryside in Małopolska in the second half of the eighteenth century), ed. C. Bobińska (Warsaw, 1957), p. 630.
140 The successors of the lord of Berdyczów deprived the Jewish community of its privileges. The community elders asked the succeeding owner and his wife for defence and protection, cf. Muzeum Narodowe w Krakowie, Zbiory Czartoryskich, 413, pp. 888–9 (n.d.).
141 Central Archives for the History of the Jewish People, Jerusalem, PL 160 (Parchment Document). See I. Baranowski, *Komisje Porządkowe (1765–1788)* (The Commission of Public Order, 1765–1788) (Warsaw, 1907). One of the results of the work of the Komisje Boni Ordinis in Poznań was 'Zbiór przywilejów i wszelkich praw Żydom synagogi poznańskiej służących oraz punktów między tymi Żydami i magistratem m. Poznania nastąpionych, tudzież dekretów wypadłych' (A collection of the privileges and all rights of the Jews belonging to the Poznań synagogue as well as matters occurring between these Jews and the Poznań magistrates and the resultant decrees) see J. Deresiewicz, 'Wielkopolskie Komisje Dobrego Porządku' (The Commission of Public Order in Wielkopolska), in *Czasopismo Prawno — Historyczne* (1960), vol. XVIII, p. 169.

142 See Maleczyński, *Zarys dyplomatyki*, pp. 23–4; H. Fichtenau, *Arenga — Spätantike und Mittelalter in Spiegel von Urkundenformel* (Graz-Köln, 1957), pp. 193–6.
143 Archiwum Państwowe, Lublin, Księga Miejska Opola, 6, fo. 290v.
144 Central Archives for the History of the Jewish People, Jerusalem, PL/We-19, p. 1.
145 Cf. Starowolski, *Stacyje żołnierskie*; see Kot, 'Polska rajem dla Żydów, piekłem dla chłopów, niebem dla szlachty', p. 7; Starowolski, *Wady staropolskie — Robak złego sumienia*, p. 87.
146 G. Podoski, *Teki* (Notes) (Poznań, 1856), ed. K. Jarochowski, vol. IV, p. 521.
147 M. Kosman, *Protestanci i kontrreformacja. Z dziejów tolerancji w Rzeczypospolitej XVI–XVIII wieku* (Protestants and the Counter-Reformation. On the history of toleration in the Republic from the sixteenth to the eighteenth century) (Wrocław-Warsaw-Cracow, 1978), p. 138.
148 Central Archives for the History of the Jewish People, Jerusalem, PL 357.
149 AGAD, Archiwum Radziwiłłowskie, XXIII, 132, fos 26r–27v.
150 AGAD, Komisja Rządowa Spraw Wewnętrznych, 185, fos 114r–117v.
151 AGAD, Komisja Rządowa Spraw Wewnętrznych, 185, fos 84r–85v.
152 See B. O'Connor, *The History of Poland in Several Letters to Persons of Quality* (London, 1698), vol. II, p. 49.
153 W. Coxe, *Travels into Poland, Sweden and Denmark* (Dublin, 1784), vol. III, p. 163.
154 F. L. de La Fontaine, *Chirurgisch — Medicinische Abhandlungen verschiedenen Inhalts Polen betreffend* (Breslau-Leipzig, 1799), p. 14.

CHAPTER 4 IMPLICATIONS OF JEWISH ECONOMIC ACTIVITIES

1 Andrzej Wyrobisz, 'Handel w Solcu nad Wisłą do końca XVIII wieku' (Trade in Solec on the Vistula to the end of the eighteenth century) *Przegląd Historyczny*, 57 (1966), p. 21; Jacob Goldberg, 'Poles and Jews in the Seventeenth and Eighteenth Centuries: Rejection or Acceptance', *Jahbücher für Geschichte Osteuropas* (1974), 22, pp. 250–1; Gershon Hundert, 'An Advantage Peculiarity? The Case of the Polish Commonwealth', *Association for Jewish Studies Review*, 6 (1981), p. 27.
2 *Volumina Legum* (St. Petersburg, 1860), vol. 4, p. 39.
3 G. Hundert, 'An Advantage',p. 27–7.
4 In Cracow, for example, there were anti-Jewish (and anti-Protestant) riots, tumults, and attacks in 1610, 1615, 1621, 1622, 1624, 1628, 1630, 1633, 1640, 1641, 1647, 1650, 1660, 1673, 1674, 1675, 1676, 1682 and 1700. In Lublin there were such outbreaks in 1620, 1646, 1650, and 1676. And see the list assembled by Bernard D. Weinryb, *The Jews of Poland: A Social and Economic History of the Jewish Community in Poland from 1100—1800* (Philadelphia, 1973), pp. 152–3.
5 Bochnia 1605; Cracow 1631, 1635; Lublin 1636, 1690; Łęczyca 1639; Sandomierz 1702.
6 Majer Bałaban, *Historja Żydów w Krakowie i na Kazimierzu* (The history of the Jews in Cracow and Kazimierz) (Cracow, 1931), vol. I, pp. 169–73; Kazimierz

Bartoszewicz, *Antysemityzm w literaturze polskiej XV—XVII w.* (Anti-semitism in Polish literature from the fifteenth to the eighteenth century) (Warsaw, 1914); Daniel Tollet, 'La littérature antisemite polonaise, de 1588 à 1668. Auteurs et éditions', *Revue francaise d'histoire du livre* 14 (1977), pp. 73–105.

7 K. Bartoszewicz, *Antysemitzm*, pp. 125–9.

8 See Jacob Katz, *Exclusiveness and Tolerance* (Oxford, 1961).

9 This is certainly the tone of Nathan Hannover's *Abyss of Despair (Yeven mesulah)* (Venice, 1653), in which, while describing the terrible disasters of 1648–9, he is careful to distinguish between the generally beneficent Poles, especially the monarch and certain generals, and the Cossacks and Ukrainian peasants. See also the section in B. Weinryb, *The Jews of Poland* entitled 'Poland through the Eyes of Polish Jews', pp. 156–76.

10 See, for example, the sermons of Sevi Hirshben Aaron Samuel Koidonover, *Kav ha-yashar* (Frankfurt a. M., 1705), chapter 76, p. 159b; chapter 82, pp. 170b–171b; chapter 83, p. 172a.

11 Andrzej Wyrobisz, 'Ludność żydowska w Tarłowie: Od połowy XVI do końca XVIII w.' (The Jews in Tarlow: from the beginning of the sixteenth to the end of the eighteenth century), *Biuletyn Żydowskiego Instytutu Historycznego* [BZIH], 89 (1974), p. 11; Tomasz Opas. 'Sytuacja ludności żydowskiej w miastach szlacheckich wojewodztwa lubelskiego w XVIII wieku' (The situation of the Jews in noble towns in the Lublin province in the eighteenth century), *BZIH* 67 (1968), p. 17; Jacob Goldberg, 'Ludność żydowska w Lutomiersku w drugiej połowie XVIII wieku i jej walka z feudalnym uciskiem' (Jews in Lutomiersk in the second half of the eighteenth century and their struggle against feudal oppression), *BZIH* 15–16 (1955), p. 193.

12 Ignacy Schiper, *Dzieje handlu żydowskiego na ziemiach polskich* (The history of Jewish trade on Polish lands) (Warsaw, 1937), pp. 27–9.

13 Ignacy Schiper, *Studja nad stosunkami gospodarczymi Żydów w Polsce podczas średnio-wiecza (Studies on the economic relations of the Jews in Poland during the Middle Ages)* (Lwów, 1911), p. 350, document 8.

14 Maria Bogucka, 'Les villes et le développement de la culture sur l'exemple de la Pologne au XVIe–XVIIIe siècles', *La Pologne au XVe Congres International des Sciences Historiques à Bucarest* (Warsaw, 1980), pp. 153–69.

15 Majer Bałaban, *Historja i literatura żydowska* (Jewish history and literature) (Lwów, 1925), vol. 3, p. 172; Mathias Bersohn, *Dyplomataryusz dotyczący Żydów w dawnej Polsce na źródłach archiwalnych osnuty (1388—1782)* (List of charters dealing with Jews in Old Poland taken from archival sources) (Warsaw, 1910), 185, p. 112; 214, p. 123; 215, p. 124.

16 M. Bersohn, *Dyplomataryusz*, 189, p. 112; 205, p. 122; 236, p. 132; 289, p. 163; *Lustracja województwa sandomierskiego 1660—1664* (Inventory of the Sandomierz province 1660–64) (Cracow, 1971), part I, pp. 59–61; *Volumina Legum*, vol. 5, p. 286.

17 Elżbieta Horn, 'Położenie prawno-ekonomiczne Żydów w miastach ziemi halickiej na przełomie XVI i XVII w.' (The legal-economic situation of Jews in the towns of the Halicz area at the turn of the seventeenth and eighteenth centuries) *BZIH* 40 (1961), p. 24; Melchior Buliński, *Monografia miasta*

Sandomierza (A monograph on the town of Sandomiercz) (Warsaw, 1879), pp. 92–93. Compare: Janina Morgensztern, 'Regesty z metryki koronnej do historii Żydow w Posce. 1588–1632' (Abstracts from the royal records dealing with the history of the Jews in Poland (1588–1632), *BZIH* 51 (1964), 56, p. 69; *Lustracja województwa lubelskiego 1661* (Warsaw, 1962), p. 57; T. Opas, 'Sytuacia', p. 9; Mordecai Nadav, 'Toledot gehillat Pinsk-Karlin, 1506–1880', in *Pinsk: sefer edut ve-zikkaron*, ed. W. Z. Rabinowitsch (Tel Aviv, 1973), p. 25.

18 Nathan Michael Gelber, 'Toldedot yehudei Zhulqiev', in *Sefer Zhulqiev*, eds Y. Ben-Shem and N. M. Gelber (Jerusalem, 1969), column 33; Salomon Buber, *Qirya nisgavah* (Cracow, 1903), p. 91; Maria Stankowa, 'Zmierzch znaczenia Lublina: Upadek (1648–1764)' (The twilight of Lublin's significance: Fall), in *Dzieje Lublina* (Lublin, 1965), p. 132.

19 G. Hundert, 'An Advantage', p. 35; S. Cynarski (ed.), *Raków, Ognisko Arianizmu* (Rakow: The centre of Arianism) (Cracow, 1968), pp. 27–8, 46; Jan Łukowski. *Dzieje miasta Rzeszowa do końca XVIII wieku* (The history of the town of Rzeszów to the end of the eighteenth century) (Rzeszów, 1913),pp. 301, 356, 362; N. M. Gelber, *Brody*, 'Arim ve-imahot be-yisra·el' vol. 6, (Jerusalem, 1955), p. 31; Bohdan Baranowski, *Życie codzienne małego miasteczka w XVII i XVIII wieku* (Daily life in a small town in the seventeenth and eighteenth centuries) (Warsaw, 1975), p. 113; Władysław Ćwik,'Ludność żydowska w miastach królewskich Lubelszczyzny w drugiej połowie XVIII wieku' (The Jews in the royal towns of the Lublin area in the second half of the eighteenth century), *BZIH* 59 (1966), p. 36.

20 For examples: W.K.Z. 'Żydzi w Lublinie i ich przywileje' (Jews in Lublin and their privileges), *Israelita* 25, 2 (January 29, 1890), p. 17; Jan Heitgeber, *Z dziejów handlu i kupiectwa Poznańskiego za dawnej rzeczypospolitej polskiej* (On the history of trade and traders in Poznań in the old Republic of Poland) (Poznań, 1929), pp. 84, 89; M. Bałaban, *Historia Żydów w Krakowie* (The history of the Jews in Cracow), vol. 1, pp. 203, 218; M. Schorr, *Żydzi w Przemyślu do końca XVIII wieku* (Jews in Przemyśl to the end of the eighteenth century) (Lwów, 1903), pp. 15–16; Wojewódzkie Archiwum Państwowe w Lublinie, Ks. Bełżyce, 5, pp. 21, 235; M. Bersohn, *Dyplomataryusz*, 244, pp. 135–8, 356, pp. 201–2; M. Nadav, 'Toledot', pp. 75, 116; Michał Baliński, Tymoteusz Lipiński, *Starożytna Polska pod względem historycznym, jeograficznym i statystycznym* (Old Poland from the historical, geographical and statistical point of view) (Warsaw, 1846), vol. 2, p. 1182; J. Leniek, *Dzieje miasta Tarnowa* (The history of the town of Tarnow) (Tarnow, 1911), pp. 119–20; Louis Lewin, *Geschichte der Juden in Lissa* (Pinne, 1904), pp. 11–12, 21; N. M. Gelber, 'Toledot', col. 54.

21 Adam Manikowski, 'Zmiany czy stagnacja? Z problematyki handlu polskiego w drugiej połowie XVII wieku' (Change or stagnation? On the problems of Polish trade in the second half of the seventeenth century), *Przeglad Historyczny*, 64 (1973), p. 787.

22 Maurycy Horn, *Żydzi na Rusi Czerwonej w XVI i pierwszej połowie XVII w.* (Jews in Red Rus in the sixteenth and first half of the seventeenth centuries) (Warsaw, 1975), p. 165; M. Baliński, T. Lipiński, *Starożytna*, vol. 2, p. 343

23 Compare the views of I. Schiper, *Dzieje handlu*, pp. 60–2. For examples of pacts

see: M. Bersohn, *Dyplomataryusz*, 62, pp. 52–8; M. Bałaban, *Żydzi lwowscy na przełomie XVIgo i XVIIgo w* (Jews in Lwów at the turn of the sixteenth and seventeenth centuries) (Lwów, 1906), 16, pp. 17–20, 34, pp. 36–9, 81, pp. 105–9; M. Bałaban, *Historia Żydów w Krakowie* (The history of the Jews in Cracow) vol. 1, pp. 200–2, vol. 2, p. 101; J. Perles, *Geschichte der Juden in Posen* (Breslau, 1865), p. 21.

24 *Lustracja województwa lubelskiego 1660* (The inventory of the Lublin province, 1660), p. 100; Bela Mandelburg-Schildkraut, *Mehkarim le-toledot yehudei Lublin* (Tel Aviv, 1965), pp. 75–7, 103.

25 This was a very common complaint. See, for example, *Lustracja województwa sandomierskiego, 1660—1664* (The inventory of the Sandomierz province 1660–64), cz. 1, pp. 62, 123; Wojewódzkie Archiwum Państwowe w Tarnobrzegu z siędziba w Sandomierzu, Akta miasta Sandomierza 10, p. 207v; Wojewódzkie Archiwum Państwowe w   Lublinie, Ks. M. Opola 9, p. 541; *Lustracja województwa ruskiego 1661—1665* (The inventory of the Ruś province 1661–1665) (Wroclaw, 1974), cz. 1, p. 21; M. Horn, *Żydzi na Rusi Czerwonej*, p. 164; E. Horn, 'Położenie', p. 27.

26 'Wojewódzkie Archiwum Państwowe w Lublinie', Ks. m. Bełżyce 5, p. 12–13, 21, 78–9, 104–5, 129, 148, 162, 169, 170, 196, 202, 224, 275–6, 371, 374, 377, 551.

27 '. . . a Jew called Kaufman went from Cracow to Prague by way of Hungary with a group of Jews.' Joshua Hoeschel ben Joseph, *Penei Yehoshu'a* (Lwów, 1860), part 2, qu. 60, p. 43a. Compare: Andrzej Wyrobisz, 'Materiały do historii kultury materialnej mieszczaństwa polskiego na początku XVIII w.' (Material on the history of the material culture of the Polish bourgeoisie at the beginning of the eighteenth century), *Kwartalnik Historii Kultury Materialnej* 19 (1971), pp. 57–67; A. Wyrobisz, 'Materiały do dziejów handlu w miasteczkach polskich na początku XVIII wieku' (Material on the history of trade in Polish small towns at the beginning of the eighteenth century), *Przegląd Historyczny* 62 (1971), pp. 703–16; Sebastian Miczynski, *Zwierciadło korony polskiey urazy ciężkie, y utrapienia wielkie, ktore ponosi od Żydów wyrazaiące synom Koronnym na sejm Walny w roku Pańskim 1618* (A mirror of the serious blows and damage which the Jews cause to the Polish crown, exposed at the Sejm in the year of our Lord 1618) (Cracow, n.d.), pp. 27–32.

28 Benjamin Aaron ben Abraham Slonik, *Sefer mas'at biniamin* (Cracow, 1633), qu. 105, p. 147a; Meir ben Gedaliah Lublin, *She'elot u-teshuvot* (Metz, 1769), qu. 110, p. 47b, qu. 128, p. 61b.

29 Israel Halpern (ed.), *Pinqas va'ad arba arasot* (Jerusalem, 1945), 48, p. 16; Simon Dubnow (ed.), *Pinqas ha-mdinah* (Berlin, 1925), 134, p. 34; Sevi Hirsh Koidonover, *Kav ha-yashar*, chapter 76, p. 159b; Dov Avron (ed.), *Pinqas ha-kesherim shel kehillat Pozna* (Jerusalem, 1966), 716, pp. 136–7.

30 I. Halpern, *Pinqas*, 50, p. 17; Joel Sirkes, *Bayit hadash* on Yoreh de'ah 157:5. Compare: Isaac ben Samuel ha-Levi, *She'elot u-teshuvot*, 1 (Neuwied), 1736, qu. 12, p. 10b.

31 Sevi Hirsh Koidonover, *Kav ha-yashar*, chapter 82, p. 171a. And see there also his castigation of Jewish women who dress like the non-Jews to the extent that

they are indistinguishable from them. Ibid., p. 170b.

32 Ibid., chapter 76, p. 159b.

33 Backvis, 'Comment les Polonais du XVIe siècle voyaient l'Italie et les Italiens', *Université Libre de Bruxelles, Annuaire de l'Institute de Philologie et d'Histoire Orientales et Slaves*, 15 (1958–1960), p. 255.

34 Elijah ben Samuel (*d*. 1735 in Hebron), who was for thirty years *av beit din* ('rabbi') in Brześć Litewski, was asked whether it was permissible to study the Torah with Gentiles and to sell holy books to them. *Yad eliyahu* (Amsterdam, 1712), qu. 48, p. 55a.

35 For examples see: I. Halpern,' *Pinqas*, 352, p. 148; Louis Lewin, *Neue Materialen zur Geschichte der Vierländersynode* (Frankfurt a.M., 1906), vol. 2, lxxiv, p. 41, lxxxii, p. 44; D. Avron, *Pinqas*, 737, p. 139; 895, p. 159; 984, pp. 170–1; 1011, p. 174; 1054, pp. 180–1.

36 I. Halpern, *Pinqas*, 896, p. 470; A. Tsherikover, 'Der arkhiv fun Shimen Dubnov: Fun Lubliner pinkesim', *Historishe shriften* (YIVO) (Wilno, 1937), vol. 2, pp. 574–6; S. Dubnow, *Pinqas*, 746, p. 186; D. Avron, *Pinqas*, 755, p. 142. This impulse to protectiveness through secrecy was not, of course, limited to Jews. The 1680 regulations of the Lublin Scottish Brotherhood included the following: 'The brethren being Conveened anie there amongst who may be fond to divulge in publiq what is Priwatelie Treatted in generall amongst our whole breethren; the Relator is to be Censured with penalties accordinglie.' A. Francis Steuart (ed.), *Papers Relating to the Scots in Poland 1576– 1793*, Publications of the Scottish Historical Society, (Edinburgh, 1915), vol. 59, pp. 123–4.

37 S. Miczynski, *Zwierciadło*, p. 50.

38 Honorata Obuchowska-Pysiowa, *Handel wiślany w pierwszej połowie XVII wieku* (Vistula trade in the first half of the seventeenth century) (Warsaw, 1964), p. 83.

39 Janina Morgensztern, 'Z dziejów Żydów w Kraśniku do połowy XVII w.' (On the history of the Jews in Krasnik to the middle of the seventeenth century) *BZIH* 36 (1960), p. 28.

40 Ibid., pp. 5–6; Jan Riabinin, *Lauda miejskie Lubelskie XVII w.* (Lauda of the city of Lublin in the seventeenth century) (Lublin, 1934), p. 22, n. 2; M. Bałaban, *Historia Żydów w Krakowie*, vol. 2, p. 107; M. Zakrzewska-Dubasowa, *Ormianie zamojscy i ich rola* (The Armenians of Zamość and their role) (Lublin, 1965), pp. 86–7; N. M. Gelber, *Brody*, p. 18.

41 M. Bałaban, *Historia Żydów w Krakowie*, vol. 2, p. 148; Leon Koczy, 'Studia nad dziejami gospodarczymi Żydów poznańskich przed połową wieku XVII (Studies on the economic history of Jews in Poznań before the first half of the seventeenth century) *Kronika miasta Poznania*, 12 (1934), pp. 353–5; G. Hundert, 'Jews, Money and Society in the Seventeenth-Century Polish Commonwealth: The Case of Kraków', *Jewish Social Studies*, 43 (1981), 261–74.

42 Jews may trade only in goods permitted by law. *Akta grodzkie i ziemskie z czasów rzeczypospolitej polskiej z archiwum tak zwanego bernardyńskiego we Lwowie* (Town and provincial records from the Polish Republic taken from the so-called Bernadine archive in Lwów) (Lwów, 1868–1931), 24 vols, here, vol. 20, 114– 41, p. 168 (1618). Jews are exceeding their rights and trading in goods not per-

mitted them. Ibid., 149–28, p. 224 (1625). There should be limitations on Jewish trade such that they do not deprive Christian merchants of their incomes. Ibid., vol. 21, 224–43, p. 429 (1666). Christian merchants must be protected against Jews who have captured all trade for themselves. Ibid., 275–66, p. 495 (1670).

43 No one, *szlachta*, burgher or Jew may travel to Hungary to import wine. Ibid., vol. 20, 100–23, p. 147 (1615); 105–26, p. 156 (1616); 215–6, pp. 464–465 (1644); vol. 21, 213–21, p. 406 (1665); 224–43, p. 429 (1666). The old prohibition is not being observed, a new law should permit travel to Hungary to import wine, except for Jews. Ibid., vol. 22, 94–23, p. 268 (1693). Compare: *Volumina Legum*, vol. 3, p. 7; Adam Przybos (ed.). *Akta sejmikowe województwa krakowskiego* (The records of the Sejmik of Cracow Province) (Cracow, 1955), vol. 2, xcv-106-37, p. 284 (1643).

44 This was directed primarily against Scots. A. Przyboś, *Akta*, vol. 2, 52, p. 264 (1641).

45 *AGZ*, vol. 20, 211–16, p. 446 (1641).

46 Ibid., vol. 22, 31–62, p. 76 (1676).

47 Merchants purchase property in the cities and suck the wealth and the marrow of all who live there. A. Przyboś, *Akta*, vol. 2, 26,p. 15 (1622). See also: ibid., 14, p. 250 (1640), 31, p. 262 (1641), 12,p. 278 (1642), 35, p. 284 (1643); *Volumina Legum*, vol. 3, p. 370; *AGZ*, vol. 24, 196–10, p. 374 (1671); 214–72, p. 417 (1678). See also the literature cited by M. Bogucka who claims that after the 1620s the nobility which had earlier singled out Jews (and foreigners), 'came to lay the blame for their financial problems on the entire bourgeois estate'. 'The Monetary Crisis of the XVII Century and Its Social and Psychological Consequences in Poland', *Journal of European Economic History*, 4(1975), p. 151.

48 'Może to być zatem wszystko taniej . . .', *AGZ*, vol. 18, no. 33–20, p. 44 (1632). And see the recommendation of Jewish participation in the fur trade, 'dla tańszego kupna'. Ibid., vol. 20, 209–39, p. 435 (1640); 211–288, pp. 455–6 (1641); vol. 21, 69–46, pp. 146–7.

CHAPTER 5 INTEGRATION OF CONVERTS INTO THE *SZLACHTA*

1 Abraham, ennobled in 1507, as was his brother Michał in 1525, both 'adopted' by aristocratic families bearing the arms *Leliwa*, in the first case Jan Zabrzeziński Grand Marshal of Lithuania, in the second Jerzy Hlebowicz Paljatine of Smoleńsk.

2 M. Mieses, *Rodziny polskie pochodzenia żydowskiego* (Warsaw, 1937), vol. II.

3 A. Heymowski, Nobilitacje, in *Materiały do biografii, genealogii i heraldyki polskiej* (Buenos Aires, n.d.), vol. VII.

4 Ibid.

CHAPTER 7 POLISH–JEWISH RELATIONS IN RUSSIAN TERRITORY

1 I. Levitats, *The Jewish Community in Russia 1772—1844* (New York, 1943); Louis Greenberg, *The Jews in Russia* (Yale, 1944) (reprinted 1976), vol. I.

2 Levitats, *Jewish Community in Russia* p. 19.

3 Centralnyj Gosudarstvennyj Istorićeskij Archiv, Leningrad, Collection 1409, opis 2, ed. 6344, p. 53.

4 Ibid.

5 Greenberg, *The Jews in Russia*.

6 D. Tollet, 'Marchands et hommes d'affaires juifs dans la Pologne des Wasa', unpublished thése d'Etat, Paris 1, 1984.

7 I. Zinberg, *History of Jewish Literature* (Ktav Publishing House, 1978), vols. 12–13. It is characteristic that it was only by leaving Lithuania for Western Europe that the 'enlightened' eighteenth-century Jew Salomon Maïmon was able to develop. Cf. S. Maïmon, *Histoire de ma vie*, tr. M. Hayoun (Berg International, 1984), p. 316.

8 J. M. Delmaire, 'La haskalah et la russification' in *Slovo* 5 (1984),pp. 77–96.

9 Greenberg, *The Jews in Russia*, pp.42–3.

10 M. Butrymowicz (H. Topór), *Sposób uformowania Żydów polskich w pożytecznych krajowi obywatelów* (A method for making Polish Jews useful citizens of the country) Warszawa,w drukarni wolnej, na papierze krajowym, 1789, 46p.

11 On the preparation of this publication, cf. letter of H. Kołłataj to J. Czech, 26 Dec. 1805, in *X. Hugona Kołłataja listy*, ed. F. Kojsiewicz (Cracow, 1844), vol. III, pp. 347–8. The influence of the Pole T. Czacki's ideas on the 1804 Statute is stressed by Levitats, *Jewish Community in Russia*, pp. 30–1.

12 J. Śniadecki to the University Curator, Prince A. J. Czartoryski, 5 April 1808, Bibl. Czart., Cracow, EW. 3069.

13 P. Kon, 'Dawny uniwersytet wileński a Żydzi' (The former Wilno University and the Jews), in *Ateneum Wileńskie* (Wilno, 1925–6), pp. 402–29.

14 A. J. Czartoryski to Alexander I, Bibl. Czart., Cracow, EW. 1283.

15 Reports of the sittings of the Wilno Schools Committee, 24 X and 7 XI 1817, 6 IX 1818, Archiwum P.A.N., Warsaw, Dossier L. Chmaj. 86.

16 Ibid., Chmaj. 87.

17 D. Beauvois, *Lumières et Société en Europe de l'Est* (Lille-Paris, 1977), pp. 868–9.

18 C.G.I.A., Leningrad, Collection 733, opis 62, ed. 1081.

19 Greenberg, *The Jews in Russia*, p. 27.

20 Bibl. Vilnius Univ., K.C. 592. A description of one of these schools is given by Isaac Paperna. Cf. Greenberg, *The Jews in Russia*,p. 59.

21 Beauvois, *Lumières et Société*, p. 867.

22 Ibid., p. 322.

23 G. J Śulkina, 'Razvitije knigoizdatelskogo dela Vilniusa v piervom tridcatiletii XIX v.' (Leningrad, 1968), thesis in Russian supervised by I. E. Barenbaum, p. 92.

24 Ibid., p. 98.

25 C.G.I.A., Leningrad, Collection 772, op. 1, ed. 170 (The Rector Pelikan's annual reports).

26 Beauvois, *Lumières et Société*, pp. 210–13.

27 W. Strojnowski, *Ekonomika powszechna, krajowa, narodów* (The general, national and international economy) (Wilno, 1816), passage on the Jews, pp. 275–7.

28 P. Chmielowski, *Liberalizm i obskurantyzm na Litwie i Rusi 1815—1823* (Liberalism and obscurantism in Lithuania and the Ukraine 1815–1823) (Warsaw, 1898).

29 Ibid., p. 128.
30 W. Marczyński, *Statystyczne opisanie gubernii Podolskiej* (A statistical description of the Podolia gubernia), t. II, 1822, pp. 87–123; ibid., p. 129–30.
31 J. Tabiś, *Polacy na uniwersytecie kijowskim* (Poles at the University of Kiev) (Cracow, 1974), pp. 36–9.
32 J. M. Delmaire, 'La haskalah et la russification', pp. 79–81.
33 A. Przezdźiecki, *Podole, Wołyń, Ukraina* (Podolia, Volynia, Ukraine) (Wilno, 1841), t. I, pp. 76–7.
34 Ibid., t. 2, pp. 26–7.
35 T. Szczeniowski, *Bigos hultajski* (Hultaj stew) (Wilno, 1845), t. II, pp. 18–27, 74. Niesecki's armorial constituted the authority in the old Poland which served to guarantee the nobility of those listed in it. 'Jarosz Beyla' was Henryk Rzewuski's pseudonym.
36 J. I. Kraszewski, *Wspomnienia Wołynia, Polesia i Litwy* (Memoirs of Volynia, Polesia and Lithuania) (Wilno, 1840), vol. 1, pp. 154–9. In volume 2 he points out that one of the favourite amusements of the rural idle rich was 'Jew hunting'.
37 H. de Balzac, *Lettre sur Kiev*, O.C., (Club de l'Honnête Homme, Paris, 1956), t. 24, pp. 560–61.

CHAPTER 8   JEWS IN LUBLIN PRIOR TO THE JANUARY UPRISING

1 Stefan Kieniewicz *Warszawa w powstaniu styczniowym* (Warsaw in the January Insurrection) (Warsaw, 1954), p. 61.
2 Thadée Tyszkiewicz, *Ecrits sur la Pologne Contemporaire* (Brussels, 1864), 186264, p. 70.
3 Charles Forbes de Montalembert, *Une nation en deuil. La Pologne en 1861* (Paris, 1861), passim.
4 Natalia Gąsiorowska, 'Mieszczaństwo w powstaniu styczniowym' (The bourgeoisie in the January Insurrection), in *Przegląd Historyczny*, vol. XXXIV (1937/38), p. 532.
5 Lublin Archives (WAPL), RGL., Confidential vol. 15, the governor of Lublin to the vice-regent of the Kingdom, 6 March 1861, p. 141.
6 Walery Przyborowski, *Historia dwóch lat* (A history of two years) (Cracow, 1893), vol. II, p. 157.
7 WAPL, RGL, Confidential Files, vol. 15, p. 192.
8 Artur Eisenbach, *Kwestia równouprawnienia Żydów w Królestwie Polskim* (The question of granting Jews equality in the Kingdom of Poland) (Warsaw, 1972), p. 330.
9 WAPL, RGL, Confidential Files, vol. 15, p. 197.
10 Ibid., vol. 16, p. 44–5.
11 W. Przyborowski, *Historia dwóch lat*, p. 203.
12 Kazimierz Gregorowicz, *Pogląd krytyczny na wypadki z r. 1861, 1862, 1863* (A critical view of the events of the years 1861, 1862 and 1863) (Lwów, 1880), vol. II, pp. 71–2.
13 N. Gąsiorowska, 'Mieszczaństwo w powstaniu styczniowym' p. 534. According to the author, the constables in Warsaw were recruited from among the youth

and the poor of the city population. This was probably the case both with the Polish and the Jewish population of Lublin.

14 K. Gregorowicz, *Pogląd krytyczny*, p. 72.

15 Ibid., vol. II, p. 72.

16 Ryszard Bender, *Ludność wiejska Lubelskiego w akcji przedpowstaniowej w latach 1861—1862* (The rural population of the Lublin area in pre-revolutionary activity 1861–2) (Lublin, 1961), p. 32.

17 WAPL, RGL, Confidential Files, vol. 1122, p. 19.

18 A. Eisenbach, D. Fainhauz, A. Wein (eds), *Żydzi a powstanie styczniowe. Materiały i dokumenty* (Jews and the January Insurrection. Materials and documents) (Warsaw, 1963).

19 WAPL, RGL, Confidential Files, p. 19.

20 Ibid., p. 193.

21 *Przegląd Rzeczy Polskich*, 20 September 1861. W. Przyborowski, Historia dwóch Lat, vol. III, p. 342.

22 Franciszka Ramotówska, *Rząd carski wobec manifestacji patriotycznych w Królewstwie Polskim w latach 1860—1862* (The Tsarist government's reaction to patriotic demonstrations in the Kingdom of Poland in the years 1860–1862) (Warsaw, 1971), p. 101.

23 Majer Bałaban, 'Żydzi w powstaniu 1863 r.' (Jews in the 1863 insurrection), in *Przegląd Historyczny*, vol. XXXIV (1937/38), p. 578.

24 A. Eisenbach et al. (eds), *Żydzi a powstanie styczniowe*, p. 19.

25 *Dziennik Praw Królewstwa Polskiego* (The Digest of Laws of the Kingdom of Poland), vol. 57, p. 339.

26 H. Łopaciński library in Lublin, manuscript 1756, Proclamation of the revolutionary and patriotic circles of July 1st, 1861.

27 WAPL files, municipal council of Lublin, vol. 25, p. 63.

28 R. Bender, 'Mieszczaństwo Lublina w wyborach samorządowych do Rady Miejskiej w 1861 r.' (The bourgeoisie of Lublin in the local government elections of 1861), in *Dzieje burżuazji w Polsce* (The history of the bourgeoisie in Poland), vol. II (1980), p. 42–3.

29 WAPL Municipal Council of Lublin, vol. 25b, p. 1.

30 *Dziennik Powszechny*, 124, 4 June 1862.

31 WAPL Municipal Council of Lublin, vol. 25b, p. 14.

32 R. Bender, 'Rady Miejskie w Lubelskiem w latach 1861–1863' (City councils in the Lublin area in the years 1861–1863), *Czasopismo Prawno- Historyczne* XIV, vol. 2, (1962), p. 158.

33 'Ruch', 6(12 October 1862).

34 In the Lublin region only the City Council of Krasnystaw was dissolved before the uprising, that is on 28 November 1862.

35 WAPL Local Club of Lublin, vol. 24, p. 481. Letter from the President of Lublin to the members of the City Council, 9 February 1863.

36 Ibid., p. 483, letter from the President of Lublin to Miller and Lichtenfeld.

37 S. Kieniewicz, *Powstanie styczniowe* (The January Uprising) (Warsaw, 1972), p. 202.

38 WAPL, RGL, Adm. Dep., vol. 1123, p. 131.

39 Ibid., p. 131.

40 A. Eisenbach, *Kwestia równouprawnienia*, p. 450.

41 WAPL. Collected files. Naczelnik Wojenny Główego Oddziału Lubelskiego, vol. 15, p. 15. Letter from the vice-regent of the Kingdom to General Chruszczow, commander of the Russian troops stationed in Lublin, 15 November 1861.

42 J. Tomczyk, 'Organizacja cywilno-wojskowa powstania styczniowego w Lubelskiem i na Podlasiu' (The civil and military organization of the January uprising in the Lublin area and in Podlasie), *Rocznik Lubelski* (1967), vol. VI, pp. 7–70.

CHAPTER 9   RURAL ANTI-SEMITISM IN GALICIA

1 Frank Golczewski, *Polnisch-jüdische Beziehungen 1881–1922: Eine Studie zur Geschichte des Antisemitismus in Osteuropa* (Wiesbaden, 1981), especially pp. 60–84.

2 For a first essay to describe the history of this party see Stanisław Antoń, 'Dzieje ruchu ludowego Sądeczyzny (!) w latach 1870–1919' (The history of the peasant movement in the Sądeczyzna in the years 1870–1919) *Rocznik Sądecki, Nowy Sącz*, 8 (1967), pp. 65–113, where only some citations hint that there might have been something like anti-semitism in its ideology.

3 For Otto Böckel's populist anti-semitic anti-conservative slogans against 'Juden, Junker und Pfaffen' in the 1880s, see for example Herman Greive, *Geschichte des modernen Antisemitismus in Deutschland* (Darmstadt,1983), pp. 68–9.

4 Stanisław Szczepanowski, *Nędza Galicyi w cyfrach i program energicznego rozwoju gospodarstwa Krajowego* (The misery of Galicia in figures with an energetic programme for national development) (Lwów, 1888).

5 Ibid., p. 125.

6 Ibid., p. 135.

7 See Ignacy Daszyński, *Pamiętniki* (Memoirs) (Warsaw, 1957), vol. 1, p. 139.

8 See Henryk Piasecki, *Sekcja Żydowska PPSD i Żydowska Partia Socjalno-Demokratyczna 1892–1919/20* (The Jewish section of the PPSD and the Jewish Social-Democratic Party 1892–1919/1920) (Wrocław, 1983), p. 301.

9 As I have tried in my book *Polnisch-jüdische Beziehungen*, p. 358–61.

10 Ibid., pp. 67–8.

11 *Wieniec Polski* (1898), pp. 138–9, 'Żydowskie majątki'.

12 *Pszczółka* (1898), p. 134: 'A woman that brings eggs, butter, cheese, etc. to the market must sell for the price the Jews like (which is fabulously low, of course), because that mob closes ranks and defines prices at will; they buy cheap and sell expensive and that is how they get rich.'

13 *Pszczółka* (1898), p. 194.

14 *Wieniec Polski* (1898), p. 189.

15 See such statements as 'They are so furious against us Catholics that you tremble with fear', or 'the Talmud orders them to kill us whenever possible . . . to cause damage to our means and our health', *Wieniec Polski* (1898), p. 188, 'O Żydowskich tajemnicach'.

16 *Wieniec Polski* (1898), p. 285.
17 Ibid., p. 286–7.
18 Ibid., p. 287.
19 Ibid., p. 352.
20 Ibid., p. 354.
21 See Golczewski, *Beziehungen*, pp. 342 ff.
22 *Pszczółka* (1898), pp. 197–8.
23 Gino Germani, *Authoritarianism, Fascism and National Populism* (New Brunswick, NJ, 1978), p. 88.

CHAPTER 10   JEWISH ASSIMILATION IN POLAND, 1863–1943

1 This paper is based in part on my 'O asymilacji Żydów w Polsce od wybuchu pierwszej wojny światowej do końca drugiej wojny (1914–1945) (On the assimilation of Jews in Poland from the outbreak of the First World War to the end of the Second World War, 1914–1945), *Zeszyty Historyczne* (Instytut Literacki, Paris, 1977), pp. 96–134. Also 'Janusz Korczak, Żyd Polski (Janusz Korczak, Polish Jew), *Więź* (Warsaw), 4 (April 1983), 'Adam Czerniakow na tle epoki' (Adam Czerniakow seen against his era), *Więź* (Warsaw), 4–5 (April–May 1982) and 'Adam Czerniaków and his times' *Polish Review*, 1–2, 1984.
2 'Jewish Assimilation in Lwów: the Case of Wilhelm Feldman', *Slavic Review*, vol. 28, 2 (December 1969). 'From Assimilation to Zionism in Lwów: the Case of Alfred Nossig', *The Slavonic and East European Review*, vol. 49 (October 1971). 'A Note on Jewish Assimilation in the Polish Lands', in *Jewish Assimilation in Modern Times*, ed. Bela Vago (Boulder, Colorado, Westview Press, 1981).
3 Polish title: *Żydzi w kulturze polskiej* (Jews in Polish culture) Paris: Instytut Literacki, 1981.
4 Jacob Shatzky (Szacki), 'Alexander Kraushar and His Road to Total Assimilation', *YIVO Annual of Jewish Social Science*, 7, 1952, pp. 146–74.
5 Celia S. Heller, *On the Edge of Destruction. Jews in Poland Between the Two World Wars* (New York, Columbia University Press, 1977).
6 Arthur Eisenbach, *Kwestia równouprawnienia Żydów w Królestwie Polskim* (The question of granting equality to the Jews in the Kingdom of Poland) Warsaw: Instytut Historii Pan, 1972.
7 Arthur Sandauer, *O sytuacji pisarza polskiego pochodzenia żydowskiego w XX wieku* (On the situation of the Polish writer of Jewish origin in the twentieth century) Warsaw, Czytelnik, 1982). See also a review of this book by Joshua Rothenberg in *Soviet Jewish Affairs*, vol. 14, 1 February 1984.
8 Helena Datner-Śpiewak 'Asymilacja narodu i asymilacja jednostki' (National assimilation and individual assimilation) *Więź* (Warsaw), 4 April 1983.
9 Joseph Marcus, *Of the Social and Political History of the Jews in Poland, 1919—1939* (Berlin; New York; Amsterdam, Mouton Publishers, 1983).
10 Lloyd Gartner, 'Assimilation and American Jews', in *Jewish Assimilation in Modern Times* ed. Bela Vago.
11 Shatsky, 'Alexander Kraushar'.

12 *Żydzi w kulturze*, p. 133.

13 Eisenbach, *Kwestia równouprawnienia.*

14 Marcus, *Social and Political History*, p. 288.

15 Arnold M. Rose, *Sociology: the Study of Human Relations* New York, Alfred Knopf, 1956, pp. 557–8.

16 *Krytyka* (Luty, 1909). This translation from Polish and several that follow are my own.

17 *Deklaracya Ideowa. Prawne rozwiązanie Kwestji Żydowskiej w Polsce* (Ideological declaration. The legal solution to the Jewish question in Poland) Lwów, Editors of *Zjednoczenie*, 1919.

18 Bernard D. Weinryb, *The Jews of Poland*, Philadelphia, The Jewish Publication of America, 1973, p. 156.

19 E. Kupfer, *Ber Meisels*, Warsaw, Żydowski Instytut Historyczny, 1953, p. 105.

20 Maksymilian Goldstein and Karol Dresdner, *Kultura i Sztuka Ludu Żydowskiego na Ziemiach Polskich*, (The culture and art of the Jewish people on Polish land) (with a foreword by Professor Dr. Majer Bałaban, Lwów, 1935).

21 Marian Fuks, *Prasa żydowska w Warszawie, 1823–1939* (The Jewish press in Warsaw, 1823–1939) Warsaw, PWN, 1979.

22 Agaton Giller, *Historia Powstania Narodu Polskiego w 1861—1864* (The history of the insurrection of the Polish Nation 1861–1864), Paris, 1870, vol. I, p. 180.

23 Ibid., p. 103.

24 Fuks *Prasa żydowska*, writes that *Izraelita* ceased publication in 1912; however, the weekly was still appearing in 1913.

25 *Izraelita*, year 47, 6 (9 February 1912).

26 As early as in 7 (5 December 1882) and as late as in 3 (20 January 1911).

27 *Izraelita*, 14 (2 April 1882); Fuks, *Prasa żydowska*, p. 100.

28 Shatzky, 'Alexander Kraushar', p. 165.

29 Ryszard Kołodziejczyk, *Jan Bloch (1836—1902)*, Warsaw, PIW, 1983, pp. 172–8.

30 *The Jewish Encyclopedia*, Funk and Wagnals Co., New York and London, vol. III, p. 252.

31 Antoni Lange, *O sprzecznościach sprawy żydowskiej* (On the contradictions of the Jewish question), Warsaw, 1911, pp. 54, 67.

32 'Lange Antoni', in *Słownik Biograficzny*, states that Lange adopted Catholicism in his later years.

33 J. Shatzky, 'Alexander Kraushar'.

34 Barbara Petrolin-Skowrońska, '*Gazeta Handlowa* i *Nowa Gazeta* (1864–1918)', *Rocznik Historii Piśmiennictwa Polskiego*, (The *Gazeta Handlowa* and *Nowa Gazeta*, 1864–1918), vol. 7, 1 1962.

35 Lange, *O sprzecznosciach*.

36 Anatol Muhlstein, *Asymilacja, Polityka, i Postęp* (Assimilation, politics and progress), Warsaw, 1913.

37 J. Baudouin de Courtney, *O Kwestii Żydowskiej* (On the Jewish question), Warsaw, 1913. This brochure was recently reprinted in the VIth volume of his *Collected Works* (Warsaw, PAN, 1983) and recently reviewed in *Nowe Książki*, 3 March 1984.

38 Kazimierz Sterling, *Państwowość Polska a Żydzi* (Polish statehood and the Jews), Warsaw, 1916.
39 *Zjednoczenie*, Warsaw, 5 May 1933.
40 Mateusz Mieses,'Żydzi w akcji wyzwolenia Polski', (The Jewish role in the liberation of Poland) *Głos Gminy żydowskiej*, XX-Lecie Polski Niepodleglej, Warsaw, Październik-Listopad, 1938.
41 *Żagiew*, Pismo Związku Młodzieży Polskiej Pochodzenia Żydowskiego, year 6, issue 1–2 (13–14), 1919, p. 11.
42 This manifesto, which is a rarity, was published in full, in Polish in *Zeszyty Historyczne*, pp. 111–12.
43 *Zgoda*, Pismo poświęcone ugodzie polsko żydowskiej, Cracow and Warsaw, 7 (15 September 1919).
44 Ibid.
45 *Zgoda*, 15 September 1919.
46 A letter reporting the decision (translated from German): 'To the Scoutmaster under the name of Col. Berek Joselewicz, S. Nr. 1 a 4004, Pot P. Warsaw, 28 September 1917. Because the Association is not legal here, it is herewith forbidden to continue its activity. At the same time attention is called to the fact that any attempt to legalize this association will be rejected in conformity with the decree of the Chief of Administration of 31 July 1917, which forbade forming new sporting associations and youth centers.' W.Z. [signature illegible].
47 *Zjednoczenie*, 15 November 1931.
48 Celia S. Heller, *On the Edge of Destruction*, p. 187, argues that 'Unity had laid dormant for almost a decade.' On the contrary, the first decade of independent Poland was a period of quickened Unity activity. It is also incorrect that assimilationists were 'overrepresented' by the 'very wealthy Jews' (ibid., p. 189). Heller, after arriving at surprising conclusions on p. 189, declares that the young assimilationists of 'Unity' 'began to refer to themselves sometimes [sic] as "Jews-Poles"' (p. 190). But Jan Ruff, the chief theoretician and ideologist of the young 'Unity' movement, categorically stated that this expression is 'a legal and linguistic monstrosity', (*Żydzi-Polityka-Polska. Zjednoczenie* (Jew-Politics-Poland. Unity) Warsaw, 1923, p. 11.)
49 Very few issues of *Rozwaga* and *Dzwon* have survived. Three issues of *Dzwon* are left and not two, as Izrael Szajn has it in his bibliography (*Biuletyn Żydowskiego Instytutu Historycznego w Polsce*, 2/78, 1978, p. 112). At least 15 issues of *Zjednoczenie* (Lwów and Warsaw) survive.
50 The 'Unity' movement wrote Jew with a small j, on the grounds that the word did not indicate nationality. Since it is now general practice to write the word with a capital letter, that is the version followed in the present essay.
51 *Pamiętnik Pierwszego Walnego Zjazdu Zjednoczenia Polaków Wyznania Mojżeszowego Wszystkich Ziem Polskich* (A memoir of the First Plenary Session of the Union of Poles of the Mosaic Faith from all parts of Poland) Warsaw: Zjednoczenie, 1919.
52 Ibid., pp. 13, 18–19.
53 *Żydzi w kulturze*, p. 147.

54 It is not without significance that, on the occasion of a birthday visit the Association paid to Marshal Piłsudski, he said: 'Yours is a difficult and hard task. Apparently pointless and hopeless. Society is clearly split into two spheres, two different nationalisms. You are rejected by both of them. Because of that, you are alone and few in number. So your ideals are not suited for people today, people who were reared in the school of slavery' *ŚWIT. Jednodniowka zokazji imienin Marszałka Józefa Piłsudskiego* (A celebration on the occasion of Marshal Józef Piłsudski's nameday) Kołomyja, 17 April 1936, p. 4.

55 *Zjednoczenie*, 15 January 1932.

56 *Sprawy Narodowościowe*, Warsaw, 6, 1937, pp. 659–60. See also a summary by Józef Orlicki, *Z dziejów stosunków polsko-żydowskich 1918–1949* (On the history of Polish–Jewish relations 1918–1949) Krajowa Agencja Wydawnicza, 1983, p. 80. Orlicki erroneously gives the date of the Congress of the Bloc as October 1937.

57 The appeal of the Association of ex-Combatants was published in the daily *Nasz Przegląd* (Our Survey) Warsaw, 2 September 1939.

58 *Żołnierz Polski-Żyd* (The Polish Jewish Soldier. A Single Publication on the Occasion of the Jewish New Year) London, 29 September 1943.

59 Ibid., p. 5.

60 The originals are in the archives of the Jewish Historical Institute in Warsaw. Yad Vashem has copies in Jerusalem.

61 Ibid.

62 Mina Tomkiewicz, *Bomby i myszy* (Bombs and Mice), London, Gryf Publications Ltd, 1966, pp. 181 and 262.

63 Marian Fuks, 'Żydowska prasa w okresie okupacji hitlerowskiej w Polsce (1940–1943)' (The Jewish press during Hitler's occupation of Poland), *Kwartalnik Historii Prasy Polskiej*, vol. 16, 2, 1977, quotes from the last issue of *Żagiew* (February, 1943) without any comment. Bernard Mark writes that the issues of *Żagiew* from 1943 were 'mystification' and provocation of Gancwajch (*Walka i Zagłada Warszawskiego getta* (The struggle and liquidation of the Warsaw Ghetto) Warsaw: MON, 1959, p. 212. Mark reiterated this opinion to me in a conversation in 1959.

CHAPTER 11   INTERWAR POLAND: GOOD OR BAD FOR THE JEWS

1 Nahum Sokolow,'Masa le-polaniya be-shnat 1933–4', *Ha-tsofe le-vet yisrael* (Jerusalem, 1961), p. 311.

2 Joseph Marcus, *Social and Political History of the Jews in Poland 1919—1939*, Berlin, NY, Amsterdam, 1983. For a review of the recent literature on Polish Jewry see Ezra Mendelsohn, 'Recent Work on the Jews in Interwar East Central Europe: A Survey', *Studies in Contemporary Jewry*, I, (Bloomington, 1984), pp. 318–24.

3 Marcus p. 231.

4 For example, Michael Stanislawski, *Tsar Nicholas 1 and the Jews*, Philadelphia, 1983.

5 'Zarys dziejów Żydów polskich w XIX i XX w.' (An outline of the history of

Polish Jews in the nineteenth and twentieth centuries), in *Żydzi polscy: dzieje i kultura* (Polish Jews, their history and culture) Warsaw, 1982, pp. 32–42. Also his review article in *Przegląd historyczny*, LXXV, I, 1984, pp. 137–41.

6 Władysław T. Bartoszewski, *Ethnocentrism: Beliefs and Stereotypes. A Study of Polish–Jewish Relations in the Early 20th Century* (University of Cambridge, 1984).

7 Ibid., p. 333.

8 Ibid., p. 337.

9 Norman Davies, *God's Playground — A History of Poland* (2 vols, Oxford, 1981).

10 Ibid., vol. II, p. 260.

11 Ibid., p. 261.

12 Ibid., p. 263.

13 Ibid., p. 408–9.

14 See Holzer's article in this book, p. 141.

15 *Nowy Dziennik*, 20 February 1936; 21 February 1936.

16 Ibid., 21 February 1936.

17 *Haynt*, 14 August 1936.

18 Ibid.

19 Moshe Kleinbaum in *Haynt*, 24 September 1936; Apolinary Hartglas in *Haynt*, 27 September 1936.

20 *Haynt*, 13 September 1936.

21 *Nowy Dziennik*, 21 April 1937.

22 *Haynt*, 16 October 1936.

23 *Nowy Dziennik*, 4 February 1937.

24 See Sommerstein's remarks in *Nowy Dziennik*, 20 February 1937, quoting Daszyński; *Haynt*, 26 February 1936, on how the peasants of Przytyk have been terrorized by the Endecja.

25 Frank Golczewski, *Polnisch-Jüdische Beziehungen 1881—1922* Wiesbaden, 1981, pp. 185–204 (on Lwów).

26 Beck is quoted in *Nowy Dziennik*, 2 February 1937, as saying: 'Poland is not anti-semitic. The key to the Jewish question is the economic and social questions, not the political question.' For Jabotinski's agreement with this position see his speech in Warsaw as reported in *Haynt*, 6 November 1936.

27 For a comparison of the situation in Poland and the Soviet Union see the article by Mordecai Altshuler and Ezra Mendelsohn in *Iyunim be-yahadut zmanenu* Jerusalem, 1984, pp. 53–64. On Hungary see my analysis in *The Jews of East Central Europe Between the World Wars*, Bloomington, 1983, pp. 85–130.

28 See Emil Sommerstein's remarks in *Nowy Dziennik*, 21 June 1936. We live, he said, in conditions 'which can be defined by one word – extermination.'

29 *Nowy Dziennik*, 6 March 1937.

30 Mendelsohn, *Zionism in Poland* New Haven, 1981, pp. 213–22.

31 *Nowy Dziennik*, 4 December 1936.

32 *Haynt*, 16 October 1936.

CHAPTER 12 INTERWAR POLISH AND JEWISH LEFT WING GROUPS

1 J. Holzer, 'Żydowskie dążenia polityczne w Drugiej Rzeczypospolitej' (Jewish Political Tendencies in the Second Republic of Poland) (*Znak*, 1983), 339–40, pp. 366–82; J. M. Majchrowski,'Problem żydowski w programach głównych polskich obozów politycznych' (The Jewish question in programmes of the main political camps in Poland (1918–1939)), ibid., pp. 383–94.

2 H. Piasecki, *Żydowska Organizacja PPS 1893—1907* (PPS Jewish Organization) (Wrocław, 1978).

3 H. Piasecki *Sekcja Żydowska PPSD i Żydowska Partia Socjalno-Demokratyczna 1892—1919/20* (The Jewish Section in PPSD and the Jewish Social Democratic Party 1892–1919/20) (Wrocław, 1982), pp. 21–82.

4 F. Tych, *PPS-Lewica w latach wojny 1914—1918* (PPS-Left during the war of 1914–1918) (Warsaw, 1960), p. 197.

5 *Przegląd Socjaldemokratyczny* VII 1902, pp. 21–5, after F. Tych (ed.), *Socjaldemokracja Królestwa Polskiego i Litwy. Materiały i dokumenty* (The Social democracy of the Polish Kingdom and Lithuania: materials and documents) (Warsaw, 1962), vol. II, 1902–03, p. 280.

6 B. Szmidt, *Socjal demokracja Królestwa Polskiego i Litwy. Materiały i dokumenty 1893—1904* (Moscow, 1934), p. 280.

7 Cf. J. Bunzl, *Klassenkampf in der Diaspora, Zur Geschichte der jüdischen Arbeiterbewegung* (Wien, 1975), pp. 1–5.

8 F. Swietlikowa, *Komunistyczna Partia Robotnicza Polski 1918—1923* (The Communist Workers' Party of Poland 1918–1923) (Warsaw, 1968), p. 19.

9 *KPP Uchwały i rezolucje* (Decrees and resolutions) (Warsaw, 1955), vol. II, III–IV Congresses (1924–9) p. 183.

10 J. Majchrowski, 'Problem żydowski', p. 393.

11 J. Holzer, *Polska Partia Socjalistyczna w latach 1917—1919* (Polish Socialist Party between 1917 and 1919) (Warsaw, 1962),p. 274.

12 J. M. Borski, *Sprawa żydowska a socjalizm. Polemika z Bundem* (The Jewish question and Socialism. A Polemic with the Bund) (Warsaw, 1937); Cf. J. Żarnowski, *Polska Partia Socjalistyczna 1935—1939* (The Polish Socialist Party 1935–1939) (Warsaw, 1965), p. 222.

13 Cf. R. Korsch, *Żydowskie ugrupowania wywrotowe w Polsce* (The Jewish Seditious Groupings in Poland) (Warsaw, 1925).

CHAPTER 14 RELIEF COUNCIL FOR JEWS, 1942–1945

1 The Central Archives of the Central Committee of the Polish United Workers' Party, mf. 2283.

2 The information on the Aid Committee to Jews and on the Relief Council for Jews contained in this paper are based on documents available in the Archives of the Jewish Historical Institute in Warsaw, Mat. podz. 114–120, in the Central Archives of the Central Committee of the Polish United Workers' Party, 202/I, 202/VII, 202/XV, 202/XVII, as well as on scores of interviews made by the author.

3 After Julian Grobelny had been arrested, Roman Jabłonowski became the president in May 1944 and held that office until July 1944; after the collapse of the Warsaw uprising, Leon Feiner was president, from November 1944 to January 1945.

4 The Central Archives of the Central Committee of the Polish United Workers' Party, mf. 203/X.

5 E. Ringelblum, *Polish—Jewish Relations during the Second World War* (Yad Vashem, Jerusalem, 1974), p. 226.

6 The statement made by I. Sendlerowa and three other women, her co-workers; in the possession of the author.

7 T. Seweryn, 'Wielostronna pomoc Żydom w czasie okupacji hitlerowskiej' (Multilateral help for Jews during the Nazi occupation), *Przegląd Lekarski*, 1 (1967).

CHAPTER 15 POLISH AND JEWISH HISTORIOGRAPHY ON THE QUESTION OF POLISH-JEWISH RELATIONS DURING WORLD WAR II

1 Emanuel Ringelblum, *Kronika getta warszawskiego wrzesień 1939 — styczeń 1943* (Introduced and edited by Arthur Eisenbach, translated from Yiddish by Adam Rutkowski), Warsaw, 1983.

2 The Yiddish version appeared in two volumes under the title *Ksovim fun geto*, Warsaw, 1961, 1963.

3 The work by E. Ringelblum *Polish—Jewish Relations during the Second World War* was published in English by Yad Vashem, Jerusalem, 1974. Edited and with footnotes by Joseph Kermish and Shmuel Krakowski. The American edition of the book, New York, 1976.

4 Władyslaw Bartoszewski and Zofia Lewin (eds) *Righteous Among Nations*, London, 1969, p. xxxiv.

5 Abraham Levin, *Mi - Pinkaso shel ha-More mi-„Yehudiyah"* (The Diary of the Teacher from 'Jehudia'), Tel-Aviv, 1969.

6 E. Ringelblum, *Polish—Jewish Relations*, ibid., p. 196.

7 Ibid., p. 247.

8 Kazimierz Wyka, *Życie na niby.Szkice z at 1939—1945*, Warsaw, 1959, pp. 198–199.

9 Archives of the Central Committee of PZPR 202/II-6, p. 105 (quoted from a manuscript written by Sh. Krakowski).

10 Archives of General Sikorski, Historical Institute, London (GSHI) PRM-K-85.

11 Yad Vashem Archives, 0–2, 89–16 (quoted from Sh. Krakowski's manuscript).

12 From a memorandum by Roman Knoll, Head of the Office for Foreign Affairs by the Delegate in occupied Poland, copy YV Archives, M-2/262.

13 About the 'schmalzovniks' see for instance the English edition of the book by Bernard Goldstein, *Five Years in the Warsaw Ghetto*, translated and edited by Leonard Shatzki, Dolfin book, pp. 198–200.

14 Stefan Korbonski, *The Polish Underground State* Boulder, 1978.

15 Kazimierz Iranek-Osmecki, *He Who Saves One Life*, Crown Publishers, New York (without year of publication), p. 135.

16 See Yisrael Gutman, 'A Report of a Member of the Polish Underground on Polish–Jewish Relations in Occupied Poland', published in Michael, *On the History of the Jews in the Diaspora*, Tel-Aviv, 1980, p. 109.

17 See the appeal in the selection of documents annexed to the book of Bartoszewski and Levin, ibid. The editors did omit the sharp anti-Jewish passage which Zofia Kossak-Szzucka included in her original appeal.

18 Ringelblum, *Polish—Jewish Relations*, ibid., p. 245.

19 See Shmuel Krakowski, *The War of the Doomed: Jewish Armed Resistance in Poland*, New York, 1984, p. 14.

20 Tandeuszbiór-Komorowski, *The Secret Army*, New York, 1951, p. 99–100.

21 See the Report submitted by Woliński about the activity of his department, in B. Mark, *Powstanie w getcie warszawskim, Nowe uzupełnione wydanie i zbiór dokumentów*, Warsaw, 1963, pp. 342–51.

22 Raul Hilberg, *The Destruction of the European Jews*, London, 1961, pp. 319–20.

23 See more details about this confrontation. Yisrael Gutman, *The Jews of Warsaw. Ghetto, Underground, Revolt*, Bloomington, 1982, pp. 416–19.

After the presentation of this paper and that of Professor Bartoszewski at the Oxford Conference there was an important discussion between these two scholars which will be published in volume 2 of *Polin*.

CHAPTER 16 POLISH–JEWISH RELATIONS, 1944–1947

1 Michael Chęciński, *Poland, communism, nationalism, anti-semitism* (New York, Karr-Cohl Publishing, 1982).

2 Hersch Smolar, *Na ostatniej linii i z ostatnią nadzieją* (On the last line and with the last hope) (Tel Aviv, J. L. Perec, 1982) (in Yiddish).

3 Louis Gronowski-Brunoł, *Le Dernier Grand Soir. Un Juif de Pologne* (Paris, Seuil, 1980).

4 'Słowo o prawdzie staje się obowiązkiem' (A word of truth has become an obligation) *Kultura* 11/133, Paris, 1958; included in my book, *Ludzie, książki, spory . . .* (People, books, disputes . . .) (Paris, Księgarnia Polska, 1980).

5 Tadeusz Żenczykowski, *Dramatyczny rok 1945* (The dramatic year 1945) (London, Polonia, 1982).

6 Krystyna Kersten,'Kielce – 4 Lipca 1946 roku' (Kielce – 4 July 1946), *Tygodnik Solidarności*, 364 (December 1981).

7 Joseph Tennenbaum, *In Search of a Lost People* (New York, The Beechhurst Press, 1948), pp. 235–41. Joseph Tennenbaum was accompanied by Professor Olgierd Górka from the All-Polish League for the Battle Against Racism.

8 S. E. Shneiderman, *Between Fear and Hope* (New York, Arco Publishing Company, 1947).

9 Schneiderman, *Between Fear and Hope*. A comprehensive record of all relevant declarations is included.

10 I experienced the truth of this personally. On announcing my own publication

against anti-semitism (M. Borwicz, *Organizowanie wściekłosci* (The organization of hatred) (Warsaw: All-Polish League for the Battle Against Racism, 1947), I had to omit two sections on this very subject when the manuscript went to print, even though they had been very carefully edited.

11 The statistics quoted by Shneiderman, *Between Fear and Hope*, and communicated to him by the spokesman of the Department of Productivity are as follows: as on 10 June 1946, the approximate number of Jews employed in Silesia was 13,101, of whom 2,000 were in Richbach and over 10,000 in Wałbrzych, Wrocław and Bielawa. The majority of Jews were employed in textile factories (1478), mines (906), in the textile industry (377), in other state enterprises (3080), in co-operatives (1561) and in other fields (5,183).

12 These two theatres were later to join forces with the Ida Kaminska Theatre.

13 Between June and September 1946 about 100,000 Jews left Poland by legal and illegal means, through Silesia to Czechoslovakia and from there to DP camps in Germany.

14 All figures regarding the size of the Jewish population in Poland after the war are approximate. Despite the sudden decrease in population, the co-operative movement continued to develop and reached a membership peak in 1948. It had 8–9,000 members in 220 productive co-operatives, a certain number of which were real factories. See P. Meyer, E. Duschinsky and N. Sylvan, *The Jews in the Soviet Satellites* (Syracuse University Press, 1953), quoted from M. Wieriorka *Les Juifs, La Pologne et Solidarność* (Paris, Denoel, 1984).

15 According to these official theories, both during the German occupation and after the war, there existed only a handful of reactionaries. As propaganda insisted on including Home Army groups among this handful together with any representatives of the Delegation in London, the official reasoning could claim little credibility.

CHAPTER 17   THE JEWISH ISSUE IN POST-WAR POLISH POLITICS

1 A. Kwilecki, 'Mniejszości narodowe w Polsce Ludowej (National Minorities in People's Poland), Kultura i Społeczeństwo (1963), vol. VII, 4, 85–103; P. Glikson, 'Jewish Population in the Polish People's Republic, 1944–1972', in *Papers in Jewish Demography, 1973* (Jerusalem, 1973), pp. 235–53.

2 'Jews in Eastern Europe after World War II: Documents from the British Foreign Office'. Introduced and annotated by Antony Polonsky, *Soviet Jewish Affairs*, vol. 10, 1, in particular pp. 61, 64–8; *Jewish American Yearbook 5706/ 1945–6*(Vol. 47), 405–7, 5707/1946–7 (vol. 48), 535–8, 5708/1947–48 (vol. 49), 383–6, 5709/1948–9 (vol. 50), 390; Bernard D. Weinryb, 'Poland', in *The Jews in the Soviet Satellites* (Syracuse, 1953), pp. 248–53; Krystyna Kersten, *Historia polityczna Polski 1944—1956* (A political history of Poland 1944–1956) (Warsaw, 'Krąg', 1982), pp. 27–8.

3 See for instance report about Ochab's statement to a meeting of Jewish PPR activists on 25 October 1948 in Hersh Smolar, *Oyf der Letster Pozitsye, Mit der Letzter Hofenung* (At the last outpost, with the last hope, Tel Aviv, 1982), pp. 43–4.

4 See Weinryb, *The Jews in the Soviet Satellites*, pp. 1–2; Francois Fejtö, *A History of the People's Democracies. Eastern Europe Since Stalin* (London,1971), pp. 8–10.

5 Flora Lewis, *The Man Who Disappeared: The Strange Case of Noel Field* (London, 1965).

6 Witold Jedlicki, *Klub Krzywego Koła* (The Club of the Crooked Circle) (Paris, 1963), chapter I, 'Chamy i Żydy', pp. 17–60. See also M. K. Dziewanowski, *Poland In the Twentieth Century* (New York, 1977), pp. 163, 198–9.

7 Edmund Silberner, *Kommunisten zur Judenfrage* (Opladen, 1983), pp. 253–7.

8 V.C. Chrypinski, 'Poland', in *The Communist States in Disarray 1965—1971*, A. Bromke and Teresa Rakowska-Harmstone (eds) (Minneapolis, 1972), pp. 11–12; M. K. Dziewanowski, *Poland in the Twentieth Century* pp. 191, 203; M. Chęciński, *Poland. Communism, Nationalism, Antisemitism* (New York, 1982), pp. 160–1.

9 Cf. Bromke and Rakowska-Harmstone, *The Community States in Disarray*, 342–4; Trond Gilberg, 'Influence of State Policy on Ethnic Persistence and Nationality Formation: The Case of Eastern Europe', in *Ethnic Diversity & Conflict in Eastern Europe*, ed. Peter E. Sugar (Santa Barbara, California-Oxford, 1980), pp. 194–202. For an official presentation of the premises of Polish national communism see Marian Orzechowski, 'Rewolucja – socjalizm – tradycja' (Revolution – socialism – tradition) in Antoni Czubiński (ed.), *Społeczeństwo Polskiej Rzeczpospolitej Ludowej* (The Society of the Polish People's Republic) (Warsaw, 1977). For a sympathetic presentation of Gomułka's 'Polish way' see Hansjakob Stehle, *The Independent Satellite. Society and Politics in Poland since 1945* (London, 1965).

10 Antony Polonsky, *Politics in Independent Poland, 1918—1939* (Oxford, 1972), pp. 240–1, 417; Emanuel Melzer, *Political Strife in a Blind Alley. The Jews in Poland 1935–39* (Tel Aviv,1982), p. 54 (in Hebrew).

11 Chęciński, *Poland. Communism, Nationalism, Antisemitism*, pp. 165–7, 201–2. See *American Jewish Yearbook 1964*, p. 278; ibid., 1967, pp. 290– 1.

12 See W. Rozenbaum, 'The Anti-Zionist Campaign in Poland, June-December 1967', *Canadian Slavonic Papers*, vol. XX, 2 (June 1978). This paper also draws attention to differences of views within the party leadership with regard to the anti-Zionist campaign.

13 See H. Gordon Skilling, *Czechoslovakia's Interrupted Revolution* (Princeton, NJ, 1976), pp. 682–3.

14 Gomułka's speech was broadcast live on television and published with some changes in next day *Trybuna Ludu* and other papers. For an annotated selected list of participants in the anti-Jewish campaign of 1968 see *Judenhetze in Polen. Eine Documentation von Simon Wiesenthal* (Bonn, 1969).

15 Institute of Jewish Affairs, *The Anti-Jewish Campaign in Present-Day Poland* (London, 1968); *Wydarzenia Marcowe* (The March events) (Paris, 1969); Paul Lendvai, *Antisemitism in Eastern Europe* (London, 1971), pp. 89–239; Josef Banas, *The Scapegoats* (London, 1979); M. Chęciński, *Poland. Communism, Nationalism Antisemitism*, pp. 225–54.

16 Tadeusz Walichnowski was at that time a high official in the Ministry of the Interior. He later became Director of State Archives, and is now the chief of the

Feliks Dzierżyński Academy of the Ministry of the Interior. His *Izrael a NRF* (Israel and the Federal Republic of Germany) a doctoral dissertation at the University of Toruń was first published in June 1967 with an introduction by Marian Wojciechowski. An English translation was published in 1968. In 1967 and 1968 many pamphlets on Zionism and Israel by Walichnowski were published in Warsaw and Katowice, including *The Tel Aviv–Bonn Axis and Poland* (Warsaw, 1968) in English. Kazimierz Kąkol was chief editor of the fortnightly *Prawo i Życie* (1957–74) which became under him a militant Moczarite organ. In 1974–80 he was head of the Office for the Affairs of Religion and later deputy director of the Radio and TV Committee. In 1985, after the death of another participant in the anti-Jewish programme of 1968 Professor Czesław Pilichowski he became Director of the Commission for the Investigation of Nazi Crimes in Poland.

17 Cf. W. Pobóg-Malinowski, *Najnowsza historia polityczna Polski, 1864–1945* (The recent political history of Poland 1864–1945) (London, 1956), vol. 2, part 1, pp. 618; Celia Heller, *On the Edge of Destruction. Jews of Poland Between the Two World Wars* (New York, 1977), pp. 254–5. This accusation had its pre-history in a view propagated throughout the nineteenth and twentieth centuries of the Jews as a propagator of revolution, see Chapters XII and XIII in Bernard Lazare, *L'antisemitisme. Son Histoire and ses causes* (a new reprint appeared in Paris, 1982); see also H. Valentin, *Antisemitenspiegel. Der Anisemitismus. Geschichte, Kritik, Soziologie* (Wien, 1937), pp. 155–82.

18 The lengthy resolution adopted by the plenary meeting of the CCP of CP of Czechoslovakia in December 1970 was published in January 1971. See for text in an English translation the special enclosure to *New Times* (Moscow), 4 (1971). See also *The Use of Antisemitism Against Czechoslovakia* (Institute of Jewish Affairs, London 1968).

19 See Dominik Morawski,'Korespondencja z Rzymu' (A letter from Rome), *Kultura* (Paris), 5308 (1973), 52; also Joseph R. Fishman, *Revolution and Tradition in People's Poland* Princeton, NJ, 1972), p. 17.

20 Cf. for example J. Holzer, 'Doświadczenia marca 1968' (The lessons of March 1968) *Kierunki* (17 May 1981). This essay was extensively summarized in *Polityka* and appeared in a Yiddish translation in *Fołks-sztyme*, 20 June 1981.

21 Cf. L. Hirszowicz and T. Shafar, 'The Jewish scapegoat in Eastern Europe', in *Patterns of Prejudice*, vol. 11, 5 (1977), 7–11; L. Hirszowicz, 'The Current Polish Crisis and the 1968 Antisemitic Campaign', *IJA Research Report*, 23 (1980); Hirszowicz, 'Jewish Themes in the Polish Crisis', *IJA Research Report*, 10 and 11 (1981); Hirszowicz, 'Poland's Jewish Policies under Martial Law', *IJA Research Report*, 3 (1982); 'Anti-semitism in Today's Poland', document introduced and annotated by Lukasz Hirszowicz, *Soviet Jewish Affairs*, vol. 12, 1 (1982), pp. 55–65.

22 See especially a letter signed by well over 100 Polish intellectuals printed in *Życie Warszawy*, 20 March 1981, and the exceptionally large number of letters received by the newspaper (20 April 1981), some of which were published; many other pronouncements by individuals and public bodies appeared in the Polish press in the spring of 1981. The PUWP CC First Secretary, Stanisław

Kania, also condemned anti-semitism in a speech on 12 March 1981.

23 See, for instance, L. Maleszka,'Uwaga faszyzm' (Beware fascism), in the uncensored Solidarity paper *Goniec Małopolski*, 25 March 1981.

24 See *Fołks-sztyme*, 23 January 1982 and 13 February 1982.

25 Cf. Nicholas Bethell, *Gomułka, His Poland and His Communism* (London, 1969), pp. 53–60, 94, 144–5; Jan B. de Weydenthal, *The Communists of Poland. An Historical Outline* (Stanford, California), pp. 53–4.

26 Andrzej Werblan, 'Przyczynek do genezy konfliktu' (A contribution to the causes of the conflict) *Miesięcznik Literacki* (June, 1968).

27 B. Syzdek, 'Spojrzenie na przebytą drogę' (A look at the road we have traversed) *Trybuna Ludu*, 21–22 February 1981, 28 February–1 March 1981 7–8 March 1981, 14–15 March 1981.

28 For instance, N. Michta, 'Nasz wspólny dom' (Our common house) *Sztandar Młodych*, 2 February 1981; W. Przelaskowski, 'Obecna sytuacja a marzec 1968' (The present situation and March 1968) *Za Wolność i Lud*, 14 March 1981.

29 See M. Mieszczankowski, 'Jednostronne spojrzenie', 'Przeoczone przyczyny' and 'Prezentyzm czy niewiedza' ('A one-sided point of view', 'Distorted causes' and, 'Presentism or ignorance'), in *Polityka*, 23 May 1981, 27 June 1981 and 25 July 1981 respectively.

Notes on Contributors

Władysław Bartoszewski is a writer and historian and is Secretary of the Polish PEN Club. From 1973 to 1985 he was Visiting Professor at the Catholic University of Lublin (Poland) and is at present Visiting Professor of Political Science at Munich and Eichstätt (West Germany). He has written about 20 books on the Second World War, Nazi crimes and the destruction of the Jews. He was co-founder of the Council for the Aid to Jews (*Żegota*) and recipient of the title 'Righteous among Nations' (Yad Vashem 1963).

Daniel Beauvois is a Professor of History at the University of Lille and Director of its Centre for the Study of Polish Culture. His publications include *Lumières et Société en Europe de l'Est* (Lille–Paris 1977) and *Le noble, le serf et le revizor* (Paris, 1985). He has edited *Les voyages de Jan Potocki* (2 vols, Paris, 1980); *Pologne: l'insurrection de 1830–31, sa reception en Europe* (Lille 1982, proceeds of a scholarly conference) and H. Sienkiewicz's *Quo Vadis*. He has also translated works by B. Geremek S. Przybyszewska and C. Miłosz.

Ryszard Bender is Professor of History and Dean of the Faculty of Humanities at the Catholic University of Lublin. His principal interest is nineteenth and twentieth century history on which he has published six books and over 200 articles, including *Ludność miejska lubelskiego w akcji przedpowstaniowej 1861–62* (The urban population of the Lublin region and its part in pre-insurrectionary political activity 1861–2, Warsaw, 1961), *Chrześcijanie w polskich ruchach demokratycznych XIX stulecia* (Christians in Polish democratic movements of the nineteenth century, Warsaw, 1975) and *Powstaniec-zakonnik. O Rafał Kalinowski* The insurgent-monk. On Rafał Kalinowski, Warsaw, 1977).

Michał Borwicz was, from 1945 to 1947, director of the Jewish Historical Commission in Cracow and deputy director of the Central Jewish Historical Commission in Poland. He was appointed as an expert by the Polish Supreme Court in war crimes trials. From 1947 he has lived in Paris where he has collaborated with *La Revue d'Histore de la II Guerre Mondiale* and the Centre Nationale de la Recherche Scientifique. He is the author of many books in Polish, French and Yiddish on the second world war including *Ecrits des condamnés à mort sous l'occupation hitlerienne*, *1939—45* Paris, (1957), *L'insurrection du ghetto de Varsovie* (Paris, 1966) and *Vies interdites* (Paris, 1969).

Andrzej S. Ciechanowiecki is an art historian and historian of culture. He has published extensively in both fields. He is a trustee of various Polish Institutions abroad and is Chancellor of the Polish Association and SMO of Malta. He is Managing Director of the Heim Gallery (London) Ltd, and holds various Polish and foreign decorations. He has lived in London since 1961.

Alexsander Gieysztor has been Director of the Historical Institute of the University of Warsaw and President of the Polish Academy of Sciences. At present he is Director of the Royal Castle in Warsaw. Among his publications are *Władza Karola Wielkiego* (The rule of Charlemagne, Warsaw, 1938), *Geneza wypraw krzyżowych* (The origin of the Crusades, Warsaw 1950) and *La Pologne et l'Europe du Moyen Age* (Warsaw, 1962).

Frank Golczewski is a Professor of Modern History at the University of the Federal Armed Forces, Hamburg. He has written on Polish anti-semitism, national minorities in Poland and the Soviet Union and the history of National Socialism in Germany. His publications include *Polnische-jüdische Bezeihungen 1881—1922. Eine Studie zur Geschichte des Antisemitismus in Osteuropa* (Weisbaden, 1981).

Jacob Goldberg was until 1967 lecturer in history at the University of Łódź. Since then he has been first Research Fellow and subsequently Senior Lecturer and Professor of History at the Hebrew University of Jerusalem. He has published over forty books and articles on the social and economic history of Poland and on the history of the Jews in the Polish–Lithuanian Commonwealth. Among his books are *Stosunki agrarne w miastach ziemi wieluńskiej w drugiej połowie XVIII wjeku* (Agrarian relationships in the towns of the Wielun district in the second half of the seventeenth and the eighteenth century, Łódź, 1960) and *Jewish Privileges in the Polish Commonwealth. Charters of Rights granted to Jewish Communities in Poland—Lithuania in the sixteenth to eighteenth centuries, Critical Edition of Original Latin and Polish Documents with English Introduction and Notes* (Jerusalem, 1985)

Yisrael Gutman is Max and Rita Haber Professor of Holocaust Studies of the Institute of Contemporary Jewry at the Hebrew University and Director of the Center of Holocaust Studies at Yad Vashem. A member of the Jewish Fighting organisation, he took part in the Warsaw ghetto uprising. His books include *Anas him Va'Efer* (Men and Ashes, Jerusalem, 1956), *Mered ha-Nezurim: Mordecai Anieliewicz ve-Milhamot Getto Varsha* (The Revolt of the Besieged: Mordecai Anieliewicz and the Revolt of the Warsaw Ghetto, Jerusalem, 1963) and *The Jews of the Warsaw, 1939—1943: Ghetto, Underground, Revolt* (Brighton, 1982).

Lukasz Hirszowicz is Editor of *Soviet Jewish Studies*, a journal on Jewish Problems in the USSR and Eastern Europe. He is the author of 'Iran 1951-1953. Oil-Imperialism–Nationalism' (Warsaw, 1958). *The Third Reich and the Arab East* (Warsaw, 1963, Tel Aviv 1965, London–Toronto 1966, Cairo 1971) and other contributions on Middle Eastern history and Soviet and Polish Jewish affairs.

Jerzy Holzer is Reader in Polish and European Modern History at the University of Warsaw. His books include *Polska Partia Socjalistyczna w latach 1917—19* (The Polish Socialist Party, 1917-1919. Warsaw, 1962), *Mozaika polityczna drugiej Rzeczypospolitej*

(The Political Mosaic of the Second Republic, Warsaw, 1974) and *'Solidarność' 1980—1; Geneza i historia* ('Solidarity', 1980–1; Origins and history, Paris, 1984).

Gershon David Hundert is Associate Professor of History and chairs the Jewish Studies Department at McGill University. Among his publications are *The Jews in Poland and Russia* (with G. Bacon); *Bitahon u-telut: yehudei ir peratit ahat be-mamlekhet Polin*; and articles in various collections and journals including *Revue des études juives*, *AJS review*, *Jewish Social Studies*, and the *Jewish Journal of Sociology*.

Stefan Kieniewicz is Professor Emeritus of History at the University of Warsaw. He has written extensively on Polish history in the nineteenth century. His books include *Społeczeństwo polskie w powstaniu poznańskim 1848* (The Polish society in the Poznan uprising of 1848. Poznan 1935), *Historia Polski 1795—1918* (The history of Poland 1795–1918) and *Powstanie styczniowe* (The January Uprising, Warsaw, 1983).

Joseph L. Lichten is Professor of the Polish University Abroad, London and representative of the Anti-Defamation League of B'nai B'rith in Rome and at the Vatican. He has specialized in Christian–Jewish and Polish–Jewish relations as well as in the history of legal and political thought in Poland. He is the author of several studies on these subjects.

Ezra Mendelsohn is Professor at the Institute of Contemporary Jewry, Hebrew University. His principal interest lies in modern Jewish history and he is the author of *Class struggle in the Pole* (Cambridge, 1970), *Zionism in Poland: (The Formative Years 1905—26* (London and New Haven, 1981) and *Jews in East Central Europe between the Two World Wars* (Indiana, 1983). He is co-editor of *Studies in Contemporary Jewry* and editor of the Monograph series of the Center for Research on the History and Culture of Polish Jews.

Teresa Prekerowa was a member of the Council for Aid to Jews (Żegota). In postwar Poland, she has worked for many years in various publishing houses. She is the author of *Konspiracyjna Rada Pomocy Żydom w Waszawie 1942—1945* (The underground council for aid to Jews in Warsaw 1942–1945, Warsaw 1982) and many articles on Polish–Jewish themes.

Daniel Tollet is Secretary-general of the Centre for Jewish Studies at the University of Paris. His thesis for the doctorate d'état on 'Marchands et Hommes d'affaires juifs dans la Pologne des Wasa (1588–1648)' is about to be published.

Index